The "New" Men of America— and ME

Mary Ellen New White

Illustrations by Gayle New Gray

AB ASPECT Books
www.ASPECTBooks.com

The author assumes full responsibility for the accuracy of all facts and quotations as cited in this book. The opinions expressed in this book are the author's personal views and interpretations, and do not necessarily reflect those of the publisher.

This book is provided with the understanding that the publisher is not engaged in giving spiritual, legal, medical, or other professional advice. If authoritative advice is needed, the reader should seek the counsel of a competent professional.

———————————————————

Copyright © 2015 ASPECT Books
ISBN-13: 978-1-4796-0546-0 (Hardback)
ISBN-13: 978-1-4796-0547-7 (ePub)
ISBN-13: 978-1-4796-0548-4 (Mobi)
Library of Congress Control Number: 2015914767

Published by
AB ASPECT Books
www.ASPECTBooks.com

Table of Contents

Dedication

Lovingly dedicated to the memory of my father,
Lt. Edward Leon New, 1917,
a man of honor, a gentleman of the South.

NEW FAMILY CHART

Richard New
of England

Robert   Edmund

Pricsilla   Edward   Mary   Rebecca   Sarah   Edmund   William   Eliz.   Ann   Henry

           David   Francis (Frank)

Jacob   James   John   Ann   Elizabeth   Judith

Jesse   Joel   David   George   Henry   Samuel   Jake Jr.   Elijah   William

5 Daughters?   Edward V.   James   Martha   Joel Green

       Susan   Luke J.   Elijah   Joel   Edward Jr.

Henry   Ed.Leon   Minnie   Marie   Lorena   Mary   Herman   Joe   Susie Mae   Irvin

Edna   Mary   Constance   Mable
Mae   Ellen   Amelda   Sue

Peggy   Patsy   James (Jim)   Janice
Jean   Ann   Monroe   Ellen

          James (Jimmy)   Brian   John
          Vernon   Lee   Vincent

A Letter to My Children

Dear children, Jim and Jan,

My ancestors, which make up half of yours, are that of a proud family with a not-so-usual surname, a family called *New*. Our line of the New family history spans a period of over three centuries of American life. It is a real story, as true as exhaustive research can make it.

The first episodes of our New family history, lacking eye witnesses, come from educated guesswork based upon facts gleaned from yellowed pages in courthouses, church records, and dusty archives. I have pored over countless historical accounts in libraries from "th'ar to th'ar" to gain insight into what was happening in our forefathers' world as they passed through on their way. Slowly, so very slowly, our "New" story unfolded.

I found the News to be a typical American family, ordinary people much as those from other clans across our nation. I found no News that were famous, nor infamous, and none that were overly wealthy, though none suffered long from want.

What our New family possessed was not bought with money. Their riches lay in a certain strength of character, a stubbornness that carried them through whatever ill tides brought. None claimed sainthood and none could walk on water, but personal pride made them hold their heads high, doing what seemed to be right. God blessed them with a goodly amount of brains; their innate ability to think and reason gave them the power to make use of the talents He gave them. None gained high political acclaim but their common-sense suggestions were respected and often heeded by their peers.

Our earliest New ancestor who came to America was Richard New, a son of an upper middle-class English family who built sailing ships at Bristol, an English seaport located in the southwestern area of the British Isles. Young Richard arrived in the Virginia Colony in America in 1636, a century and a half before there was a United States.

Bringing only his good name, he was in his early teens when he came to the colonies and worked as an indentured servant to pay his fare for passage on a ship. Through gumption and hard work, he improved his lot. He became a respected citizen that walked with dignity among the gentlemen of the land. He fought Indians when they burned his home and suffered through the hardship of an economic depression brought by the edicts of an oppressive English king and Virginia's royal governors.

Richard New had two sons, stalwart responsible citizens who carried forward the moral principles that Richard had displayed. Their standards were passed along, father to son, in the generations of News that followed.

Cherishing liberty, generation after generation of our New family fought for their rights and beliefs. To protect his home, one forefather, Francis New, battled Frenchmen and their scalp-taking Indian allies in the French and Indian War in the 1750s, helping to drive these enemies from Virginia's valleys. Having become more American than British, Francis's son, Jacob New, fought alongside other Americans in the 1770s to dispel British tyranny in a War of Rebellion that resulted in the birth of a new nation, our United States.

In the 1860s, believing the southern part of the United States had been given "the short end of the stick," the News took an active part when the South seceded from the Union to form a new Confederacy of States. The ensuing Civil War was not fought for slavery, which, contrary to Northern abolitionist beliefs, was already being phased out; the Civil War was fought to gain equal rights for all the states. Our grandfather of that era, Edward Vandergriff New, a railroad builder from Georgia, did not fight as a soldier in that war but valiantly kept the Alabama and Vicksburg Railroad—the old A&V, the "lifeline of the Confederacy"—up and running throughout the bloody hostilities. In Mississippi, after Yankee Union soldiers under Gen. W. T. Sherman destroyed the Rebel Army's warehouses and cantonments at a town called Meridian, it took Ed New and his crew but a brief month to replace the A&V Railroad's burned crossties and twisted rails and to restore the crucial rail service through the town.

To "make the world safe for democracy," in 1917 your own Pa New, my dad Capt. Edward Leon New of the U.S. Army, was stationed in China, Japan, and the Philippine Islands to take part in the "Great War," World War I.

I remember how I felt in later years, 1941, when Japan attacked our country—YOUR country—to plunge us into World War II. Having no brothers to send and myself too young for the Women's Army Corps, I in patriotic fervor joined the Cadet Nurse Corps to train to become an army nurse. The war ended before I could complete my schooling so I only got as far as the school in San Antonio, Texas. Graduating as a registered nurse about the time our soldiers returned home in 1945, I married your father James M. White in 1946. He was a returning veteran of sea battles fought in the South Pacific. The Whites are from another American family whose epic story I plan to write in the future.

So now it's up to you. You have already made me proud; I find nothing in your lives that would cause unrest in your forefathers' graves. Continue to pull your weight and live with self-respect and dignity. Remember the New blood that flows in your veins; speak out for what you believe to be right. Hold your head high, undaunted and unbowed, through life's difficult times, as did those who lead our way.

As old Abe Lincoln said, "It is for us, the living, to be here dedicated to the unfinished work … that we here highly resolve that these dead shall not have died in vain …"

Your ever-devoted mother,
Mary Ellen New White.

Chapter I
Setting the Stage

In the years following 1492 when Columbus first discovered the new world called America, Spain began to colonize on this land in the areas she claimed, which were later called the West Indies and Florida, in Mexico, and parts of South America. England, busily developing her lively trade in China and the Far East, was not interested.

But wait! By the 1570–80s Spanish galleons were returning to Europe with their holds heavily laden with GOLD! Avaricious English eyes began to glitter. Perhaps some English colonies in the Americas would prove to be most beneficial …

An adventurous British naval military officer Walter Raleigh, born in Devonshire and educated at Oxford, had cultivated friendships with English gentlemen of influence. He became established in England's royal court, and after serving in Ireland with military distinction for two years, in 1581, he returned to court where he won the high favor of Queen Elizabeth I. By rewarding him with excessive grants and estates, she made him one of her wealthiest courtiers. In 1584 he became Sir Walter Raleigh when the queen made him her knight. In 1584–86 he was a member of Parliament and also served as captain of the queen's guard.

Impressed by the Spanish gold arriving in Europe from America, Sir Walter became obsessed with the idea of English land exploration and settlement in the new world. He began taking engagements in "voyages of discovery" (and piracy) against Spanish merchant ships in the West Indies. By 1589 he had led five ships on expeditions to North America although the queen had forbidden him to take any personal participation in any fighting.

To forestall greater hostility between the countries, Raleigh bypassed Spain's Central and South American claims and sailed northward to establish claims for England on the eastern coast of today's United States. Adding urgency to his thoughts, seamen reported sightings of tall Spanish sails lurking off the North American coast. Sir Walter made haste to claim a rather large territory on the eastern coast of North America for England. He named the claim "Virginia" to honor Queen Elizabeth, his so-called "Virgin Queen."

England's first settlement in North America was established in 1585 on the coast of what later became today's state of Maine. It was a failure, its surviving settlers returning home to England.

England's second colony, sited on Roanoke Island (off today's state of Virginia) was founded two years later in 1587. Sadly, the Roanoke Colony disappeared while the leader, John White, was sailing back to England for supplies. Some surmised that the Roanoke settlers, who were starving, had been adopted by Indians and became absorbed in the native tribe. While he was there Capt. White, fascinated, made some interesting drawings of early Indian life to show when he returned home.

In 1591 Sir Walter Raleigh while leading his squadrons on expeditions to discover a northern water route to the Pacific was recalled to England—his queen had become angry after hearing of his involvement with one of her ladies-in-waiting. However, at about that time Queen Elizabeth met an untimely death and James I was crowned the new king of England.

Raleigh's jealous enemies made King James believe that Raleigh was opposed to his recent ascension. The king stripped away Raleigh's wealth and had him committed to the tower where he remained for thirteen years. He was finally reprieved but was later executed due to further infractions—King James had Sir Walter Raleigh decapitated in the Palace Yard on October 29, 1618.

Following its past failures, by the 1600s England's King James had given up the idea of establishing further British settlement in the new world. When the crown lost interest, a group of London gentlemen, seeing Spain still gaining riches, invested their own combined capital to found "The Virginia Company" as a privately owned enterprise. King James granted the new company some land in England's Virginia claim on which to found their colony.

In 1606 the Virginia Company sent a hundred and five settlers to establish a settlement in their Virginia land. They left England in a fleet of three ships—the "Susan Constant," the "Godspeed," and the "Discovery"—bound for new world adventures.

After sailing westward for weeks, the fleet reached Virginia's Chesapeake Bay. Not wanting Spaniards to dispute their presence before they were fortified and ready for "unwelcome guests," they turned their ships into the broad James River to continue sixty more miles.

According to a report of Capt. John Smith, the leader appointed by the company's council, the fleet dropped anchor at an island on the north shore of the James "where the river's deep channel came so near land ye ships used greatly tall trees as mooring posts."

Another gentleman wrote of "fair meadows and greatly tall trees, with such fresh waters running through the woods I was almost ravished with the first sight thereof!"

They proclaimed the site for their village "Jamestowne" in honor of King James I. The date was May 14, 1607.

Ah, life in Jamestowne!!

The masters of the three ships had suggested they bring laborers to build the colony but gentlemen-adventurers, spoiled scions of wealthy investors, had requisitioned all but twenty-four of the ships' berths. They planned to quickly gather gold and return home in triumph. In his *General History of Virginia,* Capt. Smith recorded, "There was no talk, no hope nor work, but dig gold, refine gold, load gold." But, alas, there was no gold to be found in Virginia.

The colony's first years were marked by hardship. The settlement—a triangular blockhouse and several thatched huts—was destroyed by fire in 1608. Somehow, under Capt. Smith's prodding a year later Jamestown consisted of fifty wooden structures, a chapel, and a storehouse all surrounded by a palisade. Gaining the confidence of the local Indians, Smith had developed trade in swapping shiny beads and trinkets for corn so the colony could eat.

Capt. Smith, unfortunately, became injured and returned to England on a ship being sent for supplies. The friendly Algonquian Indians had traded Smith their corn, but after he left the colony's hunger became rampant. The spoiled adventurers who were accustomed to a life of ease didn't know how, or weren't willing, to grow food. The winter of 1609 was remembered as "the starving time."

Hunger reduced the settlers to savagery. Like lords of the manor the spoiled settlers raided the Indians' storehouses and helped themselves. The Indians fought back and burned Jamestown to the ground.

The summer before, in 1608, the Virginia Company in London had sent out a fleet of nine vessels laden with tools, food, and supplies, and with nearly five hundred new immigrants selected from every quarter and working class of people. Ignoring express orders to proceed immediately westward, the fleet sailed south to take advantage of more favorable trade winds.

Nearing the end of their journey, the fleet ran into a hurricane and experienced all the horrors of a tropical storm. Sails were ripped from masts by fierce winds as waves swept the ships, ruining precious cargo in their holds. One small ship, a ketch, foundered and lost its entire crew.

Another ship, the Sea Venture, that was heavily loaded with people and provisions ran aground off an island called Bermuda. It was tossed onto rocks but all were saved by wading to shore and safety. (Two years later William Shakespeare wrote a play, *The Tempest*, about this shipwreck.)

Among the Sea Venture's survivors was an English family named "Wellborn," whose relatives had helped translate the King James Version of the Holy Bible from its original Greek language into English for King James I. This happened around two hundred years before our later ancestor, Joel New, married Miss Mamie Wellborn down in Meridian, Mississippi. Their story is told later.

Existing upon wild boars they found roaming the island, the shipwrecked Sea Venture's survivors made use of the island's tall trees and the ship fittings salvaged from their wrecked vessel to build two crude crafts they christened "Patience" and "Deliverance." Leaving Bermuda, the survivors began the last six hundred miles of their long voyage. Becoming short of food, they sustained

themselves by thinking of the feast they would enjoy once they reached Virginia.

Robert Howiston wrote in his *History of Virginia From Its Discovery And Settlement By Europeans* [Cary and Hart, Philadelphia, 1846]:

> ... *Seven [of the fleet of nine] vessels rode out the storm and arrived in shattered condition in Virginia in August [1609]. So considerable a fleet caused alarm and, believing them to be Spaniards, the [settlers] prepared to greet them with shots from the fort ... Had not the mistake been speedily discovered the English ships might have received a rude welcome.*
>
> *When the new colonists were landed it was soon discovered that the provisions they brought were hardly adequate to the want. This was a small evil, compared with that flowing from the James Towne inhabitants' own vicious characters; gentlemen reduced to poverty by gaming and extravagance, too proud to beg, too lazy to dig ... rakes consumed with disease, shattered in the service of impurity ... libertines packed off to escape worse dignities at home.*

These were the men who had come to aid in the founding of a nation!

In May 1610 when the survivors of the Bermuda wreck arrived in Jamestown, they were dismayed to find the settlement had already consumed the food brought earlier by the seven ships that had weathered the storm. Facing starvation, the desperate colonist voted to give up.

The few who had survived starvation and disease loaded up and set sail for England and home. They sailed down the James, but as they rounded the last tip of land and were in sight of the open sea, they met the ship of Thomas West, the Baron De La War, the first governor the Virginia

Company sent from London. He ordered them to turn back—things were going to be better. Under Gov. West conditions did improve. He ruled with a stern hand; only those that worked could eat. After 1614 when John Rolfe, a survivor of the Sea Venture, married the Indian Princess Pocahontas (real name Mataoka, daughter of Chief Powhatan), the Indians became more friendly—somewhat.

Learning from the Indians, Rolfe found a way of curing Sot Weed (tobacco) so it could be packed and shipped back to England without spoilage. No product achieved a more overwhelming acceptance in England as did tobacco. It became fashionable to chew the weed or smoke it in pipes, or to snuff it up one's nose to make one sneeze. Not even the king could stop this strange habit.

After finding this new cash crop, Virginians hastened to plant tobacco every place they could. After planting the narrow spaces between the village houses, they cleared the forest so they could grow even more.

More people kept arriving from England. In 1617 Samuel Argyll, replacing Gov. Thomas West, constituted a new form of representative government patterned after the shire structure in the British Isles. Each Virginia shire—James City, Charles City, Henrico, and Kikotan—contained a village. Virginia's first House of Burgesses, made up of two men to represent each shire (county), met in Jamestown. Inferior courts were established, and a detailed land survey was begun to quiet title disputes. These changes were good, but Gov. Argyll wouldn't, or couldn't, do much about the continuing Indian problem.

Gentleman Richard Pace of London had arrived in Virginia on the ship "Marmaduke" in 1611. A descendant of a line of court jesters, he had earlier been a jester in Henry VIII's court where his brother had been one of the king's advisors. He migrated to Virginia alone but was joined later by his wife, the former Isabella Smyth, daughter of a Virginia Company investor. The Pace home, "Pace's Pains," was built on the southern shore of the James, directly across the river from Jamestown.

In 1622 Chanco, an Indian lad working for Pace, confided that the natives were planning another attack upon Jamestown to drive the invading white men back to the sea. Alarmed, Pace had the boy row him across the river to alert the settlement.

As Chanco had warned, the "savages" came to attack. Some houses were burned and several people were slaughtered, but Richard Pace and Chanco were credited with saving the settlement from complete destruction. A metal plaque honoring them still hangs in the reconstructed Jamestown Church.

This Richard Pace was progenitor of a long line of the Pace family in America. In the 1840s Rev. Alsa Pace, in a direct line of descent from Richard, arrived in Lauderdale County, Mississippi, where he helped his brother Rev. Edwin Pace establish "Pace's Church," today's "Fellowship Baptist Church," located near Meridian. Around 1900 this Pace family became allied with our New family by marriage. More on this is to be explored in a later chapter.

After so many settlers were massacred in Virginia uprisings and after raging epidemics of cholera and malaria had taken their tolls, the private Virginia Company became bankrupt. When Virginia was taken over by the crown in 1624, there were only 1,200 persons left of the thousands who had ventured forth from England.

The Virginia Colony was thirty in 1636 when a young shipbuilder from Bristol, England, came to the new world. [As recorded by George Cabell Greer; *Early Virginia Immigrants*, Genealogical Pub. County, Baltimore, 1972.] This English lad,

Richard Newe (New), growing up in Virginia, was our first New ancestor in America.

The "Susan Constant," "Godspeed," and "Discovery" – Virginia Company ships that anchored off the Jamestown Island in 1607.

Chapter II
New Men In Old England

Bristol is a city located at the meeting of the English shires of Gloucester and Summerset in the southwestern British Isles situated near the confluence of the Avon and Frome Rivers, which flow into the Severn River that reaches the Bristol Channel and hence to the Atlantic Ocean. Bristol became a busy seaport.

Research has shown that an upper middle-class family named New was living in the town of Bristol in England's Gloucester County before Columbus discovered America. One Edmund New had died there and was buried at the Church of Saint Thomas.

Edmund New's will, dated 16 January 1491, stated that he was a member of the House of Burgesses from the town of Bristol with his occupation being that of a dyer. (Bristol, a seaport, had become a textile manufacturing center.) Edmund's death left his wife Agnes with three sons—John, Richard, Robert—and one daughter, Margaret, to mourn their loss.

A second Richard New was born in Bristol several years later, circa 1622. By this time our New family had invested in a Bristol shipyard. Which of old Edmund's three sons was father of this younger Richard has not yet been established, although we reasonably assume that our first New ancestor, Richard New II, was a grandson of the late Edmund New.

Believing that literate people made better subjects, King James I had instituted England's first public schools, so our young Richard New was probably educated—at least until he was twelve. By English law the eldest son was the heir; younger sons either joined the military or went to sea or were apprenticed to a journeyman craftsman to learn a trade.

Our Richard New was not the heir apparent as, taught by craftsmen, he learned to build boats at his father's Bristol shipyard.

Chapter III
Richard New
(circa 1620–after 1680)

Before him not the ghost of shores,
Before him only shoreless seas,
The good mate said, "Now we must
  pray
For, Lo!, the very stars are gone!
Brave Adm'r'l, speak! What I shall
  say?"
"Why, say Sail on! Sail on and on!"
They sailed and sailed as winds might
  blow
Until at last the blanched mate said,
"Why, not even God would know
Should I and all my men fall dead!"
These very winds forget their way
For even God from these dread seas
  is gone.
Now speak, brave Adm'r'1, speak and
  say—
"He said, "Sail on! Sail on and on!"
- From Columbus, by Joaquin Miller

Who can know what was going on in the mind of young Richard New on this 1636 winter crossing of the Atlantic from his father's English hearthside to an unfamiliar shore in America? He had left his safe harbor, perhaps forever, to sail into the unknown. It was the first time he had ventured onto the vast open sea, and as it was to the mate in the poem, the five-week voyage seemed interminable. He was a little scared, but exhilarated, when he thought about the drastic changes and challenges he would encounter. But with his adolescent feeling of immortality, he sailed forward to meet his destiny.

Born in Bristol, Richard was around fifteen when he was transported to the sparsely populated British Crown Colony of Virginia where artisans and knowledgeable craftsmen were in great demand. He was probably already acquainted with the shipmaster and pilot who charted their course as he, like many local lads, had been drawn to the Bristol quay to listen in round-eyed wonder at old seafarers' tales of distant places. Young Richard, when he was apprenticed to the journeymen shipbuilders and fitters working in his father's shipyard, had also met other seamen who had come there to transact business.

When our eager teenager arrived at Jamestown, the white population of the entire Virginia Colony was less than 8,000 souls, most of them dispersed in the primeval forest on isolated farms that had been cleared of trees. Accustomed to teeming English cities, Richard saw the Jamestown settlement as the "back side of nowhere."

Next to the wharf at Jamestown was the fort and a nearby warehouse storing hogsheads of tobacco awaiting shipment on a seagoing vessel. A scattering of thatch-roofed huts made of willow withes plastered with pinkish-colored clay were randomly sited along dirt streets. The town's only cobbled street led up from the wharf to the town's center (mall?)—a church and a few shops, along with the ordinary that offered spirits, food, and lodging.

At the "mall" the shops and houses were better-constructed, being built of hand-rived lumber and boasting glazed windows. Since 1608 a glassworks, located nearby, had made hand-blown bottles but had not, as yet, been able to produce windows. Little diamond-shaped window glass had served as ballast on ships from England. Leaded together, the wee panes were then framed with wood to make window sashes.

Virginia's few trading posts were largely under stocked, if not bare; the colonists remained sorely in want of necessities unattainable on the frontier. The settlers, with a hunger for English goods, eagerly sought merchandise from newly arrived ships. When an incoming sail was sighted, they began to collect at the Jamestown pier.

As sailors unloaded the barrels and bales from their ship's hold, an extraordinary spectacle began. As bundles of goods were opened, the crowd surged forward to seize whatever treasure came to light. Refined ladies and gentlemen snatched and grabbed like scullery maids did in England when a boat landed with a catch of fish.

Englishmen had to have their tea of course, as well as spices from the Orient. They watched for molasses from Barbados to satisfy their sweet tooth and to make a supply of rum. Gentlemen, as well as their ladies, were interested in the latest fashions so there was a brisk trade of velvets, brocades, silks, and satins, and of laces, ribbons and shoes. Gentlemen wore loose cotton garments to work their plantations, but on church and court days or on other special occasions both sexes dressed like peacocks.

They had great need for things made of metal—axes and hoes, cook pots and pothooks, nails and hinges. By English law it was illegal for ordinary citizens to own a gun, but Virginians, needing protection from "wild beasts and Indians," bought muskets anyway. Gunpowder, lead, and bullet molds were popular sale items.

Minted coins were scarce, so tobacco traded by the hogshead became an accepted medium of exchange. One early Virginia governor complained of the prices " … which unconscionable merchants and mariners doe impose upon our necessities," and of the "rotten Wynes which destroy our bodies and empty our purses." One

early shipmaster boasted, " … the profit from a sale of only fower butts of wyne would be sufficient to clere the whole Voiage." (A butt was a large cask holding two hogsheads; a hogshead equaled sixty-three wine gallons or about 531 English Imperial gallons.)

In *Laboring and Dependent Classes in Colonial. America, 1607–1783* [NY: Fred. Unger Publ. Co., 1931], Marcus Wilson wrote:

> … There were vast areas of rich virgin land which were usually granted in a manner to promote a more rapid increase of population of extended cultivated tracts. This system was known as the "headright system." Anyone immigrating was rewarded with a gift of land, about 100 acres. Also, since labor was needed to clear and work this land, anyone who paid for importing a servant was entitled to an additional allotment, another headright. To induce laborers to immigrate, a similar allotment was promised [the indentured servants] after they served a term of years as a servant …

It was customary for a master to furnish his bound servants room and board, along with two sets of work clothing. Their master was also required to furnish medical attention if needed and schooling for any servant that was a minor. Indentured servants were entitled to a 100-acre headright after completing their term of service and becoming freedmen, although in many this was an empty promise.

Upon his arrival at Jamestown, young Richard New became indentured to a Mr. Edward Travis who had paid for his ship passage. He was bound to Mr. Travis for four years, or until he turned twenty-one.

Edward Travis had married the daughter of an elderly Mr. John Johnson, a designated "Ancient Planter" who had been a member of the original private Virginia Company before it had reverted to the crown. Travis lived on his father-in-law's plantation, a short distance east of the main village, on the back of Jamestown Island.

In *James City County Patent Book I*, page 531, the following land patent is recorded:

> ***EDWARD TRAVIS;*** *James City County, January 25, 1637: 900 acres upon the head of upper Chippokes Creek adjoining Jeremiah Dickenson, 200 acres thereof due in right of John Johnson, his wife and two children, the daughter, an heir [ofd said Johnson, marrying the said Travis; 250 acres for 5 serv'ts transported by said Johnson & for the transport of 9 persons transported by the said Travis.]*

The above patent went on to list the nine persons transported by Edward Travis. They were Walter Travis, Katherine Douse, Thomas Bath, Thomas Simpson, Peter and John Turvey, Francis Chambers, Jon. Jennings, and Richard New.

Chippokes Creek, on the south side of the James River across from Jamestown Island, empties into the river a short distance upstream from the original settlement. This creek was located in James City County in 1637 when the above patent was recorded, but by 1652 this region's population had increased; Surry County became one of the new counties formed from this southern portion of Jamestown County.

The family and servants of Edward Travis and his Johnson in-laws moved to their new land on the upper Chippokes Creek to build a new home and clear land to plant tobacco. It was not uncommon, in those days, to see extended families and their servants living cramped together in a one-room hut, usually a makeshift shelter of hand-rived weatherboards. More rooms and outbuildings were added later if their fortune increased or if a need arose.

If the new Travis/Johnson dwelling followed the usual custom, it consisted of a great room where cooking, dining, and sleeping all took place. Bedsteads were rare—most sleeping was done on the floor on 'shakedowns,' bedrolls filled with leaves or straw, which were unrolled at night. Some huts had a loft to provide storage and/or more sleeping space. Glazed windows were not common but usually a small opening, with moveable shutters, was left in one wall to admit daylight.

The dominant feature of most great rooms was its enormous fireplace, one big enough for three fires. They took a heap of wood to operate but what the heck, wood was certainly plentiful! The largest fire was for warmth while another, of red-hot embers, supported a bake-oven. The third was a smaller fire over which an iron cook-kettle was suspended on a metal pothook, although in warm weather most cooking was done outdoors.

Walter Freeman Hawke wrote, "No day passed where the fireplace went unused ... soot would accumulate in the chimney making a hazardous thick, tarry, highly flammable coating. Brooms were used to clean short chimneys; in taller ones it was not uncommon to drop a chicken down the opening, its frantic wing-beatings doing the cleaning job quickly." [*Everyday Life in Early America*, NY: Harper and Row, p. 55.]

There were few connecting roads in the never-ending forest except for faint Indian traces where one could easily become lost. Hence, Virginia's numerous waterways served as the main routes between the scattered settlements. Most plantations had been thoughtfully sited near streams so dugout canoes, made from boles of giant trees, could be used to transport a planter's

tobacco to await shipment on larger seagoing vessels. It is now unclear if Master Travis put Richard New to work clearing tobacco fields, or if he had him working at his profession, that of building river-crafts for sale and for home use.

Mr. Johnson, the "Ancient Planter," died that winter when the families moved to Chippokes Creek. Johnson's son and heir, John Jr., inherited his father's share of the Travis/Johnson plantation, the change in ownership recorded in the *James City County Patent Book I*, page 36:

> EDWARD TRAVIS and JOHN JOHNSON, son of John Johnson, deceased, February, 1638: 900 acres upon head of Upper Chippokes Creek adjoining SW side of Jeremiah Dickerson; 200 acres by right said Johnson, the elder; 450 acres for transport of nine persons by said Travis … [*Richard New was here again listed along with the same others that Travis had transported.*]

In the year following the death of the elder Johnson, the ambitious Mr. Travis found a larger plantation with a nice house that was better suited to his needs. Upon selling his interest in the Travis/Johnson plantation to his brother-in-law John Jr., he transported twenty-one more immigrants. This enabled him to get a new patent for 1,100 acres of land. Travis' new land patent was recorded on pages 642, 643 of *James City County Patent Book I*, as follows:

> **EDWARD TRAVES:** *300 acres on Chickahominy River, James City Co, 25 April, 1639: On Warrenty Creek, westly from land of Wm. Hogg, a creek between, and southly on said Creek, due for transport of six persons … [Their names were listed but not copied here.]*

THE SAME: 800 acres ... [same county and date]; On Chickahominy River, being the neck of land called Pease Hill, one side butting down to maine River eastly, the head of the neck being on the E. side adjoining the land of Wm. Beard, due him [Travis] for his own personal advantage & for the transportation of fifteen persons ... [Their names were listed but not copied here.]

This latest Travis plantation, located on the northern bank of the James River, was in the western portion of Jamestown County on the western shore of the Chickahominy River that flows from the north into the James River. (At a later date the wide Chickahominy River became the dividing line when the new Charles City County was formed from the original James City County.)

A rising price return for their tobacco crop brought the planters more money. The newly rich planters began to construct substantial homes along Virginia's numerous waterways, mansions that bespoke of gracious living. Mr. Travis, with all his new land, had plenty of space for his new home, which was surrounded by generous fields—and taking note of the nearness of the adjoining deep water, he installed a boatyard, taking advantage of the work of his servant, the shipbuilder Richard New.

We found no record of when Richard New completed his bondage. For him it would have been around 1640 as youngsters were generally freed when they came of age.

When they completed their term of bondage, it was the custom for a master to furnish his freed servants a year's provision of corn so they wouldn't starve, double apparel, and tools necessary for them to get started. They were also supposed to receive one and a half acres of land but this didn't always happen. As no deed has been found for Richard, we assume he continued to work—this time for wages—at the Travis shipyard after he had been set free.

Sir William Berkeley, upon being appointed royal governor of Virginia by King Charles I (the son of James I), arrived in the colony in 1642. He was popular at first when he began to institute better local government. He tried to advance the colony's economic welfare by introducing the cultivation of a variety of new agricultural products, especially silk. This, he hoped, would stop Virginia's reliance upon tobacco as its only cash crop.

Tired of the Virginia planters escalating their encroachment upon Indian land, an aging Powhatan Chief, Opechancano, launched his final big attack in 1644. The aging chief, carried by litter onto the battlefield, was shot by a guard and taken prisoner. (This old chief was an uncle of the then deceased Princess Pocahontas.)

Three hundred or more white men—and goodness knows how many Indian warriors—perished in this massacre, but the Indians, although somewhat subdued, continued to raid the settlers that lived on outlying plantations. Trying to control these raids, Gov. Berkeley established forts about the area, but King Charles I was busily fighting a civil war in England with Oliver Cromwell and could not spare his troops to aid his American colonies. Each colony was required to form its own civilian militia to fight in the native uprisings.

Richard New, in his early twenties, was called for service in the Virginia militia, as were all males between sixteen and sixty.

Virginia's militia companies began holding regular musters at the respective county seats to train men to fight the "red-skinned marauders." Militia officers were picked from the more affluent leaders of the local gentry, although a few British Regulars were sent over to America to lead the civilian soldiers. Each recruit was required to bring his own musket.

William Freeman Hawkes wrote, [Ibid., p. 136], "The Militia's monthly muster days resembled a carnival to which most of the county came to watch their men stumble through their drills. Unlike uniformed British Regulars, which accepted only men of uniform height and size, the Virginia militia was not so particular. Tall or short, thin or portly, as long as they were hardy and could handle a weapon, Virginia's men were called to duty. Watching citizens pointed and laughed, making sport of the diversity of their varied weapons and dress, and their want of discipline demanded by their officers."

Hawke wrote that a typical muster day usually began with morning drill, followed by footraces or other sporting events. A record shows that one Jamestown resident paid his yearly quick-rent by furnishing capons to be roasted on spits for their noontime chow.

"In late afternoon," Hawke continued, "a hogshead of punch was rolled out which entertained all the people, keeping them drunk and fighting all evening, but without mischief."

While Indians were on the warpath, Capt. Francis Barrett of the British Regulars, a younger son of a wealthy English family, was sent to the colony to train the raw recruits being drafted into the Virginia militia. He was billeted in the home of one William Frye, but he didn't plan to remain long in Virginia. When granted a small headright for immigrating, he transferred its title to Mr. Frye.

This Mr. Frye had transported five immigrants to Virginia back in 1637 for which he was granted 250 acres of land in James City County. This land was located a short distance from the mouth of the Chickahominy River. It was in that same neighborhood that Mr. Edward Travis, two

years later in 1639, had purchased his big new plantation.

After being in the colony a while, Capt. Barrett found promising financial possibilities. He made plans to establish his home in Virginia. Sending for his wife and their two daughters, he received his second land grant, a patent on 600 acres, for transporting his wife and eleven other persons. [*James City County Patent Book I*, p. 594.]

This second land grant, located near the home of his friend Mr. Frye, was in James City County on the eastern side of the Chickahominy River. On this land the captain built a comfortable colonial home, naming it "Richahocke"

In late 1642 Capt. Barrett enlarged Richahocke by acquiring 600 acres of its adjoining land. This land was " … adjacent to John Robbins, passing through a run of water & a certain Indian field near Fowlers Shambles, alias 'the Ridge' … " [*James City County Patent Book I*, p. 843.]

It was near this time that Richard New's master, Mr. Travis, acquired "the neck of land called 'Pease Hill' " that had once belonged to the above mentioned John Robbins, owner of the land adjacent to Capt. Barrett's Richahocke.

Having found that Richard New was an honest hard worker, Mr. Travis hired him to continue working in his boatyard after Richard's period of indenture was complete. Although no deed has been found, it appears that Travis gave the young man some land, the promised one and a half acres due him after the completion of his indenture.

Thus it was that Richard New and Capt. Francis Barrett became neighbors. They already knew each other—both had drilled with the James City County militia.

Miss Margaret Barrett, eldest of Capt. and Mrs. Barrett's two daughters, fell in love with and married Alexander Shepherd, a Virginia planter. After their marriage Margaret moved several miles distant to the home of her new husband.

After Margaret left, Mrs. Barrett unfortunately died with a fever. Her death left the younger Miss Barrett to manage the Richahocke household for her widowed father. It was this younger Barrett daughter that caught the attention of our Richard New.

Richard and Miss Barrett were married sometime around 1649–1650, apparently to everyone's satisfaction. It is believed that the happy couple lived at Richahocke with Capt. Barrett until Richard could build them a home. We don't know the exact date of their wedding as the record has been lost …

(Due to fires and other calamities, many early records are missing. We have been unable to find the given name of Mrs. Barrett, nor the name of her younger daughter who married Richard New.)

England, as in the past, continued to buy Virginia's tobacco. However, Parliament made new requirements—all the colony's tobacco had to be shipped only to England, using English merchant ships. In England a high tariff was placed on the tobacco before its shipments were reloaded and sent on to foreign markets. This was an added expense for the men who sold tobacco; to make up for the factors' shortfall planters began to receive less for their produce.

Virginia planters, to maintain their present income, responded by planting even more tobacco. In order to grow enough food for the colony's need, it became necessary to pass a new ordinance requiring that for each two acres of tobacco planted, a planter must also plant an acre of corn. As enlarged fields expanded further into the forest, the Indians became more restless, the outlying plantations making easy targets for their increasing raids.

In 1653 Mr. Ed Travis, becoming fearful of raiding Indians, left the isolated area around his plantation to return eastward to Jamestown Island. The island, with its greater population, offered better protection for his family. They relocated at Black Point in Goose Hill Marsh on the island's back river. (When Travis died ten years later, "Edward Travis, Jr., son and heir of Edward Travis, deceased," took over his father's estate.)

The Travis family moved back to Jamestown Island just in time—about then Indians raided and burned Richard New's home. Richard, along with his wife and their baby, Robert, managed to escape into the woods. They lost everything they owned, but their lives were spared.

They were in good standing with the community; records show that neighbors pitched in and rebuilt their home. A man to be trusted, Richard got a job collecting church tithes for the St. James Parish where he worked for the next five years.

Although some colonies in America were founded by Protestants, the only church recognized in the Virginia Crown Colony was the Anglican Church, the Church of England that had been England's dominant religion since 1534 in the reign of Henry VIII. As the colony furnished no public welfare, each parish was expected to care for its needy. To do this, the church demanded a tithe from its members. Persons who didn't pay their tithes were brought before church elders to pay up or be excommunicated, expelled from grace.

The Richard New family had only two children of record. Their actual birth dates are lost, but in the early 1650s Richard's wife presented him with two sons—Robert, namesake of Richard's father, and Edmund, namesake of Richard's grandfather who was buried at St. Thomas in Bristol, England.

(Quoting again from William Freeman Hawkes [Ibid., chapter 6]: "The low tidewater areas along Virginia's numerous waterways was not a healthy place to live … fragility of life was contributed to a virulent strain of malaria [and] probably accounted for the high death rate of their women in childbirth and may have affected the life span of the entire population … In later years a large family was the norm, but at first the number of children born to a Virginia family was small … Parents considered themselves lucky if more than one or two children survived birth and childhood.")

Capt. Francis Barrett, in failing health with death drawing near, thought of the future of his daughters. Margaret, as his firstborn child and heir, would by English law inherit his Richehocke plantation. The old soldier wanted to insure that his younger daughter, Richard's wife, would be provided for as well.

On April 6, 1655, the following land patent was recorded in *James City County Patent Book III*, page 336:

> **RICHARD NEW;** *750 acres in James City County, on North side of the James River on the East side of the Chickahominy River, Southeast of Thomas Brooke and sidely on Mr. Rolfe's land; for the transport of fifteen persons included in a certificate to Capt. Barrett in March last and assigned to said Richard New.*
>
> *[This Rolfe was Thomas Rolfe, child of the late John Rolfe and Pocahontas. Later, in 1659 it was recorded on page 257 of the same book that Thomas Rolfe was granted "… 50 acres on Chickahominy River, NE of Richard New and NW of his own land."]*

In early Virginia women had no property rights, any inheritance becoming her husband's. For this reason Capt. Barrett assigned the above patent to Richard instead of his daughter. The land would, by law, be his anyway. Besides, the captain liked Richard, thinking of him as a son, admiring his integrity,

Capt. Barrett died soon after giving the plantation to Richard. Upon his death Margaret's husband, Alex Shepherd, claimed her Richahocke inheritance. As they were already snugly ensconced on Shepherd's own plantation, he sold the Richahocke plantation, the deed being recorded on page 55 of *James City Patent Book IV*:

> *HENRY SOANES; 2000 acres in James City County, 10 December 1656: Northeast side of the Chickhonimy River, called by the name Richahocke; Beginning at Richahocke Creek above Mattapony Neck & including John Ling's plantation, and running through Thomas Brooke's cornfield by the land of **Richard New** & including Namtpucoy [sp?] & Pemacrey [sp.?] Necks with a small island called Pepacrey [?]; due by purchase from Alexander Shepherd and Margaret, his wife, the daughter and heir of [Capt.] Francis Barrett, deceased.*

(An interesting bit of gossip told in passing: Mrs. Judith Soanes, wife of Richahocke's new owner, later obtained a court order to have the Richahocke estate registered in her name only, as Henry Soanes. "Gentleman," had deserted.)

As mentioned above, Virginia's planters were getting rich in the 1650s, but in the 1660s, in spite of Gov. Berkeley's efforts, their pockets were quite pinched. England's navigation acts of 1660 and 1663 confined the tobacco trade to England where heavy tariffs were collected before it was reshipped and sold to European markets. Merchants had to offer low prices in order to sell their tobacco at all. Gov. Berkeley objected to these new taxes to no avail. By the 1670s the tobacco farmers had become poor.

Gov. Berkeley, well-liked at first, lost the planters' esteem in the 1660s. His charm had grown thin. He had welcomed wealthy English Royalists when they came to Virginia seeking refuge from

England's civil war. He exempted them from taxes and showed them special favors. He granted them membership in his special council, which carried the most weight in governmental decisions. The House of Burgesses was supposed to be made up of two people from each county, but Berkeley wouldn't allow new elections for the citizens to oust his favored members. No elections were permitted from 1661 through 1675.

Adding to the general discomfort, in 1675 the Indians again stepped up their hostilities. In September that year a party of Virginia militia was sent on a peace mission to a warring Susquehanna tribe down on Virginia's southern border. Instead of bringing peace, the fools killed the chieftains who had come to re-associate. In January 1676 the Indians, fighting back, slaughtered thirty-six Virginians.

In a dither, Gov. Berkeley levied even higher taxes to erect more forts. (One fort was located next to the plantation of Richard New on land owned by Thomas Rolfe.) But the citizens didn't want more forts; they wanted *action* and they wanted it FAST!

Enraged over the new taxes, which they could ill afford, a self-appointed group of angry men mobilized in Charles City County. They elected Nathaniel Bacon, a wealthy young newcomer, to be their leader. Bacon, accepting, led the group on a punitive expedition against local Indians.

After frightening away a settlement of peaceful Pamunkey Indians near Richard New's home, Bacon demanded a military commission from the governor. Berkeley refused his commission but did, finally, call for a new election, the first in eleven years.

Early James Towne

Then Bacon, still without a commission, visited the friendly Occaneeche tribe on the Carolina border to have them capture some warlike Susquehannocks. Instead, through a misunderstanding, Bacon's boys killed most of the friendly Occaneechees ...

In an election held that June, Bacon won a seat in Virginia's House of Burgesses. When he went to Jamestown to claim his seat, Berkeley had him arrested but then pardoned him (because of public demand) and restored him to the council. He was still refused a military commission.

Gathering strength, a few days later Bacon returned to Jamestown with a force of 600 followers. Berkeley, overwhelmed by the number of citizens against him, finally gave Bacon his commission. However, after Bacon left, the governor denounced him again. This caused such an outcry that Gov. Berkeley fled to Virginia's eastern shore. When he returned to Jamestown two months later in September, Bacon's rebels drove him out again by setting fire to the whole town.

Thinking that after this the king (Charles II) would surely send help, Bacon began to consolidate the citizens, having them sign an oath of allegiance to the crown in case of an investigation. At this inopportune time, however, Bacon was taken by a fever and died.

When Bacon died, a Joseph Ingram took command of the insurgents, but by then Berkeley had regained control of the rivers. By the end of the year, the rebels had lost heart, and Gov. Berkeley completely restored his authority.

The following spring (February 1677) Royal commissioners finally arrived from overseas bringing a Royal Proclamation of Amnesty for all remaining rebels—along with an order for Gov. Berkeley's recall. Berkeley, refusing to leave before he "concluded his business," proceeded to have twenty-three more Virginians executed

before sailing in May. They say he didn't live long after his return.

(Charles II, King of Great Britain and Ireland who reigned from 1660 to 1685, was heard to say, "That old fool has killed more people in that naked country than I did for the murder of my father!")

"Bacon's Rebellion" had involved the entire colony; there were less than 500 men in the whole of Virginia who had not revolted. As Richard New's family lived next door to the fort constructed on the Rolfe plantation, it seems that Richard and his two stalwart sons would have found it impossible to not take part in Bacon's conflict. Yes, it is hard to imagine the News not joining with Bacon in the rebellion.

After Gov. Berkeley's recall, Virginia's problems were unrelieved by her next two despotic governors. It wasn't until the 1690s that good times returned after better governors were appointed and planters finally learned to rotate crops on their worn-out soil. Gaining control of the Indians didn't hurt their prosperity, either.

Their new prosperity brought changes. More colonial mansions and tobacco warehouses were constructed along the banks of the colony's numerous rivers. As the frontier moved westward, the Indians' woodland paths were widened to accommodate carts and carriages. Stone rolling-roads, some as much as twenty miles long, were cobbled to accommodate the rolling of large tobacco casks overland to warehouses on the river. For shorter distances the casks were rolled by hand; for longer distances they were pulled by teams of oxen. (There still remained a shortage of horses.)

Richard New was in his sixties in April of 1681 when his name appeared along with that of his deceased friend and neighbor, Thomas Rolfe, on a land patent being issued to one William Browne. (Sixty was an old age back when one's life expectancy was so short.) Browne's patent was described:

> *... the commonly called Fort formerly belonging to Thomas Rolfe, deceased, which begins at the mouth of Nantepony Neck to Nantepony Runn, to William Webb's planation, to RICHARD NEW, to branch of Revenett Runn; the 525 acres granted to Thomas Rolfe, Gent., on August 1653 and the 300 acres granted 25 April 1656, the bounds accounted as part of the Fort Land ...*

We don't know when Richard New, nor his wife, died. He likely died in the late 1680s or early 1690s at their home on the eastern side of the Chickahominy, about twenty miles west of the "Middle Plantation" (Williamsburg) in James City County. Both his sons had married and settled west of the Chickahominy in Charles City County. Their stories follow.

The Middle Plantation was located seven miles north of old Jamestown, halfway between the James and the York Rivers. New's plantation was just outside the "Middle Plantation" where, in 1693, the "William and Mary College, a Seminary of Ministers of the Gospel" was established. Two years later the Virginia House of Burgesses moved its meeting there from Jamestown, naming the settlement "Williamsburg" in honor of King William III.

After the Burgesses moved their meeting place, old Jamestown, losing population, slowly died away, its houses falling into disrepair, its swampy streets reverting to forest.

Today's archeologists are restoring the town to its former condition. Each year many tourists come to visit the site to catch a glimpse of the town's historic past.

The Children of Richard New

I. Robert New

Born: Circa 1651–1653, James City County, Virginia
Died: 1729? (His inventory was recorded in Charles City County.)
Married: ELIZBETH (___).

Robert, a mere youngster when Indians burned his parents' home, grew up on the New's plantation near the Middle Plantation settlement in James City County. He was around twenty when Bacon's Rebellion took place, so it's very likely that he took an active part in the conflict as practically all Virginia's men were involved.

We have no record of when Robert and Elizabeth married. We found them living in neighboring Charles City County on 'Possimmon' [Persimmon?] Island, a river peninsula on the James River near the west side of the wide mouth of the Chickahominy.

An old Charles City County quick-rent record, *A Full and Perfect Roll of All Land Held By Her Majesty*, dated 1704, has Robert New with Patent No. 100. We haven't a clue as to how he obtained this land, whether rented, traded, bought, or inherited, or if he gained it through his wife.

Robert New's occupation is not now known but one wonders, as he lived with all that water about, if he had learned the craft of boat building from his father.

To visit relatives Robert's family traveled northward up the Chickahominy Path—an Indian trace connecting the Chickahominy and James Rivers—crossing the Chickahominy River over "Soanes Bridge" near Richahocke. (Soanes was the fellow who had purchased the former Barrett Estate.) They may have found it easier to merely paddle a boat up the river.

Robert New's name showed up again several years later on a land patent issued to Charles Christian, as shown:

CHARLES CHRISTIAN, 10 April. 1717: 672 acres of land known . as Possimmin Island in Charles City County, adj. Mr. John Hunt and Thomas Hardaway, on Chickahominy Path near Robert New's corner.

(Charles Christian was a brother of the merchant Thomas Christian who had married Robert's niece, Rebecca New. More on them later.)

Robert's branch of the New family ended with him because he had two daughters but no sons to carry on his New family name. His widow, Elizabeth, took over Robert's estate upon his death, as widows were allowed to do.

As in its earlier days, Virginia continued to suffer from a shortage of women. Widows often remarried, being wooed with "indecent ardor" before their late husbands were decently buried. Widow Elizabeth New may have been planning to remarry in 1729 when she divided Robert's estate between her two grandsons to prevent it being taken over by a new husband. Could be, however, that she was just old and ailing and before she died she wanted to dispose of Robert's estate as she saw fit.

Children Of Robert And Elizabeth New

1. (Daughter), m. **Henry Adams**; Their son Robert inherited half the New estate.
2. (Daughter), m. **Francis Cilly**; Their son **Peter** inherited other half.

II. Edmund New

Born: Circa 1655, James City County, Virginia.

Died: 1726, in old Henrico (now Goochland) County, Virginia.

Married: MARY (____) : (In James City or Charles City County, Virginia)

Our next New ancestor; his biography in next chapter.

Children Of Edmund And Mary New

1. **PRISCILLA**, spinster.
2. **EDWARD**, m. **Sarah**, daughter of Edward and Margaret Bland.
3. **MARY**, m. **John Prior** (Pryor? Found spelled both ways.)
4. **REBECCA**, m. **Thomas Christian**.
5. **SARAH**, m. **John Tulley**, brother of James Tulley Sr.
6. **EDMUND JR.**, m. **Sarah**, daughter of James Sr. and Judith Tulley.
7. **WILLIAM**, m, **Priscilla**, daughter of Francis and Bridgett Sampson.
8. **ELIZABETH**, m. **David Patterson**.
9. **ANN**, died young.
10. **HENRY**, (We lost him: did he also die young?)

Chapter IV
Edmund New
(circa 1655–1727)

Edmund, the younger of Richard New's two sons, was born in the Virginia Colony around 1655 on his father's plantation in James City County. He and his older brother Robert grew up amidst hard times while the colony's economy was at a low point. Due to a shortage of public schools and his family's lack of money, Edmund didn't have a chance at "book-larnin"—he couldn't write his own name—but at a young age he was taught to work, how to farm, and how to make plants grow.

While in his teens Edmund took part in the Bacon Rebellion and, around 1680, he married his wife, Mary. (We don't know who she was.)

Old Mr. Richard New died near the time of Edmund's marriage. Edmund's brother Robert New, being the oldest son and by law the family heir, inherited the New plantation.

Apparently Robert disposed of—sold, traded, or lost—the family plantation and relocated a bit farther south to the north bank of the James River in neighboring Charles City County. Edmund and Mary, with a growing young family, soon followed and resettled near his brother.

At a time when small families were the norm, Edmund and Mary New were blessed with ten children, although only eight lived to reach adulthood. Some said the colonists' health had benefited after they began to drink apple cider instead of contaminated tideland river water.

Edmund New was about fifty in November 1705 when he and his son-in-law Thomas Christian, husband of his fourth child Rebecca, became business partners. They jointly patented 1,324 acres of land on the water near the home of Robert New on the James River in Charles City County. There, where shipping took place, they opened a trading post. Thomas did the merchandising while Edmund managed the growing of their tobacco.

The colony's poor economic condition, though slowly recovering, was boosted in 1707 by the union of England and Scotland. This made it possible for Virginia planters to ship their tobacco to Scotland rather than being required to send it all to England. The Scots paid more for the bright leaf than did England, while charging less for shipping. Encouraged, Virginians increased the size of their tobacco patches. In this new era of prosperity Thomas Christian and John Prior, taking advantage of the proximity of the local shipping wharves, became successful merchants in

Charles City County. (John Prior was husband of Mary New, another of Edmund New's daughters.)

In 1717 Charles Christian, a relative of Thomas, bought 672 acres of land in Charles City County "on the Chickahominy Path near Robert New's corner on the line of Thomas Christian." For this land he paid three pounds cash plus the transportation of two immigrants. [See *Chas. City Patent Book 10*, p. 311.]

Privileged upper-class planters—Virginia's gentry—were becoming more wealthy by land speculation and slave trading. Their first small number of Negro slaves increased to become the basic labor on their extensive plantations. Smaller landholders were being crowded out. New immigrants from Scotland and Wales still poured in but, not finding farmland in the coastal tideland readily available, began settling in Virginia's thinly populated piedmont as far west as the Blue Ridge Mountains.

With population increasing and the existing worn-out fields becoming depleted of nutrients, there arose a great hunger for new fertile soil. The old practice of granting a headright for each new settler had shifted to requiring cash for land. The price of a land patent was about five shillings per each fifty acres; to make a decent living one needed at least twenty to fifty acres for each farm laborer. In addition, along with land cleared for crops and pastures, a planter needed forested land to provide wood for houses, barns, barrels, fencing, and heat.

A new naval-store industry thrived as land in Virginia and the Carolinas was cleared. Farmers used their felled trees as a sideline to their tobacco cash crop by manufacturing pitch, tar, turpentine, and resin for naval use.

The tallest trees were marked by the Crown, those that were at least twenty-two to thirty-six inches across, to be used as masts for the Royal Navy—but who could tell if a felled tree was marked or not after its bark had been removed? Let's just say that the local commercial sailing ships did not suffer a want of tall masts. Those who illegally cut the Crown's marked trees were fined up to a hundred pounds, but few were ever caught.

Another forest-based industry was the production of potash used to make soap, glass, and fertilizer, and as a bleach for wool. In fact, more money was made from potash than from the raw timber. Potash was made by burning hardwood trees, oak or birch, and boiling their ashes in a kettle to produce a thick brown salt. Sometimes this salt was baked in hot ovens until its carbon had burned away, thus producing a better product, pearl ash, which was then sold for a higher price.

Tobacco is a greedy plant that quickly depletes a field of its nutrients. Growing tobacco in Charles City County on his and the Christians' jointly held plantation, Edmund New found each year their crop yield was becoming less. He entertained thoughts of moving to a fresh site that had better soil. Acting upon his need for richer land, Edmund, in his sixties, made plans to move west. Accepting a bond from his son-in-law Thomas Christian as payment, he sold his share of their business arrangement.

Their older children were already married, but the News, taking their younger children, left Virginia's tidelands for its piedmont, the foothills of the Blue Ridge Mountains. Following the James River, Edmund patented land where they settled on the headwaters of "Little Licking-Hole Creek" in sparsely settled western Henrico County. A description of Edmund's new land as recorded on page 47 of *Henrico County Patent Book 11* was:

EDMUND NEW, 17 August 1720; 400 acres, Henrico County on N. side of James River and on west side of Little Horsepen Creek; 40 schillngs.

In the next *Henrico Patent Book, No. 12*, the following was recorded on page 399:

*THOMAS BALEY [Bailey?], 24 March 1725: 229 acres, Henrico, County, N. side of James River, cornering on **Edmund New** near head of a branch of Little Licking-Hole Creek; 25 shillings.*

(Vast Henrico, one of the four large original counties, had been formed in early days when the English shire form of government had been instituted in Virginia. At first an unsettled wilderness, Henrico County reached westward from Charles City County all the way to the ridge of the Blue Ridge Mountains where only Indians roamed.)

There were no neighbors listed on Edmund New's 1720 Henrico land patent, which would indicate that he was among that area's first white settlers; the land of his neighbor, Tom Bailey, was not patented until 1725, five years after Edmund arrived.

In addition to the monumental task of clearing trees to make potash and for fields to grow the traditional tobacco, Edmund planted food crops and raised horses. It was likely his horse corral that gave title to the "Little Horsepen Creek" named in his patent.

Ever a dedicated farmer, Edmund's biggest dream for his new foothill land was to begin a nursery for apple trees. Having observed that families who drank cider appeared far healthier than those who drank the polluted tideland water, he came to believe that more people should grow apples. Seeing a need, he began the propagation of apple trees, selling their scions to others who wanted to raise their own fruit.

His new venture succeeded; to this day this area of Virginia is known for its production of apples.

Most all of the New's married children followed their parents to Henrico County where, in time, they bought land of their own. After years of hard work, Edmund and Mary spent their final years together in contentment, sharing days of happiness with their increasing number of grandchildren.

It was in the summer of 1726 that old Edmund, in his seventies, became ill. That July he dictated his will, naming his wife, Mary, with nine of their ten children. (Missing was their oldest son, Edward, who had died six years earlier in Charles City County.)

Being too ill—and illiterate—Edmund couldn't pen his will for himself, but at the end of the dictated document, he painstakingly drew the letter "N" for his signature. After he died two months later, his will was recorded on September

5, 1726, on pages 50 and 51 of the *Henrico County Will Book I*, as follows:

Will of Edmund New Of Henrico County and St. James Parish:

Executors: Wife, son Edmund [Jr.], and daughter, Prisella [sic].

- To son Edmund all land lying and being on lower side of upper branch Covold [Corral?] of the little kreek [Little Horsepen Creek?] of Little Licking-Hole.
- To son Edmund New my nursery of apple trees.
- To my daughter Prisella New all remaining part of my land lying on upper side of Little Creek Licking Hole.
- To my loving and lawful wife Mary New, son Edmund, and daughter Prisella; my personal effects to be equally divided between them and not to be appraised after my decease.
- My full right to the forty-pound bond of the Thomas Christians, to all of them and their heirs.
- I give and bequest to my grandson John New, son to my son Edward New, deceased, and to William New, Mary Prior, Rebeccer Christian, Sarah Tuley, Elizabeth Patterson, Ann New, and Henry New, one shilling money each as their full dower.

> His
> Edmund "N" New
> Mark

Witnesses: Paul Green, John Lain [Lane?], Hugh Morris. [Neighbors.]

Lying there in his sickbed and listening to his family's suggestions, Edmund got to thinking about the will that he had dictated. Upon more

consideration he thought to divide his estate differently. He dictated a second will, written thus:

Edmund New Of Henrico Co. And Charleston Parish, 8 August 1726;

Wife Mary, son Edmund, & daughter Priscilla, Executors.

- Son Edmund New, one half of land and the other half, with the plantation, to daughter Priscilla. [Priscilla was his oldest child; Edmund was his oldest *living* son.]
- To wife and my two children above named, all other effects to be equally divided between them after debts are paid.
- To daughter Mary Prier [Prior? Pryor?] one shilling and no more. --To daughter Rebecker [Rebecca Christian] one shilling and no more.
- To daughter Sarah Tuley [Tulley? Tooley?] one shilling and no more.
- To daughter Elizabeth Patterson one shilling and no more.
- To son William New, one shilling and no more.
- To son Edmund New, my nursery of apple trees.

> His
> Edmund "N" New
> Mark

Test.: M. New, Thomas Christian, John Tuley. [Wife and sons-in-law.]

[Note change in church parish; Edmund had not moved but boundaries of older. St. James Parish were changed when the new Parish was formed.]

While composing his new will, it had come to Edmund's attention that his adolescent grandson, John New, did not need his money as John, when he came of age, would inherit "Kymages," a large plantation estate that had been his late father's, Edward New. Young John was omitted in this second will.

Also, this time Edmund did not mention his former business partner Thomas Christian, nor Christian's children. Instead, he bequeathed his daughter Rebecca Christian only one shilling, the same as he had his other daughters.

Finally, Edmund's two youngest, Ann and Henry New, were not named in his second will. It is possible that these unmarried minors had died

before this second will was written. No further reference to them has been found. One wonders if they died of the same malady that took old Edmund.

Following Edmund's death, widow Mary New and his two oldest children divided his personal effects and neighbors were asked to inventory the plantation assets. This inventory, along with each item's value given in English currency, was listed thus:

Inventory Of Edmund New, Deceased:

Item	Value	Item	Value	Item	Value
Sorrell Mare & Colt	1.10.1	Bedstead	0.04.0	6 yr. heifers	4.10.0
Gray Mare & Colt	1.05.0	Lumber	0.10.0	Four sows	1.12.0
Bay Mare & Colt	1.15.0	Bay Mare & Colt	1.10.1	Ten young hogs	2.00.0
Small Feather Bed	0.10.0	Gray Mare & Colt	1.10.0	Ten shoats	2.00.0
Two Basins	0.02.0	3-yr-old horses	1.15.0	Two Barrows	1.00.0
Three small dishes	0.04.6	2-yr-old horses	1.15.0	Six young hogs	1.10.0
Pot & Pot rack	0.07.6	Four Ives	0.18.0	One Sow	0.8.0
Couch Frame	0.05.0	Six Cows	6.00.0	Two Shoats	0.04.0

Witnesses: Richard Oglesby, Richard Haynesworth Jr., This Beason.
Presented to an order of Court 5 September 1726 at a court held in Henrico County 5 June 1727.
Mary New presented this inventory upon oath and it was admitted to record.
[Signed] William Wood

Changes were made in Henrico County's boundaries near the time of Edmund's death. The eastern area of the vast Henrico County, where the New plantation was located, was changed; the governor created a new Virginia county, "Goochland," while leaving Henrico's western area intact. Hence, after 1727 any records concerning Edmund's estate were recorded in the new Goochland County courthouse instead of in Henrico.

Edmund New, comfortable but not wealthy, had built a profitable plantation in Henrico County, growing and selling apple trees and raising horses. At his death the inventoried value of his estate—31 pounds, 14 shillings, and 6 pence—would be around $3,025 in today's American currency.

As shown, old Mr. New had bequeathed half his land, the half where his home was sited, to his eldest child, Priscilla New. The other half, the part with the apple trees, he had willed to Edmund New Jr., his oldest surviving son. Being male, Edmund Jr. had no problem claiming his inheritance, but Miss Priscilla, an unwed female, ran into problems.

By law an unmarried female could not own land outright; any land she inherited was controlled either by her widowed mother, an older brother, or some other responsible male who would look to her interest. When or if the girl married her land would then become the property of her new husband.

Since Virginia's beginning, there had been a shortage of women; at one point the Crown had paid passage for boatloads of adventurous ladies who would consent to immigrate. Virginia men continued to vie for the hand of any eligible female, be she tall, short, plump, thin, or ugly. Even more in demand were the girls who had land for a dower.

As Miss Priscilla New was unmarried her widowed mother controlled her spinster daughter's inheritance. They continued to live together in the plantation home, and all went well until Mary New announced that she planned to marry Mr. Hugh Morris, and this she did, causing quite a stir!

Hugh Morris, an immigrant from Wales, had witnessed the signing of Edmund New's will. After Edmund died, Morris wooed, and won, Edmund's widow in an attempt to take over Miss Priscilla's half of the New plantation. He would have succeeded had not young William, the New's third son, intervened. The conflicts between William New and Hugh Morris are chronicled in the following chapter about the life of William New.

Records show that the ambitious Morris failed to acquire Priscilla's land, but in 1743 he bought more land on the Lower Hardware River located farther west though still in Goochland County. He and Mary moved there (with Miss Priscilla) even before he could find a buyer for his original land-holdings near the New estate at Little Licking Hole Creek.

As settlers from eastern Virginia continued their westward migration, in 1744 another new county, Albemarle, was separated from the westernmost portion of Goochland, on the steeper eastern slopes of the Blue Ridge Mountains. This new land Morris purchased, on the Lower Hardware River in western Goochland County, was included in the area that soon became Albemarle County.

Several years later in 1748, Morris finally found a buyer for his old land back near Little Licking Hole Creek. The following entry was recorded in *Goochland County Deed Bk 6*:

HUGH MORRIS, November 13, 1748:
To William Welday, for 95 pounds current money, on Branch of Little Licking-Hole

Creek and branches of Treasures Run; 730 acre of land contained in 3 parcels of land patents, 1ˢᵗ granted in 1733, 2ⁿᵈ dated 1735, and third dated 1736.

(signed) Hugh Morris

An attached note stated further that Mrs. Mary Morris had relinquished her dower for this sale.

Eventually most of Edmund New's children left western Goochland (formerly Henrico) County to re-settle on the upper slopes of the Blue Ridge Mountains in the new Albemarle County. Their stories follow.

Children of Edmund and Mary New

(It is impossible to find the exact birth dates of Edmund New's ten children; their ages written herein are estimated. The order of their appearance below follows the scant evidence now available.)

I. Priscilla New

Born: The oldest child, born in James City County in early 1680s.
Died: After 1741, in Amherst or Albemarle County, Virginia.
Married: No record of a marriage found; she probably remained a spinster.

Growing up as eldest child in a large family, Priscilla New became "Mama's helper," assisting in the management of the busy New household while being "big sister" to her lively younger siblings. She never found time to marry, or perhaps she just never found a suitable man she wanted.

Before Priscilla's father died, he had bequeathed his oldest living son and male heir, Edmund Jr., half of the New plantation, the half with his apple tree nursery and orchards. But to his firstborn, Miss Priscilla, he gave the other half, which contained his home. He had appointed his wife Mary, along with Priscilla and Edmund Jr., to be the executors of his will.

After her father died, Priscilla continued to live with her widowed mother and the younger New children in her inherited plantation home on Goochland County's Little Licking Hole Creek—until her mother married their near neighbor, Hugh Morris. As soon as her mother re-married, Mr. Morris, eager to become rich, took over Priscilla's inherited fields for his own profit, saying it was not fittin' that a single female should own property. Miss Priscilla, who had a stubborn streak and a mind of her own, did not agree.

It was not proper, back then, for ladies to appear in court in person, but Miss Priscilla, undaunted, had her lawyer brother, young William New, represent her in a court battle against her mother and her new stepfather. As a result of William's help, Miss Priscilla retained the title of her land, along with its profit. (The case was finally settled out of court.)

When William New married, his big sister let him establish his own home on 150 acres of her land. It is not clear if she sold William this land or if she graciously gave him land as a wedding gift.

Mr. Morris and Priscilla's mother, along with other neighbors, prepared to join the rush of pioneers moving west to find fertile new ground. When her mother and Mr. Morris moved to the western part of Goochland County in 1738, Priscilla left with them. Her stepfather was appointed to act as her legal guardian for the purpose of selling her remaining land.

Records show that Hugh Morris staked a claim in western Goochland on the lower Hardware River in 1743. A year later that western area of Goochland County was measured off to create another new county, Albemarle.

We don't know what became of Miss Priscilla New after they moved. No wedding record for her has been located.

II. Edward New

Born: Circa 1685, James City County, Virginia.
Died: 1720, Charles City County, Virginia.
Married: **Sarah Bland**, daughter of Edward and Margaret Bland of 'Kymages,' a 2,000 acre land tract in Charles City County. (Kymages had first been owned by an early Virginia Governor, Sir William Berkeley. q.v.)

Upon the 1690 death of Edward Bland, Gent., Kymages was entailed to his widow, Mrs. Margaret Bland and their two children, John and Sarah Bland. The widow Margaret soon remarried and with her new husband, Thomas Tanner, by law claimed her share of the Bland estate.

Then, sadly, young John Bland also died, leaving his sister, Sarah, to inherit both children's share of the estate.

About 1700 Miss Sarah Bland, the heiress, married Edward New (oldest son of our Edmund New) who took over Sarah's interest in Kymages. Their only child they named **John New**, a namesake of Sarah's late brother, John Bland.

John New was but a lad in 1720 when his dad, Edward New, a youthful husband and father, died at Kymages. We don't know the circumstances surrounding his death, whether caused by illness or accident.

William Waller, in his *Laws of Virginia, a Collection of Virginia Laws from 1619* [Vol. VT, p. 303], wrote, " ... [Sarah Bland New] entered into said two thousand acres of land, and

apperurtenances, and became seized in possession of two third parts of the same, expectant immediately upon the termination of the natural life of the said Margaret Bland Turner [Sarah's mom], and intermarried with Edward New, late of the county of Charles City, deceased, whom she survived, and by whom she had issue, John New, a son ... "

John New, a minor, was by law the rightful heir to inherit Kymages when he came of age, because Kymages, being entailed to John, was to remain in the possession of the heirs of the Bland family forever. However, in 1722 John's widowed mother, Sarah Bland New, married Alexander Horton who promptly sold her young son's Kymages inheritance to one Benjamin Harrison for fifty pounds English sterling and 1,530 acres of land located southward in Hunting Swamp in Surry County.

To make matters worse, the new husband of young John's Grandma Margaret, Thomas Turner, sold Margaret's one-third part of Kymages, which was also entailed to John, for thirty pounds sterling.

As Kymages was entailed to young John, neither his mother nor grandmother had the right to sell it. But he was just a kid—what could he do?

Child of Edward and Sarah Bland New (Grandson of Edmund New, named in will):

1. **JOHN NEW**, (circa 1710-d.1772), m. (1) **Tabitha Pennington** (2) **Frances Butts**.

    John, in his teens, moved south with his mother and his stepfather, Alex Horton when they relocated on their new Surry County land. Next to them was the land of Edward Pennington, who died in 1729. His will named his wife Tabitha along with his three sons. [Recorded *Surry County Will Book 3*]

The year following Pennington's death found John New, then around twenty, marrying widow Tabitha Pennington. John, a wheelwright and carpenter, took over his wife's Pennington plantation.

John was industrious. In 1739 he patented land of his own near the Carolina border on Fountain Creek in Spring Swamp in Brunswick County, Virginia. Later, he installed a gristmill on another acre of land in Spring Swamp he had purchased on Fountain Creek from one William Jordon.

John and Tabitha had sons—William, John Jr., and Benjamin—before she died. John, needing a housekeeper and a mother for his children, quickly married again. His second wife, Frances Butts, was a daughter of John and Judith Armistead Butts of King William County. With Frances John fathered five more children.

John New, when a juvenile, had been helpless in 1722 when his mother and grandmother sold his Kymages birthright to Benjamin Harrison, but when he became older he took his case to court. In 1741, after several years of legal writs and court hearings to decide the rightful ownership of Kymages, Benjamin Harrison died. Stubborn and determined to not give up, John New continued his legal battle with a younger Harrison, Benjamin Harrison II.

It took John around twenty years, but in February 1752 the second Benjamin Harrison gave in; the case was settled out of court. In exchange for New's right to Kymages, Harrison agreed to cede to John the 700 acres of land he owned in Henrico County near the town of Richmond, along with Harrison's water gristmill located on the James River at Richmond and some Negro slaves valued at 350 pounds British sterling.

(Who were these Harrisons? The family had arrived in Virginia early in the seventeenth century. Their descendant Benjamin Harrison II, a statesman who became Virginia's governor, was born in 1726 in Charles City County on Berkeley, a large plantation adjacent to the Blands' Kymages estate. He had become a member of the Virginia House of Burgesses and was twice its elected speaker. He took over his father's fight with John New for the ownership of Kymages, whereupon, in 1752, he ceded to John New the land in Henrico County. In 1773 he was chosen a member of the committee, which united the American colonies against Great Britain. He became a member of the Continental Congress in 1774–1777. A close friend to George Washington, he was a member of the Continental Congress where, as committee chairman, he reported on the Declaration of Independence, which he signed on July 4, 1776. Upon his retirement from Congress, he took a seat in the House of Delegates, serving as speaker from 1778 to 1781 when he was elected Virginia's governor and was twice re-elected. After a long eventful life, he died in 1791.)

(William Henry Harrison, the third son of Governor Benjamin Harrison and wife Elizabeth Barrett, was born on the plantation of Berkeley in Charles City County on February 9, 1773. Becoming famous as an Indian fighter "out west" with the U.S. Army, they called him "Tippecanoe." He was elected and became the ninth president of the United States in

1837. A month after he was inaugurated, the 68-year-old "Old Tippecanoe" died of pneumonia while in Washington. His office was taken over by his vice president, John Tyler, the first to become president of the United States without an election.)

(A *third* Benjamin Harrison, born 1833 in Ohio, was a grandson of the above president, William Henry Harrison, and great-grandson to the Virginia governor and statesman, William Harrison of Berkeley who had settled John New's property rights out of court. A well-known and respected lawyer and judge, he was elected as the twenty-third president of the United States in 1888, but was defeated by Grover Cleveland when he ran for a second term.)

Growing older, John New did not compose a will, but before he died he deeded his oldest son and heir, William New, half his Henrico County land. Later, when John became too old to manage his affairs, he deeded William the other half. William New never had to fight for his inheritance as had his father. (After the problems he had faced about Kymages, old John had lost faith in depending upon an inheritance.) With his estate thus neatly disposed, John New died intestate in 1772.

Children of John and Tabitha Pennington New:

1. **WILLIAM NEW**, (1713?–1784), m. **Edith**. This William was John's son who was deeded his father's land. (See above.) His name on Henrico County tax list in 1783, replaced by "Wm. New Estate" in 1784–1786, with "Edith New" appearing in 1787. Children were **Tabitha, William Jr., McGilvary, and Martha**. (William New Jr. fought in North Carolina's 4th Regiment under Capt. John Ashe in the American Revolution.)

2. **JOHN NEW, JR.** (173_–1782), m. **Margaret** and moved to Duplin County, North Carolina. His children were **Joseph, Betty, Tabitha, John, Peggy, William, George, and Winney**. [This younger William New was an ancestor of Janet New Huff who, with Ann Wall Allgood, both of Natchez, Mississippi, wrote a self-published book, *The Family of New*, in 1981.]

3. **BENJAMIN NEW**, (b. 1750s?), m. **Elizabeth Butlar**. He was listed on Charles City Tax List from 1789 through 1796. Children: **William, Thomas B., James W. and Jane**.

4. **JAMES NEW**, m. (____) (____). "James New" was listed on Tax List where he worked as clerk of the Charles City Court in 1782. After 1792 he began to be listed as "James New Sr." when the name of "James New Jr." also began to appear. Names of other children, if any, are unknown.

Children of John New with second wife, Frances Butts; (Birth dates unknown):

1. **SARAH NEW**
2. **JEMIMIA NEW**
3. **RICHARD NEW**, m. (1) **Elizabeth Lacy**, (2) **Joyce Ragland**.

Richard and Elizabeth migrated to sparsely settled Bedford County in southwest Henrico County. David E. Johnson, in his *History of Middle New River and Settlement* wrote, " … The origin of the name of the New River in Bedford County came from a man named "New" who, in early days, kept a ferry … " [Huntington, 1906]

When Elizabeth New died in Bedford County in 1781, Richard returned to Charles City County. with their children. In Charles City he married his second wife, Joyce Ragland. His name appeared on the tax roll there from 1781 through 1796, the year he died. His will, recorded on page 369 of *Charles City Will Book 1*, names his wife Joyce Ragland New along with his six children. The children were **Elerson Armistead, John** (and John's wife, Mary), **James Lacy, Nancy, Judith**, and **Elizabeth**. (James Lacy New fought in the Revolution and married Gulielna Ladd and migrated to Ohio.)

4. **JESSE NEW**, m. **Sally Hamlett**; children were **Nelson, Susan, Abby, and Joseph**.

III. Mary New Prior

Born: Late 1680s, James City County, Virginia
Died: Goochland County, Virginia
Married: **John Prior**, circa 1700, in Charles City County, Virginia

John Prior was an astute businessman. He and his brother-in-law Thomas Christian (q.v.) were successful merchants in Charles City County in 1720 when Mary's father, Edmund New, sold Thomas Christian his share of their business to move out to Henrico County to raise apples. In 1727 when old Mr. Edmund died, he willed his daughter Mary New Prior one schilling.

In 1728, the year following the old man's death, the partners Prior and Christian jointly patented 400 acres of land to open a new trading post in old Henrico County (which soon become Goochland County) "on N. side of James River on Edmund New's line…." (This "New's line" mentioned in their deed referred to the line of Edmund New Jr. who had recently inherited the

land with the apple trees on Little Licking Hole Creek from his father.)

It is believed that John and Mary Prior had five sons (listed below) who moved with them to Goochland County; we haven't been able to locate any daughters.

The new trading post developed a brisk trade as more and more tideland settlers came pouring into the new county. Before long all the better farmland was taken so settlers continued on westward to stake a claim. Edmund Jr., Mary's brother, put up his Goochland land for sale so he could move westward with some of their kinsmen. John Prior, remaining in Goochland, helped sell Edmund's land, and, in 1750 when the land was sold, John signed the deed as a witness.

We have no record of Mary's death, but John died in 1755 in Goochland County where, we are told, his will was recorded.

Possible Descendants of John and Mary New Prior:

1. **JOHN PRIOR JR.** came with his parents when they moved to Goochland County, but moved to Goochland's western area with his mother's relatives in 1741. There were two John Priors—Sr. and Jr.—from Amherst County listed on the payroll of Capt. William Tucker's militia Company in 1781 near the close of the war that Americans fought for independence. That was the year the British Col. Bannastre Tarleton, "Bloody Ban," made his cavalry raids on Charlottesville in Albemarle County, burning homes along the way.

   It is thought that these two Prior men were our Mary New Prior's son and grandson as her husband had died before the war began. One of them died in Pittsylvania County (south of Amherst County), his inventory recorded in 1797.

2. **DAVID PRIOR**, possible son, died in Goochland County where his inventory was recorded in 1746.

3. **NICHOLAS PRIOR**, possible son, also died in Goochland in 1746 where his will was recorded. (Another Nicholas Prior, a younger man, owned 150 acres of land in Albemarle County where he had moved before 1758. His name was on the tax roll there in 1773 and fought in the Revolutionary War in Amherst County. After the war he acted as bondsman when one Sally Prior married a Robert Nichols in 1795. Was this Sally Prior his sister or daughter?)

4. **SAMUEL PRIOR**, died in 1773, his inventory recorded in Goochland County.

5. **WILLIAM PRIOR**, m. **Margaret**, (_____). In 1747 William was living on the Pedlar River which flows into the James in the southern portion of Albemarle County in the part that soon became Amherst County. In 1772 William and his wife Margaret sold 350 acres of land situated on "both sides of the Pedlar River" in Amherst County to one Jacob Brown. A month later William bought back 93 acres of this same land "located on Brown's Creek near the south branch of Enchanted Creek" from this same Jacob Brown. Could William, owning land on both sides of a stream, have been operating a ferry?

IV. Rebecca New Christian

Born: Circa 1690, James City County, Virginia
Died: Outlived her husband, who died in 1737.
Married: In early 1700s to **Thomas Christian**, the brother of the merchant Charles Christian, who lived next to the New family.

When Rebecca married, her husband Thomas Christian worked for his brother Charles, a local merchant, but owned no land. To help his daughter get a home, in 1705 Edmund New went in with his new son-in-law Thomas to jointly patent 1,324 acres of land in Charles City County. This land adjoined the land of Edmund's brother Robert New, who was Rebecca's uncle.

The young couple had built a home and had started a family when Rebecca's parents moved westward to Henrico County. Having put down roots, Rebecca and Thomas chose to remain where they were. Thomas continued to work for his brother at the Charles Christian trading post. However, with his family growing larger, Thomas thought that it would be more profitable to open his own store. The population in Henrico County where Rebecca's folks lived was fast increasing—perhaps if he opened a trading post there it would do well.

Feeling thus, in 1717 Thomas sold his brother Charles the 672 acres of his Charles City plantation "cornering on Robert New's land on Possiomon [Sp.?] Island, a peninsula on the James River …." Ready to leave, Thomas and Rebecca Christian followed her family to live with, or near, her parents in Henrico County. Rebecca was glad; her folks were getting older, and she longed for her children to know their grandparents better.

Thomas was happy to sell his land as he needed capital to buy land and to stock his proposed store in Henrico County. He pocketed the money from this sale and gave Rebecca's father, Edmund New, a promissory note for Mr. New's interest in the Charles City land that Thomas had sold.

When the Christians arrived in Henrico County, Thomas shook hands on a deal he made with an experienced merchant, John Prior. They agreed to form a partnership, combining their capital to buy land to open a new trading post.

(John Prior, q.v., was the husband of Mary New, Rebecca's older sister.)

When Thomas and Rebecca came to Henrico County, Rebecca found her old father in poor health. Feeling "po'ly," he dictated his will in which he gave the Christians "the full right of the forty-pound bond of Thomas Christian's to them and their heirs … " But then he changed his mind. In his second will, dictated from his deathbed, he bequeathed his daughter Rebecca Christian "one shilling and no more," the same amount he gave to his other daughters.

After the old man died in 1726, in October 1727 the following two land patents were recorded on page 222 of *Henrico County Patent Book 13*:

> *JOHN PRIOR AND THOMAS CHRISTIAN: 400 acres in Henrico County, on North side of James River on Edmund New's line. [This Edmund was Rebecca's brother who had inherited land from their father.]*
>
> *THOMAS CHRISTIAN: 400 acs. in Henrico County on North side of the James River on the lines of James and Thomas Christian; 40 shillings. [James and Thomas Christian were the two oldest sons of Thomas and Rebecca; their second son was named 'Thomas' like his father.]*

The portion of Henrico County where the Christians and most of their New relations lived was changed to become Goochland County a year later in 1728 when that growing new county was inaugurated. The Prior and Christian partnership in Goochland was quite successful; their store, a trading post, did well. Thomas and Rebecca became quite prominent Goochland citizens before they died. Thomas was the first to go.

On October 16, 1736, Thomas, being "very sick," wrote his final will and testament. His brother-in-law, John Prior, his close friend and business partner, remained at his bedside and signed the will as a witness.

The following spring (May 1737) after Thomas died his will was recorded on page 32 of *Goochland County Wills and Deeds, 1736–42.* In it he appointed his wife, Rebecca, and their oldest son, James, as his executors. He bequeathed Rebecca "the land I live on, 210 acres, for life, and then to my son James." Also, to Rebecca he left his horses and his Negroes, Jack and Tom, for her lifetime, and then to go to her oldest son, James Christian.

Thomas gave small plantations, around 250–300 acres each, to each of his four sons. (We don't know the names of their wives.) To his favorite grandson and namesake, Tom Christian, he gave a cow and her calf. His other children are named below with their share of the inheritance.

After Thomas died, Rebecca continued to live in her home with her oldest son's family to care for her. Some of her progeny moved farther west to Albemarle and Amherst counties.

Children of Thomas and Rebecca New Christian:

1. **JAMES CHRISTIAN**, (b. 170_, oldest son): When James' mother died, he inherited the family home on its 210 acres of land, along with its horses and slaves. He was there in Goochland in 1740 when he witnessed a deed for his Uncle William New who was selling out. James also left the county later, moving his family westward. He died in Albemarle County in 1759.

2. **THOMAS CHRISTIAN JR.:** Lived on the 250 acres of his inherited Goochland County land. In 1730 he was called to serve on a Goochland jury, and was

later made a constable. He remained in Goochland County where he died in 1745.

3. **ROBERT CHRISTIAN**: Inherited 300 acres from his father, "it being the land where he now lives." In 1741 Robert had moved to western Goochland where by 1747 he was living on the branches of Porridge Creek in Albemarle County. (Part of Goochland County was changed to form Albemarle County.) He died there in 1749, leaving a will.

4. **WILLIAM CHRISTIAN**: Inherited 300 acres from his father, "it being my part of the land that John Prior and I took up," wrote old Thomas Christian.

5. **MOURNING CHRISTIAN COLEMON**: She was married when her father died. He left her one ewe.

6. **MARY CHRISTIAN**: Inherited a horse colt, "etc." from her father.

7. **CONSTANT CHRISTIAN**: Inherited several different small items.

8. **REBECCA CHRISTIAN (II)**: Inherited six ewes.

V. Sarah New Tuley

Born: Circa 1700, James City County, Virginia
Died: In Albemarle County, Virginia
Married: **John Tuley**, in Charles City County, Virginia

John was a younger brother to James Tuley whose daughter, Miss Sarah Tuley, became the bride of Edmund New Jr. (We have been told that the Tuley brothers, John and James, were descendants of an older John Tuley who had been imported to Virginia's Accromack County back in 1640 by a John Holliday. (Further proof needed.) We have found their name spelled Tuley, Tulley, or Tully—the "Tuley's Creek" near their home was spelled "Totier Creek" by a French mapmaker!)

In 1729, the year after Goochland County was formed from the western portion of Henrico, John Tuley with his wife, Sarah Tuley, relinquishing her dower rights, sold their small farm to Judge Edward Scott for fifty pounds. [See Goochland County Wills & Deeds, 1728–1736, p. 74.] This land was in St. James Parish, Goochland County, "on N. side of James River, bounded by Edmund New, (Jr.)"

(Judge Scott, a lawyer, had arrived in Goochland County the previous year when that new county's officials were being selected. After buying land in the neighborhood where the News lived, he had purchased John and Sarah Tuley's adjoining farm to enlarge his recently purchased Scott plantation. We'll meet him again later.)

Young Miss Sarah New married John Tuley while her parents were living in Charles City County. When the New family moved to Henrico County in 1720, the young couple John and Sarah Tuley traveled with them. In Henrico County John was able to buy a patent on the 100-acre tract of land that adjoined the land of Sarah's father, Edmund New. Upon selling their land to Judge Scott, John and Sarah New Tuley joined the surge of planters that went looking for new lands. They followed John's big brother, James Tuley, up the James River to start over in the more western—and more unsettled—part of that same large county. Both brothers patented land on a creek, calling it "Tuleys Creek." John's patent was for 250 acres, although the cunning James, who had more money, was able to patent more.

A year after the Tuley families came this western part of Goochland was again separated to form another new county, Albemarle.

Generations later a Rev. Woods wrote, " … [today's] Totier Creek, near the James and John Tuley plantations, was known as Tuley's Creek on some old maps. A small prominence on the old Irish Road, near the intersection of a road from Cocke's Mill, came to be called Tuley's Hill." [Edgar Woods, *Albemarle County in Virginia*, Harrison, Virginia: C. J. Currier County, 1978.]

It seems that the plantation John Tuley bought in Albemarle County did well. John and Sarah lived there for twenty years or more before John wrote his will on November 25, 1747. From his will we find that his estate, by then, consisted of 300 acres of land and eight slaves. In his will he named his wife, Sarah, along with their four sons and three daughters. We don't know the ages of their children or who they married; we also don't know the exact date of John's death. His will was not proved until May in 1750 when it was recorded in *Albemarle County Deeds & Wills, No. 1*, pages 14 and 15.

In his will John wrote that his "beloved wife Sarah" was to inherit all his estate land and all his Negroes to be disposed of, after her demise, to his children as follows:

- **JAMES TULEY**: A Negro woman named Abby, and to his grandson John Tuley, a Negro child named Lucy. (This grandson, John's namesake, was son of his son James Tuley.)
- **JOHN TULEY Jr.**: 100 acres of the estate land (after his mother died), along with three Negroes: Toney, Amey, and Jamey.
- **ARTHUR TULEY**: 200 acres of the estate land (after his mother died) and two Negroes named Joe and Peg.
- **CHARLES TULEY**: He and his brother Arthur were the appointed executors of John's will. He was to equally divide the remaining part of the estate goods and chattel between himself and his brothers Arthur and John.
- **MARY TULEY**: Ten pounds Currt. [current?] money raised from the estate

- **ANN TULEY**: Ten pounds Currt. money from estate.
- **HEORSLY ISOM**: One shilling. John called her his daughter, so "Isom" was, apparently, her married name. (There was a Charles and an Elijah Isom from neighboring Amherst County who later fought in the American Revolution.)

Thus, from John Tuley's will we learn that John and Sarah New Tuley's seven children were **James, John, Arthur, Charles, Mary, Ann,** and **Heorsly Isam**. We still don't know their birth dates nor the names of their spouses.

VI. Edmund New Jr.

Born: Mid–1690s in Charles City County, Virginia, second oldest son of Edmund New Sr.

Died: His will was probated in Albemarle County in 1781

Married: In Albemarle County [*Albemarle County Wedding Book*, p. 332] to Miss **Sarah Tuley**, the daughter of the older James and Judith Tuley and was niece to the above John Tuley and Sarah New Tuley, sister of Edmund New Jr. [Take time—'figger' it out.] Ed Jr. and his new wife Sarah Tuley were related by marriage, but not by blood.

Born in Charles City County, Ed Jr. became a young man in 1720 when he moved with his parents, Edmund and Mary New, to establish their home in the original Henrico County. No doubt his strong muscles were a welcome help to his father as they cleared the primitive forest to start their apple tree business. Virginians were learning to drink apple juice so more orchards were needed to produce more cider. New's tree nursery became successful.

Ed Jr. continued to live in Henrico County with his parents where he worked to propagate and maintain their apple tree nursery. He didn't have a chance to go to school but toiled their fields all year, and every spring he traveled about the country, peddling apple tree scions, and in the fall, he delivered fresh apples.

When Ed Jr.'s father died in 1727, Ed Jr. inherited half the New estate land, the half on Little Licking Hole Creek where their apple trees were grown.

In 1728, the year after Ed Jr. inherited the apple trees, Henrico's county lines were changed to form a new county. With this change Ed Jr.'s inherited apple orchard came to be sited in the new county, Goochland.

One of the New's neighbors near Little Licking Hole Creek in Goochland (formerly Henrico) County was Judge Edward Scott who had arrived in 1728, just as the new county of Goochland was being formed. The judge bought a plantation near Ed New's land and then, to enlarge this plantation a year later in 1729, he purchased the land of Ed New's sister Sarah and her husband, John Tuley.

Judge Scott commenced to tell the local folks about the wondrous opportunities to be found in the as yet unsettled far western part of Goochland County—how beautiful its far blue mountains, how fertile its virgin soil. He had already invested in land out there for himself, but said he was too busy at the Goochland courthouse to move out there just yet.

He must have been convincing. In 1741 James Tuley, more adventuresome (and more affluent) than his younger brother John Tuley, patented 4,000 acres of land in far western Goochland near the land owned by Judge Scott. Encouraging their married children to come with them, James and his wife, Judith, loaded up to travel west to relocate on their new plantation. Several of them did, establishing new homes in far western Goochland

near their parents. (Later this western portion of Goochland County was settled enough to be incorporated into another new county that was named Albemarle.)

When the Tuley's moved, Ed New, enamored with the Tuley's daughter Sarah, left his apple trees behind, not even waiting to sell his land. He moved to western Goochland to work for Mr. James Tuley.

As Ed's home and plant nursery had not yet sold, his name was still listed on the St. James Parish Church Registry. For the next two years, 1742 and 1743, the church fined him for non-attendance! After he moved, he registered in the local St. Ann Church Parish.

In May 1742, Ed, living on the land Mr. James Tuley had purchased in western Goochland (now Albemarle) County, finally found a buyer for at least part of his land that he had left back in eastern Goochland. A Mr. John Clarke bought Ed's "75 acres N. of the James [River] in Goochland County ... with houses, orchards, gardens, fences and other appurtenances, beginning at a corner Pine standing in James Christian's land, thence along Christian's line to Thomas Bailie's line to the dividing line between Edmund New [Jr.] & Thomas Thornell...." [*Goochland County Deed Book 3*, p. 554.] Edmund New Jr., who couldn't write, "X-ed" his signature and affixed his seal to the document.

The Thomas Thornell in the above deed had recently purchased the other half of the original New plantation from Ed's big sister, Miss Priscilla New [q.v.], after she inherited it from their father. Miss Priscilla, a spinster, had recently sold her part of the New plantation to Thornell so she could go west with her mother and stepfather.

Then, with his old home sold, Ed New, while living on James Tuley's plantation, asked his lady love for her hand in marriage. She consented. Ed New and Miss Sarah Tuley were married in

Albemarle County, their marriage recorded in *Albemarle County Wedding Book* on page 233.

Ed's bride, Miss Sarah Tuley, was daughter of James and Judith Tuley, and a niece of John Tuley, a younger brother of James Tuley. John Tuley's wife, also named Sarah, was another of Ed New's sisters.

Confused? I'll try again. The two Sarah's were (1) Mrs. Sarah New Tuley, Ed New's sister who had married John Tuley, and (2) Mrs. Sarah Tuley New, the daughter of James and Judith Tuley who became Ed Jr.'s wife. See?

Several years passed before Ed New had a buyer for the remainder of his land back at Little Licking Hole. In April 1749 John Laine [Lane?] bought Ed's last 150 acres of land, which was "bounded by lands belonging to Thomas Christian, deceased, John Prior, and John Bailey, thence to said John Paine's [Laine's? Lane's] beginning." Mr. Lane—however he spelled his name—paid Ed New 50 pounds sterling and Ed "X-ed" his name for his signature. [*Goochland County Deed Book 6*, p. 33.] The merchant John Prior, husband of Ed's sister Mary who had remained in Goochland County, helped sell this last of Ed's land and signed his name to Ed's deed as a witness.

No record has been found showing that Edmund New Jr. bought any more land, either in Goochland, Albemarle, or later in Amherst County. He and Sarah lived near her parents, James and Judith Tuley, on the Tuley plantation. As James Tuley had varied business interest that kept him pretty busy, one wonders if Ed Jr. became the overseer on the Tuley plantation—somebody had to see that Mr. Tuley's slaves worked to produce his tobacco.

(James Tuley's name is found on several deeds showing where he either bought, sold, or swapped land, or financed patents for settlers who needed ready money. Occasionally Ed New Jr. was called upon to witness one or another of Tuley's many deeds. This Tuley was a real go-getter!)

The News were still in Albemarle County when Sarah's father died. James Tuley wrote his will on September 3, 1779, although it wasn't probated until he died in 1781 near the close of the Revolution. [*Albemarle County Deed Book 2*, pp. 392, 393.] In his will Tuley named his wife, Judith, along with the names of nine children. He bequeathed his daughter Sarah Tuley New "a Negro girl named Mille, to her and her heirs."

We know little of Edmund and Sarah New's activities in Albemarle or Amherst counties; if they had children we have been unable to find them.

VII. William New

Born: Mid 1690s, Charles City County, Virginia
Died: After 1749, Albemarle County, Virginia
Married: **Miss Priscilla Sampson**, in Goochland County, Virginia, daughter of Francis and Bridgett Sampson from Barbados Isle in the Caribbean.

The story of William New, our next ancestor, is explored in the next chapter.

Children of William and Priscilla Sampson New:
1. **DAVID NEW**, m. **Susannah Pleasants**.
2. **FRANCIS "FRANK" NEW**, m. **Sarah Seeley** [Seale?].

VIII: Elizabeth New Patterson

Born: Early 1700s, Charles City County, Virginia
Died: After 1740
Married: **David Patterson**, Henrico County, early 1720s?

On June 16, 1714, one David Patterson patented 400 acres of land in Henrico County located "on N. side of James River & on E. side of Little Licking Hole Creek, adjoining the land of Capt. John Boling." This transaction took place several years before 1720 when Edmund New Sr. and wife, Mary, came to live on the creek, Little Licking Hole.

We don't know the marriage date, but the New's daughter Elizabeth married David Patterson before her father died. In his will, dated 1726, the senior Edmund New bequeathed his daughter, Elizabeth Patterson, "one shilling and no more." Later, when Elizabeth's relatives began to leave the Little Licking Hole area to move *west*, David and Elizabeth Patterson moved *east*. For reasons now unknown, they moved back to the Virginia's tidelands between the York and the James rivers in New Kent County, a short distance east of Richmond.

In 1740 "David Patterson of New Kent County" sold his 400 acres of land back in Goochland County "between Gr. & Little Licking Hole Creeks, adj. to the lines of Mr. Edmund New & Charles Christian" for 40 shillings. [*Goochland County Patent Book 14*, p. 135.]

We don't know if the Pattersons had children. They likely did. (A John and a Thomas Patterson of Albemarle/Amherst County fought in the American Revolution. Elizabeth's sons? Grandsons?)

IX: Ann New

Born: Early 1799s
Died: After 1726; possibly died young
Married: Unknown

Ann was not married when her father died; he willed her "one shilling and no more." Nothing more is known about her.

X: Henry New

Born: Early 1720s
Died: After 1726; possibly died young
Married: Unknown

When Edmund New Sr. composed his first will, young Henry New was to receive one shilling from his father but, when old Edmund dictated his second will from his deathbed in 1726, he omitted Henry's name. Why? Was it merely an oversight? Or had Henry already succumbed from the same malady that took his father?

No further mention of this Henry New has been found. Did the Indians get him? Was he lost at sea?

If you find this Henry New, please call home!

Tuleys
Will

In the name of god Amen I James Tuley being in my perfect health and of sound mind and disposing Memory, do make and Ordain this my Last Will and Testament, Revoking hereby all other will by me made. first Recommending my Soul to him that made it and my body to bee buried at the discretion of my Executors herein after Appointed, and my Just debts paid. Item I Lend to my beloved wife Judith Tuley, all my Stock of Cattle, hogs, Horses, Sheep and Gees and all my household furniture during of her life, my will and desire is that if She Shall see Cause to dispose of any of my Stock or household Goods among my Children before her death that it may Stand good, but if any Remaining at her death my will and desire is that it bee Equally divided among my five last Children, Item I give to my Son John Tuley a negroe woman named Luce to him & his heirs, Item I give to my Son James Tuley a negroe fellow named Samson to him and his heirs, Item I give to Daughter Sarah a negroe girl named Mille to her & her heirs Item I give to my Daughter Anna Martin, a negroe fellow named Dick to her & her heirs, Item I give to my Son Charles Tuley Seventy Three Acres of Land that I bought of Thomas Morrison

(392)

in Amherst County on the waters of Rockfish River, also a negroe fellow named Bristol to him & his heirs. Item I give to my Son William Tuley the Land Whereon I live from the upper end down below the house to the Second great Rock, also a negroe wench named Peter, and all her Increase hereafter born to him and his heirs, Item I give to my Son Arthur Tuley, The Remaining part of my Land from Williams Tuleys lower line to the Lower End, also two negroe girls to wit Hannar and winnie to him and his heirs, Item I give to my daughter Elizabeth Tuley a negroe wench named Delfe and all her Increase hereafter born to her & her heirs, Item I give to my daughter Mary Tuley a negroe wench named Pat to her and her heirs, Item I give to my daughter Judith Tuley, two negroe girls to wit eve & Anake to her and her heirs, I appoint my wife Judith Tuley, and my two Sons James & William Tuley Executors of this my Last will and Testament, my will and desire is that my estate may not bee appraised, as Witness I have hereunto Set my hand and Seal this 5th Day of September 1779

In Presence of us

John Tuley
Nath. Watkins
                 her
Mary + Mascee
      mark

                              his
                    James X Tuley
                              mark

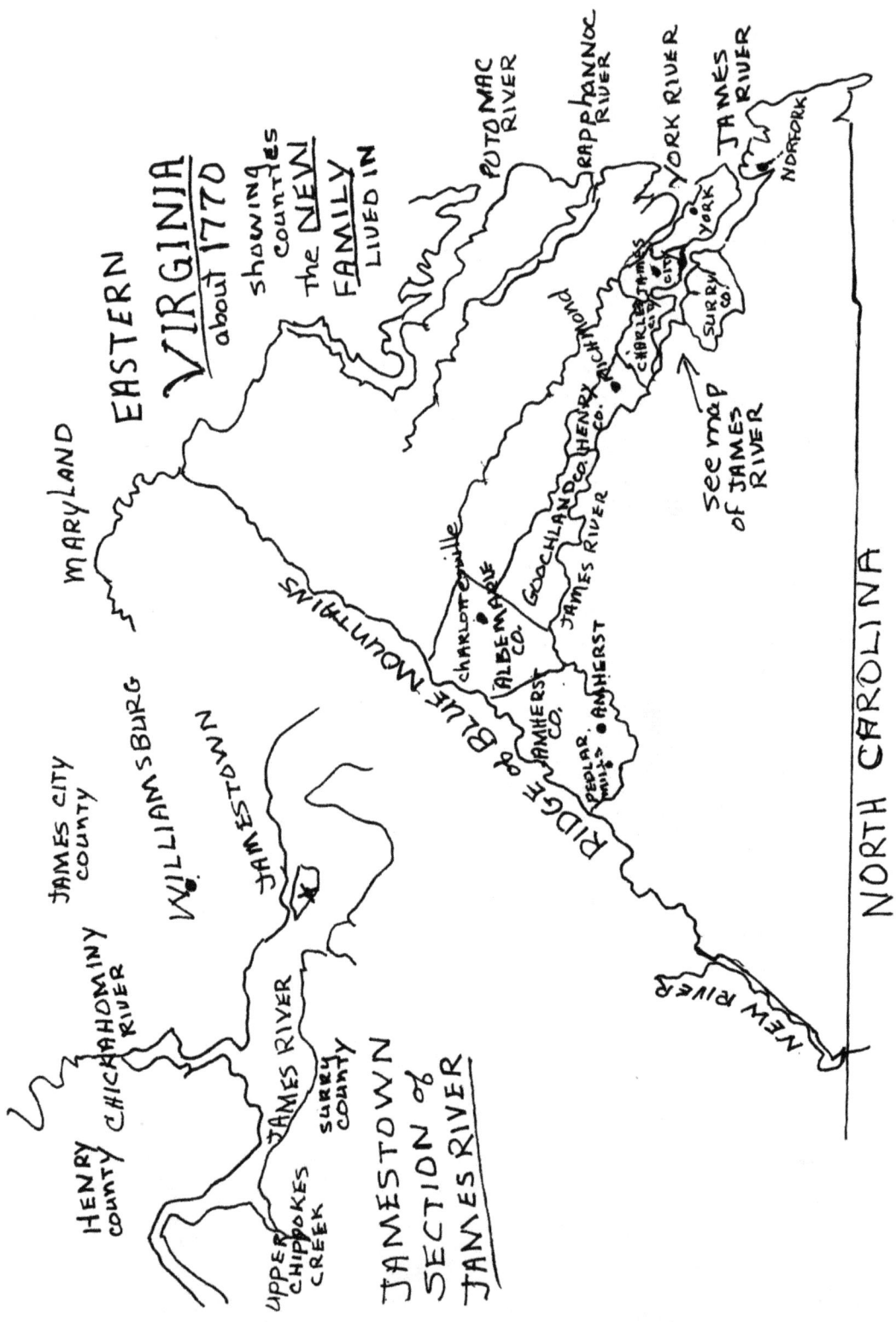

EASTERN VIRGINIA about 1770 showing counties the NEW FAMILY LIVED IN

MARYLAND

POTOMAC RIVER
RAPPHANNOC RIVER
YORK RIVER
JAMES RIVER

NORFOLK

YORK
CITY
CHARLES CITY
SURRY CO.

RICHMOND
HENRY CO.
GOOCHLAND CO.

See map of JAMES RIVER

CHARLOTTESVILLE
ALBEMARLE CO.

JAMES RIVER

AMHERST CO.
AMHERST
PEDLAR MILLS

BLUE RIDGE MOUNTAINS

NORTH CAROLINA

NEW RIVER

JAMES CITY COUNTY
WILLIAMSBURG
JAMESTOWN

HENRY COUNTY
CHICKAHOMINY RIVER

JAMES RIVER
SURRY COUNTY

UPPER CHIPPOKES CREEK

JAMESTOWN SECTION of JAMES RIVER

Chapter V
William New
(circa 1710–1775)

William New, third son of Edmund Sr. and Mary New, and a grandson of the immigrant, Richard New, was born in Charles City County, Virginia, coming along about the middle of the New's "litter" of ten children. He had grown to be a "big boy," nearing his teens, when his family moved to Little Licking Hole Creek.

The wilderness around Little Licking Hole in Henrico County was largely unsettled when the News came. Young William's help was sorely needed by his father and older brother, Ed Jr., as they cleared their forested land and made pot-ash for sale while preparing the hillsides to plant apple trees and tobacco.

A bright lad with an inquiring mind, William New loved his parents and hated to see them struggling with illiteracy. He longed to learn to read and write to help them out. Public schools, at that time, were well established in England but Virginia, as yet, had no school except for a few scattered parish schools where church-provided clergymen taught the basics. Nevertheless, from somewhere William learned to read, reading everything he could get his hands on. (Books were treasures, hard to find.)

William was around twenty when his father, Edmund New Sr., died. Missing the comradeship he had enjoyed with his father, William began to visit their neighbor, Edward Scott, who happened to be a lawyer.

When talk of forming a new Virginia county began to be discussed about the area, Mr. Scott, hoping to be appointed a judgeship, showed up and purchased the plantation next to the New's. With him he brought his impressive library of books from which William New was allowed to borrow. Seeing the young man interested, Mr. Scott began to teach him how to "read law." (By the way, Scott made it—he became a judge.)

Increasing population in the eastern portion of extensive Henrico County prompted the 1727 Virginia Assembly to create a new county from Henrico's farther western area. They named the new county "Goochland" after Maj. William Gooch, a military man who had been recently appointed to be Virginia's governor.

As long as her British merchants were protected, England, busily engaged in fighting in small wars with France, had left Gov. Gooch and the Virginia Assembly pretty much alone. Uninterested in personal gain, Gov. Gooch proved to be one of Virginia's most able and popular governors. Under his rule a hogshead weight of tobacco was standardized, preventing planters from being underpaid. He improved the quality of Virginia's tobacco by requiring growers to take their bright leaf to a warehouse for inspection, insuring that it was packed and sealed properly and in good condition; merchants would not pay for tobacco if it reached England in poor shape.

Under Gooch's leadership the Virginia Colony became the most prosperous colony in America.

The survey for the new Goochland County began at the James River and ran northwest along the path of Tuckahoe Creek. South of the James the line followed the Lower Manachin Creek and then cut westward along a blazed trail to the Appomattox River. Its far western boundary of Goochland was the ridge of the Blue Ridge Mountains.

When the new county was formed, the New's "Henrico County plantation" came to be the New's "Goochland County plantation."

The Senior Edmund New, William's father, died shortly before the county lines were altered so his will was recorded in the Henrico County courthouse. At first all went smoothly without fanfare. Ed Jr. took over his half of the plantation with the plant nursery that he inherited, and moved out. This left the widow Mary New to live in the old home with her spinster daughter, Miss Priscilla, and her third son, William.

Although Miss Priscilla had inherited the other half of the New plantation where the home was sited, by law it would remain under the widow's control unless, or until, the young lady married and gained a husband to take it over.

The debris hit the fan when bans were posted at church for the widow Mary New to marry. Perhaps she thought she needed someone stronger to take over the farm's operation, or maybe she was just lonesome. The man she chose was Hugh Morris, owner of a smaller farm near the News. She needed a husband; he needed more land. (Love had little to do with marriage back then: widows who controlled their late husbands' lands were in great demand by suitors.)

Upon hearing of the wedding announcement, William—and Mary's other children—became quite concerned; if a widow re-married, any land she had would come under control of her new husband. They were afraid that if their mother married Mr. Morris their big sister would lose her inheritance. As females did not appear in court, Miss Priscilla asked her brother William, who was studying law, to act for her in a court hearing. William was happy to speak in her behalf.

This entry was made in *Goochland Court Order Book 1* when the new county held its first session:

June 1, 1728: On motion of William New, it is ordered that Mary New be summoned to appear at the next court session to prove the late Edmund's New's will.

A month later the July Goochland Court ordered the plaintiff William New to write a brief on his complaint against his mother Mary New, to be presented at the next (August) court session.

Meantime, Mary New stuck to her wedding plans and married her land-hungry neighbor Morris from the adjoining plantation. Upon their marriage Miss Priscilla's plantation became the property of Hugh Morris, her stepfather. Priscilla was denied the use of the land as Mr. Morris prepared her fields to plant his own tobacco.

That fall this court entry was made:

November 1728: In the action of Debt between William New, plaintiff, and Hugh Morris and Sarah [Mary], his wife, executrix of Edmund New, deceased, the defendant is granted permission to argue his declaration. [The court clerk erred by writing 'Sarah' instead of 'Mary' when recording this report. In later entries he corrected his mistake and rightly penned her name 'Mary.']

William's suit against Hugh Morris dragged on, month after month, throughout the year 1729.

Finally, Hugh and Mary Morris agreed to settle out of court in the spring of 1730, whereupon these final three court entries were made:

> ***March 1730:*** *In the action of trespass between William New, Plaintiff, and Hugh Morris, Defendant, a special jurisprudence is granted the defendant.*

> ***May 1730:*** *The action of debt between William New, plaintiff, and Hugh Morris and Mary his wife, executrix of Edmund New, deceased, the plaintiff not prosecuting the same.*

> ***May 1730:*** *The action of trespass between William New, Plaintiff, & Hugh Morris, Defendant, is dismissed, the plaintiff not prosecuting.*

It seems that Morris was allowed to keep the profit from the tobacco he had grown in Priscilla's field, and William was appointed Priscilla's guardian so she could keep her land.

In the year before William New's father died, one Francis Sampson came to Henrico County with his wife Bridgett and their children. On March 24, 1725, Mr. Sampson paid 25 shillings to patent some land "on N. side of James River, beginning at John Pleasants, on Wolfpitt Br. [Branch? Bridge?] to E. side of Buffalow Br. on Amos Lad's line … " [*Henrico County Patent Book 12*, p. 394.]

The parents of Francis Sampson were the late John and Elizabeth Sampson, a couple of English descent. They had lived on the English colony of Barbados, the most eastern of the Windward Islands, in the West Indies.

Barbados was first discovered and named by Portuguese sailors, but in 1624 English sailors had laid claim to the island in the name of King James I. When the first English settlers landed there in 1627 they divided Barbados into estates where they grew cane and refined sugar, using Negro slaves imported from Africa.

The more wealthy landowners, seeking even greater profit, gradually crowded out the smaller plantations. More problems developed when the slaves, tired of the back-breaking work in the sweltering tropical heat of the cane fields, sometimes revolted, murdering their masters with their cane knives.

It would be interesting to know why the Sampsons left the island to migrate to Virginia.

William New fell in love with Francis and Bridgett Sampson's daughter, Miss Priscilla Sampson. They were married in 1737 in Goochland (formerly Henrico) County.

By tradition, Anglican marriages in Virginia were performed after a required length of time after the weddings banns were posted. This allowed any objectors to voice their complaints. More often than not the solemn religious vows were taken before a clergyman at the bride's home instead of at church. We don't know what kind of wedding William and Priscilla had; it seems likely they plighted their troth at the Sampson home in Goochland County.

Often, in the evening following the formal ceremony, an old pagan Briton ritual, "jumping over the broomstick," was laughingly practiced by the bride and groom. This ancient custom, accompanied by merriment and dancing, occurred with an abundant drinking of ale. (Often Negro slaves dispensed with the formal ceremony all together to merely "jump over the broom" to denote marriage, a rite practiced by a few blacks in America's deep South until well into the 1900s.)

On the first of January in 1738 William's father-in-law Francis Sampson of St. James Parish in Goochland County, "being sick in body," wrote his last will and testament. In it he bequeathed his five children (one son and four daughters) one shilling each. The balance of his estate was to go to his wife, Mistress Bridgett Sampson, with her and their only son, Stephen, to be his executors.

The Sampson children, all married, were: Stephen, m. Mary Woodson, captain of the Virginia militia in 1714 during the reign of George I, died in 1768; Priscilla, m. William New; Anna, m. Joseph Fuquay; Sarah, m. John Maxey; and Judith, m. Richard Couch.

Old Mr. Sampson did not die until March of 1744 whereupon his will was recorded in Goochland County. His old widow, Bridgett Sampson, did not marry again but lived her remaining years with her son, Stephen.

Even as Goochland County was being created, homesteaders and land speculators streamed into its western frontier all the way to the far ridge of the Blue Ridge Mountains. There were no roads leading through the thick forest then, except for the indistinct Indian paths. It was easy to lose one's sense of direction in the dense wilderness until guide trees were blazed at intervals along the faint traces.

The first newcomers walked—or rode horseback if they were fortunate enough to own a horse—along the narrow trails carrying backpacks of household goods and the farming tools they would need later. Homesteaders in better circumstances transported their goods, and sometimes their small children, in wicker panniers lashed across the backs of pack animals. Often larger groups of extended family members and/or friends traveled together to help each other along the way. Two men could handle a train of as many as fifteen pack mules, tethered head to tail, one man guiding the lead animal and the other bringing up the rear. Some men played it smart by paddling up the James River in dugout canoes, turning aside at various creeks along the way, in search of desirable land.

The old practice of acquiring a fifty-acre headright for each English newcomer one imported had slowly given way to having to pay cash for their unclaimed land purchase. Fifty acres of public land could be bought by paying the king's auditor 50 shillings. Land speculators, as well as homesteading pioneers, hurried to western Goochland to purchase land in the virgin wilderness.

Land speculators, men blessed with money, took up enormous land tracts for investment. Records show that in 1727 one gentleman claimed nearly 14,000 acres "near the ledge of the Blue Mountains." Another, that same year, claimed 2,600 acres along the upper James River. At a distance to the southwest, by 1739 five speculators had patented land that totaled over 50,000 acres. By dividing their outsized holdings into smaller easily sold tracts, they collected a handsome profit.

However, between 1739–1741, homesteaders, the true settlers, "seated" over 125,000 acres of land for their small plantations of less than 1,000 acres.

Since 1705 the rule to "seat" land had been that a settler had to build a dwelling of at least 12x12 feet in size, keep livestock on the premises for a full year, and pay a yearly quickrent (tax) of one shilling per fifty acres. If all these requirements were not met, their land reverted to the Crown.

Poorer settlers seated their claim themselves while others, those with money, remained in comfort "back east in civilization" and paid less fortunate farmers to become their tenants by occupying their new investment claims to establish their right of ownership.

Edward Scott, the lawyer who had befriended young William New and became one of Goochland County's first justices, had arrived while the county was being inaugurated. In October 1728 he bought 250 acres of land "on the wester-most branch of Little Licking Hole Creek" with his land line continuing "to Little Creek [Little Horsepen?] to the land of Edmund New." [*Goochland Deed Book 13*, p. 317]

A year later, in 1739, he bought the 100 acres that adjoined his home on Little Licking Hole from John and Sarah (New) Tuley. [*Goochland Will Book & Deeds, 1728–1736*, p. 74] Living so close, it is not surprising that Judge Scott became a friend of the New and Tuley families.

As new settlers continued to pass through from eastern Virginia, Judge Scott saw fit to take advantage of this movement by purchasing an early claim in Goochland's more western virgin land before it had been all taken. In 1732 the judge purchased a 550-acre tract "near the bend of the James River" on a creek in the far western portion of Goochland County.

Judge Scott spoke so well of his new western land that, by 1741, he had persuaded Mr. James Tuley to obtain a 400-acre patent of his own next to the judge's western land on the same little creek.

James Tuley and his wife, selling their plantation on Little Licking Hole, moved westward with the Judge and Mrs. Scott to settle on the same little creek, naming it "Tuley's Creek." Traveling with them were the family of James Tuley's brother John, and Edmund New, Jr. who had married James Tuley's daughter.

Preparing to leave for the west, William New and his *wife*, Mrs. Priscilla Sampson New, sold the land his *sister*, Miss Priscilla New, had given him for saving her inheritance. (Miss Priscilla had already moved west with their mother and stepfather.) William's deed, recorded in *Goochland County Deed Book 3*, page 367, was written thus:

THIS INDENTURE made this 17th day of September [1740] between William New of the County of Goochland and parish of St. James of the one part and Thomas Thornell of the same Parish and County of

the other part WITNESSETH that the said William New for Divers good Causes and Considrations thereunto moving but more especially for the Valuable Consideration of Thirty Pounds Current Money to him in hand paid by the said Thomas Thornell, he doth hereby acknowledge and himself therewith fully Satisfyed [sic] these presents do bargain sell Alien, Enfoff, and Confirm to said Thomas Thornell, to him and his heirs forever, one Tract or parcel of land lying and being on the North side of the James River containing one hundred and fifty acres more or less with Houses, orchards, Gardens, fences, and other Appurtenances the same belonging and it being the land of Edmund New, dec'd. Beginning at a corner White Oak standing in Thomas Bailey's line to Ebemezer Adam's line thence running along Adamses to Robert Rogers to a corner tree ... to the place bugun at TO HAVE AND TO HOLD the said tract and premises unto the said Thomas Thornell and his heirs forever and said William New doth hereby Covenant for himself and his heirs forever and will warrant the same unto Thomas Thornell ... Witness whereof I, the said William New, hath hereunto set my hand and seal the day above written.

William New [Seal]
Priscilla [X] New [Seal]

Signed, Sealed, and Delivered in presents of us:
    James Christian   Robert Christian
    John [X] Prior
[Witnesses were William's nephews who also moved west.]

William wrote and signed the deed after he and his wife had already moved west. Mr. Tornell had to ride all the way back to the Goochland courthouse to have the deed recorded.

As settlers and land speculators continued to pour into western Goochland, folks complained about the great distances they had to travel to and fro the Goochland courthouse to register claims, attend court, and to attend social affairs. Although roads wide enough to accommodate carts and carriages were slowly being opened on the chopped-tree trails, it was still a hardship for travelers to traverse the bumpy road such a distance to attend public meetings. Only fifteen years after Goochland County was created, another new county was needed.

In September 1744, the Virginia Assembly created a new county from the vast reaches of western Goochland. They named the new county "Albemarle" for the 2nd Earl of Albemarle, Virginia's next governor. This new county, quite large, lasted less than twenty years before it, too, had to be subdivided; eventually Albemarle was separated into five counties, with parts of three other counties being left over.

Judge Edward Scott, the New's family friend, had traveled west with the others to live on the new plantation he had purchased, which was located just down the road from the new homes of James and John Tuley. He didn't enjoy it long. While working hard to get Albemarle County incorporated, Judge Scott died. His wife inherited his new plantation.

Following the death of Judge Scott, in February 1745 the first court of the newly incorporated Albemarle County, lacking a courthouse, met at the home of his widow, Mrs. Scott. The nine justices meeting at Widow Scott's home included Peter Jefferson who had recently purchased 1,000 acres of land south of the Rivanna River. Peter Jefferson was the father of Thomas Jefferson who,

eventually, became Virginia's governor and, later, the president of the United States.

At their first meeting at Widow Scott's home, the justices selected a site for an Albemarle County courthouse. They had it built nearby, a mile north of the James River and a mile west of the little village of Scottsville.

Albemarle's first sheriffs, elected for two-year terms, meted swift and brutal punishment to those found guilty. The punishments—for crimes such as murder, theft, arson, bearing of illegitimate children, church non-attendance, cursing the king, gambling, etc.—were often public whippings. Growing tobacco was a laborious task, and workers were scarce; it seemed better to horsewhip offenders and send them back to work than it was to lock them up.

William and Priscilla New, having little money, had to seat their 400 acres of land when they came west. It was located "in the bend of the James River on the middle branch of Spring Garden Creek." To seat his land William had to build a cottage and make-do animal sheds. He had to clear it of trees and brush before he could even begin his crops. It took five years before his land brought a profit. It was lucky for him that he had studied law—he was able to pick up a little spending money by helping other settlers with their legal matters.

As currency was scarce, tobacco was often used as legal tender. Public records in early Albemarle show yearly demands for payment of "five pounds of tobacco" entered against the name of William New. This payment was for the quick-rent he owed the Crown to perfect his land claim. On the twelfth day of May in 1750 William's land was finally paid for and his land patent was registered.

In the early 1740s William and Priscilla New added two sons, David and Francis, to their family. Being unsure of their birth dates, we don't know if young David New, born around 1741, came along before the News left Little Licking Hole Creek or after they arrived at their new home. Little Francis New, namesake of Priscilla's father Francis Sampson, was born near the time of his Grandpa Sampson's death in 1744.

As far as we know, William and Priscilla had no more children. Not living long enough to see her boys grown, she died in Albemarle County. We don't know the cause of her death. It is possible that she was a frail person, and the strenuous labor required of frontier women taxed the strength of the most robust. After they did their homemaking chores, i.e., gathering food to cook on an open fire while baking bread on a covered vessel on a bed of coals, spinning thread, weaving cloth on her loom to stitch her family's wearing apparel (by *hand*, yet!), doing their laundry in streams, beating clothing against rocks with a batter-board, using the homemade soap they made by combining lye (which was made by bilin' the oak ash from the fireplace) with cookin' grease, they helped each other when their time came to birth a baby, and watched their youngsters to keep them safe when they gathered herbs to "doctor" the family illnesses. In addition to household duties, frontier women were expected to help their menfolk construct a home and work in the tobacco fields in their "spare" time!

William didn't marry again after his Priscilla died. He continued to supplement his income by working as a law clerk. He didn't become rich, his tobacco bringing him not great wealth, but it afforded him and his boys a comfortable living.

William, working at the courthouse, used farm tenants, squatters with no land of their own, to farm his plantation. He didn't have indentured servants (an obsolete practice), nor could he buy expensive slaves who were fast becoming popular, even necessary, on large plantations.

Wealthy plantation owners brought their slaves with them to the frontier and purchased more if a need arose. After 1740 the importation of African slaves increased rapidly. An indentured servant cost ten to fifteen pounds for a four-year term of service, while a Negro slave could be purchased for eighteen to twenty pounds, a bargain price when one considered that a slave would serve his master for a lifetime, and could reproduce to make even more slaves.

Albemarle County's pioneers of English descent (such as our New ancestors) who came from Virginia's tidewaters and followed the James River upstream, and those from Virginia north of the Tuckahoe River, were dubbed "Tuckahoes." The Scots-Irish and German people, coming down from Pennsylvania to settle in the Shenandoah River Valley on the western side of the Blue Ridge, were called "Cohees." In time the Cohees merged eastward through the mountain gaps to settle in Albemarle County.

The Cohees brought their religions with them—the Lutheran, Mennonite, and the Presbyterian faiths. They were industrious, plain-living people whose lives contrasted from the elegant Tuckahoe gentlemen planters who loved leisure conversation, horses, sports, politics, and chivalry. Cohees practiced a more diversified method of intensive farming based on the labor of their extended family members, while labor on large Tuckahoe tobacco plantations was increasingly done by slaves. Over the years the lives of the two groups intermingled, absorbing each other's traditions.

Frontier Tuckahoe settlers made temporary shelters where they camped until a more durable home of rock, or brick, could be built. It hadn't yet occurred to Tuckahoes to make their homes of logs; their ancestors had come from England where trees were not abundant. Learning from the Cohees, the Tuckahoes began to build their permanent dwellings of logs. As a need arose, two sturdy log cabins with a wide, roofed "dog-trot" hallway in between became the widely accepted way to build a home. Most had a gallery—a front porch—across the front.

To cut down on fires and summer heat, cooking and eating were done in a separate structure built apart from the main building. Meals were prepared on the kitchen fireplace or, in summer, on an open outdoor fire.

Several people slept in the same room, often in the same bed, as a family could include children and stepchildren, grandparents, unmarried aunts and/or uncles, and white servants. (Negro slaves had their own little cabins and never slept in the house with their master.)

Most parents wanted their children educated, at least well enough to read their Bibles and prayer books, but the Virginia Council still hadn't provided for public schools. William New, wanting his sons to learn, tutored them himself, or shared in the expense of having them taught at one of the "old-field" schools that were scattered about the countryside.

Old-field schools, a distance apart, were usually one-room cabins built by interested neighbors in abandoned worn-out old tobacco fields. They were warmed by a fireplace with each father expected to furnish a share of cut wood. Tutors' fees were collectively paid by the students' families. Some fortunate schools found a member of the clergy to teach. Clergymen tutors, educated and licensed to teach in England, were encouraged by Virginia's Anglican Church by exempting them from paying their tithes.

Mrs. Bridgett Sampson, Priscilla's elderly mother who had remained east in the old Sampson home, died in 1757. In her will she didn't name her deceased daughter Priscilla New, but bequeathed her son-in-law, William New, one shilling sterling. Bridgett's only son, Stephen,

inherited the Sampson plantation, as had been requested by her late husband, Francis Sampson.

As time wore on, William New, becoming more solvent and thinking of his two sons' future had opportunity to buy two 400 acre tracts of land that were close, but not beside, his home, one for each son. In the late 1740s, however, young Francis New, the more adventurous of his boys, left home to join a militia company that was organizing to fight in the French and Indian War. They marched over the Blue Ridge Mountains to go after marauding scalp-taking French-allied Indians. He left home with fuzz on his cheeks, barely old enough to shave.

On November 8, 1749, with young Francis gone, William New "of St. Anne's Parish of Albemarle County" sold one of his 400-acre tracts that he had been holding for this youngest son. This tract, "on both sides of the Middle Fork of Garden Creek in the fork of James River … ," he sold to a John Key for "thirty pounds good and lawful money." [*Albemarle Deed Book 2*, pp. 280–282]

Later, swaggering home from war in his buckskins and calling himself "Frank," Francis New married Miss Sarah Seeley. They settled southwest of his father in the part of Albemarle that soon became Amherst County. The story of Francis New is told in the next chapter.

William's oldest son David, whose personality was quite unlike his rambunctious younger brother, married Miss Susannah Pleasants, a local Quaker girl. The young couple made their home with William, who was beginning to feel his old age. In 1768 David New purchased a small farm, "on both sides of Garden Creek" next door to his father's plantation.

After David bought this adjoining land, old William sold the tract he had bought earlier and had been holding for David since 1750. William's deed, dated June 18, 1769, stated; "William New of St. Anne Parish, County of Albemarle of the one part & Joseph Woolton of the County of Henrico of the other part … witnesseth … that William New for the sum of twenty-two Pounds Currency of Virginia, hath sold unto said Joseph Woolton … forever … Four hundred acres in the County of Albemarle on the fork of the James River and bounded by Abraham Seay's pointers … (etc., etc.)." The document was signed and sealed by William New. [*Albemarle County Deed Book 2*, pp. 420, 421]

While other colonies in America were founded by Protestants and enjoyed religious freedom from their inception, the colony of Virginia recognized only the religion espoused by the Anglican Church. As other faiths were outlawed, Quakers, the Society of Friends, had to hold their meetings in secret, as did other religions, in private homes called a "meetinghouse."

In the mid 1660s a well-to-do planter in Henrico County was John Pleasants, a prominent man who belonged to the Society of Friends and used his home as a Quaker meetinghouse.

When John Pleasants got married, his wedding was performed by a Quaker minister instead of the Anglican clergy. As Anglicans were the only clergy in Virginia authorized to perform weddings, the couple was indicted for living in sin without the legal sanction of marriage.

Fortunately, John Pleasants received help from influential friends; he would have been ruined by heavy fines had not the then-presiding Governor Culpepper intervened. In spite of legal discrimination John Pleasants continued to hold the secret meetings at his home in Henrico's White Oak Swamp.

Finally, in 1687 King James II of England proclaimed a "Declaration for Liberty of Conscience and Indulgence in Religious Matters" for all his subjects. After that, Quakers and other dissenters, no longer having to remain secret, began to build churches. By tradition, Quakers continued to call their churches "meetinghouses." Following the king's decree, John Pleasants obtained a small plot of land on which he built a Quaker meetinghouse with a graveyard. This paved the way for other Quaker meetinghouses in Virginia.

In late 1730s the Society of Friends established a meetinghouse on Cedar Creek in Hanover, the county just north of the Henrico County line. One of its members was Master Thomas Pleasants, a relative (brother?, son?, nephew?) of the above John Pleasants. Another meetinghouse was organized on Sugar Loaf Mountain in Albemarle County. A Pleasants family was living in Albemarle County when William New's oldest son, David, married the Quaker lass, Miss Susannah Pleasants. We don't know the given names of her parents so we are unsure which Pleasants was Susannah's family.

Actually, Presbyterians were the first Protestants to organize in Albemarle County. Founded in Scotland in the mid 1500s, this religious group, the Coventers, were persecuted by the Catholic Mary Stuart, Queen of Scots, whose short reign began in 1561. Queen Mary and her advisers deprived the Coventers of their inherited fortunes, causing many to flee to Ireland.

In 1681 King Charles II had granted William Penn land to found a new colony in America. He named it Pennsylvania. Penn, a Quaker who believed in brotherly love, welcomed all religions. Soon Presbyterians from Penn's colony, seeking more land, began migrating down Virginia's Shenandoah Valley. By the 1740s they were crossing over Virginia's Blue Ridge Mountains to establish farms in Albemarle County. (There they were dubbed "Cohees.")

(One Adam White, a Scottish Presbyterian leader educated at Edinburgh, Scotland, lost his wealth and fought his way to Ireland. Two of his sons, Moses and Hugh White, continued to have trouble with the Catholics in Ireland. In 1740–41, taking their families with them, they emigrated from Ireland to Bucks County, Pennsylvania. Moses White, a Presbyterian teacher, became progenitor of a long line of Whites in America. In 1946, over 200 years later, Moses' line of Whites and a line of the New family converged when their later-day descendants, James M. White, married Miss Mary Ellen New, both natives of Lauderdale County, Mississippi. Now, back to our story ...)

The Baptist religious faith came to north Virginia around 1714 and arrived in Albemarle County in the 1750s. They believed that personal salvation could be achieved only by being baptized—completely immersed in water. They formed two groups, "regular" Baptists, who lived quietly and were legally recognized, and "separate" Baptists, who bore a more aggressive approach toward Anglicans.

The puritanical separate Baptist preachers refused to secure a required ministerial license from their county court. Their emotional ministers aroused ridicule, fear, and persecution. "Some of the preachers were beaten with clubs, cuffed and kicked, and hauled about by the hair: mobs dunked some until they were nearly drowned; live snakes and hornet nests were, upon different occasions, thrown into their meetings to break them up; and drunken ruffians insulted their preachers ... " [Katherine Seaman, *Tuckahoes and Cohees; The settlers and Cultures of Amherst and Nelson Counties 1607–1807*, VA: Sweet Briar College Press, 1992.]

In 1768 thirty-four Baptist ministers were arrested and thrown into jail, but, strangely, their incarceration brought them even more friends. Encouraged, the Baptists became the leading crusaders for Virginia's religious freedom. Among their prominent defenders was Patrick Henry. Mr. Henry, a lawyer who could sway an audience with his oratory, was a member of Virginia's General Assembly in 1771, becoming Virginia's first American governor to be elected by the people.

Nearing the end of the American Revolution in 1779, Thomas Jefferson was elected governor of Virginia for a second term. He set a goal of declaring complete religious freedom from the Anglican Church. Opposition came from the elite Tuckahoe planters who, mostly, wanted to remain Anglicans like their forefathers. Jefferson's goal wasn't reached until after the Revolution, when the "Statute for Religious Freedom" separated church and state. The Anglican Church was dis-established, but was re-incorporated, with less power, as the Episcopal Church.

Methodism, founded in England by John and Charles Wesley in 1730, was scarcely known in Virginia until after the Revolution. First taught by itinerant Methodist ministers at inns, ordinaries, on village squares or anywhere else they found a group to listen, they were quite successful in gaining converts. When the circuit-riding ministers traveled to their next meeting, they usually left a layperson to lead their congregation in their absence. Like other Protestants, they held large meetings in open fields. One big Methodist camp meeting held in Amherst County in 1785 was attended by over 4,000 people, black as well as white. It was said that their shouting could be heard a mile away.

Reaching his seventies in waning health, William New could no longer work nor oversee the labor on his plantation. His steadfast older son, David New, along with David's wife, Susannah, and their young children, remained at William's side to take care of him. David, bowing to his Quaker wife's wishes, had become a member of her Society of Friends.

William did not write a will, but in 1773 he had the following deed recorded in the Albemarle County courthouse:

THIS INDENTURE made the 5th day of February, 1773, between William New of the County of Albemarle of the one part and David New of said County of the other part, WITNESSETH that the said William New, in consideration of the natural love and affection which he bears to his said son, and also for and in consideration of the sum of ten pounds paid to him in hand … hath Granted, Bargained & Sold … unto said David New, his Heirs & Assigns forever, one Certain Tract or Parcel of land in sd. County in the fork of the James River containing 214 acres of land and the plantation whereon the said William New now dwells, bounded as followeth to wit: adjoining Walter H. and Benj. Cox's line … with rent, Issues, & Profits thereof and all Right & Title the said William New of & to the said tract or parcel of land and its appurtenances … to have and to hold unto the said David New … to the proper use and behoof of his heirs and assignes forever & the said William New, for himself and his Heirs, all and singular, the premises above granted … the said William New … unto the said David New … shall forever warrant & defend … in witness whereof the said William New hath hereunto set his hand & seal, the day and Year above written.

William New (seal)

Sealed and Delivered in presence of:
George Terry, William Tuley, James "X" Tuley, James "X" Tuley, Jr.

We don't know who the above witness George Terry was, but the Tuleys were William New's relatives who lived close by on Tuley's Creek. The elderly James Tuley (Sr.) died in 1781 after witnessing William's deed.

We also don't know the exact date of William New's death. He died sometime during the final turmoil of the American Revolution. One wonders if he lived long enough to hear that the Americans had gained their independence from England.

Children Of William And Priscilla Sampson New

I. David New

Born: In Virginia circa 1740 in Goochland County
Died: After 1788. (In Tennessee or Kentucky?)
Married: In 1768 to **Susannah Pleasants** of Albemarle County. Miss Susannah was a member of the Society of Friends, a descendant of the late prominent Quaker leader, John Pleasants (q.v.) of early Henrico County.

When their mother died, David New and his younger brother, Francis, were raised in Albemarle County by their widowed father, William New. When young Francis left home to fight in the French and Indian War, David remained behind and continued to farm their father's Albemarle plantation.

At about age twenty David became interested in the Quaker's Society of Friends whose meeting place was nearby on Sugar Loaf Mountain. Becoming a member of the group, he fell in love with and married a Quaker girl, Miss Susannah Pleasants. Their first child, little John New, was born in 1769.

David bought the land next door to his father so he and Susannah could look after old William who was getting on in years. Then, in 1773, the year of the Boston Tea Party on the eve of the American Revolution, old William New, from his deathbed, deeded his home and plantation to this more dependable son. (See copy of deed in preceding chapter.) With this much land, David, a hard worker, made a comfortable living.

In 1775 "the shot heard around the world" was fired at Concord, marking the start of the American Revolution; on July 4, 1776, the American colonies declared their independence from England. As the first battles of the Revolution were fought in the north in New York, Canada, and New Hampshire, only a handful of Virginians were engaged.

Quakers didn't believe in slavery nor being cruel to Indians, and they *certainly* didn't believe in war! Any Quaker who joined the army to fight was dismissed from the Society of Friends. David New did not enlist.

To feed the soldiers and minutemen engaged in fighting, all grain, horses, and other farm commodities that planters could produce were in great demand. On May 25, 1778, with the war in progress, David bought another 200 acres of farmland from Peter Martin and wife, Mary, for 40 pounds Virginia money. This land, near David's farm, was in the fork of the James River on the middle branch of Garden Creek near the southern edge of Albemarle County. [*Albemarle County Deed Book*, p. 207.]

David New, somewhat belatedly, took an active part in the final days of the Revolution. Toward the end the battles had shifted south to the Carolinas. The British General Cornwallis, after capturing Charles Town (Charleston) in South Carolina, then fought his way north to join the British Army stationed at Norfolk on the eastern shore of Virginia. As his men neared Virginia, Gen. Cornwallis ordered his Lt. Colonel, Sir Banastre Tarleton, to lead his light Calvary on

a raid westward to Albemarle County to capture Charlottesville where the Virginia assemblymen were holding a meeting. The assembly usually met at the capital at Richmond, but with so much fighting going on there, their regular meeting was moved out to Charlottesville in Albemarle County where it would be more safe.

Col. Tarleton, with his past record of causing unnecessary cruelty, raided his way out to Charlottesville where, in June 1781, he captured seven of Virginia's assemblymen as they met. The rest managed to get away. Thomas Jefferson, Virginia's first *elected* governor, barely escaped with his life.

On this raid Col. Tarleton laid the surrounding countryside to waste, burning homes and barns, confiscating horses, and driving off or killing livestock. All local men, those not away fighting in the Continental Army, took up arms and joined the Virginia militia to "stop that Bloody British Butcher!"

The New's plantation, a few miles south of Charlottesville, was lying in Tarleton's path. David, sending Susannah and their children down to Amherst County to stay safe with relatives, seized his firing piece and left to fight back. Both David and his cousin, John Prior, joined Capt. William Tucker's company of Virginia militia where they fought as privates.

After wreaking havoc around Charlottesville, Col. Tarleton, still looting and burning, turned eastward to rejoin Gen. Cornwallis and the British troops at Yorktown. Gen. Cornwallis fortified Yorktown but Gen. George Washington, with his Continentals, quickly and quietly slipped south to block any British escape by land while the French fleet, under Adm. Comte Francois DeGrasse, sailed up from the Bahamas to cut off any British escape by sea. With both Regulars and local Patriot forces—and with their allied

French troops arriving under Adm. DeGrasse—Washington had 17,000 men to begin a siege on Yorktown.

Out-maneuvered and out-manned, Cornwallis surrendered on October 19, 1781. The Americans had won the War for Independence! (Lt. Col. Tarleton was captured at Yorktown and was held prisoner of war on a French ship. When paroled he returned to England where, later, he represented Liverpool in the British Parliament.)

An old army payroll shows that David New received military pay for his service up to the time of his discharge on March 26, 1782, four months after Cornwallis surrendered.

David returned home that spring to find utter devastation. With home and barns burned and livestock gone, he felt his only chance was to sell his land to gain capital and start over. It was fall before he found a buyer.

That October David and Susannah New sold their 200-acre Albemarle plantation to one Henry Tuggle for 80 pounds. [*Albemarle County Deed Book 8*, p. 78.] After selling their land they moved to Amherst County. David was the only man named "New" who appeared on the 1782 Amherst Tax roll. Listed "head of household" in a family of eight, his name was on the Amherst Roll each year through 1787.

(A family of *eight*? David, Susannah, and their three sons make five. Who were the other three? We haven't a clue. Too bad they were not listed by name.)

With no apparent success in Amherst County, in 1788 David and Susannah traveled on to Kentucky with their three sons where the boys, then grown, were counted in the 1790 U.S. Census in Green County, Kentucky. Their sons were **John** (b. 1769), **Pleasant Sr.** (b. 1770), and **William** (b. 177_) who died in Giles County, Tennessee, in 1815.

We don't know where or when William and Susannah died – in Kentucky or Tennessee? Further records of their sons can be found in Giles County, Tennessee.

II. Francis "Frank" New

Born: Circa 1745, Albemarle County, Virginia
Died: Circa 1783, Albemarle County, Virginia
Married: Sarah Seeley

The story of our next New forefather—Francis New—is told in the next chapter.

Children:

1. **JACOB NEW**, m. Edith "Edy" Sweeney
2. **JAMES FRANCIS NEW**, m. (1) Cousin Martha Tuley, (2) Nancy McDonald
3. **JOHN NEW**, m. Elizabeth Martin
4. **ELIZABETH NEW**, m. James McDonald
5. **JUDITH NEW**, m. Josiah Haynes, her stepbrother

Chapter VI
Francis "Frank" New
(circa 1743–1783)

Francis New, namesake of his maternal grandfather Francis Sampson, was youngest of William and Priscilla New's two sons. Born on his parent's Virginia farm in Albemarle County in the early 1740s, he grew up in the foothills of the Blue Ridge Mountains where frontier neighbors were few and far between.

Francis and his brother, David, were mere children when their mother died. Their father, working part time as a lawyer, reared his boys with whatever help was available—relatives, a couple slaves, or perhaps the wife of one of his tenants. The boys were required to work in the fields and care for livestock as soon as they grew tall enough. Everybody was required to share in the farm labor; their living depended upon it.

Somehow William New made it possible for his boys to get some schooling—they both could read and "figger." The older David enjoyed reading and considered himself his father's helper, while young Francis, although he did his chores, would steal off at every opportunity to hunt in the forest.

As more white men came to settle in the mountains, the friendly Monocan and Cherokee Indians were pushed aside into isolated native villages. Learning from these Indians, Francis found the best way to fish and hunt. Becoming a proficient woodsman, he kept the farm table well supplied with wild game and fish.

After Albemarle County was formed by separating an area from the vast western portion of Goochland County, a steady stream of English "Tuckahoes" poured into the new county from the areas of eastern and northern Virginia. Along with the Tuckahoes in Albemarle were the Irish and Dutch settlers, the "Cohees," who had migrated from Pennsylvania down the Shenandoah Valley to enter the county from the west over the Blue Ridge Mountains. Ere long the best Albemarle farmland was patented; later arrivals found it necessary to pay premium prices for the more desirable land or learn to be content with less suitable farmland that had been at first passed over.

With most of the land in Albemarle becoming patented, in the early 1750s two English land companies, the "Ohio River" and the "Loyal Land Company," were formed to populate Virginia's far regions that lay west of the Appalachian Mountains. This outlying western land, with the rich deltas of several rivers, was a magnet to farmers, but planters who moved there ran into trouble.

France had claimed the territory west of the Mississippi River, but then her French settlers began moving east of the big river to infringe upon the English claim. Adding to the problem, Frenchmen began to enlist Indians to harass the English settlers, stealing their cattle and burning their homes—and paying the Indians a bounty for English scalps.

Robert Dinwiddie, Virginia's imperial governor at that time, sent a young Virginia surveyor, George Washington, to warn the French and their Indian allies to stay away from the Ohio River Company's land. After Washington's diplomatic and military missions both failed in 1753, England, though not yet officially at war with France, gave her colonists full support to protect their homes. The British Gen. Braddock attacked the French Fort Duquesne (later named Fort Pitt) in 1755 and suffered a calamitous defeat.

When Indians began raiding and burning unprotected English frontier homes and ripping off British scalps, the colonies called their militia into action. Thus began the French and Indian War in colonial America. (The Seven Years' War between England and France, fought mostly by ships on the open sea, began a year later in 1756 and lasted until 1763.)

Brash young Francis New, an experienced woodsman, signed on with the Virginia militia to go out against the French-allied Indians. The militia was usually not issued uniforms but dressed much as Indians and frontiersmen in short hand sewn leather shirts with double-wide collars to deflect rain. Shucking off their stylish knee-britches, they donned long-legged leather trousers to protect their shins from snakes and briars, and they made their moccasins from small animal skins. As wide-brimmed tricorn hats were easily knocked off by lower tree branches, they mostly favored coonskin caps worn with the animal's tail dangling about their neck.

The following, from *Calander of Virginia State Papers* [Ibid.] is from a letter written at a camp near Fort Cumberland by a Capt. Robert Mumford to his uncle, Col. Theodorick Bland, of Prince George County, Virginia. It pictures how a militia patrol went:

To Col. Theo. Bland of Prince George, July 6, 1758

Had opportunities offered as frequently as Inclination would have induced me to write to you, you might have read a letter from every Encampment. After being delayed at Winchester five or six weeks longer than Expected, in which Time was ordered Express to Williamsburg & allow'd but a day after my return to prepare, we pushed off into the wide 'ocean'—I was permitted to walk every step of the Way to this humble Fort to lay hard, over Mountain. thru' Mud and Water, yet as merry and hearty as ever. Our Flankers and Sentrys pretend they saw the Enemy daily, but they never approached us. A Detachment was ordered off to clear a Road thirty miles with our Companies to cover the Working Party. We are in fine scalping ground, I assure you, the guns pop around us & you may see the fellows prick up their ears like Deer every moment. Our Colonel [Col. Wm. Byrd] is an example of Fortitude, in either Danger or Hardship and by his polite Behavior, has not only the Regard but the affection of both officers and soldiers ... [Mumford's financial account to his uncle followed.]

Yr. truly Affect. & ever obliged Nephew, Rob't Mumford.

Capt. Mumford added a postscript to his letter, a personal note to his aunt, sending her his fond regards and asking her to "say hello to all the ladies"!

Fort Mayo was built by young George Washington in what is now Patrick County in southwestern Virginia near the North Carolina border. This outpost was southernmost in a line of stockades built for frontier defense in 1756 by order of Gov. Dinwiddie. Washington had been in charge of its location, design, and construction. The following is extracted from a report written [Ibid.] from a John Echols concerning a march that Robert Wade took with thirty-five men from Fort Mayo heading westward to the New River in search of hostile Indians:

> *Saturday the 12th of August 1758.*
>
> *Capt. Robert Wade Marched from Mayo Fort with 35 men to take a Range to New River in search of Enemy Indians. We Marct about three miles that Day to a Plantation where Peter Renfro formerly Lived & took up camp where we continued that night. Next morning being Sunday we continued our march about 3 or 4 miles, and* **Francis New** *returned back to the Fort, then we had 34 men besides the Captain. We marct along to aplace called Gobling Town, where we Eat our brakefast continued our march till late in the after-noon & took up camp at the Blew Ledge where we continued safe that night....*

Echol's report, continuing, related that after Capt. Wade's Company crossed the "Blue Ledge" to head west of the mountains they had minor brushes with hostile Indians and killed a few who had white scalps hanging from their belts, but no great battles took place. When they returned two months later on October 16, Echol's above report was filed at Fort Mayo. He did not say on what mission Francis New had been sent back. One wonders if Francis had been sick, or perhaps wounded, or it could be that he had been sent back to make a report. (The National Archives could not supply Francis New's military record.)

While the Virginia militia was busily fighting the hostile Indians in her valleys, the war was also being fought farther north in Canada and in upper New York, New Hampshire, near the Great Lakes, and Ontario. French-held forts in Louisburg (Harrisburg, Pa.), Duquesne (Pittsburg, Pa.), and Fontenac (Kingston, Ont.) fell to the English in 1756. In Canada, Quebec fell in 1759 and Montreal fell in 1760.

In 1763 France and England signed a treaty ceding England the territory from Canada south-ward to Spanish Florida, and from the Atlantic Ocean west to the mighty Mississippi. Americans were disconcerted when Parliament issued a proc-lamation ceding the land beyond the Alleghenies to the Indians and forbade white men to settle there. This rule could not be enforced; a few brave souls still ventured over the far mountains to set-tle in the Indians' land.

When the fighting stopped and his stint in the militia ended, Francis New returned home to Albemarle County. He was around twenty when he married Miss Sarah Seeley, although the time and place of their marriage has not been located. It is reasoned that they married around 1760 as their oldest child, Jacob New, was born in 1761 as was confirmed by a later U.S. Census.

The young couple began their marriage in poor circumstances. They lived on a farm in Albemarle County, either bought, inherited, or just merely rented. (No deed has been found.) His land was near his wife's family, as seen by a neighbor's deed that was recorded in *Albemarle County Deed Book 1764–1768*, page 485:

> *THIS INDENTURE made this 31st day of August in year 1767 between Thomas Devard and Patrick Napier of the County of Albemarle on one part and Whitehead Ryan of the other part, Witnesseth that for the sum of Ten Pounds current money paid hath granted by patent to sd. Thomas Devard and being part of a large tract to be taken forming the lines of Williams,*

Francis New, and Sam'l Jordan, to include the Planations made on the land by Whitehead Ryan.

Thomas (X) Devard
Patr. Napier

In Presents of:
William Seay   Ann Seay
Charles Richards

After the war Frank and Sarah New, with their fast growing number of children, were fighting a futile battle to make ends meet. (Francis had begun to call himself "Frank" while he was in the military.) Getting nowhere by growing tobacco on shares on the worn-out soil they rented, Frank decided to buy land of his own. Searching for land that would fit his lean pocketbook, he went to see an old family friend, Mr. James Tuley, who lived down on Tuley Creek. Old Mr. Tuley was practically family since Frank's uncle, Edmund New Jr., was married to Mr. Tuley's daughter.

A crafty operator, Mr. Tuley, in addition to his own profitable plantation, often invested in various enterprises, ever watchful for land to buy cheaply and resell for a handsome profit. Some tracts he rented out to tenants while waiting for a suitable buyer. It happened that Mr. Tuley found land for sale in Criswell's Corner.

In earlier days one Col. John Criswell, a wealthy Scottish land speculator from Virginia's Handover County, had patented 40,000 acres of land, 30,000 of which, called "Criswell's Corner," was located on Rock Fish River in what was then western Goochland County. Criswell sold portions of this land to various tobacco planters who had come to settle.

Back in 1740 one Thomas Morrison bought 2,400 acres of Criswell's Corner that was near a gap in the Blue Ridge Mountains on the south fork (called Morrison's Creek) of the upper Rock Fish River. (The name of Morrison's Creek was later changed to "Short's Creek.")

William Morrison, a brother of Thomas, operated an ordinary in the lower Rock Fish Valley. When Albemarle County was formed from western Goochland County in 1744, the new county authorized William Morrison to clear a "highway" from "the upper end of McCord's Road to Thomas Morrison's land." A village called "Rockfish" developed on the headwaters of upper Rock Fish River on the upper slope of the Blue Ridge Mountains near the river's mountain gap.

As more settlers moved in, in 1761 the southwestern half of Albemarle County was divided to form two new counties, Buckingham and Amherst, with the upper James River being the dividing line. Amherst, northwest of the Rock Fish River, included an area of Criswell's Corner.

With this division the original courthouse at Scottsville was relocated to serve what remained of Albemarle County. They built the new courthouse at Charlottesville, a village more centrally located. (Charlottesville was named for the queen, the wife of King George III.)

Another new courthouse, placed in the wilderness, was built to serve the people of the new Amherst County, with a "gaol" next door for convicts. This was followed by an ordinary and a trading post, the beginnings of today's city of Amherst, Virginia.

One spring day eleven years after Amherst County was incorporated, Francis New went with James Tuley to the Criswell Corner area to buy land; they had heard that the old Morrison estate was up for sale. Frank didn't have much money. Mr. Tuley said he would help him out.

Mr. Tuley negotiated for a 73-acre tract, a part of the deceased Morrison's estate land on Long Meadow Creek, another branch of the upper Rock Fish River. Francis New witnessed the deed, along with local neighbors Abner Witt and Samuel Lakey, and with two of Mr. Tuley's sons, James Jr. and Charles Tuley.

Mr. Tuley, along with his business associate Charles Irving, paid for the land along with three slaves, and then sold it all to Francis New. After Francis made a token payment of five shillings, they accepted his deed of trust for the balance of 80 pounds. The deed of trust, as recorded on May 29, 1772, in *Amherst County Deed Book C*, page 448, was thus:

Francis New of Amherst County on the one part and Charles Irving & James Tuley Sen'. of the other part, WITNESSETH that in consideration of … eighty pounds current money of Virginia which said Francis New is justly indebted to said Irving & Tuley and honestly desires to … pay them and in further consideration of five shillings of like money in hand … before the signing & delivering of this … Francis New hath granted bargained and confirmed … to Charles Irving & James Tuley … a tract of land lying in Amherst County on Short's Creek which makes into Rock Fish River, containing 73 acres the same where he now lives, and also three slaves, Aboy a woman, Boston a lad, and Jack a boy, with all appurtenances belonging to the premises … to hold to the proper use and behoof of them … and Francis New doth hereby grant & warrant & defend to them, Irving and Tuley, forever UPON TRUST, that said Irving & Tuley shall, after the lst day of September in the year of our Lord 1772 … call for the best price that can be gotten after ten days public notice, for the land and slaves, and out of money arising from sale shall discharge, pay, and satisfy Irving & Tuley from such sale shall discharge, pay and satisfy Irving & Tuley

the above mentioned sum of 80 pounds … with lawful interest, from the 1st day of September 1772 until the same shall be fully discharged.

Francis New [seal.]

Charles Irving, Tuley's associate, was the man with the money. A Scottish tobacco factor for the Henderson-McCaul Tobacco Company, he apparently also dealt in slaves. He planned to be the factor when Frank's tobacco plantation became productive.

Frank had already moved to his new farm that spring so he could get his first tobacco crop to growin'. (It would take several crops to get his new farm paid for.)

Frank New still loved to fish and hunt and enjoyed "socializing." As he wasn't much hand for fieldwork, and his boys were still too little to be much help, he had to hock his land a second time to buy four more slaves. [See *Amherst County Deed Book, C,* pp. 450, 451] Richard Harvie, Charles Irving, and William Mitchell, together, held Frank's second mortgage, which would come due in four years. Frank signed the necessary papers and they were in business.

(Richard Harvie, who later became an officer in the upcoming American Revolution, lived at "Albefoyle," a fine plantation on the Pedlar River in Amherst County. His father, John Harvie Sr., a noted lawyer, was young Thomas Jefferson's guardian, and his brother, John Harvie Jr., was a member of the House of Burgesses and later became a delegate to the Continental Congress. We know that Irving was a tobacco farmer, but who was William Mitchell? A slave trader?)

With debts hanging over his head, Frank New still hoed a tough row. His family lived frugally and worked alongside their slaves in their fields. Twice more Frank had to mortgage the plantation before their efforts were rewarded—eventually Frank paid off his debts.

In the French and Indian War, the Crown supplied only a fraction of the British troops and war supplies her colonies needed. Through necessity the colonial assemblies threatened to withhold their military supplies, thus forcing their royal governors to yield to their demands. England, busily fighting her own wars in Europe, let her American colonies assume more responsibility for governing themselves. These extended liberties intensified the colonies' taste for freedom, weakening the Crown's strict ruling hand.

Protracted European wars brought England to a long-lasting financial depression. British taxpayers felt their war debt was too high a burden for them to carry alone. Believing the colonies existed for the benefit of the mother country, a cry was raised from England for her colonies to shoulder part of England's obligations.

The colonies in America had never before been taxed—except for shipping and trading tariffs, which were understood and accepted. Actually, before England's Seven Years' War, the colonies had even benefited from England's wars by marketing lumber for ships, along with horses, grain, and raw materials needed for military supplies. But now Parliament began to lay taxes onto American shoulders to generate their much-needed revenue.

Parliament passed a "Paper Money Act" to prohibit colony assemblies from issuing paper money for legal tender, followed by a "Sugar Act," imposing a three-penny tax on West Indies molasses. In 1765 came a "Quartering Act" requiring colonist to supply living quarters in their private homes for British soldiers. (How they HATED that!) Next came the infamous "Stamp Act" which required colonists to buy stamps for newspapers, playing cards, dice, college diplomas, and legal documents. Well!

The colonists regarded all this as tyranny but detested the Stamp Act the most. Threatening mobs forced a few royal stamp distributors to resign. Others were tarred and feathered; a few were lynched. Except for a few in the newest English colony, Georgia, no stamps were sold in America.

With the failure of the Stamp Act, in 1767 Parliament, urged on by Charles Townsend, chancellor of the Exchequer, placed a direct duty upon colonists' imports of glass, lead, tea, paper, and paint. This inspired Patrick Henry's rhetorical speech in the Virginia House of Burgess proposing a resolution that only the General Assembly had the right and power to lay taxes in Virginia. In frustration a new royal governor, Lord Botetourt, dismissed the session, but the burgesses moved to a nearby tavern for a rump session wherein they agreed to not buy any taxed goods from England.

The colonists' boycott of British goods had, as hoped, brought a howl from British manufacturers and merchants as they felt the pinch. The failed tax act was repealed in 1770—except for the tax on tea. Henry's argument for "No Taxation Without Representation!" was rejected by Parliament. Other taxes followed. (When Gov. Botetourt became ill in 1771 and died, he was replaced by Gov. Dunmore of New York.)

Just before Christmas in 1773 a party of colonists, disguised as Indians, dumped a valuable cargo of tea overboard from a ship waiting at a Boston wharf in Massachusetts. The British barred further use of Boston's harbor until the destroyed cargo had been paid for.

After repeated attempts of appeal to King George III, in September 1774 the collective colonies (all except Georgia) sent their representatives to a Continental Congress holding a meeting in Philadelphia to assume the duties of a national government. The delegates, protesting British tyranny, called for even more civil disobedience.

There was little talk of freedom from England at the meeting—both sides wanted to patch up their quarrel.

Near the time that this first Congress met in 1774, Francis New, "planter of Amherst County," sold seventy acres of his plantation, "part of a tract patented to New," to the older James Tuley, "planter of St. Anne Parish of Albemarle County," for forty pounds. This left Frank with only the three acres where his home stood. Why? It could be that Frank, tiring again of farming, sold his fields to get rid of his debts and get ready to rejoin the Virginia militia.

Meanwhile, one thing led to another between England and her colonies in America. Violence erupted in the larger cities and seaports along America's coastline. British soldiers, unasked for and resented by the colonists, continued to be quartered in private homes. In the spring of 1775 Capt. Gage, the appointed royal governor of Massachusetts, sent British soldiers from Boston to seize the arms the American Patriots had stored at nearby Concord. They confronted each other, American Patriots and British Redcoats, on a bridge at Lexington where somebody fired a gun. Thus began the American Revolution, which would last for eight long years.

Two weeks later (June 1775) the Battle of Bunker Hill took place outside Boston. (Actually, the battle was on nearby Gage Hill; somebody had their maps mixed up.) It was a bloody battle where the colonists, out-manned and out-gunned, were defeated, although the British suffered high casualties. After this engagement Col. George Washington, late of the French and Indian War, began recruiting planters, clerks, woodsmen, and local militia to form an American Continental Army!

A second Continental Congress met in May 1776. Inspired by Thomas Paine's paper, *Common Sense*, its members resolved that "these United Colonies are, and of a right ought to be, free and independent...." Eliminating all royal political influence, the Congress united the thirteen American colonies into a national republic controlled by the states. Albemarle County's Thomas Jefferson, a recent graduate of Virginia's William and Mary College, was chosen to write a Declaration of Independence, which the representatives of the thirteen colonies signed on July 4, 1776.

The Congress then proceeded to assume supervision of all the Patriot military forces already being formed in the individual "states." It elevated the rank of George Washington from being a colonel in the Virginia militia to being a general, the commander-in-chief of the new American Continental Army.

That August, Gen. Washington, with raw untried recruits, attempted and failed to win Long Island and the town of New York; the British General, Sir William Howe, drove the untrained Continentals across the Hudson River. Checked at White Plains, New York, Howe quickly turned and captured Fort Washington, forcing the Continentals to flee to New Jersey and Delaware. With reinforcements, Washington was able to swing his ragtag army back to win small victories at Trenton and Princeton before retiring his citizen army to Valley Forge to wait out the winter. Winter gave him time to train his men for combat before the spring thaw.

From the beginning the American colonists had fought among themselves, creating a war within a war with each other. The Tories, loyal to England, were mostly the so-called upper class who had derived much of their wealth from royal grants, along with appointed royal governors, British soldiers, and Anglican clergymen. On the American Patriot's side were the rebellious Whigs who were made up of rich northern merchants and successful southern planters who owed money to British creditors; the bulk of the patriotic Whigs were small planters, frontiersmen, craftsmen, shopkeepers, and locally elected legislators.

The Virginia State Assembly met for the first time that fall (1776) where it passed an act requiring all free men between the ages of sixteen and fifty to enroll in the Virginia militia and take an oath of allegiance. That would include our Frank New who was then in his mid-to-late thirties (his oldest son, Jacob New, was just fifteen).

In other places the loyalist Tories caused havoc, but not so in Virginia's Albemarle and Amherst counties. There the Whig patriotic spirit was strong, the king's loyalist Tories causing little trouble. James Hamilton wrote, "Every Whig in the county came forward to the courthouse, drew a number and, according to the number drawn, was placed in one or another of ten militia classes." It would appear that Frank became a member of the Virginia militia.

England, still recovering from her war with France, was unable to make a great war effort when her American colonies revolted. Her acute shortage of manpower changed when Lord George Germain, the British secretary in charge of war supplies, placed 45,000 men, which included German mercenaries hired from the Prince of Hesse, into British military service. England planned to use both English and Hessian soldiers to quell the American rebellion.

After chasing Gen. Washington's raw, untrained troops across the Hudson, the British's Gen. Howe turned north to split the colonies into half. Beginning in Canada, ten thousand of Howe's combined English and Hessian forces drove the Americans southward. Winter came and slowed their campaign in upper New York State at Ticonderoga.

In January (1777) the Continentals, after being secretly refitted by France, again took to the field. Gen. Washington, under the new American "Stars and Bars" banner, defeated Lord Cornwallis in a battle fought at Princeton. Later the Battle of Brandywine took place, but this time it was Gen. Washington who was forced to retreat. The American civilian-soldiers, hungry and tired of walking in snow with feet wrapped with rags to replace their worn-out boots, were beginning to desert and go home.

Gen. Howe recaptured and occupied Philadelphia but all was not lost; in October the Battle of Saratoga took place in upstate New York where the Continentals won a decided victory.

The conflict in Saratoga began when the British Gen. John Burgoyne concocted a grandiose scheme to seize and control the Hudson River. His was an ill-conceived plan and on October 17, 1777, Gen. Horatio Gates and his Americans captured 6,000 of Gen. Burgoyne's combined British and Hessian troops. This victory saved New England and gave the Americans a much-needed psychological lift.

(Gen. Gates was a gentleman who, by political influence, had been made a general by the American Congress. He was a fine man, but he didn't know much about leading an army. His idea was to fortify Saratoga and wait for the enemy to attack. He received the credit for the American victory at Saratoga, but it was his subordinate, Gen. Benedict Arnold who, with rabble troops, engaged Burgoyne's army and captured the British soldiers outside Saratoga. Arnold, beset by false gossip, later joined the British army, married a Tory girl, and moved to England, causing history to forever brand him a traitor to America.)

(A month after the Saratoga victory, the 'Articles of Confederation Perpetual Union' was adopted by the Continental Congress. This influenced King Louis XVI of France, England's enemy, to formally recognize the United States as a *nation* with whom he signed a treaty pledging France's full military support.)

The British and Hessian soldiers, captured with Gen. Burgoyne, were marched to Boston to be exchanged. They were encamped near Boston at nearby Cambridge, but Congress thought it wise to transfer them farther inland for safer keeping. One of Virginia's delegates to Congress, John Harvie Jr., offered land in Albemarle County outside Charlottesville as a site for a war prisoner camp. His offer was accepted.

Congress awarded Harvie's brother, Richard Harvie, a $23,000 contract to hire civilians to construct log cabin prisoner barracks on the site. (Remember Richard Harvie? He had earlier financed Frank New's second slave purchase in Amherst County.)

Because of food shortages in that winter of 1778–79, it was thought prudent to not wait for spring to move the mass of prisoners farther south. Virginia's Col. Theodorick Bland (of Prince George, Virginia) began to march the six divisions of prisoners toward Virginia. Crossing the Potomac River on New Year's Eve in the dead of winter, they arrived at Charlottesville on January 13, 1779. They covered the 623 miles in two months.

In Virginia, Gov. Patrick Henry, not notified of the prisoners coming until they were already en route, had little time to prepare. A few days before Col. Bland delivered the captured enemy, Congress approved a resolution made by the Continental Board of War that "a battalion of 600 men be forthwith raised on the Continental establishment in Virginia for the space of one year … that these troops be stationed at, and not removed … from the barracks in Albemarle County."

In late December 1778, Gov. Henry gave Albemarle County authorization to raise a hundred militiamen, a small battalion, to become prison guards. While these men were being raised by Lt. Col. Francis Taylor, Gov. Henry asked six other neighboring counties for another hundred men each, ASAP.

Richard Harvie, racing against time, hired more men to work on the unfinished prisoner huts (called "the barracks") near Charlottesville. He offered handsome wages to those not in the military to leave their plantations to work for him building the barracks.

Records show that Frank New moved his family from Amherst to Albemarle County near this time. Whether Frank was hired by Harvie to work on the barracks being built on Ivy Creek near Charlottesville, or if called by the militia to become a prison guard, is not clear. At this time some interesting land exchanges were taking place in Amherst County that probably had something to do with the militia, guards, and carpenters leaving for Charlottesville.

On January 14, 1779, the day after the prisoners arrived at the barracks site, John Witt Sr., Frank's Amherst neighbor, sold David Witt thirty-four acres of land near the mountain crest at the head of Short's Creek near the head of Rockfish River. A month later other land sales took place; Sam'l and Mary Woods, also Frank New's neighbors, sold thirty acres of land on that same Short's creek "on the lines of John and David Witt" to John Witt Jr … Next, John Witt [Sr. or Jr.?] sold Littleberry Witt sixteen acres of land near the top of the mountain "on the lines of David Witt and Samuel Lackey."

(The Witts were Patriotic Americans—the names of Abner, Elijah, John, Lewis, Littleberry, and William Witt, all from the same family, appear on a roster of revolutionary solders from Amherst County, Virginia.)

Before the above land exchanges, Abner Witt had offered to buy seventy-six acres of Frank New's farm, along with Mr. James Tuley's seventy acres that Tuley had first purchased with Frank. However, Mr. Tuley, now getting along in years (but just as foxy as ever), advised Frank to hold out longer and, sure enough, in December 1779, Abner Witt paid 500 pounds *each* to James Tuley and Frank New for their land. Tuley realized quite a profit; he had paid Frank only 40 pounds for that same land five years earlier. Frank and Sarah New also realized a sizeable profit on their home.

(After this sale old Mr. James Tuley did not live long; he died at his home in Albemarle County in 1781. In his will he named all his children; his daughter, Sarah Tuley New, wife of Edmund New Jr., inherited one slave.)

After selling their home, Frank New with his wife Sarah, their six children, and three slaves moved back to Albemarle County. We still don't know if Frank was hired to work at finishing the barracks for Col. Harvie, or if he joined one of the four Amherst County militia units assigned to guard the Hessian prisoners of war at Charlottesville. Knowing Frank, it seems more likely that he joined a militia company.

Without positive proof, we surmise that Frank enlisted in either the Amherst County militia led by Col. Richard Ballinger, or in the Convention Army Guard Regiment under Lt. Col. Francis Taylor. (Taylor's Regiment was designated, at various times, as "Col. F. Taylor's Guard Reg't," "Taylor's State Guard," "Albemarle Ce. Battalion," or "Convention Guards.")

In the first cold winter months of 1779, the Convention guards and Virginia militiamen stayed busy putting on roofs and chinking logs on the unfinished huts. The guards had completed the cabins by springtime as the countryside was turning green. The guards and prisoners planted vegetable gardens between the cabins and began to build churches and clear roads. By summer recreational huts with billiard tables in a coffeehouse had opened as well as a trading post comparable to today's PX. They still had to contend with food shortages, and sometimes the guards went without pay for months. Their essential clothing became threadbare; by April 1780 there were 121 men without shoes and by July, thirty-eight men were reported "naked."

The prisoners fared better than did their guards, only a few tried to escape. Those who did were easily spotted in their inmate garb—short linen coats, or coatees and linen overalls, carrying their regimental coats in their knapsacks.

The captured enemy officers, usually of a higher class than their troopers, were allowed to rent comfortable lodgings anywhere within a hundred-mile radius of the camp. Gov. Henry, alarmed when he found enemy officers strolling freely about Virginia's capital at Richmond, shortened their roaming radius to twenty-five miles.

Henry's successor, Gov. Thomas Jefferson, at his home near Charlottesville became friends with several enemy officers, i.e., Baron Geisman. Geisman and Jefferson played their violins together, and Louis de Unger was given free access to Jefferson's library.

By 1780–81 the guards at the barracks were on the verge of mutiny. A Federal Convention guard's pay, though little enough, was vastly superior to state militia wages. The thought that their prisoners, still paid by the British, earned good money while their own families suffered, was intolerable. From lack of money in 1781 the state guard was cut back to only three companies, with most of the men sick, poorly clad, and half starved. Their officers petitioned Jefferson for relief, but the beleaguered governor could offer but little help.

Back in early 1780 British Gen. Wm. Phillips had spearheaded an army of invasion onto Virginia's Atlantic coastline. That summer, to prevent their military prisoners from escaping to rejoin the British, two new prisoner barracks had been constructed at a greater distance from the invaders. Both new prisons were sited in far western Virginia on the other side of the Blue Ridge Mountains, one at Warm Springs, one in Bath County, and another farther north at Winchester, the residence of Col. James Wood.

With the war growing closer, Gov. Jefferson moved the Virginia Assembly's meeting place from Williamsburg westward to Charlottesville—"just in case…." He advised Col. Wood, the post commander at the barracks, to stay on the ready to remove his prisoners to the new Winchester camp at a moments notice.

In early February in 1781, the Tory turncoat Benedict Arnold led a raid on Richmond. At the height of Arnold's invasion, the German internees at the barracks at Charlottesville were transported on wagons over the mountains to Warm Springs and Winchester with Capt. Edmund Read's state cavalry as their mounted guards. In March, a month later, Col. Francis Taylor reported that the German prisoners, "very orderly and easily governed," had safely reached their destination.

In June Lt. Col. Banastre Tarleton—yes, the "Bloody British Butcher"—was dispatched by Gen. Cornwallis to make a raid out to Charlottesville where the Virginia Assembly was holding their meetings. Tarleton was to capture the assemblymen and free the captured German mercenaries so they could return to active military duty. The prisoners had already been moved out of his reach, but he was able to capture seven Virginia assemblymen where they sat before the rest, somehow, managed to slip away.

Along his path in and out of Charlottesville, Tarleton left the Albemarle and Amherst countryside in tatters, burning homes and barns, confiscating grain and horses, and driving off what cattle his men didn't butcher to eat. The local men, those too old or ill for the militia, took up arms to protect their families and property. Doing their

best, they couldn't stop him. (It was about then that old Mr. James Tuley died. One wonders if all this commotion had anything to do with his passing.)

Frank New, having recently moved his family to Albemarle County, was there when Tarleton led his cavalry on his dastardly raid. Frank had joined the Virginia militia and took part in warding off the marauding invader. Frank's older brother, David New, had become a Quaker but set aside his religious beliefs to join the Virginia militia. Frank's second son, James Francis New, age seventeen, was with the militia who fought to save their homes. (Frank's oldest son, Jacob, was not there; a Continental soldier captured by the British, he was being held as a prisoner of war.) Most of the civilians and militia followed to harass Tarleton on over to Yorktown where he rejoined Col. Cornwallis.

Gen. Washington, with combined American troops and with the French under Adm. Comte Francois DeGrasse, laid siege on Gen. Cornwallis at Yorktown until at last, on October 19, 1781, the British army was forced to surrender.

Tarleton, captured along with Cornwallis at Yorktown, was held prisoner but was allowed out on parole. Recorded in the *Calander of Virginia State Papers, II* on page 567 is a letter written October 26, 1781, by one William Fontaine that tells of an incident involving Col. Tarleton and a young man named Giles. Mr. Fontaine wrote:

> *All property taken from the inhabitants by the British is liable to be claimed by them. In consequence, Master Tarleton met a most severe mortification the day before yesterday. The 'hero' was prancing thru' the streets of York on a very fine elegant horse, and was met by a spirited young fellow of the country who stopped him, challenged the horse & ordered him*

to dismount. Tarleton halted & paused a while thru' confusion, then told the lad if it was his horse, he supposed he must be given up, but insisted to ride him some distance out of town to dine with a French officer. This was more, however than Mr. Giles was disposed to indulge him in, having been forced when his horse was taken, to travel a good part of a night on foot at the point of a bayonet, He therefore refused to trust him out of his sight & made him dismount in the midst of a street crowded with spectators ... The people who have been insulted, abused, nay, ruined by him, give him no quarter ...

The surrender of Cornwallis effectively ended the Revolution, America's War for Independence, although the final treaty was not ratified by the American Congress until April 1783. The British did not leave New York until November.

Francis New was listed as "Frank" New on the 1782 Albemarle County tax record. This record shows him as a free white male "over twenty-one" who owned three slaves, seven cattle, and with three "horses, mares, colts, or mules." His tax levy was 2 Pounds, 7 Shillings.

"Francis" New was again listed on the tax roll in 1783, the year he died; in 1784 the "Estate of Francis New" was listed. The name of his widow, "Sarah New," began to appear on the Albemarle tax roll in 1785 as "head of household."

Nothing has been found to suggest the cause of Francis New's death. He wasn't an old man—he was hardly into his forties. He could have died from a pox or pneumonia, or maybe he was thrown from his horse. One wonders if he had been wounded in the war, perhaps in those last days when Tarleton made his raid through Albemarle County. We don't know—he died before he could apply for his veteran pension.

After Frank died, Sarah New returned the family to Amherst County. The 1787 Amherst tax roll shows Sarah paying tax on three slaves while living with, or next to, her three sons—Jacob, James F. and John. Her boys, all old enough to vote, had to pay a poll tax, but her three daughters—Ann, Elizabeth and Judith—as they were female, were not allowed to vote; therefore their names were not registered.

As she owned no land, it is thought that Sarah New and her children lived on the farm of her brother-in-law, David New, who upon returning from war to his burned out farm, had moved to Amherst County. (It could be that the News lived as tenants on land belonging to a friend, or perhaps with Sarah's relatives. Of all this we have found no record.)

Frank's widow, Sarah New, must have had a busy family life over the next few years. One by one her children, young adults, were finding mates and were thinking of marriage. In her late forties, widow New remained a youthful vigorous woman. When William Haynes, a recent widower, came calling to ask for Sarah's hand, she accepted.

Widower William Haynes and the widow Sarah New were married on the sixth day of December in 1794. Their two witnesses were Sarah's youngest son John New and his new wife, "Betsy" (Elizabeth Martin).

Who *was* this William Haynes? Will had been born in Bedford County, Virginia, in 1740, which made him a few years older than Sarah. His late father had been William V. Haynes Sr. (1710–1781), who had married his mother, Elizabeth, in 1734, and in 1758 he had served as a militia captain in Bedford County.

His son, William Haynes Jr., was first married, in 1764, to Miss Hannah Ellis, and they produced nine children. In 1774 he purchased 150 acres of estate land from the heirs of Hannah's relative, Capt. Charles Ellis, deceased. The Ellis estate, "Red Hill," was on the Pedlar River on the north side of Amherst County's Tobacco Row Mountains a few miles south of Frank and Sarah New's former home near Rockfish Gap. When the Revolution came, William enlisted and served as a private in the 11th Virginia Regiment.

After the war and with the older Haynes children all married, widower William Haynes and widow Sarah New met when his son, Josiah Haynes, and Sarah's youngest daughter, Judith New, married in April of 1794. William and Sarah were married that December before the year ended. They made their home on William's farm.

The nine children of Will Jr. and Hannah Ellis Haynes were:

1. **Thomas Handing "Harden" Haynes**, the oldest, was married with a young family. (He later bought his father's farm.)
2. **Charles Ellis Haynes**, b. 1765, m. Nancy Goodrich on January 1, 1783. Their fathers, John Goodrich and Will Haynes, giving consent.
3. **William Haynes III**
4. **Jesse Haynes**, m. Mildred "Hilly" Tinsley in 1793
5. **Susannah Haynes**, m. George McDonald on September 6, 1793
6. **Elizabeth Haynes**, m. Henry Searcy
7. **Josiah Haynes**, m. **Judith New** on April 8, 1794, with her mother Sarah New and her older sister, Elizabeth New Martin, giving content. (Josiah acted as surety when John New and Betsy Martin married.)
8. **Hannah Haynes**, m. a Mr. Thomas (Thompson?)
   1. **John Barton Haynes**, m. Rhoda Huff

Many Virginia veterans who fought in the Revolution left the Virginia colony (now the state of Virginia) following the war. Virginia had been largely spared from much of the war's physical destruction but suffered greatly from the loss of her sons struck down in battle and from the poor health of her returning veterans that were damaged by the unbelievable hardships they had endured and/or by their drastic wounds.

The departure of the experienced British tobacco merchants left a gap in the marketing process, which caused a great decline in Virginia's tobacco production. Planters trying to raise tobacco on worn-out land turned to less profitable crops—corn, wheat, and a little rye, along with cotton. Many vets, upon being offered land by the new United States government in lieu of their soldier back-service pay, opted to leave Virginia for new territories. It was reported that for every veteran remaining to Virginia, two migrated to other states—to Tennessee, Kentucky, North and South Carolina, and Georgia.

In 1797 William and Sarah New Haynes, selling their Virginia farm to William's son Harden Haynes for 125 pounds of current Virginia money, migrated to Ohio County, Kentucky. (See copy of deed) Some of their children, both his and hers, but not all, followed.

We don't know the date of Sarah's death. We judge it was before the death of her second husband; Will Haynes lived to be quite old, dying in Kentucky on August 23, 1827, a day short of his eighty-seventh birthday.

Children Of Francis "Frank" And Sarah Seeley New

I. Jacob New

Born: 1761, Albemarle County, Virginia
Died: November 16, 1835, Newton County, Georgia

1797

This Indenture, made this eighteenth day of September in the year of our Lord one thousand seven hundred and ninety seven between William Haynes and Sarah his wife of the County of Amherst of the one part and his son Harden Haynes of the aforesaid County of the other part Witnesseth that the said William Haynes and Sarah his wife for and in consideration of the sum of one hundred and twenty five pounds Current Money of Virginia to them in hand paid by the said Harden Haynes the receipt whereof they do hereby acknowledge, have granted bargained sold and delivered and by these presents do grant bargain sell and deliver unto the said Harden Haynes his heirs and assigns for ever a certain Tract or parcel of Land situated in Amherst County, on the north side of the Tobacco-row mountains on waters of Horsley's Creek Containing one hundred and fifty acres be the same more or less and bounded as followeth Viz by Philip Thurmond's lines on the north East by the lines of Edmond Goodrich on the South West by the lines of John Eubanks and Caleb Ralls on the north west and north. To have and to hold the said Tract or parcel of Land with its appurtenances unto the said Harden Haynes his heirs and assigns for ever and the said William Haynes & Sarah his wife for themselves their heirs and assigns do covenant and agree with the said Harden Haynes that the above sold Land and premises will for ever warrant and defend unto the said Harden Haynes his heirs and assigns for ever free from all incumbrances and all other claimants whatsoever. In witness whereof the said William Haynes and Sarah his wife have hereunto set their hands and affixed their seals the date above written.

In the presence of
John Ware
Charles Haynes
Tho. Goodrich
Thos Goodrich Junr.
Thomas Shedd
Jno. Eubank

Wm Haynes

Married: Edy (Edith?) Sweeney on March 17, 1785, Amherst County, Virginia. Our second Revolutionary ancestor. Biography in next chapter.

Children of Jacob and Edy Sweeney New:

1. **Jesse New:** ca. 1788, Virginia
2. **David New:** 1790, Virginia
3. **George New:** 1792, Virginia
4. **Joel New (I):** 1795, Virginia
5. **Henry New:** 1798, Virginia
6. **Samuel New:** 1800. Virginia
7. **Jacob New Jr.:** 1802, Georgia
8. **(Daughter) New:** ca. 1804, Georgia
9. **Elijah New:** 1806, Georgia
10. **William New:** 1808, Georgia

II. *James Francis New*

Born: October 27, 1764, Amherst County, Virginia

Died: April 12, 1848, Scott County, Illinois

Married: (1) **Martha Tuley** on April 28, 1788 in Amherst County, Virginia; (2) **Nancy McDonald** (1783–1860) in 1804, Warren County, Kentucky

Born in Amherst County, James Francis New moved to Albemarle County with his family when a young lad. Around eighteen when Tarleton's calvary raided the countryside, he joined the military to fight back. After his father (Frank New) died and with the war ending, in 1784 he returned to Amherst County with his mother. He was twenty when he was listed on the Amherst poll tax roll next to his mother.

James F. was twenty-four in 1788 when he married young Miss Martha Tuley with the consent of her father, John Tuley of Albemarle County. (This John Tuley was a son of Mr. James Tuley and wife, Judith; when James Tuley died in 1781, he had bequeathed one male slave "to my son John Tuley.")

Martha Tuley didn't live but a short while after she and James F. married. Some say she had given him a son, Anthony, although this is unproven.

In the mid 1790s James F. moved with his mother and stepfather—and other relatives—to homestead in Warren County, Kentucky. There, in 1804 he married Miss Nancy McDonald, daughter of Argus and Elizabeth McDonald. With Nancy he fathered his ten children.

Not satisfied in Kentucky, James F. moved his family to Scott County, Illinois, where, at age eighty-four, he died. His will named all ten of his children. (His will did not mention a son named Anthony.)

Children of James Francis and Nancy McDonald New:

1. **Argis McDonald New**: 1805
2. **Asa C. New**: 1807
3. **Celia J. New**: 1810
4. **Paulina C. New**: 1812
5. **Rev. James Francis New**: 1813
6. **Lucinda New**: ca. 1815
7. **Nancy New**: ca. 1817
8. **Elizabeth New**: ca. 1819
9. **William Fletcher New**: 1821
10. **Emeline New**: 1823

III. *John New*

Born: In the mid 1760s in Albemarle County, Virginia

Died: (?)

Married: **Elizabeth "Betsy" Martin** in Amherst County on February 1, 1794. She signed her own consent after John's brother, James F. New and neighbor Archilles Ballinger testified that she was of legal age. John's friend, Josiah Haynes, was John's surety.

Betsy was a member of a prominent Amherst family. Joseph Martin, (her father?), younger son of an English merchant, owned a mill in Rockfish River Valley. Twice married, he sired eleven children. "Trinity," the Martin's fine brick colonial home, was built circa 1762 on an old grant land that the Martins purchased from a Mr. John Lyon. (If interested, check today's Nelson County Historical Society's files.)

We have been unable to find, for sure, which Martin was Betsy's father. On one roster of Revolutionary soldiers there are listed six Martin American soldiers from Virginia, i.e., Capt. Azariah, James, John Sr. and Jr., Joseph, and William.

It was at John and Betsy's wedding that John's mother, Sarah New, and William Haynes met. Josiah Haynes, John New's surety, became his stepbrother when John's mother and Josiah's father married. The newlyweds John and Betsy New, apparently living in his mother's home, witnessed their wedding.

As farmers were leaving Virginia to find fresh land elsewhere, on October 1791 one Chas. and Peggy Isom sold their Amherst County land to move to Mercer County, Kentucky. Witnessing their deed was their neighbor, John New.

This is all we know of John and Betsy New. Did they immigrate to Kentucky with others of the family, or did they remain in Virginia?

Children of John and Elizabeth "Betsy" New: Unknown.

IV. Ann New Martin

Born: 177_, Amherst County, Virginia
Died: (When? Where?)
Married: The veteran **Obediah Martin** on January 17, 1791, in Amherst County. Her widowed mother, Sarah New, gave consent to the wedding and the groom's older brother, George Martin, acted as his surety.

The will of Obadiah's father, James Martin, was written on September 25, 1771 but wasn't probated until he died in March 1775. It was recorded *in Amherst County Will Book I*, page 279. His estate was inventoried (Ibid., p. 284).

In his will James Martin named (Capt.) Obediah Martin, his youngest son, to receive a token inheritance; his oldest son, Azariah Martin, inheriting the 300 acres of land "on north branch of Rock Fish River where I now live."

In the recent Revolution Azariah Martin was appointed captain of a Virginia militia company that was led by the American Gen. Gates who, in August 1780, fought the British soldiers under Gen. Cornwallis in a battle that took place at Camden, South Carolina. In this battle the Americans gave a poor account of themselves, due the inept leadership of their General, H. Gates. Forty-five Virginia soldiers, in disgust, deserted the field and headed home. Among the militiamen that remained with Capt. Martin was his kinsman, Sgt. John Martin.

After the Camden fiasco, Gen. Washington replaced Gen. Gates with Gen. Nathanael Greene, who had fought well with his "Green Mountain Boys" in battles up in New England. Under Gen. Greene the tide of the war turned in the Carolinas. Gen. Cornwallis, with his causalities running high, began a retreat to Virginia to join the British stronghold there near Yorktown. While retreating, Cornwallis sent Col. "Bloody" Tarleton with his light calvary on the devastating raid, as told earlier, through Amherst and Albemarle to capture the Virginia assemblymen's urgent meeting at Charlottesville. It was on Tarleton's raid that so many Virginia kinsmen and neighbors so greatly suffered, losing homes, livestock, and their lives.

We don't know if, due to the economic depression following the war, Obediah and Ann New Martin left Amherst County for Kentucky with their relatives or if they remained in Virginia.

Children of Obediah and Ann New Martin: Unknown.

V. Elizabeth New Mcdonald

Born: 177_, Albemarle County, Virginia
Died: In Kentucky?
Married: **James McDonald**, thought to be brother of Argus McDonald whose daughter, Nancy McDonald, had married Elizabeth's brother, James Francis New (q.v.)

Children: Unknown.

VI. Judith New

Born: 177_, Albemarle County, Virginia

Died: In Kentucky?

Married: **Josiah Haynes** on April 28, 1794, after the war, in Amherst County. A son of William Haynes, Josiah was her stepbrother, but no blood kin.

Josiah and Judith married as their families were preparing to migrate to Kentucky. We presume they all traveled together. We don't know what became of them after they moved.

Children: Unknown.

Chapter VII
Jacob "Jake" New
(1761–1834)

Jacob New, the firstborn child of frontiersman Francis "Frank" New and his wife, Sarah, was born in Amherst County, Virginia, in 1761, the year Amherst was formed from the vast Albemarle County. Jacob's father, a gregarious man who enjoyed hunting and socializing with friends more than reading a book, was not one to overly tax himself with farm labor. Frank had been taught to read and write by his lawyer/father but saw no need, nor had the patience, to pass these accomplishments on to his son. (Jacob "Jake" New had to sign his name with an "X.")

Jake was about ten when his father made the arrangement, as previously mentioned, with "Uncle" James Tuley to purchase a farm and a few slaves. The farm, located in Amherst County, was on Short's Creek, which fed into the upper Rock Fish River near the crest of Virginia's Blue Ridge Mountains. (Having grown in population twenty years following the American Revolution, this area was separated to become today's Nelson County.)

New's slaves did the bulk of the farm labor but young Jacob, growing bigger, also worked in the fields. Selling the tobacco they raised, Frank was able to pay for his mortgaged farm. The family didn't suffer from want, but they didn't accumulate wealth.

As young Jacob New was growing up, political unrest had become the main subject of conversation between Virginia's planters. Proud of his bright oldest son, Frank often took the boy along when the men talked of their grievances against England, even boldly speaking of abolishing Virginia's House of Burgesses. Jake was too young to voice his opinion, but he listened with interest.

Jake was fourteen in March 1775 when on one spring day a group of concerned Virginians met at St. James Church in Richmond to discuss what could be done about their growing dissatisfaction with England. Amid talk of boycotting British goods and refusing to pay the ever-increasing taxes England levied, the subject of a war came up as a way to set the colonies free, an independent nation. Assemblyman Patrick Henry, at the end of an impassioned speech, shouted his celebrated words, " … Give me *liberty*, or give me *death*!"

As the American unrest heightened, echoes of Henry's speech resounded throughout the thirteen American colonies. In April, a month later, the first shots of a revolution were fired outside Boston. A number of red-coated English soldiers were killed, but the Americans, out-numbered, lost the battle and fled.

That May, groups of American patriots from all the thirteen colonies held a second Continental Congress at Philadelphia. Assuming supervision of all Patriot forces, it appointed a planter/surveyor, George Washington of Virginia, to be the commanding general of the new American Continental Army.

Over the next few years the untrained and ill-equipped Continental citizen-soldiers and the polished British Army engaged in historic battles from Virginia's coastline and northward as far as Canada. While these armies clashed in the north, in the south—in eastern Georgia, the Carolinas, and along Virginia's coastline—the numerous Tory party members that lived there, remaining loyal to England, were bringing grief to their out-numbered American Whig neighbors. They burned Whigs' homes and confiscated their horses and cattle. They arrested Whigs for treason, taking a few "traitors" out to be lynched.

It wasn't as bad as this in Amherst County where our New family lived. There, as in Virginia's other western counties, the American quest for freedom continued strong. The few Loyalist or Tories living there caused little problem to the American Patriots as they organized to fight.

Back in 1771 New York's governor, Lord Dunmore, (John Murray, 4th Earl of Dunmore) had been appointed to replace Virginia's Gov. Norborne Berkeley (the Baron Botetourt) who had died of an illness.

Now, in June 1775, the new Gov. Dunmore, alarmed by Virginia's growing rebellion, ordered British sailors to guard his palace at Williamsburg and had them confiscate a powder magazine the Americans had stored and had them stash it on a nearby British ship. This action caused Patrick Henry, chairman of the Virginia Assembly, to call for an armed force to recover the Whig's seized gunpowder.

Responding to Henry's order, Capt. James Higginsbotham, Lt. Joseph Cabell, and Ens. Nicholas Cabell hastily called a meeting at "Warminster," the Cabell home on Swan Creek in Amherst County a short distance from our New's home. A group of fifty Virginia militia was

sent on a march to Williamsburg to retrieve the Patriots' gunpowder. One member of this group was Francis "Frank" New, a veteran of the late French and Indian War.

Upon being warned of the approaching militia, at two o'clock in the early morning of June 8, 1775, Gov. Dunmore sneaked off with his family to board an English ship that waited at nearby Queen's Creek. He later transferred to another ship, the "Fowey," which anchored off Yorktown in Chesapeake Bay.

The Virginia militia at Williamsburg watched for Dunmore's return for three months before they were dismissed. They had been unable to rescue their powder, although the deposed governor later paid them 330 pounds.

Later that June with Gov. Dunmore gone, the Virginia House of Burgesses adjourned to meet no more. Without governor nor legislature, Virginia citizens called a meeting and elected an eleven-man "committee of safety" to ready a defense against further English aggression. The committee was to control both military and civilian matters. Mr. Patrick Henry, of course, was its elected chairman.

Shortly thereafter, in July Virginia's "committee of safety" held its second meeting. With rebellious thoughts running high, it planned three types of military service and required that all her men between age sixteen and fifty come forth to register for some type of military involvement. It divided Virginia into fifteen military districts, which, altogether, would form two full fighting regiments. Amherst County was placed in the Buckingham district, which was composed of the counties of Buckingham, Amherst, Albemarle, and the eastern part of Augusta.

Each of the fifteen districts was to furnish two companies of sixty-eight full-time riflemen to be supported by a militia. A captain for each company was appointed, but he could choose his officers—two lieutenants, one ensign, and four sergeants. Each company was allowed one drummer and a fifer. The riflemen and their supporting militia were to be housed in camps unless ordered onto the field.

Another type to be registered for service were the "minutemen," a part-time militia (like today's National Guard) who remained at home but were ready to respond at a moment's notice in emergency, to come only when needed.

Another decision the committee of safety made at the July meeting was the design of Virginia's army uniforms. Their commissioned officers were to wear white shirts with wrist ruffles to be worn under a white vest topped by a short blue broadcloth coat. They were to wear short breeches with silver knee-buckles. They were issued a buckskin hunting coat to wear when needed.

Sergeants' coats had white cuffs while the cuffs of drummers and fifers were dark. A private's coat had no cuffs at all and was so different from the tailored red coated British uniforms that the Tories made fun of the privates, calling them "shirt-men."

Militia uniforms were long-legged buckskin suits much like those of a civilian frontiersmen. They wore their hair short and wore round hats, while the riflemen wore tricorns. Boots and shoes were hard to come by; many had to furnish their own or go barefoot.

As might be expected, our Frank New was among the first to register for service in Buckingham's military district. His son, Jake New, at age fourteen, was still a mite too young to register. He stayed home to look after his mother and his five younger siblings while his father was away.

That September (in 1775) the delegates of Buckingham district met in the lower Rockfish Valley at the home of one James Wood. They chose Charlottesville, the county seat of Albemarle County, as the site to receive and review their new rifle company.

At Charlottesville the district organized its second battalion of men to be trained for combat with Col. George Matthews (of Augusta County) to be its commander. Col. Matthews promoted Ens. Nicholas Cabell (of Amherst County) to be the captain in charge of the new company.

Looking for a place to train, the new recruits built a camp three miles from Rock Fish Gap where the road, following Rock Fish River, crosses the Blue Ridge Mountains. This site was almost within "hollerin' distance" of the New's home.

Can you imagine the thrill the young boys from the Rockfish area must have felt as they watched their fathers and brothers turning and wheeling, drilling with guns at shoulder? Jacob New, living nearby, was among the group of young admirers. In another year he would be old enough to join them.

While this activity was happening in western Virginia, in eastern Virginia Lord Dunmore had his English ships anchor off the seaport town of Norfolk. Encouraged by so many Tories living near the coast, he raised two Tory regiments—the "Queen's Own Loyal Regiment," and the "Royal Ethiopian Regiment." Raiding Virginia's coastline, they freed the indentured servants and black slaves who joined them. With this enlarged force, Dunmore led another series of raids around Norfolk to search and destroy the cannons left over from the recent French and Indian War. His raids were mostly successful.

In late October Dunmore set out to burn Hampton, another coastal town a few miles north of Norfolk. However, a group of Whig riflemen under a Col. Woodford took cover in buildings along Hampton's main street. Their withering gunfire forced Dunmore's men to withdraw.

Heading south, on November 14 Dunmore encountered a company of inexperienced

Virginia militia. Firing too soon, the militia lost and ran, leaving behind twenty-five men—seven dead, eighteen captured.

The following month (December 1775) a company from Virginia's 2nd Regiment encountered an English Tory force who were guarding "The Bridge," a causeway, the only overland route across the Elizabeth River to enter Norfolk. Held there a week in deadlock, the impatient Dunmore force initiated an attack. Having learned from past experience, the Virginians at first held their fire.

With the enemy almost upon them, the Americans began point-blank decimating rifle fire. In thirty minutes most of the English soldiers had been hit, some as many as ten or twelve times, breaking arms and legs, and dashing out brains. The Americans, firing from cover, had only one casualty—a bullet had nicked one fellow's finger, his little pinkie!

Col. Woodford's force chased Lord Dunmore's men back across the bridge to Norfolk. Upon reaching Norfolk Dunmore loaded his men onto ships and set the town on fire. The closely pursuing Virginians doused the fire and remained there on watch the rest of that winter. When they finally left, they burned the remaining town, rendering it useless, of no further interest to the enemy.

After losing Norfolk, Dunmore shifted his base of operation. Sailing up to the mouth of the James River, he anchored off Tucker's Point at Portsmouth, twenty-five miles from Jamestown.

In January (1776), a Virginia Convention, the committee of safety, met again at Williamsburg. Needing a larger fighting force, an ordinance was passed that required each county to recruit even more men into their military. As with the other counties, Amherst County was required to furnish one company of sixty-eight riflemen along with its proper number of officers. The deadline for their recruitment was the last day of February. Any officer who failed to recruit his assigned number of men was in danger of losing his commission.

With this new requirement Jacob New, upon becoming sixteen, was recruited into Capt. Nicholas Cabell's company of Amherst County militia.

In May the Virginia Convention ordered two battalions of men to aid the out-numbered American Patriots who were desperately fighting battles against Tories in the Carolinas. However, fifty men of the Virginia militia under Capt. Cabell were diverted to Jamestown in pursuit of Gov. Dunmore. Most of Cabell's men were recruited from Amherst County. (One of them, it is believed, was our Francis "Frank" New.)

Cabell's men were canoed down the James River to Jamestown but then had to march the last twenty-five miles overland to Portsmouth. They arrived too late. Due to poor food supply and with his men becoming sick and dying in an epidemic of small pox, Dunmore had already demolished his Portsmouth post. He had sailed northward up the Chesapeake Bay to Gwynn Island, thirty miles from Williamsburg. He left behind 300 British graves.

On the fourth day of the following month, July 1776, the American Continental Congress, at their meeting in Philadelphia, declared the American colonies a *new nation, free and independent of England*. This caused much celebration throughout the colonies, but England wasn't yet ready to give up; the American Revolution continued for several more long years.

Four days after the Americans made their "declaration of independence," on July 8 Gen. Andrew Lewis (of Albemarle County) arrived at Gwynn Island with a force from the 6th Virginia Regiment. Setting up a battery, his men began lobbing cannon balls at Dunmore's British fleet, burning some boats, capturing others. The ship with Gov. Dunmore aboard was hit at least a dozen times, and Dunmore was slightly wounded. Completely surprised, Dunmore withdrew, sailing off to New York. This time he left 150 of his unburied dead, as well as thirty of his black soldiers who were too sick to move. The Americans lost only one man.

The newly formed General Assembly of Virginia passed an act that required *all* her men between the ages of sixteen and fifty to take an oath of allegiance and become enrolled in some type of military service. The Amherst militia and minutemen were encouraged to join the regular Continental Army.

Young Jacob New, having just turned sixteen, joined the Virginia militia and, for the first time, left home.

While the above was happening in Virginia (as told in the preceding chapter), the American Continental Army, under its commander in chief George Washington, was fighting a discouraging war with the British in the northern colonies. The ragtag Continental Army, despite being untrained and poorly equipped, were doing their best and kept on fighting. After England hired the German Hessian Mercenary troops, the Americans were greatly out-numbered.

As told earlier, in October (1777) up at Saratoga in New York, the American Gen. Gates, thanks to one of his generals, Benedict Arnold, captured the British Gen. Burgoyne and his Hessian soldiers. Upon consideration the Americans thought it safer to incarcerate their prisoners of war in western Virginia to be further away from British strongholds.

As their prisoners were being marched to Virginia, the plans were underway to build a prisoner camp outside Charlottesville in Albemarle County. (It was at this time Jacob New's father sold his Amherst County farm and moved the family to Albemarle County where he worked on the new prisoner barracks.)

Jacob, having completed his term of enlistment in the militia in 1779, volunteered to serve six months in Virginia's Convention Army Guard Regiment at the new prisoner barracks. Greatly needed and gladly accepted, Pvt. New was assigned to Capt. Holman Rice's 2nd Company of the Convention Army Regiment under Col. Francis Taylor.

Due to a lack of money, the Convention prisoner guards were poorly paid, sometimes missing an entire paycheck. One payroll record of Capt. Rice's company shows Jacob receiving 4 pounds for one two-month pay period.

The German prisoners confined in their new barracks were treated well. They were allowed to plant vegetable gardens. One observer said the prisoners' poultry, pigeons, and other preparations "put one in mind of a company of farmers rather than a camp of soldiers."

The teenager Pvt. Jacob New, still damp behind the ears, became bored with the inactivity of guarding the docile prisoners. Seeking excitement, when his term of enlistment in the militia ended, he joined the 1st Virginia (Woodford's) Brigade of the 2nd Virginia Continental Regiment. His new officers were Col. John Nevil and Lt. Col. Nicholas Cabell, both of whom he had known back in Amherst County. His captain was Benjamin Teliferro, Jacob's former neighbor who was also from Amherst.

At about the time Jacob signed up in his new outfit, it received orders to report to South Carolina. The enemy there, led by Gen. Lord Cornwallis, was causing a heap of trouble.

[For some reason our veteran, Jacob New never applied for a pension, which makes it difficult to trace his military actions. The National Archive has furnished what scant military records they have that concerns him. By tracing the steps of his military officers, we shall here make an attempt to establish his Revolutionary role.]

One of Jacob's officers, Lt. Col. Nicholas Cabell, was the son of one William Cabell, a doctor who had left England back in 1726 to settle in the colony of Virginia. Establishing his home on Little Licking Hole Creek in Henrico County, he became a neighbor of our New family. When one of Jacob New's ancestors, Edmund New, died a year later, Dr. Cabell had been the attending physician in his final illness.

Speculating in land, in 1751 Dr. Cabell moved his wife and their three small children ten miles upstream on the James River to settle on Swan Creek in southwestern Albemarle. That area of Albemarle where they had settled was soon separated to form Amherst County. (After the Revolution this area of Amherst County became today's Nelson County; as more settlers moved westward, Virginia's frontier boundaries were again changed to meet a growing demand for closer courthouses.)

Dr. Cabell eventually chopped out and patented 25,000 acres of frontier land, which was located on both sides of the James River. By selling smaller portions of this land to new settlers, he became quite wealthy. He kept a large plantation on Swan Creek for himself where he built his fine colonial home "Warminster."

Including his two younger sons who were born at Warminster, Dr. Cabell fathered four sons, all of whom later became officers in the Continental Army. The youngest, Lt. Col. Nicholas Cabell, Jacob New's officer, lived at Warminster, which he had inherited when Dr. Cabell died.

Like Jacob's father, Nicholas Cabell had been an explorer and an Indian fighter. In the summer of 1775 he became an ensign in a volunteer company of minutemen who had marched to Williamsburg after Gov. Dunmore had confiscated the Patriot's gunpowder. That November he became the elected captain of one of the two Amherst companies of militia who had trained at

Rock Fish Gap while the admiring young Jacob New had watched. In May 1776 Capt. Cabell's company of fifty militia were at Gwynn Island when the deposed Gov. Dunmore had escaped to New York.

That summer in South Carolina around 3,000 Indian warriors from the Cherokee Nation, armed with muskets by the British, were attacking white settlements in a brutal warfare that had lasted for months. When Capt. Cabell's company of militia were sent to Virginia's back-country to serve in the Cherokee Indian Campaign, young Jacob New was a member of the group.

In fierce fighting from Virginia and on down into Georgia, Indians and whites fought each other in death battles. Settlers had learned, by tragic experience, how merciless their adversaries could be. Soldiers from Virginia, Georgia, and both Carolinas fought fire with fire, burning out whole Cherokee villages in the mountainous area. The Cherokees lost over 2,000 men, women, and children before they would sign a treaty.

In the treaty, made in May of 1777, the Cherokees ceded a part of their territory to the Americans, making it a part of South Carolina. The treaty, however, did not end the hostility; peace with the Indians didn't come until sometime later.

That October the Virginia militia was encouraged to enter the Virginia line of the Continental Army, which most of them did. Capt. Cabell's group that joined the Virginia line of the Continentals included Pvt. Jacob New!

The first battles between the Americans and England were largely fought, back and forth, in the north. This changed late in 1778, the states in the south becoming the major center of conflict. In December the British Gen. Sir Henry Clinton sought to take advantage of the South's Loyalist strength. From his headquarters in New York, he sent down British ships loaded with troops who, after meeting with some resistance, captured the Georgia city of Savannah.

A few months later the Gen. Clinton, himself, sailed down with a fleet of ships and 8,000 men. His aim was to capture Charleston in South Carolina. (Back then it was called "Charles Town.")

But Charleston, an important seaport, was heavily fortified. Unable to take the city by force, the British laid a siege and continued to bombard the town with cannons.

Opposing Clinton, Gen. Benjamin Lincoln (of Massachusetts) in command of the Continentals in the south, somehow gathered a force of 5,000 Virginia and Carolina Continentals along with their militia. The Virginia Continentals under Commander Lincoln were Brig. Gen. Woodford's three regiments of the 1st Virginia Brigade. Woodford's men entered Charleston after a 500-mile thirty-day forced march. Col. John Nevil was the senior officer of the 2nd Regiment of Gen. Woodford's brigade, with Lt. Col. Nicholas Cabell being his second in command. Capt. Ben Teliaferro, Pvt. Jacob New's captain, was one of Cabell's captains.

(Capt. Cabell's rank had been increased to lieutenant colonel. Good! Before the war ended he was made a full colonel. In another promotion, Ensign Benjamin Teliaferro was made a captain. He had been an ensign earlier when he drilled recruits back at Rockfish gap where young Jake New had watched. Promoted, he was now Pvt. Jacob New's captain.)

Gen. Lincoln became concerned that Charleston could not be held against the larger British Army and the big guns of its fleet. He had a mind to evacuate the city and let the British have it. But then, giving in to the pleas of the important civilian authorities, he decided to stay and defend.

In resignation Gen. Lincoln had his troops—along with its civilians—reinforcing Charleston's defenses against the coming attack. He even had them setting out bear traps in the outlying backwoods to discourage any invasion from the rear. All this while in the harbor enemy ships were bombarding the hapless city. Concerned over a lack of men, Lincoln repeatedly sent messages for more troops. There were none to send.

(Virginia had already been obliged to rearrange her troops back and forth to form brigades. Already stripped of troops, she had been an easy prey when Gen. Benedict Arnold, who had turned traitor, had burned her new capital at Richmond. The Virginians weren't too keen about sending more of their sons to die in South Carolina, thinking that the Carolina men should enlist and fight for themselves. They didn't realize how many Tories lived there, nor the extent of their mischief.)

In April 1780 Lt. Col. Banestre Tarleton of the British Legion, commanding a mixed force of cavalry and light infantry, effectively severed all Charleston's land communication. With her only overland escape route gone, Charleston was completely surrounded by enemy.

The British increased their bombardment, lobbing off a shell every five minutes. Charleston's situation became desperate. Food was reduced to such a point that dogs were shot to conserve the small available rations. Firewood became so scarce that barrels of turpentine, instead of bonfires, were lit at night to provide light at guard posts.

When, on April 24 and on May 7, the Americans at nearby Haddrel's Point and six miles away at Ft. Moultrie surrendered to the British, Gen. Lincoln knew that all was lost. He surrendered Charleston on May 12, 1780. In a diary one soldier wrote that it was the first time in fifty-five days that he was able to remove his clothing when he slept.

The captured American militia were allowed to return to their homes, but the Continental officers and their enlisted men, which included Pvt. Jacob New, were made prisoners of war. Incarcerated at Haddrel's Point, Jake New, a soldier of the Virginia Continental Line, remained their prisoner, not being released until the end of the war.

The Marquis Charles Cornwallis was the British Army major general who had helped Gen. Clinton capture New York and had then chased Gen. George Washington halfway across New Jersey back in 1776. He was second in command to Sir Henry Clinton at the siege of Charleston. When Charleston fell Clinton returned to New York, leaving Gen. Cornwallis in charge of the British Southern Theatre of Operation.

With Charleston occupied by the British, Col. Tarleton's light cavalry pursued and destroyed an American force led by Col. Buford in South Carolina's Waxhaws. Tarleton's men, mostly Tory Loyalists who hated the American Whig "rebels," gave no quarter when the Americans surrendered. After their white flag was raised, Tarleton allowed his men to continue cutting down Buford's men, including the men already wounded and out of the fight. After this slaughter Tarleton was named "the Butcher" and the American's new defiant battle cry became, "Give 'em' Tarleton's quarter!!"

With the loss of so many Patriot Whigs, the American cause in Carolina nearly collapsed. The Loyalist Tories, with little opposition, went from farm to farm confiscating grain, horses, and foodstuffs to furnish the British menace.

While Jacob was in prison, on August 8, 1780, the English Cornwallis and the American Gates met at Camden, South Carolina—Cornwallis led a smaller force against Gates larger, less experienced, Continentals and militia. After a long hot march south, existing on half-ripe fruit and green corn, the half sick Americans gave a poor account of themselves—partly due to the poor leadership of Gen. Gates who, to save his hide, fled the field.

After this and other fiascos, Gen. Washington, from up north, sent down his most reliable general, Nathanael Greene, with his "Green Mountain Boys" from Vermont, to replace the undependable Gen. Gates.

Gen. Greene has been described as "a tall, handsome young man who limped slightly and had a marked asthmatic wheeze." He had fought with honor in the north and was an excellent choice to lead the southern campaign—he knew how to accomplish much with limited resources. He divided his army, himself to lead half and placed Brig. Gen. Daniel Morgan over the others. To give himself time to raise more men, Greene began chasing Lord Cornwallis around the countryside, engaging in small fights. With his smaller American force he didn't try to win, but to cut down the greater number of men in his opposing enemy.

Cornwallis, used to winning, was stunned when word came that on the fourth day of October, 940 buckskin clad frontiersmen had practically annihilated a body of almost 900 Tory Loyalist in a fight at King's Mountain. It had been a battle of neighbor against neighbor.

The patriotic American frontiersmen who fought at King's Mountain, mostly of Scot-Irish decent, were from the backcounty of Georgia, the Carolinas, and Virginia. They had been led by Col. William "Billy" Campbell and Lt. Col. John Sevier. In the battle their opposing commander, Maj. Gen. Patrick Ferguson (from Scotland), had been killed, along with several of his officers. His men, also Scot-Irish, were Tories, American Loyalists fighting for the king.

Fighting for America, the Highland Scot, Col. "Billy" Campbell, a Whig, charged his Patriots up King's Mountain with his ancestral Highland broadsword raised high.

"Here they are, my brave boys," he shouted. "Shout like Hell and fight like Demons!"

(These frontiersmen, called "Long-Rifles" by the Indians, were the first to use the wild Cherokee war scream when they charged an enemy. This cry, immortalized, became the South's "rebel yell" some years later in America's Civil War.)

The enemy killed or wounded at King's Mountain was estimated to be 300 men, with 800 more being taken prisoners. The Patriot force lost only thirty or forty men. A few of the captured Tories, those notorious for killing Whig civilians, were shot—or were "strung up."

Soon afterwards, the British forces received a further blow when the hated Lt. Col. Tarleton and his light cavalry were trounced by the old Indian-fighter, Brig. Gen. Daniel Morgan and his riflemen at "Cowpens," a place where farmers took cattle to be sold.

In early dawn on January 17, 1781, the fighting at Cowpens began in the verdant Carolina meadow where cows were grazing peacefully in the warming sunshine. In the ensuing battle over 600 British soldiers were killed or taken prisoner. Tarleton, with a few of his men, somehow escaped to fight again. (History doesn't tell us what happened to the poor cows …)

Gen. Cornwallis and his men came to give chase and rescue the prisoners. Catching up with the Americans, they began firing on them while they forded a river. Their shooting stopped, however, when the Americans threatened to kill the prisoners. After that incident the prisoners, with only minor mishaps, were safely housed in Virginia.

Enraged at losing so many of his men, Cornwallis continued to skirmish with Gen. Morgan's riflemen all about neighboring North Carolina. Gen. Greene, a master of the fighting retreat, rushed to Morgan's aid, hoping to crush the battle-weakened British.

Brig. Gen. Daniel Morgan, who had joined the Continentals and had been fighting in the war since its beginning, began suffering terribly from sciatica and hemorrhoids. Increasingly unable to ride his horse, he had to fight the war from an army supply wagon. With health failing, he realized it was time to go home, and he did.

Who was this interesting officer, Daniel Morgan? Born in New Jersey, at seventeen he went to Virginia where he became a teamster, hauling supplies for the British Army. With his reputation of being an expert Indian fighter, in 1755 he fought with the British in the French and Indian War.

A hard-drinkin', hard-cussin' brawler, he was court-martialed for knocking down a British officer who had hit him with the flat of a sword. His sentence—500 lashes with a whip—left his back permanently scarred.

Later, after being shot in his face by an enemy musket—which took away his lower teeth with a part of his jaw—Morgan took up some land in Virginia, ten miles east of Winchester, a raw tavern town. Marrying a local farmer's daughter, he fathered two girls.

Morgan, in 1771, had been appointed by George Washington to captain a militia company who, siding with the colonies in 1775, had fought in the battle of Bunker Hill. Afterwards, Gen. Washington sent Morgan on a march up to Quebec where he was captured by the British. Following a prisoner exchange a year later, in 1776 Washington made Morgan a brigadier general in command of 500 Continental soldiers. Most of Morgan's men, expert riflemen, hailed from Amherst County.

With his health failing, Morgan retired from military duty and built his home, "Saratoga," in Virginia's upper Shenandoah Valley. But, in 1780 Gen. Washington called him back into military service. Keeping his rank of brigadier general,

Morgan joined Gen. Greene in replacing Gen. Gates after Gates' miserable military failures.

As told above, in the 1781 Cowpens conflict, Gen. Morgan had whipped the ruthless Tarleton and won the day. His rifle corps is said to have been one of the best small armies that young America ever fielded.

(But I digress. Back to our story …)

While Cowpens and other battles were taking place, our trooper, Pvt. Jacob New, had remained incarcerated, a prisoner of war, at Hadrell's Point near the enemy-occupied Charleston. Unable to read or write, he welcomed new prisoners to learn what was going on in the war. He was told that after Charleston fell the Americans under Gen. Greene continued to engage the British in small battles where neither side won a clear victory.

In 1781 Cornwallis had chased Greene to South Carolina's Guilford Courthouse where Greene abruptly turned to engage the enemy in battle. The British won the fight at a dear price; as Greene had hoped, Cornwallis lost over a fourth of his small remaining force.

After this battle Cornwallis moved his depleted army to Wilmington, North Carolina, to give his exhausted men a brief rest before marching them on to join the other British forces along Virginia's coast. With Cornwallis gone Gen. Greene continued to skirmish with the local English-loving Tories all the way back down to Charleston. At last he and his men sealed off British-held Charleston in an arc, which held until the war ended and the last enemy soldiers left by sea.

While Jake New remained in prison, in April 1781 the Cornwallis force—which included the "Bloody-Butcher" Tarleton and his light cavalry—had reached St. Petersburg in southern Virginia. Gen. Cornwallis continued his march on to Richmond but sent Col. Tarleton westward to free the British prisoners held at the Barracks at Charlottesville near where Jake's family lived. (An account of this raid was given in the preceding chapter.)

Planning a new base of operation, Gen. Cornwallis, after sending Tarleton westward, marched from Richmond to the Virginia coast. Along the way he collected an additional 7,000 men from British-held outposts. Upon reaching the Virginia coast, he received a new order from his commanding officer, Gen. Clinton in New York. Fearing an attack, Clinton ordered Cornwallis to return north. While waiting at

Yorktown for naval transport, Cornwallis had his men further fortify the town.

Earlier that year France had sent Adm. Comte de Grasse with a fleet of French ships from across the Atlantic to aid their American allies. When the Royal British Navy sailed down to transport Cornwallis and his men to New York, it found Adm. de Grasse waiting for them in the Chesapeake Bay. After a heated naval battle, the British ships, leaving the French fleet anchored off Yorktown, returned to New York for repairs.

In the previous summer, 5,500 French soldiers, led by Lt. Gen. Jean Rochambeau, had arrived in the north to aid Gen. Washington and his Continental Army. Together these leaders planned to capture British-held New York in a joint military action. Now, however, upon learning that Adm. de Grasse had Gen. Cornwallis bottled up in Virginia, they quickly slipped their men south to trap the "Redcoats" at Yorktown.

By late summer, Cornwallis, having come under siege at Yorktown, must have "figgered" he was in deep trouble. He desperately tried to escape by ferrying his men across the York River, but a violent storm (a hurricane?) drove them back. He surrendered the next day on October 19, 1781. As their band played "The World Turned Upside Down," more than 8,000 British troopers laid down their arms. This represented about a fourth of England's entire military force in America.

This American victory did not end the Revolution. The war dragged on in other areas for two more years. The American Congress and England signed a final Peace Treaty on September 3, 1783.

Time in prison had matured Jacob New; at age twenty-two he felt like an "old man" when the Peace Treaty was finalized and war prisoners were, at long last, set free. Having no ready transportation, they were sometimes able to hitch a ride to Virginia on a passing wagon, but many walked the entire distance home. To Jacob it was an enjoyable trip, sucking in the fresh air of freedom, feasting his glad eyes on September's colorful autumn leaves.

Jacob arrived at his parents' home near Charlottesville with mixed feelings. His great happiness at coming home was severely dampened when he learned of the recent death of his father, Francis "Frank" New. He hadn't had a chance to give his father, his "best friend," a loving goodbye. Oh, if he had been freed earlier he could have been there … !

Indeed, Virginia suffered much from the loss of her men who were either killed or maimed in the recent war. Her tired soldiers, finally returning home, found many homes and/or barns destroyed. Many veterans left to seek new land further west rather than starting over on Virginia's depleted worn-out tobacco fields.

Nobody had money. Upon returning home Jacob had tried to find a job, but there were none to be had. He couldn't go back to his old job of guarding German prisoners at the Barracks; at the war's end the incarcerated British and Hessian soldiers, as had Jacob, had been set free.

Somehow Jacob got in touch with his boyhood friend, Joseph Sweeney, who lived over in Amherst County where he and Jacob had grown up. After the war Joe Sweeney had returned from military service to live on his family's old Amherst plantation. He told Jake to come on over—together they could try to raise some tobacco.

Hence, just before Christmas in 1784 when Jacob received pay (50 pounds, 19 shillings, 8) for his past military service, he walked, or hitched a ride, over to Amherst County to take advantage of Joe Sweeney's offer. With money in his pocket, he quickly renewed his relationship with an Irish colleen, Miss Edith "Edy" Sweeney, Joe Sweeney's sister. About six months later Jake and Edy were married by Rev. Joseph Ballinger of Lexington

Marriage record of Jacob New and Edy Sweeney

Parish on May 1, 1785. (See *Amherst County Court Order Book*, p. 111.1)

Perhaps a word is needed here about Edy's family:

Joseph Sweeney, a year older than our Jacob, was enlisted in a different Virginia regiment so was not, by lucky chance, in Charleston when it fell and Jacob was captured.

While Jacob was detained in a military prison, Joseph fought in battles in both North and South Carolina. He fought under Capt. White at Camden, and under Capt. William Harris in Samuel Hawes' regiment, he took part in the fight at Guilford Courthouse. He was at Eutaw Springs when Gen. Greene and his Continentals forced Gen. Cornwallis to withdraw his troops to Virginia.

After the Eutaw Springs battle, Joe Sweeney was sent to Richmond where he was made a wagon master, in command of a brigade of nine army supply wagons.

Near the end of the war, on December 5, 1782, Pvt. Joseph Sweeney was married to Miss Nancy Whitten, also of Amherst County. [See *Amherst County Order Book, 1783–1784*, p. 73.] Their wedding, performed by the Rev. Benj. Coleman, took place while he was at home on sick leave.

(Joseph's younger brother, Charles Sweeney, testifying later when Joseph was applying for a pension, stated that he was a young man still living at home with his parents when Joseph was furloughed home on sick leave. He said that after Joseph's recovery he had helped when Joseph returned to the army.)

Finally, after taking part in the siege of Yorktown when Gen. Cornwallis surrendered, Joseph was dismissed from the army with a certificate worth $80 for pay. Using this voucher he bought a mare and rode home to his wife and babies.

Joe and Nancy Sweeney had three children—William, Elizabeth, and Moses—all born in Amherst County before 1792 when they migrated to Washington County, Kentucky. Joseph began receiving a pension in 1828, which ended when he died on June 17, 1846.

It appears that Joe and Edy Sweeney, siblings, were grandchildren of an Irishman, one HENRY SWEENEY, an early Virginia frontiersman. Henry had settled in Albemarle County in 1745, the year before a portion of that county was divided to form the county of Amherst. He patented 100 acres of land in Amherst County, located "hard by the Dutch Settlement on Steven's Branch of the Rock Fish River."

We don't know when or to whom the Irishman Henry Sweeney was married, but records show that in 1757 one MOSES SWEENEY (Henry's son?) was an overseer on a nearby tobacco plantation. It is our belief, though unproven, that this young Moses Sweeney later became the father of Jacob New's wife Edy and her older brother Joe.

By December 1767, Moses Sweeney became able to buy some land for himself from Henry and Elizabeth Martin. About three years later Moses, wanting to enlarge his tobacco fields, had the adjoining eighteen acres of land surveyed. His new land was next to the property line of a wealthy attorney John Harvie. (A native of Scotland, this Harvie became the legal guardian of young Tom Jefferson and, at one time, had business dealings with Jacob New's father, Frank New, q.v.) During the war he fared very well when the Barracks were built at Charlottesville.

Shortly before the outbreak of the Revolution, the planter Moses Sweeney "of Amherst County" petitioned the Virginia House of Burgesses as follows:

> ... *your petitioner had a Hhd.* *[Hoghead] of Tob'o lodged, the 22 day of* *May 1771, either in Shoccoe's or Byrd's* *warehouses by a person who he had* *imployed to Waggon it thither, but before* *your Petitioner could get it inspected it was* *carried off with the Fresh and he never has* *received any Satisfaction for the same; he* *therefore prays the Consideration of this* *House and such Allowance for the same as* *they shall think reasonable.*

As the war ended, Moses Sweeney was listed on the 1782 Amherst tax roll, charged one poll tax and a tax on two Negroes, sixteen cattle and horses. Also that year, Moses filed a claim for "Property Impressed or Taken for Public Service in 1773–1774." [See *Amherst County Order Book*, pp. 474, 500.]

Moses' answer came in 1784: "Referring to the Committee of Public Claims, Mr. Cabell is to search the Comm'rs (Commander's) Books for this (Sweeney's) Tob'o." [vol. 18, pp. 274, 275.]

An aside to the above, which one may find of interest, JOEL WALKER SWEENEY, inventor of the five-string banjo, lived in Appomattox County, Virginia, about twenty miles as the crow flies, southeast of the county of Amherst, the Fluvanna River being the dividing line. This Joel W. Sweeney was born in 1810, probably in Amherst County.

On today's "Virginia Roadside Marker No. M–66," placed near the National Historical Park at Appomattox, is inscribed:

Inventor Of The Five-String Banjo

Nearby is buried JOEL WALKER *SWEENEY (1810–1860), musician and* *developer of the five-string Banjo. In* *1831 Sweeney launched himself and his* *two brothers, Sam [Samuel] and Dick* *[Richard] on a series of minstrel tours* *that continued until his death twenty-nine* *years later.*

A short hop up today's road from this roadside marker is a Sweeney family graveyard. It has only three graves: (1) Joel Walker Sweeney, 1810–1860, (2) Virginia Sweeney Rosser, 1844–1877, and (3) Robert M. Rosser, son of William Rosser, February 1, 1869–August 3. 1888.

In the 1890s one Lieut. Col. W. W. Blackford, a Confederate veteran of the Civil War, wrote in his book, *War Years With Jeb Stuart* [New York: Chas. Scribner Sons], as follows:

> *We were picketing at Fairfax* *Court House ... with General Stuart's* *Headquarters not far off, and I often* *visited there. Stuart had organized a*

band of stringed instruments and singers which afterwards became well known.
Associated with them was SWEENY [Joel
W. Sweeny's brother] the banjo player
who had brought the banjo into European
notice by his skill upon it, was one of the
band; he played the banjo and sang. Bob,
the General's mulatto servant, worked the
bones, and then there was a violin player
and a guitar player and quite a number of
singers among his staff and couriers.

The Cavalry command was extended
over a long front, sometimes as much as
thirty or forty miles ... Stuart would have
an eye not only to the reliability of man
and horse, but sometimes to the man's
accomplishments in the line of enlivening
a march or beguiling the time around
a campfire ... he collected around him a
number of experts, not only in music, but
in theatricals and tricks of various kinds,
adding much to the pleasure of camp life.
Sweeny and his banjo and his Negro melo-
dies were the favorites.

Sweeny always carried his instrument
slung at his back on marches and often in
the long night marches the life of the men
were restored by its tinkly. [pp. 50, 5]

Gen. Stuart had a warm heart, and
though a member of the church and a con-
sistent, conscientious Christian, he was
fond of gay company and of ladies' society
and of music and dancing ... I have often
seen him busy arranging for some of his
brilliant cavalry movements, and then
come out of his tent, call for Sweeny and
his banjo, and perhaps for some of his men
to dance for him, and then, to our amaze-
ment, order everybody to mount and be off
after the troops who were already on the

march ... The gayer he was the more likely
it was that we were about to move soon ...
I have never seen his superior in the battlefield. [pp. 89, 90]

Jacob and Edy had named their second son
Joel. Maybe "Joel" was a Sweeny family name
and the famous banjo picker Joel Sweeny was a
nephew or a great-nephew of Edy Sweeny New.
An interesting thought.

But enough about Grandma Edy Sweeney
New's relatives. Let's get back to our News.

We aren't sure where the newly wedded Jacob
and Edy Sweeney New lived their first year, but
in their second year, 1786, Jacob New's name, No.
0073, was listed on the Amherst County Tax Roll.
It showed that Jake owned nothing but his horse.
He was making arrangements for his widowed
mother, Sarah New, and her younger children
in Albemarle to join him and Edy in Amherst
County.

The 1787 Amherst County Tax Roll showed
the widow Sarah New, No. 1005, listed as "Head-
of-Household" who owned two horses and seven
cattle. (She no longer had her three slaves. Due to
the hard times following the recent war, she sold
them to make ends meet.)

Listed next to Sarah were her three oldest
sons, Jacob, James Francis, and John, who lived
with, or next to, their mother. (Sarah's unmarried
daughters were not listed; girls couldn't vote, so
they were not required to pay a poll tax.)

Jake New still had his horse and had bought
a milk cow as Edy was expecting their first baby.
His brother James F. New had only his poll tax to
pay as he owned nothing and was preparing to
leave the state. Jake's younger brother John New
was listed with four cattle.

On the next tax roll, in 1788 Sarah New,
head of household, No. 1038, had only one of
her two horses left and had no cattle at all. Jake

New had lost his horse, but had two head of cattle. (Apparently his cow had produced a calf.) Poor John New owned nothing at all …

With the war being over, Amherst, along with Virginia's other counties, faced the "joys of freedom" along with harsh financial uncertainty. Justices were overwhelmed by citizens who demanded payment for the goods and services they had furnished for the war, as well as their crowding of the courts by lawsuits being brought by debt-creditor problems. Also, with the British gone, the Anglican Church was no more, and with it went the welfare of the poor and destitute which the church had heretofore handled. The state had to find a new way to help its newly poverty-stricken people.

Amherst County had been spared much physical destruction but suffered from the loss of her men who were either killed in battle or returned home wounded and disabled—or were diseased. There was a loss of tobacco profit when the British merchants left, and it had become harder, anyway, to raise an abundance of tobacco on the soil-depleted farms. The planters began to grow more grain and cotton, but there wasn't as much money to be made there. They began to sell their slaves "down the river" to the plantations farther South, where the climate was better suited for the growth of cotton.

The most troublesome problem for Virginia was the migration of her families to the West or the South where veterans were offered land instead of pay for their recent war service. Many took advantage of the offer and left. Jacob New, one of the lucky soldiers who had been paid for his military service at the time of his discharge, was not qualified for free land.

As his brothers and sisters were getting married and moving away and after his mother found a new husband, Jake and Edy thought it was high time that they, too, left Amherst County. He didn't have to worry about his mother anymore as she and her new husband, the veteran Will Haynes, had moved to Kentucky. There just didn't seem to be much left to keep him and Edy in Virginia. Their next question was *where* should they go?

Then Jake heard that the state of Georgia was offering a free headright to newcomers in Wilkes County after they staked a claim on virgin land and lived on it for three full years. (Wilkes County, in the northeastern corner of Georgia, was right across the upper Savannah River from South Carolina.)

Jacob New was thirty-nine years old—in another year he would be *forty*! In spite of his hard work as a tenant farmer, he had little to show for his effort. By that time Edy had presented him with six healthy sons, and it didn't appear that she was about to be finished. With such a poor opportunity to acquire a home for them in Virginia, perhaps he would have a better chance down in Georgia. How else to acquire a permanent home for his growing young family? Yes, Edy, with her usual cheerfulness and her good Irish humor, followed his lead.

So, with the turning of the new century in 1800, Jacob and Edith New, with their young boys—Jesse (age 12), Joel (10), David (8), George (6), Henry (4), and their infant Samuel—loaded up their meager belongings and left Virginia to move to Georgia. Desperately Jacob New's family, stifling their fears, traveled south in anxious anticipation.

Chapter VIII
Jake in Georgia

In the early 1700s General James Edward Oglethorpe, English philanthropist and soldier politician, had been the moving force behind the establishment of another English colony in America. He had come to realize that the disputed territory lying between the existing South Carolina English colony, the Spanish Florida territory, and the French territory in Louisiana, was the military key to North America. Adding to the foreign threats, the Cherokee Indian Nation claimed a stronghold in the disputed territory's northern mountainous area while its southern region was inhabited by smaller tribes of the Creek Nation, although the Indian population, overall, was relatively small.

When Oglethorpe and his board of trustees received a charter from King George II for a large land grant in America, they set out to colonize this new territory. They gave it the name of "Georgia" and named Gen. Oglethorpe its first governor.

Gov. Oglethorpe, with 114 settlers, founded Georgia's first settlement, "Savannah," on February 2, 1733. A tropical grassland, it was sited next to South Carolina where the Savannah River empties into the Atlantic Ocean. His organization had handpicked the first settlers from indigent but well-deserving Englishmen, as well as German Lutherans and other persecuted Protestant religious sects. It was designed to protect the British Carolinas from a military force from Spanish Florida. With this in mind, Gov. Oglethorpe soon established a coastal fort on St. Simons Island (near today's Brunswick, Georgia) to serve as a defense against invasion.

The original Georgia grant, the largest ever made by the Crown, extended from sea to shining sea. Gov. Oglethorpe adopted a policy that allowed his settlers to purchase a homestead from Indian land for a nominal fee. Interested in making the colony more financially sound, the planters were encouraged to experiment by raising mulberry trees to provide food for silkworms, as well as other exotic plants—indigo, grapes, hemp, olives, and medicinal plants—that England had to buy from foreign countries.

Methodists John and Charles Wesley, along with George Whitfield and others, began to preach their religion in the new Georgia settlements. In 1740 Whitfield founded an orphanage in Savannah. Called "Bethesda," it was the first institution of its kind in the American colonies.

In 1742 Gov. Oglethorpe's forces overwhelmingly defeated an invading Spanish army in the Battle of Bloody Marsh. This victory opened the colony's interior for further development.

As a bulwark against the French and Spanish, the colony proved successful but, as a philanthropic and economic experiment, it sadly failed. Georgia's trustees finally surrendered their charter to the Crown in 1752 and it became a British colony. John Reynolds was appointed its first royal governor.

In sympathy with the other colonies, Georgia sent representatives to the Continental Congress meetings to resist the policies of King George III. In 1775 the governor's powder magazine at Savannah was seized by thirty Whig volunteers to send to the Continental Army. In 1776 when America's Declaration of Independence was written, all three of Georgia's delegates to the Congress voted for freedom by signing the historic document.

In 1777 Savannah, near the Atlantic coast, became Georgia's first capital, only to be overthrown a year later when the British army seized the city. The British captured Georgia's other towns of Augusta and Sunbury in 1779, but the Whig Patriots in her upcountry region were successful against the British Tories in 1780. The Continental Army and Patriot Whigs finally drove the British from Georgia and the Carolinas in 1782. The American prisoners of war (which included our Virginian Jacob New) were released to return to their homes when a treaty was signed and the war ended. On January 2, 1788, Georgia became the fourth state to ratify the United States Constitution.

At the close of the Revolution when the Paris Peace Treaty was signed, Georgia's vast land west of the Mississippi River tacitly came under the jurisdiction of America's allies, France and Spain. The state of Georgia still held claim to her land east of the Mississippi River that reached the Savannah River, the dividing line between Georgia and South Carolina.

Georgia quickly recovered after the war, its population increasing as new settlers arrived from the Carolinas and Virginia. Aiding its growing prosperity, in 1792 Eli Whitney, while staying near Savannah at the home of Maj. Gen. Nathanael Greene's widow, invented the cotton gin. His machine, which mechanically removed the seeds from cotton, revolutionized the southern cotton industry.

Georgia had been the largest grain producer in the southern states, but larger profits gained from cotton, especially the long-stapled variety that grew nowhere else better than in Georgia, completely changed the area's agriculture. To produce more cotton, the number of black slaves increased, which led to significant political and economic development.

In early colonial days, headrights of land were allotted by Georgia's trustees under the authority of the king, but later headrights were granted by royal governors until after the war when Georgia became a state.

As newcomers began to arrive from Virginia and the Carolinas to homestead in Georgia's under-populated counties, the new state legislature reserved "bounty land" for veterans who had served in the Revolution. This intention, while good, turned into a fiasco as civilians and ex-militiamen took up much of the reserved land, leaving less for qualified veterans.

The wide unoccupied lands between Georgia's Chattahoochee River and the Mississippi tempted land speculators. In 1795 smooth operators bribed members of the legislature to pass an act giving them title to more than 50,000 square miles of land—the site for the present states of Alabama and Mississippi—for less than $10 per square mile. This fraud was repealed by the following legislative session in 1796. This scandal, the "Yazoo Land Fraud," was named for the Yazoo River area in today's Mississippi.

This was how things stood five years later in 1800 as Jake New entered Georgia, moving his family down from Virginia. We would give a nickel to know how they made the long arduous trip. As poor as they were, they could not have paid for ship passage, as those with money did, to go by sea and then sail up the Savannah River.

The News probably traveled by an ox-drawn wagon, alone or in a wagon train. They may have simply walked, though with their several children that hardly seems likely. They likely built rafts to travel down the rivers, although it was hard to find streams deep enough to float all the way without involving a lot of portage.

However they traveled, one has to admire the strength and fortitude of our ancestors. Sipping a cold drink in front of our TV, it is hard for us to even visualize what hardships they must have experienced.

Wilkes County, one of Georgia's original counties, was formed following the 1777 Cherokee Indian land cession. A rather large, narrow county on the upper Savannah River in the northeastern corner of the state, it was one of the counties Georgia reserved for veterans, although its land was claimed more by civilians rather than former soldiers.

A new county, Elbert, on the Savannah River, had been formed in 1790 by separating it from the large original Wilkes County. When Jacob and his family arrived in Georgia in 1800, Jake somehow acquired land in this new county. As his deed has not been found, it is unknown if he received his land as a bounty grant or if he had claimed his land by headright. Jacob and his family were living in Elbert County in April 1802 when Jake X'ed his name (he couldn't write) as a witness when his neighbor, Wm. D. McAlpin and wife Agnes, sold their home with 200 acres of land for $2,800. McAlpim's land was situated in Elbert County on the south fork of the Broad River. [*Elbert County Deed Book J,* p. 28.]

In January 1810 Jacob New witnessed another deed when one Sarah Deskin sold Josiah Hopkins, both of Elbert County, 100 acres of land, "being part of a tract granted to Richard Aycock on Scull Shoal water ... adjacent on East side by Jacob New." [*Elbert County Deed Book M,* p. 104.] From

this we learn that our News were living on Scull Shoal, a tributary of the north fork of the Broad River, in the western part of Elbert County.

There were a few Indians, mostly Cherokee, still about when they settled. Though somewhat subdued by white men, the Indians still caused trouble, stealing horses or robbing corncribs. A watchdog would have come in handy. Georgia had been divided into state militia districts (a National Guard?) to be on call if a need arose.

In 1802, two years after our News arrived, Georgia agreed to cede her largely unoccupied land that lay west of the Chattahoochee River to the United States if the federal government would, in exchange, remove all Indians from Georgia's remaining eastern borders.

The United States, agreeing, took over Georgia's western land (today's states of Alabama and Mississippi) calling it a Federal "Mississippi Territory." They didn't break into a sweat to get this done; it took a number of years for the new country to accomplish the Indians' removal, finally herding them west to the Oklahoma Territory.

Due to a burgeoning number of new settlers coming into Georgia from the battle-torn north, another new county was needed. (The newcomers were dubbed "Chesapeakes," a name given folks who moved down from Virginia.)

On December 11, 1811, Georgia's Gov. David Mitchell signed a bill forming a new county to be created from the western part of Elbert and parts of four other counties. The new county, Madison, was to be included in Georgia's 4th Militia Brigade.

After this change, Jacob New's farm, located on Scull Shoals Creek in Elbert County, was listed as being in Madison County.

Madison County's 1813 Poll Tax Records listed Jacob New owning 269 acres of land at Scull Shoals. Following Jacob's name was "Joel New," Jacob's next-to-oldest son. Joel, twenty-three years old and married, had to pay a poll tax only as he owned no land but lived with Jacob and Edy. The names of other members of the family were not listed.

On this same tax record was the name of "Henry Swinney" (Sweeney), thought to have been a brother of Edy New. He owned 200 acres of land on "B.C." (We have no inkling what these initials stand for. Broad Creek? Beaverdam Creek? There was a Bluestone Creek next to Scull Shoals where the News lived. All three creeks were in Madison County.)

Henry Sweeney lived in Capt. A. B. Strickland's militia district, while Jacob and Joel New were listed in the district of Capt. Joseph Ware.

The 1820 U.S. Census of Madison County listed both Jacob and Joel New, and also Henry Sweeney, each as "Head of Family." The census gave their family members no names, but listed them by age brackets.

On page 7 Jacob New was listed as being over age forty-five, with his male family members being four males age eighteen to twenty-six, one male age sixteen to eighteen, and one male age ten to sixteen. The females of the family were one over forty-five (Edy), and only one daughter, age ten to sixteen. He owned no slaves, but reported that five members of his household were engaged in agriculture.

Jake's second son—our next New ancestor—was listed on page 9 of the same 1820 census. His name, Joel New, twenty-six to forty-five years old, was the only male in his family. His wife was also aged twenty-six to forty-five. They had no boys but had four daughters, all less than ten years old. His occupation was agriculture, and he, like his father, owned no slaves.

Henry Swinney, Edy New's older brother, was also counted in that 1820 Madison County census, giving his age as being over forty-five, with one son age ten to sixteen and two more under the age of ten. His wife, a little younger than Henry, was

listed as age twenty-six to forty-five. Their daughters were two girls between ten to sixteen, and three under age ten. Henry gave his occupation as agriculture, but owned no slaves.

The War of 1812, the second war between England and America, mostly fought in and near Canada, didn't have much impact on the Georgia farmers and cotton planters. However, in 1813 the Creek Indians from the Deep South, tired of the white men's land encroachments and inspired by the great Chief Tecumseh, went on a rampage to kill white men and drive them from their land. On August 30, 1813, Fort Mims near Mobile in the Mississippi Territory was captured by the Creeks, its garrison massacred. The war that followed was called the "1813 Alabama Indian Uprising."

Gen. Andrew Jackson of Tennessee led his American force in the last big encounter of the war where the Creeks were soundly defeated in a big bloody fight, the "Battle of Horseshoe Bend," in March 1814.

As a result of this war the Georgians brought even more pressure for the Indians to be removed from their state. The Creek Nation was compelled to cede a large portion of their territory in 1821. In 1825 the Creeks signed a treaty at Indian Springs, Georgia, in which they ceded all their Georgia land, as well as a part of their land in Alabama. Around 1840 the last of the Creeks were removed west to the Oklahoma Indian Territory.

Following the Creek cession of January 1821 and by the authority of a Georgia Act passed that May, Henry County had become one of five large Georgia counties formed from the former Creek land. As swarms of people wanted to homestead in this newly gained land, Georgia set up a land lottery (her fourth) to pick which of the hopefuls could settle.

The new Georgia counties were divided into lots of 2,021 acres each. Any Georgia citizen who met certain requirements was eligible to put their name in the hat, so to speak. After the respective counties collected the names, they sent them to Milledgeville, Georgia's state capital at that time.

The surveyors who had marked the land lots wrote the numbered lots on pieces of paper to be collected in one drum, while the names of eligible men who had registered were placed in another. Each fortunate citizen whose name was drawn received whichever land lot he drew from the surveyors' drum. Georgia was the only state that distributed new land in this manner.

The rules that established those eligible to draw were simple. Jacob New, registering in Madison County, was entitled to *two* draws by meeting the requirements of being a married man with a wife, having a minor son under eighteen, and/or an unmarried daughter, and was a three-year resident in Georgia who had been a U.S. citizen for over three years. (He did not gain an extra draw by being a veteran of the Revolution; in this lottery veterans were not given preference as they later were.)

On one of the draws Jacob New Sr. won! (His seventh son was Jacob New Jr.) For a fee of $19 Jake became the proud owner of 202½ acres of rich cotton land in Henry County! One can imagine that Jake and Edy made haste to move to their new home—as soon as a house could be built.

Several of Jake and Edy New's children moved to live with, or near, them on the new plantation. Their oldest son, Jesse, after being a captain in the War of 1812, had already purchased land in Jackson County, just up the road a way from Madison County's Scull Shoals. He chose to stay there with his new wife. But Jake's second son, Joel, remaining close to his father's side, moved with his wife and daughters to look after his parents—by then Jake and Edy were both well into their sixties.

The other New boys—David, George, Henry, Samuel, Jake Jr., Elijah, and William—either single or about to be married, came along to settle in or near Henry County. It seems they were a close-knit family, always keeping in touch.

The boys must have had a lively time together on the frontier where neighbors pitched in to help each other in times of need. It was a hard life, building their homes and barns and clearing ground for cotton fields. But it wasn't all bad. The men enjoyed hunting together and gave community parties in their "Georgia cracker" homes on Saturday nights where most everyone square-danced to the tune of a fiddle. (Those unable to dance patted their feet.) Most everyone met at church on Sundays.

Georgia had, beginning in her early days, provided for public schools. The neighborhood schools were mostly small with only one or two teachers. Jake New, never having had an opportunity to learn to read or write, made a great effort for his boys to not be so handicapped. All his sons were literate.

We don't know what became of Jake and Edy's only daughter. Her age but not her name was given when she was living with her parents in the 1820 Madison County U.S. Census. She was not living with them when they were counted for the 1830 Census. Likely she had married, but we don't know to whom, so we lost her …

Following the great influx of new settlers that came after the lottery, in the last month of 1822 the northern part of large Henry County was measured off and separated to become DeKalb County. Thus it was that Jake New's Henry County land came to be located in DeKalb County. His allotment was a short distance east, about ten to fifteen miles from a stream that flowed around the base of a large rock elevation known as Stone Mountain. Soon a little trading post was opened at Stone Mountain where Whitehall Inn was established. This was before there was a town called Atlanta.

STATE OF GEORGIA.

By His Excellency *George M Troup* Governor and
Commander in Chief of the Army and Navy of this State and
of the Militia thereof.

TO ALL TO WHOM THESE PRESENTS SHALL COME, GREETING:

KNOW YE, That in pursuance of an act of the General Assembly, passed the 15th of May, 1821, for making distribution of the land lately acquired of the Creek Nation of Indians, and forming the counties of Dooly, Houston, Monroe, Fayette and Henry, in this State, I HAVE GIVEN AND GRANTED, and by these presents, in the name and behalf of this State, DO GIVE AND GRANT, unto *Jacob New Senr of Baugh's district Madison County his* heirs and assigns forever, all that Tract or Lot of Land, containing two hundred two and a half acres, situate, lying and being in the *Sixteenth* district of *Henry* county, in the said State, which said Tract or Lot of Land is known and distinguished in the plan of said district by the Number *Two hundred and thirty* having such shape, form and marks as appear by a plat of the same hereunto annexed : To have and to hold the said tract or lot of land, together with all and singular the rights, members and appurtenances thereof, whatsoever, unto the said *Jacob New his* heirs and assigns ; to *his* and their proper use, benefit and behoof forever in fee simple.

GIVEN under my hand and the Great Seal of the State, this *Sixteenth* day of *June* in the year of our Lord eighteen hundred and *twenty four* and of the forty *eighth* year of American Independence.

G M Troup

Signed by His Excellency the Governor, the
16 day of *June* 182 *4*

E H Pierce S. E. D.

Registered the *16* day of *June*. 182 *4*

Jacob New's lottery win in Henry County

The Muskhogean Indians were one of the most important confederacies of American Indians living north of Mexico. When the English colony of South Carolina was settled in 1670, one large section of Muskhogeans claimed much of the land of today's lower United States. Many had homes grouped along Carolina's Ochese Creek. They were called the "Ochese Creek Indians," or more simply, "Creek Indians."

The Creeks gave refuge to Tories and fought with the English against the Americans in the Revolution. Then, after the war they signed treaties with the new United States government, bringing an uneasy peace.

Following the "Creek Indian Uprising" (in today's Alabama) in 1813, Georgia began to call for all Indians to be removed from the state. This led to the Creek land cession in 1821 and Georgia's fourth land lottery in which the name Jacob New Sr. was drawn.

After ceding this part of their land in 1821, the Creeks still claimed a sizable long chunk of Georgia land, which was located along the eastern border of today's Alabama. With Georgia citizens clamoring for more land to grow more cotton, political pressure brought about the last Creek Indian land cession. (Another Indian tribe, the Cherokees, still claimed a sizable portion of ground in the northwest corner of the state.)

By authority of a state act on June 9, 1825, the state of Georgia began the paperwork for its fifth land lottery. It took two years before the actual name-drawing took place.

The large area of this fifth lottery was first divided into five new Georgia counties: Carroll, Coweta, Lee, Muscogee, and Troupe. When surveyed, these counties were sectioned into land lots of 2,024 acres each, as was done in the fourth lottery. Persons who had been a winner in the previous lottery were excluded, unless they were

a veteran of the Revolution. Jake New, a veteran, was allowed one single draw.

For that 1827 drawing Jacob New, who still had sons needing land, placed his name in the drum and sure enough, he won again! He received 2,024 acres of new land in Carroll County!

As Jake and Edy had developed their cotton plantation in DeKalb County and had built a substantial home, they didn't feel up to starting again in a new place. Getting on in years, they sent one of their sons to see about the Carroll County land that Jake had won.

Jake New Sr. was sixty-nine when he and Edy were counted in the 1830 U.S. Census of DeKalb County. The census showed them living alone, all their children having left the nest. In the house next to the older couple was their faithful son, Joel New, who was listed along with his wife, Catherine, and their eight children. More and more it was necessary for Joel to take over the management of the New plantation.

On the neighboring plantation was Edy's brother, Henry Sweeney, with a wife and six children. They had followed the News to DeKalb.

The Cherokee Indians had been established in the southern Appalachian Mountains for at least two or three centuries before their first contact with Western civilization. Their first contact with white men was with frontier traders who bought their animal skins, especially deer hides, and sold them guns.

By 1750, however, white men had so invaded their land that, in defense, they began to kill the encroaching settlers. Near that time a calamitous smallpox epidemic, a disease brought by the whites, came and greatly weakened the tribe, making it ill-equipped to handle their conflict with land-hungry settlers.

After the Revolution, in 1802 Georgia ceded nearly two-thirds of her land to the federal government in exchange for the government agreeing to remove all Indians from Georgia's remaining borders. The western part of Georgia that was taken over by the United States became the Mississippi Territory, today's states of Alabama and Mississippi.

Displacement of the Cherokee Indians became more rapid as white families continued to move forward. The discovery of *gold* on the remaining Cherokee land in northwestern Georgia brought the final pressure for Cherokee removal. Georgia passed laws that extinguished the Cherokee government and made plans to distribute the Cherokee's land by another lottery as it had already done with the Creek's.

On December 21, 1830, Georgia declared that the Cherokee land in her northwest corner henceforth belonged to the state. This large area was called "Cherokee County" when Georgia held its sixth land lottery—the "gold" lottery—in 1832.

For the gold lottery those deemed eligible could draw for either a prospector's "gold lot" of forty acres, or for a "homestead lot" of 160 acres. After the drawing, Cherokee County was divided into ten smaller, but still large, counties.

In December 1835 the Cherokees ceded all their remaining land, that which was in the Mississippi Territory, in exchange for land out west in the Oklahoma Indian Territory and $5,700,000. This did not please the majority of the tribe—in 1838 the last of the Cherokees had to be forcibly moved west by an armed force of the United States. Many Indians died along the way. The Indians remembered it as "The Trail of Tears."

Jacob New Sr., Jacob New Jr., and Jesse New were all fortunate winners in the sixth Georgia land lottery, the "gold lottery." Jacob Sr., after swearing an oath that he was a Revolutionary veteran, was entitled to one draw. Old Jake would have been allowed two draws had he not been a winner in two previous lotteries. After Cherokee

County was later sub-divided, Jake's land was found to be in Carroll County.

Jacob New Jr. was entitled to two draws because he was a U.S. Citizen who had lived in Georgia for three years, had a wife, and had either a son or a daughter under eighteen still living at home. His brother, Jesse, who was still living in the old New home in Madison County, met the same requirements so was also entitled to two draws. (We don't know if he won.)

After winning land in the gold lottery, old Jake and Edy New, still living on their plantation in DeKalb County, again did not move. Jacob, at age seventy-four, began "feelin' po'ly" after the cotton was picked and the corn had been gathered. His Edy wasn't feelin' none too pert, either. Their son Joel's house was just next door, but they didn't want to burden him to take care of old sick folks—Joel's house was bursting with young 'uns and didn't seem like a quiet place to get well.

One of their younger sons, either Elijah or William, or perhaps both, came to get the old couple to take them to their home to nurse them back to health. Leaving Joel to operate their DeKalb County farm, they moved to nearby Newton County.

On November 16, 1835, Jacob New died intestate at his son's home in Newton County after Dr. George K. Hamilton had made a final visit. Edy Sweeney New died soon after. As she had done in life, she had continued to follow her Jake, even unto death.

Records show that William and Elijah New were appointed the executors of their father's estate on December 2, 1835. [Newton County Estate Records Vol. II, L–Z, 1822–1900.] The Honorable Inferior Court of Newton County, sitting as a court of ordinary, met for their January 1836 term on Monday, January 4. It ordered that William and Elijah New, after furnishing a bond for $4,000, be duly sworn in as administrators of the estate of Jacob New Sr. An inventory of the estate was ordered, which was completed on January 16. In Jake's papers they found a receipt from the sheriff of Carroll County showing that he had sold some of old Jake's Land, Lot #7 in Carroll County's 9th District, the 2,021 acres of land that Jake had won in Georgia's fifth lottery.

Jacob's estate sale took place on February 18. Buyers there with the New surname were Henry, Joel, Samuel, Jesse, Jacob Jr., William, and Elijah. All were Jake and Edy's sons. (More about them to follow.)

That July, in 1836, the Newton County court of ordinary gave Elijah and William New leave to sell all real estate of said deceased Jacob New, and on November 1838 the administrators sold Jacob's 2,021 acres of land (Lot #4, Dist.) in Carroll County to one E. B. Martin.

We have found no record of when the New's home and plantation in DeKalb County was sold, nor do we know where Jake and Edy were buried. It is thought that their son Joel inherited their cotton plantation.

Many interesting happenings took place during Jacob New's lifetime. Born in 1761 near the end of the French and Indian War in which his father Frank New had fought, he was six when the Mason-Dixon Line between Maryland and Pennsylvania was established. He was eleven in 1773 when the Boston Tea Party took place, and was fifteen when the Americans declared their independence from England and he became a soldier and was captured.

He was in his early twenties in 1783 when England recognized the United States as a sovereign nation, and he was released from a prisoner camp where he had been held for two years, and he was twenty-eight when George Washington was inaugurated as the first president of the new country in 1789. The U.S. Post Office was inaugurated that same year.

In 1793, when Whitney patented his cotton gin, Jake was thirty-two, and he was forty-two when President Thomas Jefferson made the Louisiana Purchase in 1803. He was forty-nine when Chile and Mexico declared their independence from Spain and was fifty-one when the War of 1812 began. He was fifty-eight in 1819 when the United States purchased Florida.

Jacob was 71 in 1832 when the first railroad was constructed in the United States. He was seventy-four when he died in 1835, the year that Samuel Morse developed the telegraph and Samuel Colt patented his six-shooter revolver.

Yes, much happened while Jacob New was alive. In whatever Jacob accomplished, he had been ably helped by his dear, faithful wife, Edy. Together they left behind nine able sons and a daughter to carry on in whatever triumphs and tragedies their future might bring.

Children of Jacob and Edy New

I. Jesse New

Born: 1788, Amherst County, Virginia
Died: Georgia?
Married: **Elizabeth Griffin**, August 7, 1814, by Henry Ware, J.P., in Madison County, Georgia. [*Madison County Wedding Book*, p. 5]

Jesse was twelve when his folks moved to Georgia from Virginia. He fought in the War of 1812 and married the year after the war ended.

In 1817 Captain Jesse New was listed in the *1808–29 Militia Record Book* in Jackson County where he was also named in the 1820 U.S. Census of Jackson County, Georgia. (Jackson County adjoined Madison County, the home of his father.) In 1820 Jesse New of Jackson County had a fortunate draw in Georgia's third land lottery, being picked for a 250-acre land lot [Lot #2, Section 2, in Winters' Military Dist.] in Habersham County.

When his father moved to Henry County in the 1820s, Jesse returned to Madison County where, on September 29 1829, he bought 250 acres of bounty land on the Main Broad River from a Samuel Groves for $200. That same day Jesse sold 100 acres of this land to a James O'Kelly for $100. (Ole Jess knew how to strike a bargain.)

In Georgia's sixth lottery, the gold lottery, Jesse New of Madison County put his name in for a draw and was granted Lot 221, Dist. 12, Sec. 1 in Cherokee County, Georgia in 1832. When Cherokee County was divided, this part of Cherokee became Lumpkin County, one of the places where gold was discovered.

Jesse New sold his last Madison County land, 239 acres, to Thomas McCollister for $700. [Deed Book F, p. 1] In this deed the house and other apertures went with the land, but Jesse reserved a half interest in the river so he could fish in the river shoals. It would appear that Jesse left Madison County to move up to Lumpkin County to look for gold.

Jesse New was listed in the 1830 U.S. Census of Madison County, but had moved away by 1840. The last we heard of him was when he showed up at his father's estate sale in Newton County in 1836. We could not find him in the 1840 Georgia census.

Children: Unknown.

II. Joel New (I)

Born: 1790, Amherst County, Virginia
Died: After 1865

Married:
>   (1) **Catherine (?)**, (b. 17__, North Carolina) in Georgia
>   (2) **Jane Cromwell** (b. 1830, Georgia) on December 15, 1851, in DeKalb County

Joel New is the subject of the next chapter in this "New" book.

Children of Joel and Catherine New:

>   Nos. 1–5: **FIVE DAUGHTERS**, listed by ages in both 1820 and 1830 censuses. The girls apparently died or were married in the 1840s as they were not listed with Joel New in the 1850 census, which would have given names and ages.
>   6. **EDWARD VANDERGRIFF NEW** (b. 1825, Georgia), m. **Margaret Bishop**
>   7. **JAMES NEW** (b. 1828, Georgia), m. **Caroline**
>   8. **MARTHA NEW** (b. 1833, Georgia)
>   9. **JOEL GREEN NEW** (b. 1837, Georgia)

III. David New

Born: 1792, Amherst County, Virginia
Died: (?)
Married: (?)

David was eight when he moved to Georgia with his folks, and was thirty when he went with them to Henry County. He was thirty-eight when he was listed in the nearby Newton County 1830 U.S. Census. He must have been married by then as he no longer lived with his father.

We could not find David in any Georgia census in 1840. Don't know what became of him. Maybe he went to join Crockett at the Texas Alamo in 1836. (Wild guess.)

Children: Unknown.

IV. George New

Born: 1794, Amherst County, Virginia
Died: (?)
Married: (?)

He was age six when he came to Georgia, was living with his father in the 1820 Madison County, Georgia, census, moved to Henry County with parents when they moved there in 1822–23. He was listed in Newton County, Georgia, census in 1830. George and his brother David left the state (or died) about the same time, as neither were found in the 1840 Georgia census. Looks like they left together.

Children: Unknown.

V. Henry New

Born: 1796, Amherst County, Virginia
Died: DeKalb County, Georgia, after 1880
Married: **Loucina** _____ (b. 1801, North
    Carolina) (Lusie? Louisa? Lucy? Her name is
    spelled differently each time you see it.)

He was four when he moved to Georgia, was twenty-four when he was listed with his parents in the 1820 Madison County, Georgia, census, and married soon after. In 1821–22 he and wife moved to Henry County with his parents and settled near them in the part of Henry County that later became Newton County. He was listed as "head of household" in both the 1830 and 1840 Newton County censuses. In the 1840s he moved his family to DeKalb County to work on the coming railroad line whose track was being laid from the east.

The 1850 census of DeKalb County shows fifty-four-year-old Henry and wife, Louisa (Lucina?), age forty-nine, living with eight children in the Crop Row District near Decatur, the seat of DeKalb County. (Their oldest son, William N. New, lived several houses away with a wife and three small children.) At that time Henry's real estate was valued at $150. In 1860 Henry, age sixty-four, and Louisa, age fifty-nine, still had their three younger children living in their DeKalb County home, their older children having married and gone. Their real estate was valued at $200, personal property $250. Henry survived the Civil War and the Yankee Sherman's devastating march from Atlanta to the sea. Lucina died first; the 1880 census shows Henry, at age eighty-four, living with his oldest son William.

Children of Henry and Lucina New:

1. **WILLIAM N. NEW** (b. 1822, Georgia), m.
    (1) **Elizabeth** _____, (b. 1826);
    (2) **Arminda** _____ , (b. 1845, Georgia)
    In 1860 William and Elizabeth lived in the Crop Row District in the little community of Lithonia in DeKalb County where William worked for the railroad. His property was worth $100, his real estate worth $200. Living with his family was a twenty-four-year-old boarder, John H. Raden, a stonecutter. When the Civil War began in 1861, it is not known if William, age thirty-nine, joined the Confederate Army or if he continued to work to keep the railroad open, the major way Confederates fighting in the northeast were kept supplied.
    Wife Elizabeth died during the war, and when the fighting ended, William married his second wife who was a year younger than his oldest daughter. He went to work as a stonemason. There was much work available for masons as war-torn Atlanta was being rebuilt.
    In 1880 his widowed father came to live with him at his home in Phillips

District near Flat Rock. He took care of Henry until the old man died.

William and Elizabeth's Children:

A. **Sarah A.**, 1846
B. **Mary Seleta**, 1849
C. **Nancy F.**, 1852
D. **James F.**, 1855
E. **William A.**, 1857

William and Arminda's Children:

F. **John**, 1867
G. **Jacob**, 1870
H. **Henry**, 1873
I. **Emma**, 1876
J. **Olive**, 1880

2. **JACOB C. NEW** (b. 1830, Georgia), m. **Julia Ann C.** (?), (b. 1830, Georgia) around 1850 while living in Newton County, Georgia.

Moved to Decatur, county seat of DeKalb County, and went to work for the Georgia Railroad Company in the 1850s. He fared better in wartime than most folks; he bought and sold land and loaned money at a high rate of interest. There are deeds recorded in Decatur Courthouse dated in the 1860s–1870s showing his land transactions. In 1870 he lived in Gwinnett County (adjoining DeKalb) with real estate worth $3,300, personal property worth $2,205. (A fine antebellum home?)

Children:

A. **William S.**, 1852
B. **Thomas H.**, 1854 (m. Mary A., 1879)
C. **Sarah A.**, 1856
D. **Julia D.**, 1859
E. **Luke H.**, 1861
F. **John**

3. **MARY J. NEW** (b. 1830, Georgia), nothing is known about this daughter
4. **ELIJAH G. NEW** (b. 1832, Georgia), m. **Tilithia Regan** (b. 1835, Georgia) in Newton County. Moved from Newton County to Lithonia, DeKalb County, where he farmed. Pvt. Elijah G. New fought in County C, Cobbs Legion, in the Civil War. (Information provided by Ms. Lena New McMichal of Decatur, Georgia, her parents Luke and Ella New listed below.)

Children:

A. **Henry**, 186_, a daughter, named for her Grandpa New
B. **Elmira**, 186_, lived to be "very old"
C. **James "Jim,"** 1867, a minister
D. **Elizabeth "Betty,"** 1869, married, moved to Alabama
E. **Georgia**, 1870
F. **Parks**, 1873
G. **Edward "Eddie,"** 1875
H. **John**, 1878
I. **Bert** (Albert?), 1880, worked for Georgia Railroad
J. **Luke Lawson**, 1882–1979, m. Ella Eliz. Walker, DeKalb County. Luke, raised by his "very old" unmarried sisters, lived in Lithonia, DeKalb County.

5. **ABAZENIA NEW** (b. 1835, Georgia), (Abergenia? Avarazena?) Named for her Uncle Elijah New's wife.
6. **MARTHA NEW** (b. 1837)
7. **LYDIA A. NEW** (b. 1843)
8. **ELIZABETH E. NEW** (b. 1845)
9. **JOHN H. NEW** (b. 1845), m. Ellen _____, fought in the Confederate Army in County C, 3rd Battalion. Infantry, and also in County D, 3rd Battalion Sharpshooters. Married at end of war, lived in DeKalb

County working as a stonecutter. Children listed in 1880 census;

   A. **Georgia**, 1869
   B. **David**, 1872
   C. **Lula**, 1875

10. **LUKE H. C. NEW** (b. 1849, Georgia), in 1870 census he was unmarried, living at Stone Mountain, DeKalb County, a railroad section foreman.

VI. Samuel New

Born: 1800, Amherst County, Virginia
Died: (?)
Married: **Nancy Dudley** (b. 1800, Georgia) in Elbert County, Georgia on October 5, 1820, by C. W. Christian, J.P.

Sam was a second lieutenant in the U.S. Army, having joined February 3, 1830. [*Georgia Mil. Record Book*, p. 4] He was in Butts County, Georgia, a county formed from the original Henry County, as listed in the 1830 census. He moved his family to Carroll County shortly after the Creek Indian cession of 1826. He had two sons and a grandson who fought with the Confederates in the Civil War. In 1870 Sam'l and Nancy, both fifty years old, were living in Carroll County, Georgia, near their children. He was a blacksmith.

Children:

1. **JARRETT NEW** (b. 1820, Georgia), m. **Sarah** _____ (b. 1820, Georgia), was in Carroll County in 1850 where he was a miner—gold or coal? Was in DeKalb County when the Civil War began, fighting with the Confederates in Company D, 42nd Georgia Infantry, alongside his brother Joel and his son Samuel C. New. Unknown where he went after the war, if he wasn't killed. His children were:

   A. **Mary**, 1841
   B. **Samuel C.**, 1844 (fought in Civil War)

2. **JOEL NEW** (b. 18__ ,Georgia) was a private in the same CSA outfit as his brother Jarrett and his nephew Samuel C. New.

3. **ELIJAH NEW** (b. 1827, Georgia), m. **Minah** _____ (b. 1827, Georgia)

4. **NARCISSA NEW** (b. 1835, Georgia)

VII. Jacob New Jr.

Born: 1804, Elbert or Madison County, Georgia
Died: (?)
Married: **Sylvia** _____ (b. 1806, Tennessee) around 1824

Moved from Madison County to Henry County with his parents when a young man. By dint of being head of a family and a U.S. citizen with a three-year residency in Georgia, he was allowed two draws for a 40-acre gold lot in Georgia's sixth land lottery in 1832. He won a 40-acre gold lot in Cherokee County but didn't strike it rich; a few years later on December 7, 1843, he sold it to Jesse C. Farrar of Cobbs County, Georgia, for $40. His was Lot #1024 in 3rd District, 2nd Section of Cherokee County, forty acres by survey. The 1850 Carroll County census finds Jacob Jr. and Sylvia New living on their land worth $300.

Children:

1. **JAMES NEW** (b. 1826, Georgia)

2. **NICHOLAS NEW** (b. 1828, Georgia). There was a Nicholas M. New in Company D, Cavalry, Georgia State Guards in Civil War.

3. **JESSE NEW** (b. 1829, Georgia), m. **Narcissa** _____ around 1850.

4. **MARTHA NEW**, (b. 1836, Georgia)

5. **MATILDA NEW**, (b. 1850, Georgia)

VIII. *Elijah New*

Born: 1804, Madison County, Georgia
Died: (?)
Married: **Avarazena** ____, (b. 1806, Georgia);
her unusual name is spelled differently each
time noted. A nice lady, had two nieces
named for her. (They couldn't spell her name
right, either.)

After his pa took him to DeKalb County and
he became twenty-one, Lige took a two-year hitch
in the U.S. Army, from June 7, 1824, through June
28, 1826, a commissioned officer with the rank of
lieutenant. When discharged he got married; his
oldest child, Luke, was born in 1827.

In 1830 and 1850 the Newton County census shows him living in Newton County, his
plantation valued at $1,500. Don't know when
he died, nor if Sherman burned his home when
he marched through Atlanta's countryside in the
Civil War. By then Elijah was too old to do much
fighting; he was nearly sixty when the war began.

Children of Elijah and Averazena New:

1. **LUKE NEW (b.** 1827 Georgia), m.
   Elizabeth ____ (b. 1829, South Carolina)
   circa 1849. Their first child, **Mary**, was
   born in 1850, but they likely had more.
2. **JESSE NEW** (b. 1829, Georgia), m. **Sarah**
   ____ (b. 1831, South Carolina) (Daughter
   Elizabeth, b.1850. More later?)
3. **JOHN NEW (b.** 1834)
4. **JAMES NEW** (b. 1836)
5. **MARY NEW** (b. 1840)
6. **HENRY NEW** (b. 1845)

IX. *William New*

Born: 1808, Georgia
Died: (?)

Married: **Lydia** ____ (b. 1811, South Carolina)
in Georgia, 1828

Moved to DeKalb County with parents in
the early 1820s, married and bought a farm in
Newton County after the new county had been
separated from DeKalb. William New and Luke
Robinson, both of Newton County, jointly owned
200 acres of land in DeKalb County. (One wonders if this land had been inherited from William's
deceased father, Jacob New. It was in the same
neighborhood as Will's older brother, Joel New,
who always lived next to Will's parents.)

On January 4, 1844, William paid Robinson
$50 for his share in the DeKalb County land,
described as "Lot 202, 16th District, DeKalb
County, originally Henry County." [*DeKalb
County Deed Book H, p. 594*]

William and Lydia moved to DeKalb County
after this sale where Will was elected a justice of
the peace. In 1848 he, as J.P., performed the marriage ceremony for his brother Joel's son when
Edward V. New married Miss Margaret Bishop in
DeKalb County. (See next chapter.) William and
Lydia, with their seven children, were counted in
the 1850 census of DeKalb County.

On February 17, 1850, William sold his
Newton County farm to James Kilgrove of DeKalb
County for $707. This farm, located in "Lot #67,
17th District of Newton County, originally Henry
County" contained only 1,971 acres, as it did not
include a five-acre plot William had reserved in
its southwest corner. [*Newton Deed Book G-Q, p.
187*] Did he save the five acres for a home, for a
business, or was he simply preserving the family
gravesites?

Children of William and Lydia New:

1. **LUKE NEW (b.** 1830), a carpenter.
   Recorded on May 5, 1855 in *Deed Book
   0*, page 110: "Luke M. New of DeKalb

County, Georgia, claims an encumbrance on the house and premises on which is __?__ of Jesse J. Robinson, adj. the town lots in town of Lithonia, who owes $183 for building house.
(signed) Luke M. New"

2. **SARAH NEW (b.** 1833)
3. **JOHN NEW** (b. 1839)
4. **JAMES NEW (b.** 1840)
5. **ABAZENA NEW (b.** 1843)
6. **NANCY NEW** (b. 1846)
7. **MARTHA NEW (b.** 1849)

Now we know why there are so many people named "New" in today's Atlanta telephone book.

NORTH
GEORGIA
EARLY 1800's

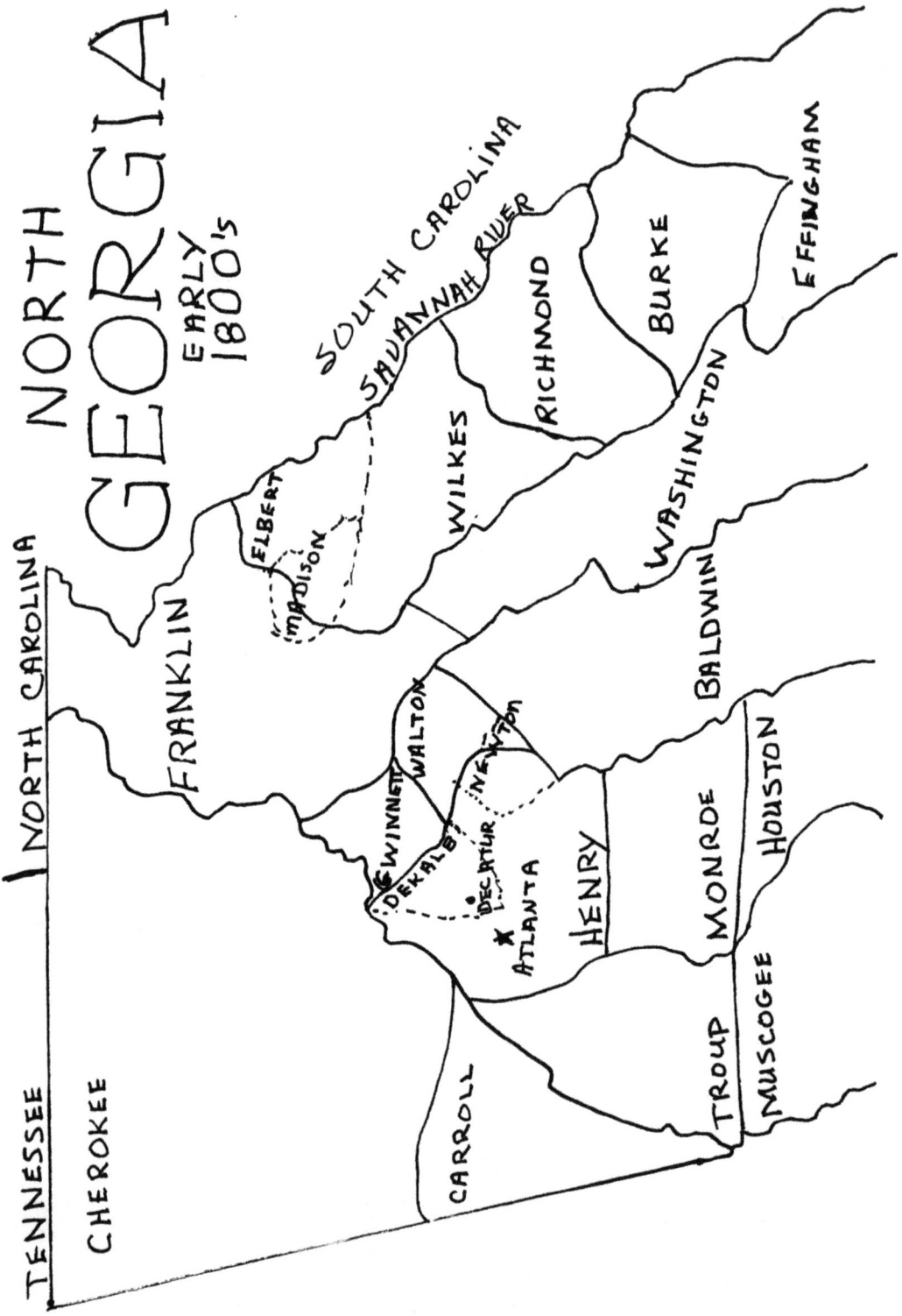

TENNESSEE

NORTH CAROLINA

SOUTH CAROLINA

SAVANNAH RIVER

CHEROKEE

FRANKLIN

ELBERT

MADISON

WILKES

RICHMOND

BURKE

EFFINGHAM

WASHINGTON

GWINNETT

WALTON

NEWTON

DEKALB

DECATUR

ATLANTA

HENRY

MONROE

HOUSTON

BALDWIN

CARROLL

TROUP

MUSCOGEE

Chapter IX
Joel New (I) of Georgia
(1790–1864?)

Joel was a big boy, ten years old in 1800, when his pa, Jacob New, decided that they should move to Georgia since making a decent living in Virginia appeared bleak. The prospect of their acquiring a homestead in Georgia sounded good.

Joel's older brother, Jesse, almost twelve, helped Pa drive their ox-team that pulled their wagon, and he helped the other men as they herded the train's livestock to keep them headed in the right direction.

As next oldest son, Joel was Ma's main helper. He gathered wood and toted water and helped her watch after his younger brothers. At ages eight and six, David and George could be a handful to manage on the long tiring trip. They wanted to fight Joel when he warned against straying too far from camp, unbelieving when he said that Indians still lurked about in the woods. Four-year-old Henry, a brave little soldier, believed everything Joel said and tried hard to please his big brother.

Ma mostly rode in the wagon where she sometimes took a turn at driving the team while looking after baby Sam'l—not that little Sam caused much trouble. All she had to do was to keep his 'hippin' dry and open her ample bosoms when he cried.

As the wagons inched through the southern Appalachians, they sometimes saw Indians. Pa said they were Cherokees who didn't cause much trouble. He said they used to be real mean but now they mostly lived on farms like white men. Sometimes the wagon trail crossed one of their farms, and Pa would trade with them for fresh vegetables. As they continued south, Pa said to watch out for the Creeks; sometimes Creek Indians still liked to fight. "Cain't blame 'em," he said, "they are protectin' their land."

It seemed they had traveled forty-forevers before they finally reached Elbert County, Georgia, where Joel's pa, Jake New, staked his land claim for their new homestead on Scull Shoal Creek, a tributary of the upper fork of the Broad River.

It is not now known if Joel's father gained their new Georgia farm by "headright" (as was done earlier in Virginia) or if he received it "on bounty," the land offered to Revolutionary vets. Shortly after Joel's family came, in 1809 Georgia repealed all laws relating to headrights and began portioning unsettled public lands, the lands ceded from Indians, by lottery.

The whole family had to work to establish their new Georgia farm. Where they settled in the Appalachian piedmont, level fields were hard to come by unless, like the News, the land was situated in the delta of a nearby river. It required great effort to cut the large trees for their home and barns and to open up the forest for their fields.

Georgia's early day settlers had founded schools and, when it wrote its first state constitution in 1777, it had provided money for a school in each county. Joel New and all his brothers were taught to read and write.

As newcomers kept arriving, in 1811 another Georgia county was formed and given the name of Madison. The area of this new county, Madison, was composed of parts of five other counties that had earlier been taken from the large original Wilkes County. The New farm happened to be in the western portion of Elbert County, which was sectioned off to become part of Madison.

All this came about in the year that Joel New turned twenty-one. With the county seats changing, we have been unable to find Joel's wedding record, but it was about this time that he got married.

Although his wedding record has not been found, the 1820 U.S. Census of Madison County listed Joel and his wife with four young daughters, all under ten years old. They were living in house #17 next door to Joel's parents, Jacob and Edy New, in house #16. From a later census we learn that his wife's name was "Catherine," a young lady near the same age as Joel. We haven't been able to learn her family name, but it was recorded that she was a native of Georgia, having been born there in 1790.

Joel and Cathy didn't own land but lived in a house on his father's farm. Joel's six younger brothers and their only sister were still living with their parents who were, by that time, sixty years old. Joel's oldest brother, Jesse New, had joined the military, married, and lived not too far away in neighboring Jackson County, but Joel New, ever faithful and responsible, was still standing by and helping his old parents.

On January 8, 1821, the Creek Indians ceded another large portion of their land to the state of Georgia. Located in the western half of the state, it was divided into five large counties. By authority of an act of the state that May, it was decided to hold the state's fourth land lottery to open this

new land for settlers. We don't know if Joel and/or his brothers drew for land or not, but their pa did. Old Jacob New won 202½ acres of land located in Henry County.

Immediately plans were laid for the News to move to this new location. Old Jake, leaving his son Jesse to take over his Madison County farm, took the rest of his New family with him when he and Joel moved westward to Henry County.

The area where they moved in Henry County had fairly level ground, well suited to raise the preferred long-stapled cotton for their cash crop, better than their old farm in Madison County. However, when they arrived they hardly had time to unpack their wagons before Henry County was subdivided into smaller counties. One of the new counties formed (from Henry) was DeKalb County, with its courthouse being established in a settlement called Decatur. Following this division, Jacob and Joel's homes were located in DeKalb County.

The next ten years were a busy time for the News. Old Jake's family became smaller and smaller as, one by one, his younger sons matured and moved, but Joel New's family became bigger and bigger as he begot more children.

After Joel and Catherine came to DeKalb County in 1821 their *fifth daughter*, Martha, was born. Joel had about given up hope for his having a son until little Edward was born in 1825. At last! A son to carry on the family name! He was again pleased when their second son was born in 1828. They named this son James.

The 1830 DeKalb County census, still not recording names other than the "head of household," showed six families that we find interesting. Living next to each other, they formed a little neighborhood community.

Living in house #1 was Henry Swinney, Joel New's maternal uncle, with his wife and their six children. Uncle Henry, a younger brother of

Joel's Mama, Edy, had followed the News from Madison County. He was then between forty to fifty years old, his youngest child being between ages ten to fifteen.

In house #2 was Jacob New, age sixty-nine. He and his wife (Edy Swinney New) were living alone, all their children having married and left home.

In house #3 we find our Joel New, age forty, with his wife Catherine. With them were listed, by age but not by name, all their seven children. (They later had two more.) Their two oldest daughters, between fifteen and twenty, had reached "marrying age" but were still at home. Their fifth daughter and their two sons were all under ten years old.

In house #4 in this census there lived a William Holly. We have no idea who he was. He could have been husband to one of the New girls, or it may be that he was a plantation owner or a slave overseer.

(We find no evidence that the News owned slaves. While more affluent planters bought more land to plant more cotton and kept well-stocked slave quarters for plantation labor, Joel New maintained his father's smaller farm and earned less money. He well provided for his family, but did not get rich.)

In house #5 there lived Reuben Bishop, age forty to fifty, with a wife and seven children. We also find this family interesting as one of his Bishop girls (Margaret) later married one of Joel and Catherine New's sons. (See next chapter.)

In the final house we noted, house #6, lived rich old Mr. Thomas Wooten, over ninety years old, and his younger wife, who was in her fifties. His sister was Nancy Wooten Bishop, wife of Reuben Bishop in house #5. When the wealthy Mr. Wooten died later, the children of this sister benefited from his will.

When Joel New's father died in 1835 his death was a great loss to Joel—as well, of course, to old Jacob's other children. Joel, perhaps more so than the others, had always stayed beside his father, each helping the other when times got rough. When the old man died, his family agreed that his plantation should go to Joel; the others were more interested in their own pursuits.

As more local cotton gins came into operation, the planters' cotton was ginned and baled to be sent by wagon to warehouses along one of Georgia's several rivers. Next, it had to be barged down to the coast to be shipped by sea to America's northern weaving mills as well as to other parts of the world. It was a long, slow way to get their cotton to market.

A few cotton textile mills were beginning to open in the state, but they couldn't compete with the North's many industrial factories. They were all driven, in those early days, by water power.

Railways first began in England in the late 1700s. (Americans called them "railroads.") The first railway carriages, built to run on parallel iron rails laid on cinder or graveled roads, were first drawn by horses, although some early trains were pulled along by windsails, or by gravity. It wasn't until the early 1800s that railroads crossed the Atlantic to take home in the United States.

After the United States became larger following President Tom Jefferson's Louisiana Purchase in 1803, it occurred to our forefathers that an easier way for the States' senators and representatives to get to the nation's capital needed to be found. It was said that even by the speediest route possible it took four times longer for a congressman from the West to reach the capital at Washington than it took one to travel down from Boston. Some voiced fears that our new nation would become divided, not pulling together as a unit; those living near Washington could exert more influence than those who served from the west. Also, as more settlers moved across the continent, a better means of hauling freight to-and-fro from raw producer to manufacturer, and from seaports to interior regions, needed to be found. Railroads became the answer to the "American dream of empire."

In the first part of the 1800s there were experiments with railroads in the United States as well as those in England. The early models weren't too exciting until 1825 when John Stevens, an intelligent advocate of railroads, built a little workable steam locomotive in New Jersey where it was tried on a circular track in Hoboken. News of Steven's invention went quickly to England where they "grabbed the ball and ran"! Most of the first steam locomotives were made in England—as late as 1838 nearly half of America's steam locomotives were imported from Great Britain.

The planning of routes for new railroad lines fell to the individual states after some quarreling in Congress. (Some thought that any influence of the federal government would be unconstitutional.) For twenty years the national government paid nothing toward building railroads other than paying for the carriage of U.S. mail and providing army engineers trained at West Point to survey routes for new lines to be built. It did, however, lower tariffs on steel rails from Great Britain when steel rails replaced those of iron. (Before long the enterprising Americans forged their own steel rails.)

Early railroad companies, privately owned, were first opened along the east coast between seaports, and across the nation's northern states. Somewhat belatedly the railroads caught on and were developed across the South.

In 1833 the South Carolina Railroad Company opened its line from Charleston to Savannah, its 136-mile track being the longest privately owned railroad in the world. Soon other companies opened up railroads to establish more southern routes.

The "Western and Atlantic Railroad" (the W & A) began laying line in 1835, coming from South Carolina and heading west across the state of Georgia. It selected the area around Stone Mountain in DeKalb County as its terminus where the old Whitehall Inn had stood on the old stagecoach line. This site, originally called "Whitehall," soon came to be called "Termanis."

After 1842 when rail service began to operate on the W & A Railroad, the settlement that developed at the end of the line, "Termanis," came to be called "Marthasville" to honor Martha Lumpkin, daughter of Georgia's presiding governor. Upon the completion of the "Georgia Railroad," another line to Marthasville in 1845, the town's name was changed to "Atlanta," the feminine version of part of the name of the "Western and Atlantic." In 1847 the town of Atlanta was chartered as a city.

As Atlanta became a rail center, it grew culturally and economically as well as in size. By 1853 it had such a large population that the area in DeKalb County around the city was made into a new county, Fulton. (Joel New lived on the opposite side of Stone Mountain so he still lived in what remained of DeKalb County.)

While the W & A Railroad was being constructed, Joel's sons—and some of his nephews—found working for the railroad profitable. They found the work no more laborious that plowing and picking cotton, and it was nicer to receive a monthly paycheck rather than having to wait for their money until the fall when cotton crops were sold.

The story of the building of America's railroad lines is epic. Railroad camps, called "hell on wheels," were loaded onto flat cars and were moved forward as work on the roads advanced. Before the Civil War, slaves, with white men acting as foremen, did a lot of the work, but strong, stalwart young white men worked alongside the blacks. It was no place for ladies. Married men who worked on railroad work gangs had their wives wait at home. The men were sometimes allowed to visit them at intervals, more often if the track work happened to be in the area of their homes.

As time went on some railroad men became folk legends with songs being made about them. Who could forget the black man, "John Henry, The Steel Drivin' Man," and the ballad of "Casey Jones," the railroad engineer who told his fireman to "get ready to jump" before their train left the track?

As more train tracks were laid in Georgia, several of the New men left their farms to move to Atlanta to get jobs with the railroads. Some worked at laying track but others became flagmen, or train engineers, or firemen who stoked the locomotive engines to generate steam. Others, however, became miners, or perhaps stonecutters who worked in the granite quarries located around Stone Mountain. (Granite was plentiful in that part of the state; new buildings used stone slabs to form floors and walls, and granite slabs for grave markers were shipped—by rail, of course—to other areas where there was no igneous stone to be found.)

The 1850 U.S. Census recorded that Joel and Catherine New, both in their sixties, were still living on their plantation. They lived in house #60, which was located in the Diamond District of DeKalb County. Their youngsters had all left home except for their daughter Martha New, age seventeen, and Joel Green New, age thirteen, their third and last son.

Also living with them was Miss Catherine (Caroline?) Swinney, age seventeen. One wonders if she was Joel's niece, daughter of Joel's Uncle Henry Swinney who had at least five children. (Uncle Henry, being so old, must surely have died

by that time. We did not find him in the census but two years we did find a Sarah Caroline Swinney—Henry's daughter Catherine?—who married one James Madison Lamarr in DeKalb County.)

The 1850 census next listed James (Jim) New, age twenty-two (Joel's second son) living in House #61 with his bride, also named Caroline. Owning no land, he and his new wife lived on his father's plantation. One wonders if he worked on his father's farm or if he worked on the railroad.

In the next house (#63) was Joel's oldest son, Edward V. New, age twenty-five. Ed, married for two years, worked for the railroad, a job which required him to be away from home a lot. He was listed with his wife, Margaret Bishop New, age twenty-one, and a young lady named Elizabeth Owens. age seventeen, who stayed with Margaret to keep her company when Ed was absent. Elizabeth was a daughter of Benjamin and Judy Owens, formerly of South Carolina, who owned a nearby plantation in DeKalb County's Flat Shoal District near Decatur, the county seat.

Joel New's sixty-year-old wife, Catherine, must have been "feelin' po'ly" when that 1850 census was taken; soon thereafter she died. Old Joel, feeling his age, didn't feel none too good himself. That summer, feeling unable to operate his farm by himself, he sold off fifty acres of his land to his neighbor, Joseph E. Bishop. (Bishop was father of Mrs. Margaret Bishop New, the wife of Joel's oldest son, Edward V. New—as is detailed in the following chapter.)

Lonely without his beloved Catherine, old Joel New married again. The second Mrs. Joel New was Miss Jane Cromwell, a young lady half Joel's age. Their wedding took place on December 15, 1851, in DeKalb County and was recorded on page 142 of DeKalb's *Wedding Book A.*

The wedding must have breathed new life into Joel, or maybe he wasn't as old as he thought he was. For some time he had secretly hankered

State of Georgia   ))   This indenture made the fifteenth day of March the year of our Lord,
DeKalb County   ))   1855 between Joel New of the same state, Cherokee County, of the one
part Jacob Chuff of state and county aforesaid Witnesseth that the said Joel New for and in
consideration of the sum of one thousand twenty-five dollars to him in hand paid at and before
the sealing & delivery of these presents the receipt of which is hereby acknowledged hath granted
bargained and sold & conveyed & and doth by these presents grant bargain sell & convey all that
land or parcel of land situated lying and being in the sixteenth District of originally Henry
now DeKalb County known & distinguished as Lot No. 186 the same being the southwest corner of
said Lot containing fifty acres more or less to have and to hold said parcel of land to the
said Jacob Chuff his heirs & assigns together with all & singular the rights members and
appurtenances to the same in any maner to his & their own proper use benefit & behoft forever
in fee simple and the said Joel New for himself and his heirs Executors & Admins. the said
bargained premises unto the said Joseph Chuff his heirs & assigns will warrent and forever defend
the right and title thereof against themselves & against the claim of all other persons whatever
In Witness thereof the said Joel New hath hereunto set his hand & seal the day and year above
written.   Joel New   [Seal]
Delivered in presence of))
D.P.Marbut   ))
Davod Chuff, J.P.   ))   Registered this 21st day of August, 1856
                                              R.M.Brown, Clk.

to go search for gold in northern Georgia where nuggets were being found on the old Cherokee land, but family responsibility had kept him tied to DeKalb County. Now, however, following the marriage of his youngest daughter Martha, he had only his young wife and his last son, the teenager Joel Green New, to think about. Joel felt free, at last, to go adventuring. His energetic young wife Jane and his son young Green were as excited as he was. Reserving their home on Joel's remaining DeKalb County land "just in case," they set off by wagon to go prospecting for gold.

Joel, with his wife and son, camped out or stayed with relatives while they searched for their fortune. It is believed they visited, for a while, in nearby Carroll County with Jacob New Jr., Joel's brother. (Jake Jr. had been awarded a forty-acre gold lot in Georgia's sixth land lottery. Seeking gold had not panned out so Jake Jr. had sold his gold lot and bought a farm in Carroll County.)

In the 1850s, the decade before the Civil War, antebellum Georgia was in its heyday, its "golden age," when cotton was king, slaves abounded, and good cropland was purchased at a premium. On March 15, 1855, Joel New, now in Cherokee County, sold his old home in DeKalb County to one Jacob Chuff. (See copy of deed.) Joel had asked for and received $1,025 for this last fifty acres.

With the proceeds of his land sale, Joel bought another farm located in northwest Georgia near Canton in the Woodstock District of Cherokee County. He, Jane, and Green New were all listed there together in the 1860 U.S. Census.

In this census Joel New, age sixty-nine, gave his birthplace as Virginia and his occupation as farmer. His real estate was valued at $400, his personal property worth $100.

Joel's wife, Mrs. Jane New, age thirty, her birthplace was Georgia. (Somebody goofed in recording Jane's age. Ten years later in the 1870 census her age was recorded to be forty-five.)

J. Green New, age twenty-four, was the third and last member of the New household. He still lived with his father. Planning to marry, he had already picked out his bride.

Joel New, in his seventies, died around 1864 during the Civil War. It was said that he died while defending their home when Gen. Sherman's Yankee soldiers came marauding across Cherokee County on their way from the Chickamauga Battlefield to cripple the Atlanta's rail center. Green New wasn't there; a soldier, he was away serving in the Confederate Army.

After the war Jane and Green New, both having survived the terrible war, were named in the 1870 Cherokee County census. Joel G. New, "head of household," was a farmer, age thirty-five, born in Georgia, with real estate valued at $200, personal property worth $100. (Green began signing his full name, "Joel G. New," after his father died.) Green's wife, a Georgia girl Mary A., age thirty-one, listed her occupation as "keeping house."

At that time they had four children, all born in Georgia: Missouri (8), Catherine (6), Thomas J. (4), and Mary (2).

At the end of this household's list of names we find Green's stepmother, Mrs. Jane Cromwell New, age forty-five, "without occupation." We wonder if Jane ever married again.

Children of Joel and Catherine New

1–5. *Five Daughters, Names Unknown*

Listed with Joel New by age and gender but not by name in the U.S. Census records up through the year 1830. Apparently all had married—or had died—before the 1840 census, which began to include names:

1. (Daughter) Under age ten in 1820, age fifteen to twenty in 1830
2. (Daughter) was under ten in 1820, age fifteen to twenty in 1830
3. (Daughter) was under ten in 1820, age ten to fifteen in 1830
4. (Daughter) was under ten in 1820, age ten to fifteen in 1830
5. (Daughter) Born 1820s, age five to ten in 1830

VI. Edward Vandergriff New

Born: 1825, Lithonia, DeKalb County, Georgia

Died: Circa 1910, Meehan Junction, Lauderdale County, Mississippi

Married: **Margaret Bishop**, September 3, 1848, Lithonia, DeKalb County, Georgia

His biography follows in the next chapter.

Children:

1. **SUSAN**, 1857–1931, m. **John W. Clark**
2. **LUKE J.**, 1859–1903, m. **Hattie J. Elam**
3. **ELIJAH**, 1861–1935, m. **Alice Nichols**
4. **JOEL (II)**, 1863–1931, m. (1) **Mamie Maude Wellborn**, (2) **Ellie Pratt**
5. **EDWARD VANDERGRIFF, JR.**, 1866–1912, m. **Rosa McNulty**

VII. James "Jim" New

Born: 1828, DeKalb County, Georgia

Died: "Out west" in California

Married: **Caroline** _____, (b. 1828, Georgia)

James "Jim" New and his bride, both age twenty-two, were living next door to his father, Joel New (I), when they were listed in the 1850 DeKalb County, Georgia, census. We don't know what Jim did over the next few years, but several years later he came, alone, to visit his brother Edward New who had moved to Mississippi. (We don't know what happened to Jim's wife.)

Jim tried to persuade Edward to accompany him "out west" to seek their fortune. But Ed had a steady job with a railroad, and a wife and children. Jim continued west alone.

Years later, around 1890–1900, Edward New heard from California; someone sent word back that Jim New had died and they wondered what to do with his personal effects. Edward's daughter Susan related this story to her young nephew, Joe New. She did not say what their reply was or what was contained in Jim New's belongings. Probably didn't amount to much.

In the 1960s this writer was touring San Luis Obispo, an old Spanish Mission on the California coast. Displayed under a glass countertop was a faded yellowed register of the old mission's former guests. Displayed on an opened page, James New had signed his name sometime in the long gone days of yore.

Children: None known.

VIII. Martha New (Richardson?)

Born: 1833, DeKalb County, Georgia

Died: 1930, buried in the Goodwater Baptist Cemetery, Meehan, Lauderdale County, Mississippi

Married: Unknown (In Georgia's *DeKalb County Wedding Book A*, p. 325, was recorded a Martha New who married Thomas J. Richardson on December 18, 1854. Was this our Martha?)

Lorena New White (b. 1908) recalled seeing "old Martha" when she was a little girl visiting in the home of her grandfather, Edward V. New. Lorena didn't know who the old lady was; they just always called her "Martha." Lorena remembered when old Martha got sick and Grandpa told Aunt Sis to take her to the doctor. (Aunt Sis was Lorena's father's only sister, Susan New Clark, the youngsters called her "Aunt Sis.")

Martha, having become feeble, usually sat huddled next to the warm fireplace. That morning Aunt Sis took special pains in bathing her, cleaning Martha up for the visit to the doctor. Something came up, however, and their trip had to be postponed. Unaware of this, when Grandpa came in that evening he looked at old Martha and said, "I donno what Doc did but he sure knows what he's doin.' Marthie looks a whole heap better'n she did this mornin'!"

Martha lived to be nearly a hundred years old. She lies, buried next to the News, in the nearby Goodwater Baptist Church graveyard.

IX. *Joel Green New*

Born: 1837, Lithonia, DeKalb County, Georgia
Died: ? (Cherokee County, Georgia?)
Married: **Mary A. ____** , around 1860, probably in Cherokee County, Georgia

Green New was twenty-four when he was listed with his father and stepmother, Jane, in the 1860 U.S. Census of Cherokee County. Soon after his marriage, he fought in the Civil War (1861–1865) when all available men were called to arms to fight for their beloved South.

In the next Cherokee County census, in 1870, he was recorded with his wife and four children, their oldest having been born in 1862. By that time his father had died and his widowed stepmother, Mrs. Jane New, was living in his home.

A farmer, Green apparently inherited his father's land near the Woodstock post office in Cherokee County; his real estate was worth $200 and his personal property worth $100.

Children: (Possibly had more born after 1870 census.)
1. **Missouri New**, 1862
2. **Catherine New**, 1864
3. **Thomas J. New**, 1866
4. **Mary New**, 1868

Chapter X
Edward Vandergriff New
(1825–ca1905)

After first producing five daughters in Madison County, the first Joel New and his wife Catherine happily welcomed their first son, baby **Edward Vandergriff New**. Little Edward, born in February 1825, came soon after they moved to DeKalb County, Georgia. We don't know how they chose his name; the name Edward is common enough, but about his Dutch/German name, Vandergriff? We are told that an esteemed Georgia representative, J. Vandergriff, was popular about that time, or perhaps Edward's middle name was associated with his mother's family. (Other than the fact that Mrs. Catherine New was from South Carolina, we know nothing about her.)

Edward, growing up on his father's DeKalb County farm, was ten years old when the Western and Atlantic Railroad began laying track from South Carolina to cross Georgia. Some of his uncles and cousins got jobs with the railroad, and he listened with interest to their exciting tales. As soon as he was old enough, he also went to work for the railroad, hauling crossties and laying track. Railroading was hard labor. It kept him away from home a lot, but it was a steady reliable way to earn a living.

After pounding spikes to install rails for several years, young Ed New, hard-working and intelligent, was promoted to be a crew foreman with a nice raise in pay. Earning more money, he felt that he could afford to take a wife. On a visit home Ed discovered that a former schoolmate, Miss Margaret Bishop, had grown into a biddable young lady. A laughing girl of Irish descent, she was a daughter of Reuben and Nancy Wooten Bishop. Ed had known her most his life as she lived on the farm next his parents in DeKalb County.

Edward V. New (age twenty-three), and Miss Margaret Bishop (age twenty-one) were married in DeKalb County at her rich Uncle Joseph Wooten's fine plantation home on the fifth of September, a colorful fall day, in 1848. As Ed was a Baptist and Margaret was a Catholic, they had Edward's grand-uncle, William New, a justice of the peace, to take their vows.

Edward New, a serious taciturn sort of man whose speech, like his straightforward mother's, was direct and to the point, while Margaret was a gregarious person with a ready laugh, seldom at a loss for words. Ed's mouth would twitch with a little half-smile when she made some humorous whimsical remark with her pronounced Irish brogue. Their personalities complemented each other, him the straightforward man with her his comic relief.

Ed and Margaret New began housekeeping in a log cabin located on Ed's father's farm. Ed, working for the railroad, was often away from home. After the W. & A. Railroad completed its track to Atlanta, Edward got another railroad job

[handwritten wedding license document in left column]

WEDDING LICENSE OF EDWARD V. NEW AND MARGARET BISHOP

State of Georgia   )
DeKalb County   ) To any Minister of the Gospel, Judge, Justice of the Inferior Court, or Justice of the Peace to celebrate, These are authorize & permit you to join in the Honorable State of Matrimony Edward New of the one part & Margaret Bishop of the other part according to the Rites of your Church, provided there be no lawful cause to obstruct the same and this shall be your authority for so doing Given under my head as clerk of the Court of Ordinary for the County aforesaid this 32st day August 1848.   H.G.Johnson, C.C.O.

Georgia   )
DeKalb County)   I do hereby certify that Edward New and Margaret Bishop were joined together in the Holy Bonds of Matrimoney by me on the 5th day of Sept. 1848.
William New, J.P.

that took him even farther away to northern Georgia. Margaret, to be closer to Ed, followed him up to the Georgia/Tennessee state line in Whitfield County.

Living in Whitfield County, Ed worked for the East Tennessee Valley and Georgia Railroad Company, the E.T.V. & G. (Years later Edward New's young grandson, Charley New, asked what E.T.V. & G. stood for. Grandma Margaret told him it stood for "Eat Tough Vegetables and Grunt.")

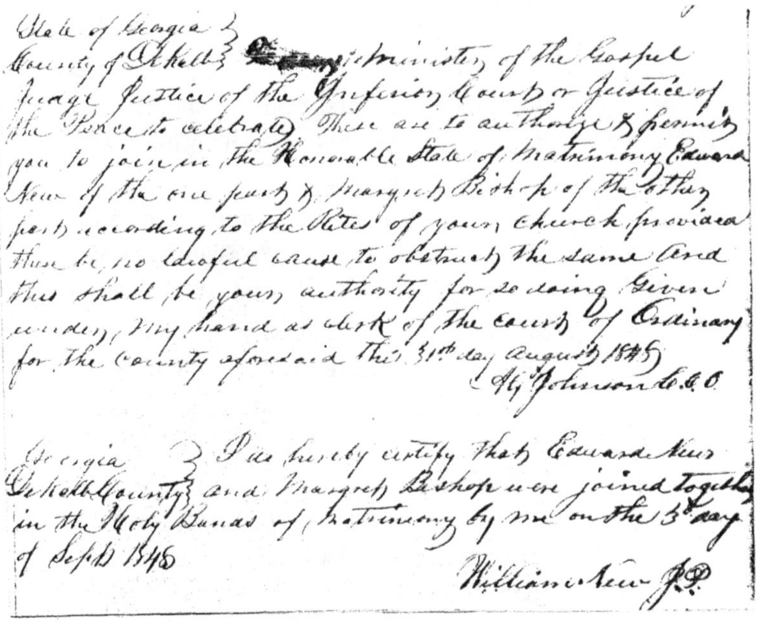

The uncle of Edward New's wife was a Mr. Joseph Wooten of DeKalb County, the brother of Margaret's mother, Mrs. Nancy Wooten Bishop. Uncle Joseph, having reached an advanced age, found himself growing feeble. Not expecting to live much longer, in October 1854 he wrote his last will and testament. In his will, Uncle Joseph named his wife, Mrs. Avis Wooten, and his "good friend Samuel Potts," to be his executors.

Uncle Joseph had accumulated considerable wealth in his long lifetime but, having no children,

Early railroad train

desired to leave part of his sizable plantation to his dear sister, Mrs. Nancy Bishop (Margaret New's Mama), with whom he enjoyed a close kinship. Living with her husband in the house next door to her brother, Nancy was a source of great comfort to him and Avis as they grew older.

Mr. Wooten didn't think it prudent to leave his sister land; her Irish husband, Reuben Bishop, with his strong propensity for drink, would probably take it over. Old Joseph thought it best, therefore, to insure his sister Nancy always had a home by giving land, jointly, to her three married daughters: Margaret, Susan, and Avis. Her girls would see that Nancy Bishop retained a home in her old age.

With this in mind, on September 24, 1855, old Joseph Wooten deeded 205½ acres, a part of his plantation in District 16, Lot 41, of DeKalb County, for "natural love and affection" to his three nieces. The deed included the house where Nancy lived with her husband, Reuben Bishop. Joseph reserved a small plot of this land for a "burying ground," a family cemetery where he planned to be buried.

They didn't have to wait long for his funeral; Joseph Wooten died soon after he wrote his will.

Margaret's Aunt Avis Wooten was a good bit younger than her late husband. A widow with land and money who had no children, she was considered a "good catch." Shortly after Uncle Joseph died, Aunt Avis married their mutual friend, Samuel Potts.

When Avis and Sam Potts married, Avis wrote her own will to insure that when it came her time to die her first husband's wishes would be carried out in the manner he had requested.

In his will Uncle Joseph had bequeathed his wife, Avis Wooten, his entire estate for the duration of her lifetime but, upon her death, *half* of his estate was to go to anyone of Avis' choosing.

The other half of his estate was to be divided (upon her death) between the nine children of Joseph's sister, Mrs. Nancy Bishop. Avis was free to split this half between them in whatever manner she chose.

In her will she bequeathed her new husband, Sam'l Potts, her half of the Wooten estate.

The other half of the Wooten estate Avis divided, as Joseph had wished, among Nancy Bishop's nine children as follows:

> To Susan Bishop Spinks, wife of John Spinks, $300.
> To Joshua J. Bishop, James Bishop, and Luke Bishop, $5 each.
> To John T. Bishop, Elijah Bishop, and Edmund Bishop, $300 each.
> To Avis Bishop Braswell, her namesake, wife of Wm. H. Brasswell, $400.
> And lastly: To Margaret Bishop New "of Whitfield County," wife of Edwund V. New, the rest and residue of the Bishop Childrens' half of the Wooten Estate!

One wonders how much Margaret's "rest and residue" amounted to. At any rate, she would not collect her inheritance for several more years, not until after her Aunt Avis Wooten Potts died.

Edward and Margaret New's first child, a daughter they named Susan after Margaret's favorite sister, was born in 1857. Their second child, a son they named Luke, was born in 1859 in Whitfield County when rumblings of political unrest were being openly discussed whenever men met. Whispers—nay, *shouts* of "secession!" and "war!"—were heard throughout the South.

In the early days it took five yokes of oxen to haul 3,000 pounds of baled cotton over poor muddy roads. Many oxen, worked to death, died along the way. Then, in 1831 the Clinton and Vicksburg Railroad Company was incorporated

WILL OF MRS. AVIS WOOTEN POTTS, MARCH 4, 1859 (See opposite page.)

In the name of God amen. I, Avis Potts of the County of DeKalb & State of Georgia, wife of Samuel Potts of said County & State, widow of Joseph Wooten, late of said County, deceased, being of sound & disposing mind and memory and desirous to settle my worldly affairs and matters left at my disposal by my said deceased husband, Joseph Wooton, while I have the strength to do so, do by this my last will and testament in writing do hereby revoking all former wills by me at any time heretofore made, dispose of my estate both real & personal and that left to my disposal persuant to & in accordance with the authority given to me given in & by the last will and testment of said deceased husband Joaesh Wooten, dated the twenty seventh day of October 1854 and by virture of said will and & authority to me given therein in the manner following.

Item 1st. I give & bequeath unto my dear husband Samuel Potts my two Negro women Malinda & Harriet & Amy Ann the child of Harriet and also all of that half of the Estate of my deceased husband both real and personal which he bequeathed to me during my life with power to dispose of it at my death at my will and pleasure, It being my will that the whole of it together with the said three slaves shall be at my death be the property of the said Samuel Potts....[?]..

Item 2nd. In accordance with the 4th Item of my said deceased husband's will I see proper to give, devise & bequeath unto the children of Nancy Bishop, his sister, the one half of the Estate bequeathed to me in & by the will of my said deceased husband during my life & at my death to be bequeathed to them in any manner & way I may see proper, as follows, To Susan Spinks, wife of John Spinks and daughter of Nancy Bishop, I give $300. To Joshua J. Bishop, Elijah Bishop, & Luke Bishop I give each of them $5 (They being the sons of Nancy Bishop) To John T. Bishop, Elijah Bishop, & Edmund Bishop, sons of Nancy Bishop, I give each one of them $300. To Avis Braswell, wife of Wm. H. Braswell, & daughter of Nancy Bishop, I give $400. To Margaret New, wife of Ed New & daughter of Nancy Bishop, I give all the rest & residue of that half of the estate of my deceased husband which I am directed in & by his will to bequeath give and devise to the children of Nancy Bishop, his sister.

Item 3rd. I do hereby appoint my husband Samuel Potts Executor of this my last will and testament.

Item 4th. I desire to commit my Soul to God who gave it & my body to a decent & Christian-like burial.

In witness whereof I, Avis Potts, to this my last will & Testament hereto set my hand & seal this 4th day of March 1859.

Avis Potts   [seal]

by authority of the state of Mississippi to build a twenty-to-thirty-mile long railroad from Clinton (Mississippi) to the Mississippi River to replace the slow-moving oxen being used to transport baled cotton to the paddle-boats on the river.

Lacking money, the construction of the new railroad didn't begin until 1833 when the C & V (Clinton & Vicksburg) Railroad was taken over by the Commercial and Railroad Bank of Vicksburg, and was chartered to build its railroad line from Vicksburg all the way east to Jackson, the Mississippi state capital.

Starting out at Vicksburg, several miles of track had been laid by 1837, and in 1838 its first locomotive, the "Commercial," arrived at Vicksburg and was pressed into service. By fall two daily trains were scheduled to run between Vicksburg and the Big Black River.

Although it was difficult to excavate earth cuts and build a sturdy railroad bridge across the Big Black, construction of the track slowly continued eastward. By July 1839 the track was completed only to the Edwards' plantation, eighteen miles east of Vicksburg.

The first railroad tracks used in the South were wooden rails, which were fastened into place by strips of iron held by iron spikes. The spikes, called "snake heads," were easily loosened by use so trackmen had to make daily trips to tighten "snakeheads."

Making every effort to complete their railroad, slaves were bought, or rented, from planters along the route. By the end of 1840, the railroad was complete from Vicksburg to Jackson, a cause for big celebration; the advertised round-trip fare from Jackson to Vicksburg was five dollars, about eight cents per mile.

The C & V Railroad Company spent all its money building its road, and after it was sold at a sheriff's sale in 1848, its name was changed to the "Vicksburg to Jackson Railroad Company."

While this was going on another railroad, the Jackson & Brandon Railroad, was chartered to build a line heading east out of Jackson for a distance of eighteen miles. Financed largely by state funds, it was built almost entirely by slave labor. It opened for operation in 1849.

In March 1850 the Southern Railroad Company (NOT today's Southern Railway System) began laying track from Brandon, Mississippi, that was to continue eastward all across the state. At the state line, in Lauderdale County, it was to connect with another track (the Alabama & Vicksburg road, the A&V) that was being laid across Alabama. The two tracks were to join in eastern Mississippi near a small village that had collected around a Mr. John T. Ball's log store.

After the Southern Railroad track was completed, in 1855 the "Mobile and Ohio Railroad Company" (the M & 0), on its way north, intersected with the Southern Railroad's line in Lauderdale County. Before long the sleepy southern village around Ball's store developed into a bustling railroad center. On February 10, 1860, Mr. Wm. C. Smedes, president of the Southern Railroad Company, gave the busy little Mississippi town its permanent name—he named it "Meridian."

In the 1850s Edward V. New, our "railroad man" who was working up in Whitfield County, Georgia, took a job with the Southern Railroad Company to help lay the Mississippi track from Brandon to Meridian. An intelligent, honest, hard-working man with hands-on experience, Ed was hired to be a foreman in charge of a group of track laborers. (Old-timers said that the sixty men could lay a mile of track in one day—barring any unusual obstacles.) Near the time that Ed New came, the name of this Southern Railroad Line came to be called the "A & V," the "Alabama and Vicksburg Railroad."

Ed New moved Margaret and their two children—little Susan and baby Luke—with him when his work took him to Mississippi. The 1860 U.S. Census listed them in their rented rooms where they boarded just outside Meridian.

In 1861, the year after the A&V was completed, their third child, Elijah New, was born. Little "Lige" was born in April, three months after January 9, the date that the state of Mississippi seceded from the Union. In the month that Baby Lige was born, the first shots of the Civil War were fired in South Carolina.

Who can say the precise cause of the costly Civil War that wrought holocausts in the South and brought so many unnecessary deaths to men from both contestants? Truth to tell, there was no one reason that caused the conflict. It was not a civil war wherein anarchist sought to overthrow an existing government, but rather a war fought over the attempt of the South to withdraw and form a new independent nation. There was right as well as wrong on both sides.

Many still say that the war was fought to free the slaves, but this was not the true reason. Although President Lincoln emancipated the slaves while the war was in progress, a large majority of the people in the North didn't care whether the South owned salves or not, the abolitionists being only a small but loud vocal minority.

The Southern states believed, with some truth, that their "state rights" were being violated by the industrial North, and the North fought to preserve the Union of the United States when the southern states seceded to form a new nation. South Carolina was the first of the southern states to pull away.

South Carolina seceded from the Union on December 10, 1860, closely followed by the state of Mississippi who withdrew on January 9, 1861. By the end of May nine other southern states had withdrawn. On February 8, 1861, delegates from these states, meeting in Alabama at Montgomery, formed a new government: "The Confederate States of America."

This Southern Convention selected a provisional president and vice president, Jefferson Davis of Mississippi and Alexander H. Stephens of Georgia, both being chosen again by popular vote in an election held that fall. Richmond, Virginia, was the selected site for the new nation's capital.

The actual fighting began on April 12, 1861, when Confederate forces under Gen. Pierre Toutant Beauregard (of New Orleans) fired upon the Federal Fort Sumter from the bay off Charleston, South Carolina. Thus began the long bloody war, the "Civil War," between the North and South.

Ten miles west of the Mississippi/Alabama state line and at a shorter distance from Lauderdale County's courthouse at Marion was the little Mississippi town called "Meridian." With a population of nearly 200, Meridian had, in addition to a scattering of private homes, a small hotel and a couple boarding houses.

A busy little town, Meridian had a cotton gin with warehouses, a sawmill, and two gristmills. It also had, in addition to Ball's general store, a tavern owned by Lewis A. Ragsdale (a lawyer from Alabama), and another general store owned by W. F. Brown.

The Meridian post office was located inside Brown's store, along with the ticket office of the new M & O Railroad. Brown also ran a drug store and a saloon in his store where he kept a barrel and sold whiskey by the tin cup.

Crossing through the state, the A & V Railroad track was completed from Vicksburg through Jackson to a point east of Brandon when the Civil War came in 1861. As throngs of hot-blooded southerners rushed to join the Confederate Army,

Ed New just kept on laying track on the line as it neared Meridian.

Desperate to open the A & V so trains could be utilized to move troops and war supplies, a contingent of Confederate soldiers were sent to assist in the completion of the track. With the soldiers' help the work went faster, but in their haste they took shortcuts and the track was laid in a makeshift way. The shoddy tracks required numerous repairs.

After reaching Lauderdale County and building a bridge across the Chunky River, the A & V track had reached near seven miles from its proposed junction with the M & O at Meridian when the building crew encountered a steep hill. Rather than extending the line by going around, a railroad tunnel was dug to go right on through. This slowed progress a bit, but at last the Alabama & Vicksburg line was finished. When it joined the line coming from across Alabama, its name was changed to the Montgomery & Vicksburg line. (It all eventually became part of today's Illinois Central.)

On May 28, 1861, the "Meridian Invincibles" and three other southern volunteer troops left going northward on the M & O to join the first Civil War battles that were starting up in Virginia and North Carolina. The next day, May 29, the Montgomery & Vicksburg Railroad's first steam engine, a little locomotive called "Mazeppa," arrived at Meridian Station from Alabama with a hundred and eleven volunteer Confederate soldiers, the "Vicksburg Southerners"—along with its civilian passengers.

Upon this occasion Meridian played host at a huge barbecue given to honor their brave soldiers. Who could doubt that Edward and Margaret New were among the throng of citizens who gathered to dance and celebrate as they waved the fighting men goodbye?

When the railroad track was completed and came into full operation, Ed New was made a section foreman of Section No. 1, the first section heading out of Meridian toward Jackson. He "bossed" a crew that maintained and repaired their assigned section of track to keep it in full use.

The army from the South, outnumbered by the North, had so many boys killed or wounded that first year that, in 1862, the Confederate Congress resorted to conscription. It passed the first national draft law in American history. The age limits of the draft were eighteen through thirty-five. (Ed New was thirty-seven.)

Two years later, in 1864, the Confederate Army's acute manpower shortage led to the extension of the draft-age to range between seventeen and fifty years. Ed New would have been drafted that time but he had an occupational exemption; he had to keep his railroad running, a job vitally important to the war.

As the war progressed, there came acute shortages of manpower to carry on the work at home. Ed continued to work long hours keeping up his track, but he opened a wood-yard, upon Margaret's suggestion, to supply firewood for the locomotives' steam engines. (The coal normally used was in short supply as so many miners had gone to war.)

While Edward New worked long hours on his regular job, his wife took the un-ladylike chore of running their new business where she sold firewood for private homes as well as for train locomotives. Margaret didn't have to do the hard work herself—if you qualify supervising three young children and selling wood while being pregnant as being easy. Owning no slaves, she hired young boys and old men—those unfit for the army—to cut and bring wagons of firewood to stock her yard so she could supervise it being loaded onto train coal-tender cars.

In the midst of wartime, Margaret's baby, the New's fourth child, was born on May 10, 1863. Edward named him "Joel," a namesake for his own father, the baby's grandfather, the aging first Joel New back in Georgia. It was about then that they heard from their Georgia relatives that the first Joel New had died.

After the Civil War began in South Carolina, its battles soon shifted northward to be fought in and about Virginia near the national capital in Washington, D.C. As fighting progressed its conflicts ranged further south across Tennessee and north Mississippi as Union soldiers ("dammed Yankees") under command of Gen. Ulysses S. Grant sought to gain control of the entire Mississippi River.

Yankee riverboats had advanced down the river as far south as Vicksburg before they were stopped by Rebel cannon fire that damaged, or sank, their gunboats. The Yankee's venture failed, primarily, because the boats' guns could not be effectively directed against the Confederate batteries that were mounted upon Vicksburg's high bluffs.

Failing the river onslaught, in December 1862 the Union Army, under Gen. Grant, planned an overland movement against Vicksburg from north Mississippi. He sent Maj. Gen. William T. Sherman with a force of 30,000 men to attack the Rebels at Chickasaw Bluffs, a distance north of the city.

The land attack also failed. The Rebels at Vicksburg were greatly outnumbered but had excellent defenses. As the Yankees withdrew northward, Confederate cavalry units under Generals Nathan B. Forrest and Earl VanDorn destroyed Grant's principal military base at Holly Springs and wrecked his line of communication.

Not to be outdone, the Yankees made a third attempt to capture Vicksburg. The Yankees loaded boats with soldiers and crossed the Mississippi at a point higher upstream. Then, by digging canals and passing through the bayous of eastern Arkansas and Louisiana, they bypassed Vicksburg to re-cross the river downstream to approach the targeted city by land.

Upon reaching the backside of Vicksburg, the Yankees laid siege, their steady cannon fire sending Confederate soldiers—and civilians—underground to survive in caves.

Due to an outbreak of measles and a shortage of food, many soldiers and civilians died in the caves. Before the long siege ended, they had resorted to eating their horses and mules. Some survivors later reported that they also ate rats!

Surrounded and starving, Vicksburg finally surrendered. The Confederate defeat at Gettysburg on July 3, 1863, and the fall of Vicksburg on July 4, marked the turning point of the Civil War and signaled the doom of the Southern Confederacy.

Earlier that year (in February 1863) a contingent of battle-ready Confederate soldiers left Meridian on the A & M Railroad on their way to aid in the defense of Vicksburg. The rains had been unusually heavy that winter, causing creeks and lowlands to be flooded.

The train leaving Meridian the day before had slowly crossed Lauderdale County's Chunky River as floodwaters lapped high on the bridge timbers. Near dawn the next day when the train transporting Confederate soldiers and some civilians crossed the bridge, the swift water lapped at the steel rails; in places the track was completely submerged. The engineer had been warned, but knowing how desperately the soldiers were needed to defend Vicksburg, he decided to take a chance on crossing the creaking bridge.

Traveling at a snail's pace, the locomotive started across the bridge, the engine creeping across the swaying bridge inch by inch. It had gained the other side when the whole bridge structure collapsed. As the train split in half, the last cars of the crowded train became uncoupled and fell, followed by heavy bridge timbers, into the rushing flood. The entire train crew, along with their soldier and civilian passengers, were plunged into the swirling waters.

On higher ground a short distance west of the fallen bridge was, fortunately, a training camp of friendly Choctaw Indians who had enlisted in the Confederate Army to fight alongside their white brothers. Hearing cries for help, the Choctaws rushed to the river to rescue the drowning passengers. Diving again and again into the cold water, they brought out ninety-six passengers; among who were five seriously injured civilians who were taken to area homes for treatment.

Only twenty-two soldiers survived the tragic accident, the bodies of their dead comrades being buried in unmarked graves facing east, head to toe, along the railroad right-of-way. Other bodies, impossible to recover, were left buried beneath crushed boxcars and bridge timbers.

As soon as the flood had somewhat subsided, Edward V. New, track foreman for the A & M Railroad, worked overtime throughout the next few weeks replacing the washed-out Chunky Bridge and shoring up rain-weakened tracks. It was vital to the war that the A & M Railroad be kept open.

Since the war's beginning, the quiet little Meridian railroad crossroad had become a bustling military center, as important to the South as the large railroad center at Atlanta. It only covered an area of a square mile, but it had become "Confederate Army Headquarters" for Mississippi, Alabama, and Louisiana, and it housed a jail for captured Yankee soldiers. Draftees from several surrounding counties were sent to Meridian to get their physical examination before being sent to various training camps. On a hill northwest of town was a hospital for wounded soldiers (from both sides), and when one of their patients died, he was buried next to the hospital.

Along Meridian's tracks where the trains passed through, huge warehouses had been built, arsenals to store ammunition and other army equipment as well as bales of cotton and food crates waiting to be shipped. In addition to its mercantile stores, Meridian had two churches, a Methodist and a Baptist, the two-floored unpainted board Ragsdale Hotel, and two boarding houses as well as about seventy private homes.

After Gen. Grant's large Yankee force whipped the outnumbered Confederates at Jackson and Brandon, and then captured Vicksburg, he sent Maj. Gen. W. T. Sherman eastward to shut down the Rebels' military action at the Meridian railroad center.

In a report to Gen. Grant written in Vicksburg on February 27, 1864, Gen. Sherman wrote of his trip to Meridian:

> *... We reached Jackson February 6, crossed Pearl [River] and passed through Brandon to Morton where the enemy made dispositions for battle but fled in the night. Pushed on over all obstacles and reached Meridian on February 14. Gen. Polk [of the C.S.A.], having a railroad to assist him in his retreat, escaped across the Tombigbee [a River just inside Alabama] on the 17th.*
>
> *We stayed in Meridian a week and made the complete destruction of the railroads ever beheld— south to below Quitman, east to Cuba Station, 20 miles north to Lauderdale Springs, and west all the way back to Jackson ...*

Completing his report, Gen. Sherman continued:

... Although [enemy] cavalry moved on our flanks they gave us little concern, save in scaring in our stragglers and foraging parties. At the Tallahatta [Creek], 20 miles from Meridian, we found the road obstructed by fallen timbers, and, satisfied the enemy was trying to save time to cover the removal of railroad property from Meridian; I dropped our trains with good escorts and pushed on over all obstructions straight for the Okatibbee where we found the bridge burning ...

Old-timers, who then lived in the Pine Springs area, later told their grandchildren about how Sherman was turned back in Okatibbee Swamp by their civilian gunfire when he tried to cross the Okatibbee Creek Bridge on today's Allen Swamp Road in the Pine Springs community.

As his men were being shot, Sherman didn't cross the creek there but instead turned south to march along the western creek bank toward Meridian.

Finding that the next bridge had been set on fire, he had his men rip boards from a nearby gin to build another bridge to cross the Okatibbee Creek. (This crossing was near today's State Boulevard Extension Road.) After crossing the creek, the Yankees camped on a nearby farm for the night, stabling their horses in the barn.

Meeting little resistance, the Yankees marched on up Kennedy Hill and entered Meridian in the area of today's Highland Park.

Sherman's report to Gen. Grant continued:

... We entered Meridian at 3 p.m. of the 14th [in February, on Valentine Day!!] with little opposition, and that was overcome by a battalion of Col. Winston's Cavalry fighting on foot. So, on the 15th I rested the army on the 16th I began a systematic destruction

of the railroads centering in Meridian ... Through it the enemy has heretofore transported his armies and vast supplies, and by means of the railroads large amounts of corn, bacon, meal and produce have been distributed to his armies.

For five days 10,000 men worked hard and with a will in the work of destruction with axes, crowbars, sledges, and with fire and I have no hesitation in pronouncing the work well done. Meridian with its depots, stores, houses, arsenal, hospitals, offices, hotel and cantonments, no longer exists ...

And what havoc and destruction Maj. Gen. Sherman did wreak! In his report Sherman failed to mention how he burned practically all of Meridian's private homes. He did save one that he used for his headquarters and another where the town's ladies had taken refuge. We have heard no reports of personal injury to civilians, but after the federal troops left, the women and children were without food for several days. With their homes burned, many were left with only the clothes they happened to be wearing.

The house outside Meridian that Edward and Margaret New had rented was not burned. Ed, out trying to stop the marauding Yankees, was not home, and Margaret, with her small children and their new baby, refused to leave the house. Taking pity, the Yankees spared the house but raided the smokehouse, taking all their hams and bacon.

Years later Margaret New told her grandchildren that their hog-lard had been stored in the smokehouse in clay molasses jugs. In the cold February weather, it could not easily be melted so, in a hurry, the soldiers carelessly pitched the jugs of lard into a ravine behind the house. After the soldiers left Margaret sent her two oldest children, little Susan and Luke, scrambling down the hill to retrieve her "cookin' grease."

"For a while there, o' course, I didn't have much to cook," she laughed.

Reporting to the Confederate Gen. Polk after a tour of inspection to survey the damage on railroad lines in and about Meridian, Sam Tate of Demopolis wrote, " … On the Southern Railway between Jackson and Meridian, four bridges entirely destroyed, aggregate length 950 ft.; 47 bridges entirely destroyed, aggregate length, 3,248; 4 miles of track torn up, iron badly burned and bent and most of the crossties were burned. Five thousand crossties will be required, 300 bars of iron, and 500,000 feet of bridge timbers to complete the work. It can be done in forty days."

(The name of the old A & V Railroad, owned by the Southern Railway Company, had been changed to the V & M, the Vicksburg and Montgomery, after it connected with its line from the east.)

Needless to say, Edward New was a busy man after the Yankees rode off. He had a railroad to get back into service and he feverishly worked his men long hard days to get this accomplished. We don't know how long it took to get all his line back into service, but it was reported that the tracks in and about Meridian were open and ready for traffic in twenty-eight days!

After leaving Meridian and fighting his way north, Damn Yankee Sherman launched his invasion into Georgia starting from Chattanooga, Tennessee, on May 5, with 100,000 men organized into three armies. Opposed to Sherman was Gen. Joseph E. Johnston's Army of Tennessee, about 60,000 men.

Despite Johnston's skillful military tactics (he had been trained at West Point), Sherman engaged in running battles with the Confederates as he demolished the track of the W & 0 (Western & Ohio) Railroad and slowly fought his way down to Atlanta. At an engagement at Pine Mountain on June 4, 1864, Gen. Leonidas Polk, CSA, was killed by a Federal cannon ball.

Pushing southward along the W & O, Sherman crossed the Chattahoochee River eight miles from the Atlanta Railroad Center on July 7, 1864. That same day, upon receiving an order from the Confederate Government at Richmond, Gen. Johnston turned his command over to young Lt. Gen. John Bell Hood, who had a reputation of being a daring fighter.

Three days after his promotion. Gen. Hood attacked Sherman in a bloody battle at Peachtree Creek on July 20, and again at Atlanta on July 22. Hood, already outnumbered, suffered heavy casualties in these fights and was forced to retire to the Atlanta entrenchments. After being constantly bombarded with cannon shells for forty days, and believing Sherman when the Yankee said the citizens and their property would not be molested, Hood's men evacuated the town on September 2, 1864.

After Hood retired Sherman, breaking his word, proceeded to evacuate Atlanta's private citizens and torch their city and its surrounding countryside, much as he had done last February in Meridian.

We don't know how Ed and Margaret's relatives, the News and the Bishops, those living in and around Atlanta, fared when they were caught in this latest Sherman holocaust. The Georgia state archives in Atlanta has a list of names of Georgia soldiers who fought in the Civil War; on it are names of at least a dozen men with the "New" surname. One wonders how Edward New's father, old Joel New, having moved to Cherokee County, made it through the Yankee raids. He was in his seventies when he died near the time that Sherman came through Cherokee County where Joel lived.

Leaving Atlanta in ruins on the morning of November 16, Gen. Sherman and his force began a trek to the sea, creating a swath of burned homes, death, and destruction sixty miles wide and 300 miles long. As they marched the Yankees sang, "John Brown's Body Lies A'Moulderin' in His Grave."

Meeting only token resistance, the Yankees reached Savannah on December 10, 1864, and soon occupied the city. On Christmas Eve, Gen. Sherman sent President Lincoln a wire that stated, "I beg to present to you a Christmas gift, the City of Savannah with 150 heavy guns and plenty of ammunition, and also about 15,000 bales of cotton."

Leaving Georgia, Sherman then pillaged both Carolinas on his way northward.

Up in Virginia that spring, Gen. W. T. Grant broke through the Confederate lines and the Rebels evacuated Richmond on April 2, 1865. Fighting under Gen. Robert E. Lee, they withdrew to the Appomattox Court House where Lee surrendered his depleted, ragged, hungry army to Gen. Grant on April 9, 1865.

This ended the Civil War, but a number of Southerners wouldn't accept Lee's surrender, and for a while they kept on fighting for their lost cause. Gen. Joseph E. Johnston capitulated to Gen. W. T. Sherman in North Carolina on April 26, and Gen. Richard Taylor surrendered the Department of Alabama and Mississippi on May 4. Confederate President Jefferson Davis was captured at Irwin Ville, Georgia, on May 10.

(On April 14, five days after Gen. Lee surrendered; John Wilkes Booth shot President Abe Lincoln at Ford's Theatre in Washington. When Lincoln died the next morning Vice President Andrew Johnson of Tennessee was sworn in to become the nation's next president.)

When the war ended, the South was left in shambles and was invaded by "carpet-baggers"—scamps arriving with nothing more than a cheap bag to carry a change of clothing who came to make a fortune by swindling worn-out Southerners of their land and gold, if they had any left. The freed slaves, with no "ole' masta'" to see to their needs, were more deprived than they were before. Without a roof to cover their heads, they roamed about freely in search of food.

To make sure that the South paid for their "sins," the federal government took over Mississippi's political arena. Under Mississippi's Gov. Benjamin G. Humphreys, who took office the year the war ended, military rule was enforced by Northern troops and black soldiers. The 1868 Reconstruction Legislature was mostly composed of former slaves elected under the Republican's control. Often scalawags backed an uneducated black who they could control, appointing him a judge or to some other responsible position.

Local railroads, along with big farms and business enterprises, also fared badly during the days of reconstruction. One railroad official reported that his line's rolling stock had been reduced to a fourth of what was deemed necessary and even that was in bad condition. Ed New was thankful that he was able to keep his railroad job at all. He had been able to save the money he and Margaret had made from their wood-yard enterprise; they had kept their gold and coins well hidden when the Yankees had come through.

The 1870 U.S. Census shows that the New's still lived in Township six, just outside Meridian. They shared a house with a Davis family, and also with a young fellow named James Smith, age twenty-three, who also worked for the railroad.

That year, 1870, Ed New, age forty-five, and Margaret, age forty-three, were listed with all five of their children: Susan, Luke, Elijah, Joel, and Edward Jr. (The youngest, Ed. Jr., had been born in 1866.)

The head of the Davis family (that lived with the News) was Widow Martha Davis, age thirty-six, with her four children: Louis (17), Barbara (15), Joseph (13), and George (11), all born back in Georgia. We don't know the name of her late husband; perhaps he had been killed in the recent war.

(Do you suppose that this Mrs. Martha Davis from Georgia could have been the youngest sister of Edward V. New? Ed's younger sister, Martha New, was the same age as Martha Davis. We never found, for sure, who Ed's sister Martha New married. Makes one wonder …)

Some early Lauderdale County deed records are missing, having been mislaid and/or burned. (Let's blame Sherman for that, too.) We have found no record showing when Edward V. New bought his first farm, but it was located in Beat 4 in the southwestern corner next to a railroad siding the old A & V Railroad had built to allow trains to pass. One wonders if Ed purchased his land from the Southern Railroad Company or did he, as did his two oldest sons, obtain unclaimed land patents from the U.S. Bureau of Land Management?

The hills surrounding the railroad siding were still largely unsettled when the News first moved to this part of Lauderdale County. The steep terrain surrounding the Tallahatta Creek, still covered with virgin forest, had been largely passed over by early settlers who were looking for better farmland to grow cotton.

As was the custom back then, to keep down fire and to make bedrooms cooler in summer, the log house that Ed built on their land had a kitchen separate from the main house. Their children used to laugh when telling of the time when a panther invaded Margaret's kitchen.

Hearing a commotion in the kitchen, Margaret peeked in to see what was making all the fuss. Seeing a panther, she quickly closed the kitchen door and ran around to open wide a shuttered window. When Ed came he asked Margaret why she hadn't kept the big cat shut in so he could shoot it when he came home.

"Faith!" she replied. "I dinna want'a trap him! I jest wanted Mr. Painter to go whenever he finished whatever he was doin' and felt like leaving!"

Ed and Margaret New appear better off than were a lot of their neighbors. They had Margaret's small inheritance from her Aunt Avis Wooten, they owned their own home, and Ed had his regular railroad job. In fact, in 1874 Ed financed a Mr. John Daniels who wanted to buy a farm, loaning the gentlemen $500 at 6 percent interest. Later, Ed loaned a Mr. Dollar $165 for the same purpose. In fact, he loaned this Mr. Dollar money twice!

Just before Christmas in 1879, Edward V. New and his neighbor, Carmel Turnage, *each* gave a "sliver" of land, totaling eighty-eight square yards, to Mt. Zion Episcopal Methodist Church, South, "because we bear to the cause of Christ." The Methodist built their church there [Sec. 28, Township 6, Range 14E.] near the middle of the Siding community. To make it legal they charged the church one dollar.

When our New family was listed in the 1880 U.S. Census, Edward V. New was fifty-five and Margaret was fifty-two. They were still living on their farm in Beat 4 of Lauderdale County. Their oldest child and only daughter, Susan, was not with them; she had married John Clark, another railroad man, and had left home. Ed's four sons were still living with him, but his two oldest boys were planning on getting married. His two youngest sons were still in school.

The first Mississippi *public* schools weren't established until 1868 "after de wah" when state and/or local taxes began paying for part of school expense. In 1879 Rev. S. S. Robinson, pastor of Goodwater Baptist Church, opened a school where he held classes during the week in the church building. Respected local fathers, B. O. Allen, John Elam, and Elijah Nichols, were the school's elected

Carmel Turnage and Edward V. New } Filed for Record Jany 17th 1880
To } Deed } Recorded Jany 20th 1880
Zion Hill Church } McRae Mosby, clerk
State of Mississippi
Lauderdale County } Know all men by these presents that we Carmel Turnage and Edward V. New for and in consideration of the Love that we bear to the cause of Christ and for one dollar to us in hand paid, a give and grant and by these presents convey unto the Trustees of M.E.C. South and their successors in office a certain parcel of land, on which Zion Hill house of worship now stand (Enterprise circuit Meridian Dist Miss Confe to wit twenty four yds in the SW. corner of the SE¼ of NE¼ Sec. 28. T6. R14 and 44 yds in the SE corner of the SW¼ of the NE¼ Section 28. T6. R 14 East and 44 yds in the NW corner of the NE¼ of SE¼ Sec 28. T6. R 14 East and 44 yds in the N.E corner of North of SW¼ Sec. 28 T.6. R 14 East in all 88 yds Square all in State of Mississippi Lauderdale Co and Trustees aforesaid to have & to hold said property aforesaid for the use and benefit of M.E.C. South free from the claim or claims of ourselves our heirs our executors and administrators and from the claims of all others whatsoever, In witness whereof we have set our hand and seal this 6th day of December 1879

Carmel Turnage (seal)
E.V. New (seal)

State of Mississippi }
Lauderdale County } Personally appeared before me E Nicholas an acting Justice of the Peace in and for said county aforesaid said Carmel Turnage and Ed V New who acknowledged that they signed & sealed the foregoing deed as their act & deed and the purpose therein set forth witness my hand and seal of office this the 6th day of Dec 1879

Elijah Nicholas J.P.

DEED OF CARMEL TURNAGE & EDWARD V. NEW TO ZION HILL METH. CHURCH, DEC. 6, 1879:

Carmel Turnage and Edward V. New) Filed for Record Jany. 17th 1880
To: Deed) Recorded Jany. 20th 1880
Zion Hill Church) McRae Mosby, Clerk.
State of Mississippi)
Lauderdale County) Know all men by these presents that we Carmel Turnage and Edward V. New for and in consideration of the Love that we bear to the cause of Christ and for one dollar to us in hand paid give and grant and by these presents convey unto the Trustees of M. E. C. South and their successors in office a certain parcel of land on which Zion Hill House of Worship now stand (Enterprise Dist. Miss. Conference) to wit twenty-four yds. in SW corner of the SE¼ of the NE¼ of the NE¼ Sec. 28, T6, R14E, and 44 yds. in the SE corner of the SW¼ of the NE¼ Section 28. T6, R16 East and 44 yds. in the NW corner of the NE¼ of SE¼ Sec.28, T6, R14 East and 44 yds. in the NE corner at north of SW¼ Sec. 28, T 3, R 14E in all 88 yds. Square, in State of Mississippi, Lauderdale Co. and Trustees aforsaid to have and to hold said property aforesaid for the use and benefit of M.E.C.South free from the claim or claims of ourselves our heirs our executors and administrators and from the claims of all others whatsoever, In Whitness whereof we set our set our hand and seal, this 6th day of December 1879

Carmel Turnage (seal)
E. V. New (seal)

LAUDERDALE CO. DEED BK. 1. ppg. 568/569:

E. V. New   )   Filed for record Jany. 8th 1881 at 3 o'Clock PM,

To: Deed   )   Recorded Jany. 11th 1881

C. Turnage)   McRae Mosby, Clerk.

Know all men by these presents that I, E.V.New of Lauderdale County and State of Mississippi in consideration of Five Hundred Dollars received from C. Turnage of the same County and State of Mississippi do grant bargain sell and covenent unto the said C. Turnage the following described premises situated in the County of Lauderdale and State of Mississippi and described as follows, the $S\frac{1}{2}$ of $NE\frac{1}{4}$, $SW\frac{1}{4}$ of $SE\frac{1}{4}$ of Sec. 28, Township 6, Range 14E containing one hundred and twenty acres, more or less, To have and to hold the above described premises with the appurtenances thereunto belonging unto the said C. Turnage his heirs and assigns forever And the said E. V. New for myself and hy heirs , executors and administrators do covenent with the said C. Turnage his heirs and assigns that I am seized in fee of the above described premises and have good right to sell and convey the same; that they are free from all encumberances to and I will warrent and defend the title of said premises to the said C. Turnage his heirs and assigns forver against all lawful claims whatsoever in evidence whereof I have hereunto set my hand and seal the 8th day of January 1881=   E. V. New   (SEAL) trustees. (By the way, two of Ed New's sons later married into the Elam and Nichols families.)

After Edward and Margaret New, who were Baptists, bought their farm, they moved their church letter to Goodwater Church as it was nearer their home. In 1885 Ed New was elected a trustee of the Goodwater School, along with one John Brown and Rufus Tillman.

To find how many schools were needed, that year the Lauderdale County School Board took a countywide school census of its school-age children. Ed and Margaret's youngest child, eighteen-year-old Edward Jr., was the only student in the county's Beat 4 with the New surname. The New's three oldest children, Susan, Luke, and Elijah, had married but as yet had no children of school age. The New's third son, Joel New, was unmarried and lived at home, but he had a job with the railroad at Vicksburg.

In the late 1880s one W. J. Osborne homesteaded at a distance of three or four miles northeast of Siding, at a village owing its growth to a small sawmill. Mr. Osborne had built a small schoolhouse for his and his neighbors' children, and in 1890 he established the LaPlace post office with himself as the postmaster. Less than a year later the LaPlace post office and school closed when the sawmill and turpentine factory relocated at Siding. After the move the local post office became the Siding post office.

The school at Goodwater Baptist Church closed when the new Osborne School reopened in Siding. The site of the new school in Siding was on a lot next to the commissary/boarding house of the Cotton States Lumber Company in an old field that once belonged to Ed New, the field that Ed had sold to Carmel Turnage.

While a Mr. Meehan was establishing the Cotton States Lumber Company in Siding, the Tallahatta Railway track was being laid. The Tallahatta Railroad, a spur track junctioning with the A & M Railroad at Siding, roughly followed the Tallahatta Creek northward to Battlefield, a village near the upper Newton/Lauderdale County line. The spur was being built to transport the Virgin Pine logs through the steep Tallahatta hills to be sawed into lumber at the Cotton States Sawmills at Siding. From Siding came finished boards, bridge timbers, and crossties to be shipped over the regular railroad routes to other parts of the country.

Having lived through race riots and the terrible days of reconstruction following the Civil War, the 1880s brought needed prosperity to the people of Lauderdale County. As "good times" arrived, the whole county thrived. Cotton was "white gold" to farmers who lived in the county's eastern rolling slopes while in its steep western hills its seemingly unending forest was waiting to be harvested. Meridian's railroad center made it possible to ship these products to other parts of the nation—cotton to the hungry textile mills in the North, and lumber to other parts of the country where wood was not plentiful. Meridian's railroads made it possible to send the local goods to the Mobile and New Orleans seaports for worldwide distribution.

The city of Meridian, due to its railroads, factories, hotels, banks, and its fine mercantile establishments, became the new seat of Lauderdale County when, in the late 1870s, the old courthouse at Marion was moved to Meridian. Having become the most populous city in Mississippi, its citizens dubbed it "The Queen City."

Because of its timber and sawmills, sleepy little Siding, about fifteen to eighteen miles west of Meridian, also began to come alive. It became a regular boomtown! In the village, streets were laid out and private homes were built, but when the company's boarding house became full, their workers had to sleep outdoors in tents. On Saturday nights the tent city became quite rowdy, reminiscent of the "'49er" prospector's camps in California's gold rush days.

Elijah New, Ed's second oldest son who had married in 1881, lived in the nearby Tallahatta Hills on unclaimed land he patented from the U.S. government in 1895. "Lige" tried farming but he complained that his land was so steep "his mule would fall out'en the field if'fen he tried to plow." He found it more lucrative to distill and supply the working railroad men and timber jacks with a ready source of good corn whiskey.

Lige New's Tent Bar: From left - Elijah, unidentified children, unidentified man, cousin Oscar Clark

With his moonshine business doing well, Lige bought a tent he turned into a bar, selling drinks to the lonely working men who needed refreshment. His bar had no tables nor barstools, but Lige placed boards across barrels where men could "belly up" to buy whiskey by the tin cupful. It wasn't a fancy place, but it served its purpose.

After the state legislature established a system of free public schools, the Lauderdale County School Board, after taking its school census, organized school districts to make choosing school sites less haphazard.

In 1891 the trustees of the Osborne School hired a young accredited teacher, Miss Mamie Wellborn, to teach its twenty-four pupils. The school trustees were Luke J. New and John W.

Clark, a son and a son-in-law of Ed New. Miss Wellborn, whose home was in the county in the nearby Suquelena community was offered room and board near Siding at the farm home of Mr. Edward New. She accepted.

[In an effort to upgrade the quality of its teachers, the school board began to test its teachers on their teaching abilities. If one failed she—or he—would have to wait two years before they could repeat the exam. Miss Wellborn had received her teaching certificate in 1887, the same year that her father, Dr. David M. Wellborn, had received his. Home-schooled, she began her teaching career by working as her father's assistant when she was fifteen. After earning her teaching credentials "Miss Mamie" taught at the Vincent School in the Pine Springs community (just N.W. of Meridian) for the 1889–1890 and the 1890–1891 school terms, but transferred to Osborne School at Siding, as above stated, for the fall term of 1891.]

The 1900 U.S. Census shows Edward and Margaret New living alone on their farm near Goodwater Church. Ed had reached the age of seventy-five while Margaret was seventy-three. A boarder, Edward Doller, was renting their spare room. Luke New and his wife Mattie lived on the next farm with their first four children. Luke worked for the railroad but helped his old father with the farm work.

That fall Charley New, age six, Luke's oldest son—Ed's grandson—began his scholarship by entering first grade at Osborne under the instruction of Miss Mamie Wellborn. When Luke asked, little Charley said he didn't like Miss Mamie. Asked why, Charley said because she switched him. "Why?" "She saw me peeing in the school spring."

While Mamie Wellborn boarded with Ed and Margaret New, their son, visiting home from his railroad job, fell in love with the ladylike young

The United States of America

TO ALL TO WHOM THESE PRESENTS SHALL COME, GREETING:

Homestead Certificate No. 7433

Application 16,735

Whereas there has been deposited in the GENERAL LAND OFFICE United States a CERTIFICATE of the Register of the Land Office at Jackson Mississippi, whereby it appears that, pursuant to the Act of Congress appr. 20th May, 1862, "To secure Homesteads to actual settlers on the public domain," and to supplemental thereto, the claim of Elijah New has established and duly consummated in conformity to law for the South West quarter Section Thirty five, in Township Six North, of Range fourteen East Choctaw Meridian in Mississippi, Containing one hundred Sixty nine acres and Seventy Six hundredths of an acre according to the Official Plat of the Survey of the said Land returned to the GENERAL LAND OFFICE by the SURVEYOR GENERAL.

Now know ye, That there is therefore granted by the UNITED STATES unto the said Elijah New the tract of land above described: TO HAVE AND TO HOLD the said tract of Land, with the appurtenances thereof the said Elijah New and to his heirs and assigns forever.

In testimony whereof, I, Benjamin Harrison President of the United States of America, have caused these letters to be Patent, and the Seal of the General Land Office to be hereunto affixed.

Given under my hand, at the City of Washington, the Eighth day of August, in the year of Our Lord one thousand eight hundred and ninety two, and Independence of the United States the one hundred and So.

By the President: Benjamin Harrison

By E. Macfarland, Ass.

R. R. Roberts, Recorder of the General Land

[L.S.]

Land grant to Elijah New

The United States of Americ

TO ALL TO WHOM THESE PRESENTS SHALL COME, GREETING:

Homestead Certificate No. *5696*

Application *14065*

Whereas there has been deposited in the GENERAL LAND OFFICE *United States a* CERTIFICATE *of the Register of the Land Office at Jackson Mississi, whereby it appears that, pursuant to the Act of Congress ap 20th May, 1862, "To secure Homesteads to actual settlers on the public domain," and supplemental thereto, the claim of* Luke New *established and duly consummated in conformity to law for the* South half of i North West quarter and the North West quarter of North West quarter of Section three in Township North of Range fourteen East of Choctaw Merid in Mississippi containing one hundred and ten acres and fifty nine hundredths of an a

according to the Official Plat of the Survey of the said Land returned to the GENERAL LAND *by the* SURVEYOR GENERAL.

Now know ye, That there is therefore granted by the UNITED STATES *unto the said* Luke New *the tract of above described* TO HAVE AND TO HOLD *the said tract of Land, with the appurtenances there the said* Luke New *and to his heirs and assigns forever.*

In testimony whereof I, Grover Cleveland *President of the United States of America, have caused these letters to Patent, and the Seal of the General Land Office to be hereunto affixed.*

Given under my hand, at the City of Washington, the ninete *day of* June *, in the year of Our thousand eight hundred and* ninety five *, an Independence of the United States the one hundred and*

[L.S.]

Land grant to Luke New

340

White Teachers Examined for 86-87. mo.Aft 86

Cutif. Iss. 18 Aft 13/86	Miss Rassie Hoskins	1st grad	Paid	.50
" " " "	" Willie Brown	1st "	"	.50
Failed	" E. A. Gibson	2d "	"	.50
Cutif. Iss. Aft 13/86	Jas. F. Boydston	1st "	"	.50
" " " "	Miss Innie Boydston	1st "	"	.50
" " " "	H. J. Fry	1st "	"	.50
Failed	Dr. D. M. Welborn 2d G. ifs	1st " G. av. 58%	"	.50
Cutif. Iss. Aft 13/86	Mrs. M. J. Murphy	1st "		.50
" " " "	" V. R. Hooper	1st "		.50
Cutif. ifs. 3 Aft 17/86	Miss Kate Griffin	2d "	Paid	.50
	" Celia Cohen	1st "	"	.50
Failed for 1st grad	" Minnie Cohen	1st " G. av. 64%	"	.50
Cutif. Iss. Aft 18/86	Mrs. F. J. Mosby	1st "		.50
Cutif. Iss. Aft 18/86	" A. B. Andrews	1st "	Paid	.50
Cutif. Iss. 18 Aft 17/86	Miss Nettie N. Orone	2d "	"	.50
Cutif. Iss. Sept 18/86	Mrs. L. N. Gully	1st "	"	.50
Cutif. Iss. Aft 18/86	Miss F. A. Holladay	1st "		.50
Cutif. ifs. ---	" Maud Rogers	1st "	"	.50
Failed	" Lena Davidson	1st "	"	.50
Failed	" Lula Keller Gn av. 60%	2d "	"	.50
Cutif. Iss. Sept 18/86	" Susie Montgomery	1st "	"	.50
Cutif. ifs. Aft 17/86	M. L. Camp	1st "	"	.50
Cutif. for 2d	Miss Mamie M. Welborn	1st "	"	.50
" " 2d	T. G. L. Keane	1st "	"	.50
Cutif. Iss. Aft 18/86	J. B. Tisdale	1st "	"	.50
" " "	W. B. Ramsay	1st "	"	.50
Cutif. Iss. Sept 17/86	G. A. Holly	1st "	"	.50
Cutif. for 2d	B. D. Pace	1st "	"	.50
" " 2d	T. J. Houston	1st "	"	.50

Partial list of teachers examined for a Teacher Certificate in 1886. On the list are Miss Mamie Wellborn and her father Dr. D. M. Wellborn, along with her future brothers-in-law B.D.Pace, and T.J.Houston. Not listed was Allie Wellborn, Mamie's younger sister who earned her Credentials a year later.

teacher. They were married at Christmastime in 1891.

With the festivities of the wedding and Christmas, there were big to-dos being planned around the Goodwater Church community. As they dressed for one occasion old Ed New told the family that he didn't feel like going. Mamie sent her visiting younger sister, Miss Allie Wellborn, to persuade the old gentleman to come along.

Edward Vandergriff New

Miss Allie, a teacher like Miss Mamie, considered herself a "Southern belle." She batted her big brown eyes as she placed her soft hand on Ed's arm, saying, "Oh, Mr. New, DO join us! We'll be SO disappointed if you don't come!"

Ed, with great dignity, replied, "Miss Wellborn, please remove your hand. I know what I feel like

and I don't feel like goin.' I choose, in this instance, to remain at home."

Surprised, Miss Allie lifted the hem of her long skirt—in a ladylike manner of course—and retired from the room.

The name of Siding post office was changed to Meehan Junction in the winter of 1902, renamed in honor of the gentleman who had brought the Southern States Lumber Company to Meehan. A tragedy came in 1903 when forty-four-year-old Luke New was killed by a train in Meehan Junction.

It is not known if Luke was drinking and had gone to sleep on the tracks (as some gossips said), or if he was robbed and murdered, his body placed on the rails to hide evidence. The mystery was never solved.

Edward and Margaret New took the controversy over their son's death pretty hard. Luke, a good father and husband, had lived near them, making sure the old couple's everyday needs were met. In Luke's absence their widowed daughter, Mrs. Susan Clark, moved in with them to care for them in their final days.

It is believed that Margaret was first to go, followed by Edward. Their children buried them, side by side, in the Goodwater Baptist Church graveyard. Susan had their graves covered with cement to keep "varmints" from disturbing their rest. (It was still wild country.)

We don't know the dates they passed, but they were gone before the 1910 census was counted. With time the dates that Susan had scratched on the wet cement on their grave coverings have eroded—nowadays one cannot tell exactly the year they died.

The New children scattered like the wind after Ed and Margaret died. A few years later the whole little town of Meehan Junction lost many of its citizens after the lumber company had harvested most of the big timbers and had moved on.

In an effort to provide better education in the 1920s, the small eight-grade level schools were consolidated to provide more high schools. The one-room Osborne School, renamed Meehan Consolidated, was rebuilt on the same site in Meehan Junction but was enlarged to become a sturdy two-floored building that boasted an indoor gymnasium. In 1922 it had three teachers for its average of eighty-four students. Several years later the school was closed and Dr. Rueben Johnson, M.D., bought the unused school for its building materials (but not the land) for use in building the nearby Pine Forest Academy and Sanatorium, sponsored by the Adventist Church.

The name Meehan Junction became simply Meehan in 1950 before it was discontinued in 1956, its mail being sent to Meridian. Today the town of Meehan remains a small community of homes and a couple of gas stations/stores off U.S. Highway 80, with most of its residents commuting fifteen miles to work in Meridian. There is a small sawmill operating there, but the spindly logs they use now would not have even been considered worth sawing in olden days.

The A & M Railroad that Edward V. built has long since become the Illinois-Central, and its cars no longer stop at Meehan but still pass to and fro between Meridian and Jackson, Mississippi.

———◆———

Children of Edward V. and Margaret Bishop New

I. Susan "Aunt Sis" New Clark

Born: DeKalb County, Georgia, 1857 (the New's only daughter)

Died: 1931, at home of her son, Woody Clark, in Vicksburg, Mississippi

Susan "Aunt Sis" New Clark

Married: **John W. Clark**, March 24, 1872, by Rev. W. B. Hines. Joseph Baum was his bondsman. [*Laud. County Mar. Book 24*, p. 265.]

John Clark was a railroad man from Virginia. They lived with or near Susan's parents, and in 1892 John Clark, along with Susan's brother, Luke New, became the trustees of the one-room Osborne School at Meehan Junction. Their teacher that term was Miss Allie Wellborn, a substitute for her sister Miss Mamie Wellborn who had recently married Joel New, another of Susan's brothers. The Clarks had six children when John died, their seventh being born after he passed away. Susan went to live with her parents to care for them in their old age. She remodeled the New's old log home (in early 1900s), which she inherited. After their death she went to Vicksburg to live with her son Woody Clark, leaving her oldest son, Oscar Clark, in possession of the old homestead.

It became a family joke about how Susan was so grumpy in the morning. They used to laugh that it was dangerous to speak to "Aunt Sis" before her morning coffee.

Children of John W. and Susan New Clark

1. **EDWARD OSCAR CLARK** (June 31, 1874–March 4, 1941); m. **Rachael McCraw** (June 26, 1874–June 15, 1941), in late 1890s. Both buried at Goodwater Baptist Church near Meehan. Were listed in 1820 Lauderdale County census living near Tunnel Hill (Beat 4) near Meehan. Oscar's son, John E. Clark, bought Ed New's old homestead when it was sold for delinquent taxes in 1934.

Children of Oscar and Rachael McCraw Clark:
A. **Edward Fletcher Clark** (1901–19__), died young
B. **Susie Clark**, died as a child
C. **Henrietta "Etta" Clark**, m. **Charles Brown**, a well digger, in 1910, lived at Enterprise in Clark County, Mississippi
D. **John Ervin Clark** (1904–197_); m. **Christine Dewett**; both were teachers, redeemed old Ed New homestead when it sold for taxes in 1934 during the depression. No children.
E. **Ida Eloise Clark** (1906), m. **Guy Boardman** in 1926. Daughter **Delores**, m. **R. R. Joiner, Jr.**, lives in Meehan. Her granddaughter, **Veronica**, married to **Dennis Hicks**, took over the old New home after its original log walls had been covered with lumber and painted by "Aunt Sis." In the 1980s the Hicks covered the old house with brick and added a two-car garage.
F. **E. Louise Clark** (1909), m. (1) **Willie Lewis**, lived at A & M Railroad water tower at Point near Meehan Junction; m. (2) **W. F. Parker**. No children.
G. **Sybil May Clark** (1911), m. **Wm. Leander Martin** in February 1945. Their Martin children: **Wm. L. Jr.** (1946), **Elizabeth Ann** (1946), and **Oscar Ray** (1948).
H. **Floyd Clark**, m. **Sadie Jennings** of Enterprise, lived in Clinton, Mississippi. Buried at Goodwater Baptist Church.
I. **Van Clark**, m. **Pearl Coughman**; temporary postmaster of Meehan Junction in 1921 then followed railroad to Monroe, Louisiana.
J. **Lucile Clark** (1916–1918), died during a flu epidemic at the age of two.

2. **FLETCHER CLARK** (1876–19__), was age nine in the 1885 school census; have been told he died young, unmarried.
3. **FANNIE CLARK** (1879–18__), died young.
4. **WOODY CLARK** (188_–19__), m. **Mary Winstead.** A railroad man, he lived in East Texas, then in Vicksburg. After his father died, his mother, Susan New Clark, spent her final days at his Vicksburg home.
5. **WESLEY CLARK** (1888–19__), m. **Annie Winstead** and died in Louisiana.
6. **EMMA EVELYN CLARK** (1899–1947), m. **Joseph L. Mathews** (1884–1949); both buried at Goodwater Baptist Church.
7. **EDA CLARK** (190_–19__), m. (1) **Lee Cooper**, (2) **Kenneth Wall** and (3) **Hassel Carr**. Had one daughter, we've been told.

Luke and Mattie New, 1884

II. Luke J. New

Born: 1859, DeKalb County, Georgia, was an infant when his parents came to Mississippi and was but a lad when Sherman razed Meridian.

Died: 1903, buried at Goodwater Baptist Church near Meehan.

Married: **Mattie J. Elam** (1871–1941), ca 1892, a daughter from an Elam family who lived just south of Luke's parents.

Luke, a carpenter, also worked in some capacity for the railroad. When they married they homesteaded on 160 acres of government land in Sec–3 T–5, R–14W adjacent to his parents' farm. Luke's homestead, just down the road, was about a mile south of the Siding post office (early Meehan Junction).

Three years later, on June 19, 1895, President Grover Cleveland signed his patent and the homestead was his to keep. [Patent #8696]

When Luke and Mattie's oldest child came of school age in 1891, Luke and his friend James Henry Tillman built a one-room schoolhouse at Siding on land that had once been owned by his father, Ed New Sr. Luke J. New and James Henry Tillman were trustees of the one-teacher Osborne School the next two school terms.

Luke was forty-four when he was run over by a train at Meehan Junction in 1903. Accident or murder? It is an unsolved mystery. (Siding, renamed Meehan Junction in 1902, had become rather wild near the turn of the century.)

In the early 1930s Luke's widow Mattie, getting older, married again. Her second husband was widower James Henry Tillman, age seventy-five, who still lived in the neighborhood. Tillman's first wife had been Addie Lee New, oldest child of Elijah New, and niece of Luke New (q.v.). When Mattie died in 1941 she was buried beside the grave of her first husband, Luke J. New at Goodwater Baptist Church.

Children of Luke and Mattie J. Elam New:

1. **CHARLES "Grandma" NEW** (June 21, 1885–June 14, 1973), a house painter. Charley was fourteen when his father died and, feeling responsible, he took over the job of being "the man of the family." He ordered his younger siblings about, and they began to call him "Grandma," a nickname he was stuck with all his life.

   Charley never married. After his brothers and sisters married and his mother died (in 1941), he lived alone. As he grew older, he became overly fond of alcohol. He fell from his ladder and broke his neck and, visited by "church people," he "found religion." He said, "The good Lord had to break my neck to make me see the light!" (Ironically he did lose his eyesight near the end, going completely blind.) Refusing to live with relatives, he continued to live blind and alone. Kind neighbors and "church people" brought Charley food until at last, he consented to be admitted to a Meridian nursing home where he died.

Being somewhat eccentric, Charley New became well known, remembered with fondness by today's old folks around Meehan—those few who are alive. They chuckle when you ask about "Grandma New."

2. **MAGGIE NEW** (1887–19__), m. **George Fikes** in 1903, son of Andrew J. (1844–1922) and Rebecca Speed Fikes (1847–1916).
3. **BOURBON NEW** (1889–1___), did he die young or did he go somewhere else to live? Nobody today remembers him.
4. **EMMA EVELYN NEW** (1891–1970), m. **Howard Strickland**, lived in Vicksburg. Begged her brother Charley to live with her, but he refused.
5. **BENJAMIN NEW** (1894–19__), m. **Lela _____** , lived Tuscaloosa, Alabama
6. **ALLIE NEW** (1896–19__), m. **James "Jim" Ponds** of Alabama
7. **LEE NEW** (1898–19__), moved to Louisiana. Brother Charley said Lee was so bow-legged he couldn't catch a hog in a ditch.

III. Elijah "Lige" New

Born: 1861, Lauderdale County, in or near Meridian, Mississippi

Elijah and Alice New, 1881

Died: 1934, in an auto accident, buried at Goodwater Baptist Church
Married: **Mary Alice Nichols** (b. 1865), m. December 14, 1881, in Lauderdale County by L. E. Fairchild, J.P.

Elijah and Mary Alice homesteaded 160 acres of densely forested government land (SW½ of Sec.35, T–6, R–14) for which Lige received patent #7433, signed by President Benjamin Harrison on August 8, 1882. Located in the Tallahata hills west of Meridian near Siding, his land was really too steep to farm—Lige said his mule "would fall out'en the field when he tried to plow."

Lige and his sons began to make whiskey to sell to the influx of lumberjacks and sawmill hands who arrived at the Siding post office with the booming Cotton States Lumber Company in the 1890s. When the 1919 prohibition law made the sale of whiskey illegal it slowed but did not stop the New's whiskey business. His boys became bootleggers who knew which sheriff could be paid off and which customers could be trusted and how to hide from federal "revenuers."

Lige died at age seventy-three, killed in an automobile accident while on his way to Meridian to aid a son who was having trouble with the law. He ran off curvy old U.S. Hwy. 80 West, landing in a deep ravine. His grave, covered with cement, lies alone in the Goodwater Baptist Church cemetery with no wife beside him. (We don't know when or where his wife died.)

Children of Elijah and Mary Alice Nichols New:

1. **ADDIE LEE NEW** (January 3, 1883– March 19, 1934), m. **James Henry Tillman** (November 1864–June 1939) on December 27, 1899. They had a son, **Martin V. Tillman** (1900–1969) who married Jeanette Kitchens, and a daughter, **Emma Tillman** (b. 1903) who married a Mr. Phelps and moved to Ohio. After Addle died, her widowed husband, Henry Tillman, old and lonely, married Mattie Elam New, widow of his friend Luke New.
2. **ALMA BRUCE NEW** (August 1874–190_), died young and unmarried
3. **ALBERT SIDNEY JOHNSON NEW** (September 1887–19__), m. **Bessie Maxwell** in 1916, worked for railroad, moved to Monroe, Louisiana.
4. **WALTER EDWARD NEW** (April 1889– 19__), m. **Maude Singleton**
5. **JOEL ELIJAH NEW** (November 1891–19__), soldier in World War I, m. (1) **Etheline McLaney**, m. (2) **Ethel McMillian** in 1934.
6. **SAMUEL EUGENE NEW** (September 1895–19__), m. **Thelma Meadows** in 1921.

She "ran away," and then he left, too, "for parts unknown."

7. **HOZA B. NEW** (September 1897–19__), a named "son" in 1900 census, but now nobody has heard of him. Died?
8. **JAMES GRADY NEW** (ca.1901–19__), m. (1) **Callie Hambrick**, (2) **Winnie Mills New**, the widow of his brother Jake New. Grady and brother Jake both moved to Alabama (Clarke County?).
9. **JAKE BITTERMAN NEW** (February 14, 1905–July 4, 1961), m. **Winnie Mills**. His veteran headstone in Goodwater Baptist Church cemetery shows that he was a combat veteran, a private in Hd. Det. Station, in World War II. His brother Grady married his widow (as stated).
10. **RUBY GRACE NEW** (1907–197_), m. **Charles Mayerhoff**, lived in McComb, Mississippi.

IV. Joel New II

Born: May 10, 1863, Meridian, Lauderdale County, Mississippi

Died: February 18, 1931, Pine Springs, Lauderdale County, Mississippi, buried Fellowship Baptist Church cemetery northwest of Meridian in Center Hill.

Married:
(1) **Mamie Maude Wellborn** (1870–1900) on December 22, 1891,
(2) **Ellie M. Pratt** (1870–1926) on June 5, 1901.

Joel's story is the subject of the next chapter.

Children of Joel and Mamie Wellborn New:

1. **JOEL HENRY NEW** (1894–1944), m. **Olga V. Ziechka of Russia**
2. **EDWARD LEON NEW** (1895–1955), m. **Maebelle Edna Burnham**

3. **MINNIE LEE NEW** (1896–1946), m. **Curtis Gray Snowden**
4. **MARIE NEW** (1898–1978), m. **William Bennett "Ben" Pace**

Children of Joel and Ellie Pratt New:

1. **VIVIAN LORENA NEW** (1902–1987), m. **Laurence Lavell White**
2. **MARY M. NEW** (February 5, 1904–May 9, 1904), infant
3. **HERMAN JACKSON NEW** (1907–1950), m. **Hettie Jane White**
4. **JODIE "JOE" NEW** (1909–1979), m. **Ruby Katherine Chisolm**
5. **SUSIE MAE NEW** (1912–1988), unmarried
6. **IRVIN DEASON NEW** (1916–1963), m. **Louise Harper**

V. *Edward Vandergriff New Jr.*

Born: August 5, 1866, Lauderdale County, Mississippi
Died: February 9, 1912, buried Goodwater Church, Meehan, Lauderdale County
Married: **Rosa McNulty** of Memphis, Tennessee, on March 2, 1896, (Lauderdale County)

A stonecutter, Ed New Jr. had a good job in Meridian where he worked for J. H. O'Neil Marble Works. Needing a home after they married, Ed Jr. and wife Rosa talked old Ed Sr. into putting up the farm as security so he would rebuild New's old log homestead which, by then, was sadly in need of repair. In exchange for Ed Jr.'s time and money, the old man was to place the farm in his son's name. A Lauderdale County record, dated April 4, 1900, shows that $400 was borrowed from the British-American Mortgage Company of New York, putting up old Ed New Sr.'s farm as security. It was signed by E. V. New and E. V. New Jr. A couple years later in 1903, Ed Jr. renewed the loan, this time for $5,600, from the same company using the same security, signed and co-signed as before.

We don't know all the circumstances, but old members of the New family have told that Ed Jr. was "bad to drink." Soon after this second mortgage was made, Ed Jr.'s wife, Rosa, left him, taking their four children back to her home in Memphis.

Apparently losing hope, Ed Jr. kept on drinking. Ed Jr. never completed renovating the old log house, leaving his sister Susan Clark to finish the job. Susan ("Aunt Sis") Clark, moving in with her parents, took over Ed Jr.'s re-building project and, paying off the mortgage, inherited the old New family farm.

Ed New Jr. died fairly young in 1912 at the age of forty-six. Susan saw that Ed Jr. was properly buried at Goodwater Baptist Church.

Children of Ed Jr. and Rosa McNulty New:

1. **THOMAS NEW** (ca.1897–19__)
2. **LAWRENCE NEW** (ca.1899–19__)
3. **RUBY NEW** (1901–19__), married, moved to California?
4. **MILDRED NEW** (1902–19__), m. **William Wosick**, lived in Gary, Indiana

Chapter XI
Joel New (II) Of Mississippi
(May 10, 1863–February 8, 1931)

I don't remember my grandfather, Joel New, having met him only once when I was less than a year old, but I remember when he died—that happened in 1931 when I was five years old. We were living, at that time, on Bigmama's goat ranch at Fischer Store, Texas. When I asked Mama where my daddy (Leon New) was, she told me that he was on a trip back to Mis'sippi to visit his sick old Papa.

When Daddy finally came driving home in his old truck, he brought me and my big sister, Edna Mae, some stalks of sugar cane, saying it was Blue Ribbon, the goodest kind. We sat on the flat rock kitchen step while Daddy took out his pocketknife and peeled us a stalk, cutting it into little sweet hunks of goodie. He showed us how to chew a chunk and swallow its juice and then spit out what was left. We'd never had sugar cane before, and I remember thinkin' that folks must eat pretty good in Mis'sippi …

Grandpa Joel New, fourth child of Edward V. and Margaret Bishop New, had been born outside Meridian, Mississippi, back in 1863 in the midst of the Civil War. He was almost two in 1864 when the Damn Yankee Sherman went on his rampage and burned the town.

Joel was still quite young after the war when his father, a section foremen on a railroad, relocated his family to a growing community near a siding of the East-West A & M Railroad line (today's Illinois-Central) in Lauderdale County's western hills. This siding was sited near a spur track built to transport the state's untouched virgin timber through the steep unpopulated Tallahatta Hills. In time this community became a small town and opened its own post office, "Siding," a name later changed to "Meehan Junction."

Old-timers have said that Joel's father, Mr. Edward New, was strict but dealt equally and fairly with all. Accustomed to being "the boss" on his job, he taught his children to quickly "move out" when told to do something. The family, who were Baptist, faithfully went to church, and young Joel adopted their firm religious beliefs. From the examples set by his parents, he developed a sound moral character. His devotion to hard work he inherited from his paternal grandmother's Dutch ancestors, his sense of dry humor coming from the Irish ancestors of his short plump mother, Margaret, who seemed ever ready with a droll remark.

Joel was eight in 1871 when Lauderdale County established its first public schools. We don't know where he got his first schooling, but from somewhere he learned to read and write and to "figger." His father believed in education; Edward V. New had helped found the Goodwater School at Siding and had been one of its early trustees. However, by the time a small public school was established, young Joel was old enough to get a man's job.

Joel was taught to farm on his father's land near Siding, but when he became eighteen, he followed his father's footsteps, going to work for the railroad. Placed on a bridge gang, he learned about controlling water erosion and a little about carpentering as he helped to build bridges and trestles for trains.

Since the early days when the railroad track from the east was being laid, the line that reached Vicksburg ended at the Mississippi River bluff. Having no bridge, for years it had been necessary to transfer rail freight from Vicksburg to Delta Point over in Louisiana by hauling the goods across by riverboat. This, of course, was expensive, causing costly delays in shipping.

In the 1880s the company leaders thought it was high time to do something about this. They thought to build a track down through the river bluffs to facilitate their trains bringing their cargos directly to the boat wharves. Why not, they thought, instead of unloading and reloading the freight, why not just send the entire train across to the other side by boat? Why not, indeed!

Joel New lived to tell his grandchildren how he, as a young man, had helped sight the route that the A & V was to take when the track was being laid down the bluffs at Vicksburg. He must have been a good worker with some intelligence because the railroad company promoted him to be one of its foremen.

The next big problem was the differing gauges of the railroads. The V & M track between Vicksburg and Meridian was built to a wide gauge, the rails laid five feet apart. The Vicksburg, Shreveport & Pacific (the V. S. & P.), the western extension of the Vicksburg route through Louisiana, had been changed to today's standard gauge—4 feet, 8½ inches.

This meant that the gauge of the V & M across the entire width of the state of Mississippi had to be changed to the standard gauge before its trains could cross the river. Calling out all crews, this feat was accomplished in sixteen hours on October 22, 1885, so the same trains could run on both sides of the river.

In 1889 the V & M became the Alabama and Vicksburg Railroad. It and the Delta Point, Shreveport & Pacific Railroad came under common management. In 1926 they both became part of the Illinois Central System, and in 1930 at Vicksburg a train track/automobile highway bridge was opened and train ferryboat service over the Mississippi River was discontinued.

In 1890 the County School Board assigned Miss Mamie, oldest daughter of Dr. David and Esther Powell Wellborn, to teach at the Osborne Public School at Siding/Meehan Junction. While school was in session, Miss Wellborn boarded at the home of a school trustee, John W. Clark, husband of Joel New's only sister. The Clarks, who had several children, were somewhat crowded, so another trustee, Joel's brother Luke New, made arrangements for the teacher to stay with his parents, Edward and Margaret New.

A Baptist like the News, the new school teacher attended the local Goodwater Church. Joel began to squire her to "preachin" and to other social events. She was an intelligent handsome girl with raven hair and gentle brown eyes, a refined lady. At age twenty-eight, Joel New fell in love.

Joel must have been a persistent suitor, for on the morning of December 22, 1891, his younger brother, E. V. New Jr., rode with him to the courthouse in Meridian to apply for a wedding license. That evening, Joel New and Miss Mamie Wellborn were married, with Preacher E. Nicholas performing the ceremony.

Now, for those interested in genealogy, Mamie's branch of the Wellborns has been traced

Marriage license of Joel New and Mamie Wellborn

Joel and
Mamie Wellborn New, 1891

to an early Wellborn ancestor in England who was instrumental in translating the Holy Bible into English for England's King James. Her first American forefather arrived in Virginia's Chesapeake Bay area in the early 1600s soon after Jamestown was founded. Family tradition has it that one of his sons married an Indian maiden of the Powhatan tribe of which the celebrated Pocahontas had been a member. Following those early days in America, subsequent generations of Wellborns—from Samuel to Curtis Sr. to Curtis Jr.—migrated south to North Carolina and then over to Georgia.

Before the American Revolution, in 1761 the Junior Curtis Wellborn married Drucilla, daughter of Absalom and Elizabeth Thurmand of Wilkes County, Georgia. This Curtis Wellborn fathered five children, which included two sets of twins. (It seems that the Wellborns were blessed with twins perhaps a bit more often than others.)

In 1775 Curtis Wellborn Jr. fought in our Revolutionary War under Brig. Gen. Elijah Clark of the 3rd Georgia line. After the war he was granted 287½ acres of land along the Oconee River in Washington County from Gov. Houston of Georgia. Later he received an additional 538 acres in Greene County for his military service.

The father-in-law of Curtis Wellborn Jr. was Absalom Thurmond who, when in his fifties, fought in the Continental Army. Curtis Jr.'s oldest set of twin sons, David and Johnathan Wellborn, were only twelve when the war began but fought in battles before the war ended.

At the close of the war, in 1784 David, one of the Wellborn's twin boys, married Mary Robertson, daughter of Thomas and Mary Robertson of Franklin County, Georgia, and became a prosperous cotton plantation owner in nearby Newton County. The two oldest of David's eight children were twins, Sanders and Curtis (III) Wellborn. His fourth child, born in 1790, David named Josiah. This Josiah Wellborn became the grandfather of Joel New's wife, Mrs. Mamie Wellborn New.

Little Josiah Wellborn grew up and married Margaret Robertson in 1817 and established their home near Madison, the seat of Morgan County, Georgia. (His wife, Margaret, was a daughter of William and Jean Robertson of Franklin County, a first cousin of Josiah's mother, the above Mrs. Mary Roberson Wellborn.) Josiah and Margaret Wellborn had twelve children, which included *another* set of twins! Their fifth child, David Mercer Wellborn, born in 1824, later became the father of Mrs. Mamie Wellborn New.

This same David had been twenty-four when his father, Josiah Wellborn, died. As the oldest unmarried son who was still living at home, David took over the family affairs to replace his deceased father. He helped his aging mother operate the plantation and acted as an adviser to his younger siblings. When the last of the Wellborn children

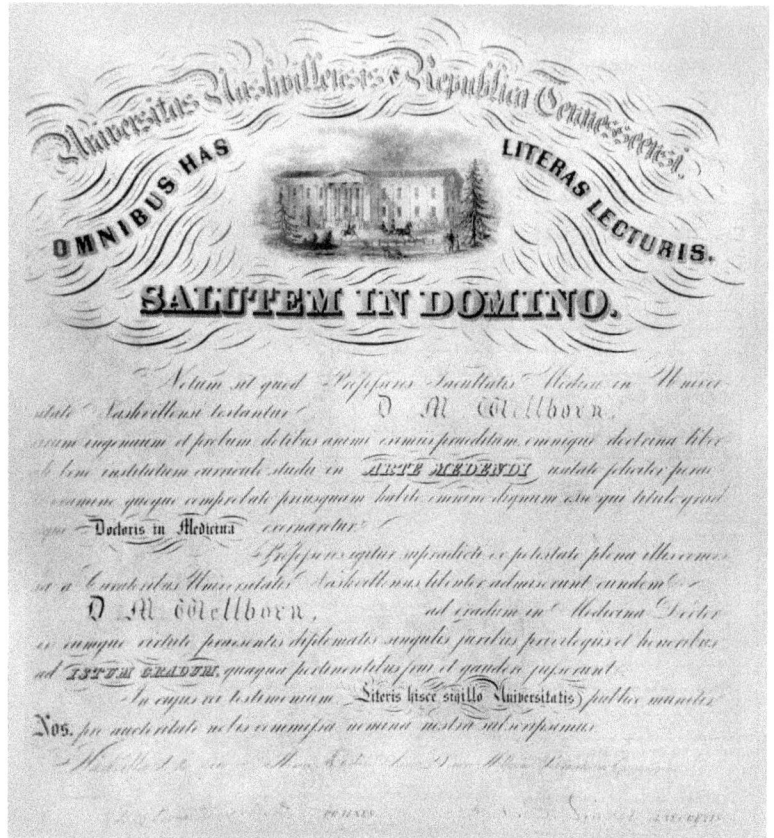

D.M. Wellborn's diploma from medical school

had come of age and/or married, the Wellborn estate was divided between the Wellborn heirs.

After collecting his share of the Wellborn inheritance, David M. Wellborn left for the University of Nashville to study medicine. He had a late start but on March 1, 1859, at age thirty-one, he received his "sheepskin." (See photo.) His diploma was written in Latin on a sheepskin parchment, but translates into English as follows:

University of Nashville Republic of Tennessee
Greetings in the Lord
Be it known that the Professors of the School of Medicine of the University of Nashville hereby testify that D. M. WELLBORN a man of nobleness and

*probity gifted with an exceptional mind,
is endowed with all the literal doctrines
in the curriculum of this institution in the
study of Medical Arts, having successfully
passed his exams and proved he is worthy
of being granted the title of DOCTOR OF
MEDICINE.*

*The undersigned professors, with the
full authority granted them by the cura-
tor of the Univ. Of Nashville, freely accept
D. M. Wellborn as a practicing Medical
Doctor along with the duties, privileges
and honors adherent to this degree.*

*We hereby stamp THE SEAL OF THE
UNIVERSITY, furnished to us by the people,
and sign with the authority invested in us.*

March, 1859

David's older brother, James R. "Jim"
Wellborn, was a schoolteacher at Blakely in Early
County down in the southwest corner of Georgia.
After graduation David visited his brother, liked
the country, and stayed to begin his medical practice. The brothers, Dr. David and Jim Wellborn,
together opened a pharmacy in Blakely.

When the Civil War began in 1861, almost
all available men hastily joined the Confederate
Army to fight for the South. David tried to enlist
but as he was slight of stature and had a frail build,
the other men told him to stay home to look after
the health of their ladies; they would soon whip
those Yankees and return home. (Ha, ha! The war
dragged on for four long, devastating years.)

Soon after the war began, in August one
Rev. Hiram Powell, a prominent Early County
Baptist minister who loved the South, died of an
illness. Dr. Wellborn was his attending physician.
Becoming acquainted with the Powell family, Dr.
Wellborn fell in love with Miss Esther Powell, the
patient's daughter, a pampered Southern belle
who was nineteen years his junior.

But alas! Miss Powell was already betrothed
to a dashing young Confederate soldier.

But fate intervened: Miss Powell's soldier did
not return from the war so Dr. David began his
courtship in earnest. On November 8, 1867, amid
the terrible time of the South's reconstruction,
Dr. David M. Wellborn and Miss Esther Pamelia
Powell were married in Blakely, Georgia.

Miss Esther, a "flower of the Old South," had
been reared in luxury. Accustomed to having her
personal slave to help her dress, she didn't know
how to manage her own coiffure, let alone how
to manage a home. But David loved her dearly.
Seeing her as helpless as a kitten, he gave her a pet
name, "Miss Puss." Miss Puss had a lot to learn.

During the war all business in Early County
had come to a standstill. Folks had no money to
pay a doctor, causing David's medical practice
to suffer. A railroad friend traveling through
Mississippi reported that the town of Meridian,
a railway crossroad in Lauderdale County, was
thriving and was fast becoming a city. In desperation, in May of 1871 Dr. Wellborn traveled up
to Mississippi and, dipping into the last of their
savings, he bought a home in Marion (outside
Meridian) where they could live and he could
open a medical office. It cost him $1,500.

Returning to Georgia, David loaded "Miss
Puss," their young son Jesse, and their baby
Mamie onto wagons, along with their belongings, to begin the long tiring trek westward across
the entire state of Alabama. When they set off
some blacks, faithful ex-slaves came along to
help. Esther's brother Adolphus "Dolph" Powell
also joined them and came along. Dolph Powell,
becoming a Baptist minister in Lauderdale County,
Mississippi, married Mrs. Anne Scarborugh, a
local war widow with a young son.

One of Dr. Wellborn's brothers, Elijah Jones
Wellborn, and his wife, Mary Adeline Rutledge,
were also having a hard time making a living in

post-war Georgia. Dr. Wellborn wrote and asked his brother to join him in Mississippi; the area around Meridian, fast recovering, would offer a better opportunity to get back on his feet. Elijah came and bought a small farm just south of town at Sageville where they raised a family of eight children.

Dr. Wellborn never attained the wealth he had before the war, but he was able to keep his family in some degree of comfort. They had two more daughters born in Marion—Minnie Mozell born in 1873 and the youngest of their four children, Allie Henri, was born in 1875.

Dr. Wellborn home schooled his children while continuing his medical practice, and for a while, he bolstered his income by obtaining a teaching certificate to teach philosophy in a new county public school. His son Jesse became a minister and his middle daughter Minnie married Joseph L. Houston and raised a family in Collinsville in Lauderdale County. (Joseph L. "Jodie" Houston was grandson to heroic Sam Houston of Texas.) His daughters Mamie and Allie Henri both became teachers before they married.

Miss Puss—Mrs. Esther Wellborn—used to tell how she stood in awe of her oldest daughter, Mamie, saying how Mamie was so resolute when she set out to accomplish a goal. She recalled that once Mamie, as a young girl, was given a calf that her father had accepted in lieu of his medical fee. She bottle-fed it milk, and when it matured, she sold it to buy one of the recently invented sewing machines. Mamie said she was tired of hand-stitching her mother's and younger sisters' garments.

But enough about the Wellborns—back to our New family …

When Joel New and Mamie Wellborn married, Joel bought a land patent for public land from the U.S. government. A few miles from Meehan Junction, this land was near Mamie's parents who had recently moved from Marion to the Suquelena/Collinsville area in western Lauderdale County. Their first child, Joel Henry New, was born there in 1894.

Still working for the railroad, Joel didn't have time to farm. He sold his place to a dentist, Dr. G.W. Davidson (a friend of Dr. Wellborn), and rented a house closer to the railroad so he would be closer to his job.

The rented house was at a place called Point, a village on a narrow strip of land owned by the railroad, lying between the railway track and the Chunky River. With a population of less than thirty, Point had collected around a water tower near the Meehan Junction not far from the home of Joel's parents. Their second son, Edward Leon New, was born there in 1895.

(Point, Mississippi, was never more than a flag station on the A & M—today's Illinois Central Railroad. It got its name when, in early days, old Edward V. New was working with the engineers who sited the path that the original track was to follow. When they arrived at this point, their compass needle went haywire because of the area's vast quantity of submerged minerals. Today there is little left of the small village, just traces of brick to show where people once lived.)

One day Mamie and her two little boys walked over from Point to visit her in-laws who lived near Meehan. Pregnant again, Mamie found it difficult to walk down through the hollows and up the steep hills. On the way home she led the boys on a shorter path across a train trestle built for locomotives to cross a deep ravine.

That evening little Henry couldn't wait to tell Papa about their adventure. Joel, "fit to be tied," became quite angry. It frightened him to think that anything bad should happen to his beloved little family.

"What if a train had come long while you were out there in the middle?" he cried. "Did you think you could hang over the edge by your fingernails, or did you plan for you and the boys to jump?"

Their third child, born at Point in 1896, was a daughter they named Minnie Lee New.

When the New boys reached school age, they moved again, this time to Chunky Station near the Lauderdale/Newton County line. Joel rented a house in Chunky near the railroad, two blocks from the school where Henry and Leon would began their education, and where Mamie was able to teach. She continued teaching until their fourth child, baby Marie, was born in 1898.

After this last baby was born, Mamie was never quite well. She tried to keep going but suffered bouts of nausea and abdominal pain. Joel, seeing that Mamie didn't seem to improve, in desperation took her and the children over to stay with her younger sister, Mrs. Allie Pace; Allie would give her big sister loving care.

Allie Wellborn, married to Dr. Bennett Deason "Dee" Face, lived in Lauderdale County north of Meridian near Gumlong Baptist Church in the Obadiah community. Joel thought if anybody could make his Mamie well, it would be Dr. Dee.

(Dr. Dee Pace, having graduated from a Memphis medical school, had gone into practice with Mamie's father, Dr. David Wellborn. When Dr. Wellborn and his wife grew older, they moved to live with Dr. Dee and their daughter, Allie.)

Under Dr. Dee's care, Mamie's health did appear to improve. As the Pace home was somewhat crowded, when Mamie felt better Joel took her and their children over to Collinsville to stay with Mamie's other sister, Mrs. Minnie Wellborn Houston, until she was able to go home. Joel, feeling relieved, returned to Chunky Station to continue working. On weekends he rode his horse,

Dixie, over to Collinsville to check on his little family.

An interesting bit about the Houstons: Miss Mamie's sister, Miss Minnie Wellborn, had married Joseph Luther Houston Jr. His father, J. L. Houston Sr., was reported to be the bastard son of the famous Gen. Sam Houston, gained from Sam's early alliance with an Indian maiden. Sam later became a hero in 1836 when he fought for Texas independence from Mexico.

Gen. Sam Houston's son, young Joseph Houston Sr., was an embarrassment to his socially prominent stepmother when "Big Sam" began politicking to become governor of Texas. Before the election the young man was sent to Mississippi for the Hambrick family to keep out of sight.

History writes that the Hambricks, before moving to Lauderdale County, Mississippi, had become Sam Houston's friends when "Big Sam" had fought alongside Capt. John Hambrick under Gen. Andrew Jackson at New Orleans in the War of 1812.

Dashing young Joseph Houston Sr., his Mexican saddle decorated with bright conchos as big as silver dollars, met Miss Elmira Hambrick, and they eloped. They settled near Elvira's folks in the Collinsville community and raised a houseful of children. (Some say they had nineteen kids, although this did include two sets of twins.)

Miss Minnie Wellborn, Mamie's sister, met one of the Houston's sons, Joseph L "Jodie" Houston Jr., and they married. Their home was in Collinsville where Joel took Mamie to recuperate.

Instead of gaining strength, Mamie relapsed. Suffering acute abdominal pain, she died at the home of her younger sister. Joel was beside himself with grief.

Little Marie, Mamie's baby, had not long learned to walk. While she and her big sister Minnie played in Aunt Minnie Houston's yard, they picked flowers and brought them into the house. Hand in hand, the little girls tiptoed over to place them on the bed beside their mother's body. Four-year-old Minnie nodded sagely to her little sister, "Mama will get up 'terectly and put them in some water."

Joel, sitting near, got up and left the room.

Back then Mamie New's illness was diagnosed as "cramp colic." Short year's later physicians discovered "appendicitis" and how to surgically remove an inflamed appendix. Later Dr. Pace said that Mamie had died when her appendix ruptured. He could have saved her life. "Oh, if I had only *known!*" he said.

Mamie Wellborn New was buried in the Hamrick cemetery near Aunt Minnie Houston's home in Collinsville. On her tombstone Joel had inscribed, "Mamie M. New, born December 21, 1870; died August 30, 1900; we trust our loss will be her gain, and that with Christ she's gone to reign."

(With time the weather beaten stone cracked and shattered. In the 1970s a new headstone was placed at Mamie's grave by Mamie and Joel's youngest daughter, Mrs. Marie New Pace.)

Following Mamie's death, Joel rented a house on the Brown farm in Obadiah. Living directly across the road from Aunt Allie and Uncle Dee Pace, the Paces—with Grandpa and Grandma Wellborn—could babysit the children while Joel was at work. This was before the Paces had children of their own. Allie begged Joel to let her adopt little Marie.

"I do not have any children to give away," Joel said gruffly.

One Sunday afternoon Dr. Pace's brother, Albert, came visiting from nearby Pine Springs. The brothers suggested that Joel should re-marry to provide a real home for his children. Joel replied that he didn't know anybody suitable that could take his Mamie's place. Albert Pace said his wife 'Betty' (Mrs. Elizabeth Pratt Pace) had a

sister that would be ideal. True, Miss Ella Pratt was a thirty-year-old spinster, but she was a fine woman. The eldest of three daughters, she had never married because she had to teach school to support her family after her father had taken ill.

The Pratts, William and Rosa Linda Everett Pratt, had seven children in 1853 when they arrived in Lauderdale County from Georgia. William was a master carpenter and his two oldest boys, Sherrod and John, were his apprentices until the Civil War came, when both joined the Confederate Army. John had been killed in battle in front of the Atlanta courthouse but Sherrod, a railroad engineer, returned and settled just north of Meridian to become the first postmaster at Bailey Store, serving from 1883 through 1889.

One of William Pratt's younger sons, Joseph Aaron Pratt, living near his brother Sherrod at Bailey Store, became a machinist at Col. Bailey's cotton gin and sawmill. He married Mary Isabelle Thrash, a daughter of poor Irish emigrants Jackson and Elizabeth Thrash. Joseph and Mary T. Pratt had three daughters when Joseph was elected a public school trustee for neighboring Cook School.

In 1900 Joseph Pratt became ill with some sort of stomach malady. Unable to keep his job with Col. Bailey, he was forced to move to a tenant house on his son-in-law Albert Pace's farm in nearby Pine Springs. He developed dysentery so badly that crushed wild blackberries was all he could eat. Joe Pratt died that summer on June 6.

Joe and Mary I. Pratt's second daughter, Miss "Betty" Pratt, had married Albert Pace who had inherited the Pace farm from his father. The eldest Pratt daughter, Miss Ellie Mable Pratt, upon earning a teaching certificate, was teaching at a public county school.

Joel New, upon thinking things over, went calling on the teacher, Miss Ellie. She consented to be his wife, and they were married on June 5,

1901. Miss Ellie turned out to be a fine wife and a wonderful mother. Their marriage, with its un-romantic beginning, turned into a rich rewarding experience that lasted throughout their lifetime.

Joel and Ellie New—with Joel's four children—continued to live in Obadiah in Joel's rented house in front of Dr. Pace's home. Ellie's widowed mother, Grandma Mary I. Pratt, brought her old spinning wheel and came to live with them. In 1902 Joel and Ellie's first child was born, a daughter they named Vivian Lorena New.

Joel and Ellie Pratt New, 1901

In February 1904 Joel and Ellie had another baby, another little girl. Born early, she weighed only three pounds. Her tiny hand was so small that when Ellie placed her wedding ring about the baby's wrist it fit as a bracelet. They named the infant after her grandmothers, Mary Pratt and Margaret New.

Joel, agreeing with Dr. Pace, thought the infant could not survive, but Grandma Pratt would hear of no such thing. Taking over the care of her little namesake, she kept the baby alive in a box warmed with hot bricks from the fireplace. When necessary to pick little Mary up, she had to be held on a pillow.

Amazingly, Grandma Pratt kept the infant alive for three months. They buried her wee body in the nearby Fellowship Baptist Church Cemetery near the grave of Ellie's late father, Joseph A. Pratt.

The death of their baby served to make Joel and Ellie's relationship closer. The deep respect they held for each other developed into an abiding love.

Mr. George T. Lockhard, whose store and home were halfway between the Pine Springs Store and Meridian, customarily bought land for its standing timber, re-selling it after harvesting its big trees.

Joel New's deed for Pine Springs property

In 1904 Joel New bought an 80-acre farm in the Pine Springs community from G. T. Lockard, in Section 3, Township 7, Range 15 East. The farm cost Joel $600, but on it was a dilapidated log house where the News could live until Joel could build something better. Joel gave up railroading then because he wanted to be at home more with his growing family—and because he liked working with the soil.

The old house in Pine Springs, built by pioneers before the Civil War, was a two-room log cabin with a detached kitchen. Moving his family there, Joel and his two boys, Henry (10), and Leon (9), went to work.

Joel bought lumber to build three large rooms north of the cabin. Moving into these three rooms, they poled the old log cabin down the hill behind the house. With the cabin out of the way, they built two more good-sized rooms of sawn lumber, connected to the first three rooms by an enclosed hallway. A front porch extended halfway across the house. (Mamie's sister, Aunt Allie Pace, with her greater finesse, called it the "front gallery.")

The original log kitchen was left in the back-yard to serve as a smokehouse, the back room of the new house becoming the new kitchen. Joel built a spacious country back porch where, next to the new kitchen, a cedar water bucket hung with a gourd dipper. A used marble-top dresser was placed by the kitchen door to hold a washbasin and soap where they washed up before coming in for dinner, drying their hands on a cotton feed-sack which Miss Ellie had hemmed to make a towel.

The back porch was a cool place in summer where the girls in the family sat to shell peas or to churn the weekly supply of butter and buttermilk. The back steps was a meeting place where young'uns sat to do their nightly foot-washing ritual before climbing into Miss Ellie's clean beds. The youngsters went barefoot all summer, and Miss Ellie didn't like it if they hopped into bed with dirty feet.

There was no running water or electricity, but their coal oil (kerosene) lamps served them well. They had plenty of water, but it had to be carried in buckets from an all-weather spring. An unwritten rule: Whoever took the last dipper of water was expected to grab the bucket and fetch more from the spring.

Pine Springs Home built by Joel and Ellie New, painting by Mary Ellen New White

1910 census for a section of Pine Springs Road

They, of course, had no bathroom but a two-hole privy down past the chicken house served its purpose. Joel had left the old log hen house intact for Miss Ellie's black-n-white "Dominicker" hens. He had to replace the rickety pole fence around the old garden site to keep her hens from peckin' the ripe t'maters.

The ancient barn, also made of logs, was in danger of caving in, but Joel, running short on money, said they would have to make-do until he could build another.

On the front of the barn was a shed-roof covering two stables across a wide hallway, just right for Joel's horse, Dixie, and his stubborn little tan mule, Lucy. In the main barn, on opposite sides of a wide hallway, were two large cribs for corn, all covered by a spacious loft for hay.

Behind the barn was another lean-to room that covered a row of milking stalls for cows to be milked out of the rain. It opened onto a calf pasture where calves were kept from the mama cows during the day. Milk from three teats were milked for household use, but a back teat was left for her calf. This gave rise to the old saying, "I've been handed a back tit," when one felt slighted.

In addition to Joel's four older children and Ellie's little Lorena, he and Ellie had four more kids born while they lived on their Pine Springs farm. They had **Herman Jackson** in 1906, **Jodie "Joe"** born in 1908, and **Susie Mae**, born in 1912. The last baby came in 1916, his name recorded in the family Bible as **Irving Deason**, a name he later changed to **Irvin**. Joe New also changed his name. He refused to be called Jodie and became, simply, "Joe New."

Much of the New's farm was uncultivated rather steep hills. Although there was some flat land near a creek that was good for grazing cows, it was subject to flooding during wet spells. Joel had one small field near his house but his largest field was a flat crawfishy bottomland next to the "Old Slough," a creek that ran across the back of his farm. He had, however, a rather large sandy hill that would be good for planting corn and cotton but was too steep to be saved from washing away by merely plowing terraces.

But Joel had learned water control by working as a youth on a railroad bridge gang—and he was stubborn when he made up his mind. Never one afraid of work, he and his oldest two boys resolutely took up hand shovels and undertook the enormous task of digging deep ditches around the steep hill's contours to control soil erosion.

Making a good-sized A-frame out of 8 foot 2x4's with a crosspiece to secure his carpenter level, Joel began laying out the sites for the Sand Hill ditches. Starting at the top, they worked downward. It took them all winter to complete the job, but next spring they planted the Sand Hill with corn and peanuts.

(Joel New's bottom-land field now lies under a swimming area in today's Okatibbee Lake. The weathered Sand Hill, now covered with Kudzu Vines, can still be seen between the Pine Springs swimming area and boat landing, a monument to the old-timer's laborious achievement.)

Joel continued to improve his farm and expected his children to do the same. As they grew taller, the boys worked in the fields, plowing

and planting, chopping cotton, hoeing weeds, and thinning corn. He required that all fields had to be cleaned after fall crops were harvested. Together they cleared grass weeds, cornstalks, and rotting cotton stems from their fields, making them ready to be plowed and replanted when spring returned. Every winter they cleaned out the ditches on the Sand Hill, cutting away any bushes and wild blackberry briars that had sprouted along the ditch banks. The boys used their two-man cross-cut saw to cut firewood from their woods for winter warmth, hauling it by wagon to the woodpile at the house. They made sure that Miss Ellie had enough stove wood for her cook stove, enough to last all year.

The girls helped Ellie in the garden, picked wild plums and blackberries, and helped boil heavily soiled clothes outdoors in an iron kettle

Ellie New (right) with her sister, Mary

to be scrubbed in washtubs. They shelled peas, canned tomatoes for winter use, and peeled and sliced apples to be dried in the sun. The girls became adept at cooking—especially Lorena, who made food taste "just right."

(My mother, Minnie's sister-in-law, said that Aunt Minnie could turn off a lot of work quickly; at a drop of a hat Minnie could go into a cold kitchen, turn around twice, and before you knew it she'd lay out a scrumptious meal on her dining room table.)

Their cows gave more milk than they could use, and they raised hogs, feeding them on corn, hay, and peanuts grown in their fields. Some hogs they sold, but they butchered as many as they needed, for hams, sausages, bacon, and lard.

Joel traded for a cane mill from his neighbor, Fred Johnson. Joel became quite adept at making molasses. He made a name for himself by farmers who hauled their wagons of sugar cane to be squeezed and cooked into molasses, a service for which Joel charged a toll.

Molasses provided most of the sweent'nin they used, tho' sometimes Miss Ellie would have Joel buy some white sugar from Mr. Ratcliff's Pine Springs store if she wanted to bake a cake or maybe a blackberry pie.

Ellie spent Saturday afternoons cleaning house, even shining the brass bands around the cedar water bucket hanging on the back porch. (She scoured the bands with sand from the yard.) The News worked all week but on Sunday, the Lord's day, all labor came to a halt. They didn't always go to church but would clean themselves up, put on their Sunday clothes, and sit on the front porch and sing gospel hymns. The children would play baseball or go fishin' on Saturday afternoon, but didn't dare to go fishing or hunting on a Sunday!

Being Baptists, the News attended the Fellowship Baptist Church, which was about five miles up the road. Sometimes they went down the road a mile to the Union Church that old Mr. Sam Bozeman had built across the schoolyard from Pine Springs public school.

The Bozemans were members of the Church of God (Holiness) Church but from time to time this local Union Church invited various Bible-thumping preachers to shout out the Lord's message. It is remembered that one summer the famous evangelist Gipsy Smith set up his tent in the schoolyard where he preached a week of hellfire and damnation. It isn't known how many souls were saved, but he made a lot of folks "powerful uncomfortable."

Eventually, in the 1920s a census was taken to determine which kind of church the community wanted. This census showed that more Methodists were living in Pine Springs than any other faith. Hence, a local Methodist congregation was organized and began holding Sunday school and preachin' in the schoolhouse. Joel and Ellie New joined their neighbors and moved their church letters to the Methodist Church.

Joel New was a short man that walked "slue-footed." It was said that one could pick out his tracks in the sand by the way the toes on his right foot pointed outward. (One wonders if he had experienced some kind of accident in his younger days.) He wore a heavy mustache and often one could catch a hidden twinkle in his eye. Well liked, he was respected by his neighbors, and he never cheated in his life. He was friendly but had an abrupt, straightforward manner of speech that left no doubt about how he stood on a matter. He was kindly with his family but remained a strong father-figure.

Several years ago the late Dr. Reuben Johnson told how he remembered Mr. Joel New. The Johnson farm, owned by Dr. Johnson's father, Fred Johnson, touched on the backside of the

New's place. Dr. Johnson, then just a boy, thought of Mr. Joel as the wise community philosopher.

Dr. Johnson said, "Mr. New spoke in parables, using common things—dogs, mules, coons, etc.—as characters in his simple stories that brought out some moral truth."

"Lee Ratcliff, who owned the store across the road from the schoolhouse, was our local Justice of the Peace." He continued, "He held court in his store where neighbors could settle their differences—such as one farmer bringing charges against another whose cows broke down a fence and ate half his corn patch. They respected Mr. New and someone would ask him what he thought. His answer would be down-to-earth and *right*!"

Joel New expected much from his children, but they all had a happy childhood. They hunted, fished, swam in the creek, went to church and community socials, and attended the local eighth grade school. It is interesting to note, however, that none of his sons, except one forced by circumstances, ever returned, as adults, to the farm to make a living. As soon as they became old enough to leave, they found "outside" jobs.

Around 1912 Joel's two oldest boys, Henry (18) and Leon (17), found work at a sawmill in Alabama near Mobile. Feeling badly about leaving, each month they sent their papa part of their paychecks so he could hire plow hands to take their place. Joel hired a black man and let him live in the log cabin that had been left standing after they had poled it down the hill. The hired help came in handy as Joel's younger boys, Herman and Joe, were a mite little for man-sized jobs.

The original Pine Springs Road, roughly following the N/S mid-section line of Section 4 between Joel New and his neighbor Frank Vincent, passed directly across the New's front yard. To straighten a curve in the road, however, in 1916 Lauderdale County constructed a new road that crossed Vincent's land a little further up the slope directly in front of Joel's house.

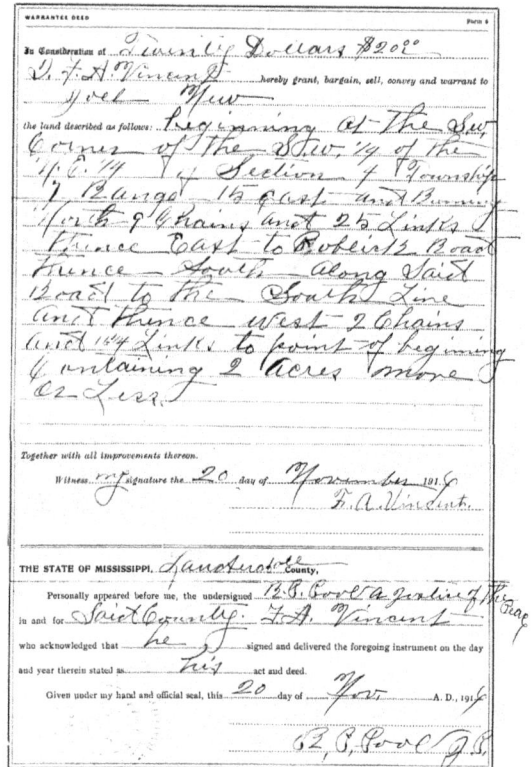

Joel New's deed from F.A. Vincent

Joel, feeling cut off, didn't like the idea of anybody owning land between him and the public road. He talked Vincent into selling him the small portion of land that lay between the old and the new public roads. That November Vincent sold Joel the two acres (more or less) that was directly in front of Joel's house for $20. (See copy of deed.) Come spring Joel planted cotton on the little hill, pleased that he had a bit more land to plant.

With the "Great War" raging in Europe, in 1918 cotton prices were high. Joel wanted more land so he could plant more cotton.

Old Mr. Hillard C. "Hill" Wolfe, who owned the farm just south of Joel's, sold Joel three acres of farmland that adjoined the New farm. The aging old gentleman was no longer able to work so he sold Joel this part of his farm for $55. It was purchased in March, just in time for Joel to break ground for another cotton patch. (See deed.)

Joel missed seeing his New relatives. About twice a year—in summer after crops were laid by and again near the Christmas holidays—he loaded Miss Ellie and their young'uns into the farm wagon to travel the several miles over to Meehan Junction to spend a week with his folks. It was good that the children got to know their New and Clark cousins, and Joel enjoyed rehashing old times with his sister and brothers.

Usually Joel came home with a couple of jugs of his brother Lige's whiskey. Joel was by no means a drunkard, but he did enjoy a bedtime toddy to ease his aching muscles so he could sleep.

In 1919 Congress passed the Volstead Act, which prohibited the manufacture, sale, and transportation of intoxicating beverages. Elijah "Lige" New, whose whiskey was located on his isolated farm in the Tallahatta Hills, went temporarily out of business as he was being watched by federal revenuers. The "feds," knowing that Lige made moonshine, kept his place under close surveillance.

Joel, concerned about losing his yearly liquor supply, talked his big brother into bringing his still over to his Pine Springs farm. After some hesitation, Lige agreed. He came over, bringing his paraphernalia and setting it up out of sight, at Joel's spring behind the workshop where Joel sharpened plows. (The spring had not been used since Joel had a well dug in his yard.)

Lige was an old hand at it but 'twas all new to Joel. Joel began testing the fiery liquid as it slowly dripped from the coil, making sure all was working properly. After a while Joel, becoming merry, began to sing;

O'Possum up de 'Simmon tree,
   Raccoon on de ground,
Raccoon say, "You Possum you,
Shake dem 'Simmons down!"
Possum b'gin ta shake, 'Simmons b'gin
   ta fall,
Raccoon say "You possum you,
Didn't say I want 'em all!"

It appeared that Joel had got himself quite tipsy. Lige became worried because Joel was making so much noise. He made several trips up the rise, peeking from behind the bushes to see if any strangers were coming.

Next morning Lige told Joel that he was gong to take his stuff and head home. When asked to stay and visit longer, he said, "Naw, I'm too tired. I'm plum tuckered after traipsing up that hill watchin' for them rev-noorers!"

(That day the New's friendly neighbor, Ed Hooks, who was quietly passing across the farm on his way to set out hooks on Okatibbee Creek, had been amused when he heard Joel singing. A few days later Mr. Ed, keeping a straight face, teased Joel, asking when he planned to open his distillery business. Joel's curt reply was unrecorded.)

Joel was one of three responsible local fathers (along with John White and Kirby Smith) who served several years as trustees of the Pine Springs school. Believing in education, Joel sent his children to the local school, although it was an elementary school that offered only eight grades.

In 1919 the Lauderdale County School Board combined some of its up-county schools to form the "Center Hill Consolidated High School," a school that offered twelve grades. The Pine Springs school remained open, but their students had to travel five or six miles if they wanted to graduate with a high school diploma.

Joel New began sending his school children up the road to the Center Hill school by farm wagon, his sons Herman (13) and Joe (11) driving his mules, Mack and old Lucy. By that time the two oldest New boys had joined the Army, his daughters Minnie and Marie were married, and his next daughter, Lorena, was engaged to marry Lawrence White. This left only Herman, Joe, Susie Mae, and young Irvin to enroll at Center Hill.

The New's neighbors offered Joel a fee to transport their students to Center Hill along with his, seeing how his wagon was going that way. Joel agreed to take Mr. Kirby Smith's two boys and the two older sons of Mr. Tom Wolfe. It is unknown who else hitched a ride, but when Mr. Nate Byrd asked for his young'uns to ride, Joel had to say no—his farm wagon had reached its capacity.

Most of their trips to school were uneventful, but some days, while at school, a "gully-washer" rain would come that caused the creeks to overflow. When this happened they couldn't cross the flooded Bales Creek with the wagon. The boys would leave the girls to stay the night at the nearby Stamford Avera farm, unhitch the wagon, and swim the mules across the swollen creek. Once across, the boys doubled up and rode Mack and Lucy on home to do their evenin' chores. Next morning they returned to re-hitch and pick up the girls to return to school.

Ralph Snowden, Joel's oldest grandchild, son of Curtis and Minnie New Snowden, in later years recalled when he was beginning school at Center Hill in 1921. Back then school wagon-owners had a row of stalls, or pens, so their teams could be unhitched during the school day.

"Grand-daddy New," Ralph said, "was the first to have a motor school-bus to park among the horse-drawn carriages. He was so proud of his bus that he built two 'ge-rages' fer it—one at home and another at school. He didn't want his fine bus left out in the rain! His first school bus was small, held about twenty kids if they all jammed in. It was a Ford Model 'T' with a factory-built body. They had given him his choice of colors: Black, or Black!"

Ralph also remembered when his Aunt Lorena New married; Ralph was then about three years old, his favorite playmate being his Uncle Irvin New, who was near his own age. In March 1919 Aunt Lorena married Lawrence "Humpy" White (son of neighbors John and Lidie White), the solemn ceremony taking place on the New's front porch.

Uninterested in what the grown-ups were doing around the front porch, young Ralph and Irvin went exploring. They found a "nest" of baby kittens in a dirt-covered potato bank where potatoes were kept in the garden behind the smokehouse. The News kept about twenty cats roaming about the place to keep rats from raiding their corncribs and making dents in their stashed peanuts.

Pine Springs School - Later remodeled to be Pine Springs Methodist Church.

Concerned because the kittens' eyes wouldn't open, the boys loaded their arms with the little fellows and took them to the kitchen in search of help. Finding nobody there, they went on through the house and out the front door right into the middle of Lorena's wedding!

Their exit caused quite a stir! Grandpa Joel, in consternation, grabbed the youngsters, one under each arm. Shedding mewing kittens all over the place, he bustled them back inside. Ralph couldn't understand why everyone was laughing. Why were they laughing at the poor blind kittens?

Old Mr. Hill Wolfe, living next door to the News on what was left of his farm, was further crippled in Meridian when hit by a streetcar. He died two weeks before Christmas in 1922 and was buried beside his wife Lucile (Miss Luly) in the local cemetery adjacent to the Pine Springs school.

On December 28, Tommy Wolfe, Mr. Hill's heir, sold the remainder of his late father's farm—sixty acres less the three acres Joel New had purchased earlier—to Joel New for $500. [See copy of deed.] Joel had to borrow the money, but with this sale the New's total land holdings increased to 162 acres. (After this sale Tommy and his wife, Julia Wolfe, moved to Meridian where he worked in the office of the tax assessor, W. W. Denton. Roy Wolfe, oldest of their four sons, graduated from Millsaps College in Jackson and became a well-known Methodist minister. Invited to preach at Pine Springs from time to time, Roy was probably instrumental in having Joel and Ellie New move their church letters to the Pine Springs Methodist Episcopal Church.)

On the "old Wolfe place" there was an old log house where Mr. Hill and his wife Luly had lived since 1901 when they first moved to Pine Springs. The house had been built following the Civil War by a Confederate veteran, "Uncle" Jimmy Wright, on gentle rolling land that had since been cleared

Deed from Tom Wolfe to Joel New

for plowing. Other than the old house and its garden site, it was all field except for a small crib and shed in a grazing area big enough for one horse and perhaps a couple of cows.

Joel New began to rent his "Wolfe House" to sharecroppers, folks who had no land of their own but worked for landowners for a share in what they produced. With more cotton being grown, the New farm became a profitable enterprise.

Joel finally became able to build a good-sized barn for his growing herd of cows. He set it further up the hill behind the sagging mule barn. To go with the anvil and foot-operated grindstone in his farm blacksmith shop, he bought a coal-burning hearth complete with a bellows. This made it easier to sharpen plows, shoe horses, and build and/or repair farm machinery.

KNOW ALL MEN BY THESE PRESENTS: FORM 3

THAT *H. C. Wolfe*

of *Lauderdale County* and State of *Mississippi*

in consideration of *Fifty-five* _____ Dollars received

from *Joel New* of *Lauderdale County*

and State of *Mississippi* do grant, bargain, sell and convey unto the

said *Joel New* _____ the following described premises,

situated in *The* _____ County of *Lauderdale*

State of Mississippi, and described as follows:

Beginning at Northwest corner and running east along said line one hundred (46) and forty yards to wire fence, and South from said corner One hundred (189) and eighty-nine yards, and then North east along wire fence to where it intersects east line. This being Northwest corner of the N. E. ¼ of the S. W. ¼ of Sec 4, T. 7, R 15 east and containing Three (3) acres more or less.

To have and to hold the above described premises, with the appurtenances thereunto

belonging, unto the said _____ *Joel New* _____ *his*

heirs and assigns, forever. And I _____ the said *H. C. Wolfe* _____

_____ for *myself* and my

heirs, executors and administrators, do covenant with the said *Joel New*

his _____ heirs and assigns, that *I am* seized in

fee of the above described premises and have good right to sell and convey the same,

that they are free from all encumbrances, and that *I will* warrant

and defend the title of said premises to the said *Joel New*

his _____ heirs and assigns, forever, against all lawful claims whatsoever.

IN WITNESS WHEREOF *I* hereunto set *my* hands and seal

the *21st* day of *March* _____ 1918.

H. C. Wolfe [Seal]

Deed from Hill Wolfe to Joel New

The frame house that Joel and his boys had built when they first came to Pine Springs remained sturdy and comfortable, but it had never been painted. Now that times were better Miss Ellie, thinking Joel should do something about that, had him send to Meehan Junction for his nephew, Charley New. Charley, called "Grandma," was in his thirties, the oldest son of Joel's late brother Luke. (Luke had been run over by a train.) Charley had become an excellent housepainter, if one could keep him sober long enough to finish a job.

Charley came and was doing a fine job of painting his Uncle Joel's house—until the weekend approached. Takin' nips from his jug of moonshine, he soon began laughing and talking a mile-a-minute. Joel was working in the field but the women grew tired of Charley's shenanigans. Lorena, visiting her mother, lured Charley to the barn; she told him that was where Papa hid his jug.

Charley stumbled into the crib and rooted through the ears of corn, looking for Uncle Joel's 'stash.' Lorena quickly barred the door so he couldn't get out.

"Lo-REEN-a! Lo-RENAL," Charley hollered, "Pu-LEESE turn me loose!" Poor Charley called and called until he finally went to sleep.

That evening when Joel came from the field he went to the barn to feed his mule. He heard Charley's pitiful plea, "Please, Please, Uncle Joel, *pu-leese* open the door. That Lorena's done shut me in the crib. I can't get out and I gotta PEE!"

After this episode Charley finished painting Uncle Joel's house with no further incident.

Then, in the midst of the good times of the early 1920s, Joel's wife Ellie suffered a stroke. When Ellie became an invalid, a trained nurse, Miss Ruth Johnson, moved into the New home to provide constant bedside care. Ellie's mother, Grandma Mary Pratt, had grown feeble but helped Miss Ruth all she could. Despite their efforts Mrs. Ellie New died on the thirteen day of October in 1926. Joel had her buried in Fellowship Baptist Church cemetery beside the graves of their premature infant, Mary New, and Ellie's father, Joseph A. Pratt.

The above Ruth Johnson, a registered nurse, was the oldest daughter of the New's near neighbor, the late Fred Johnson, a widower, who was killed by a falling tree. The teenaged Johnson boys, with no parents, worked their farm alone. Joel checked on them every week to offer suggestions and help. They had learned to love Mr.

Joel and Miss Ellie, and wanted to furnish special music for Miss Ellie's funeral.

In later years Dr. Reuben Johnson recalled that at the funeral the Johnson boys, one playing violin and the other a trombone, played a hymn while family and friends filed past Ellie's casket. The music was moving and the mourners went to pieces.

"The sobbing from the congregation sounded like doomsday," Adolph Johnson said. "We said we'd never again play for a funeral."

Joel wanted to pay Ruth Johnson for her nursing Ellie in her final illness. Ruth refused his offer. Joel then went to the courthouse and recorded a land deed to Miss Ruth, a deed giving her twenty acres of his farm. This plot, which bordered on the Johnson farm, was a wee part of Joel's "old Wolfe place."

In the late 1920s the Lauderdale County school board didn't own school busses but began the practice of paying private motor-bus owners to transport the students. Bus owners were required to bid for a school route and Joel New's bid was accepted as one of the two school routes reaching from Pine Springs to Center Hill High.

With money borrowed from his son-in-law, Curtis Snowden, Joel traded his old Model 'T' school bus for a new Model 'A' Ford. The Model 'A,' a 'step-down,' had no body, but had a windshield and two folding seats behind the steering wheel.

Joel, in his sixties and feeling his age, hired a local carpenter, Odie Snowden, to construct a handmade wooden school bus body with a door at front for passengers. Mr. Odie didn't have glass for side windows but left long openings above the padded front-to-back seats—benches down each side with a double bench down through the middle. The side openings had black waterproof tarp curtains that could be strapped up or be lowered in cold or rainy weather. The New boys, Herman,

Joe, and Irvin, painted the body of the new bus black and, switching to white, printed "Center Hill Consolidated School" down each side.

Ralph Snowden related, "The new bus had four cylinders. Larger than Grandpa's old bus, it held about forty kids. It had a sweet-running engine. Granddaddy used to take fishing trips on that bus with Herman or Joe being his drivers." (They also took turns at being their father's school-bus drivers until they graduated from high school.)

Joel became lonesome after Miss Ellie died. With better transportation, he went fishing more often with his brother, Elijah (Lige) New. To look at the two men one could hardly believe they were brothers. Joel, two years younger than Lige, was a short little fellow while Lige was tall as well as being just naturally big. They both shared the same sense of humor and both enjoyed laughing, as had their long deceased Irish mother, Margaret Bishop New.

Joel New, getting the mail

Miss Ellie's death left Joel and the youngest of their children—Herman, Joe, Susie Mae, and Irvin—to continue their life on the Pine Springs farm. With the help of the sharecroppers living in the Wolfe house, Joel and his boys carried on the grueling farm work. Susie Mae, a teenager, was the only girl left to do the "woman's work" around the house. Joel began to have old Blannie White, a black woman born to former slaves, to help with the cooking, washing, and ironing. Joel didn't have to pay her much.

The blacks, very poor, would work for meager wages. One black lady complained that all she got for dong the weekly wash for a large family was "a worn out man's shirt an' hit a-needin' patchin'!"

White folks usually turned a blind eye when they found black servants filching leftover food or an item of worn clothing. They likely felt guilty for paying them so little.

On the days that Blannie worked for the News, she walked the two miles from her home in the morning but usually one of the boys took her home after she finished her work. One evening Joel came into the kitchen to tell Blannie that it was time to go. As he walked in he saw Blannie empty a bag of salt into her wide apron pocket

"Hold on Blannie!" he cried, "You takin' all my salt?"

"Lardy Mercy, Mr. New," she replied. "If'in I knowed that was all you had I wouldn't have too-ken it!"

Joel, finding this amusing, did not make her put it back.

As Joel became too frail to do hard work, Herman gradually took over the farm operation. At Christmas in 1929, Herman married Miss Hettie Jane White, one of the four daughters of Mart and Sarah Brett White of Obadiah. He brought his bride home to live with his folks.

Come spring, Herman, assisted by his two younger brothers, took over the plowing and plantin' but old Joel, still calling the shots, made all the important decisions. By summer-time Herman's young wife had become quite dissatisfied.

Hettie Jane found managing the busy New home a daunting experience. Even with Susie Mae's help, the gardening, cooking, canning, raising chickens, and milking cows was still more than she felt she could handle. Growing up with a mother and three sisters, she was not used to managing this much work, and her father-in-law's abrupt manner brought more discomfort. Not understanding his personality, she thought him the meanest man she had ever met.

(Lorena, in a frank manner like her father's, called a spade a spade. She said that "Het" was just lazy. She reported that Hettie Jane didn't iron her fresh-washed sheets as did other wives, but folded and placed them in chairs where folks sat around the fireplace at night. "Het had their 'hinies' doin' her ironing!")

After harvest Herman and Hettie Jane moved to Obadiah to live with an older widow who lived alone on her farm with no one to work her land. When Herman spoke of leaving, Joel wrote to Henry New, his oldest son who had returned from the "Great War" (World War I) and found a job in Texas. He wrote Henry that if he would return home he would deed him the farm.

Henry didn't enjoy farming. To get away, he had talked his brother Leon into leaving home with him and, together, they had joined the U.S. Army near the time the United States became involved in World War I. They were sent to the Philippine Islands but were separated when Henry was sent to Russia and Leon was sent to China. When the war ended Henry came back with a girl he met and married while stationed in Siberia.

Henry's wife couldn't speak much English but pronounced her maiden name **Olga Vinona**

Zienka. (Not sure of the spelling, but that's the way it sounded to Pine Springs folks, who thought "foreigners" a curiosity. They found her fascinating and called her, simply, Olga New.)

Henry and Olga, with their two little girls, Lorena and Louise, came back at a bad time. The year before (in 1929) the stock market had crashed, marking the beginning of a great financial depression. However, unlike "city folks," families could at least raise food so their children didn't have to go to bed hungry.

Ready money soon became non-existent. Money suddenly vanished. If a fellow managed to get a dollar bill, he ran around proudly showing it to his neighbors. So many textile mills closed that there was scarcely any sale for cotton. Unsold bales of cotton had to be stored in Meridian's warehouses.

Henry New, among others, gave up planting cotton; it cost more to produce than it brought when it was sold. He used the profit from Joel's school bus to pay bills. Even this small stipend ended when public schools ran out of money and the school board began to issue vouchers, IOUs, to teachers and bus owners to be honored if, or when, times improved.

After using all available cash, Henry began to sell the milk cows. Joe, Susie Mae, and Irvin, worried that there would be no money for taxes, complained to their sick father.

After listening to his children, Joel sadly burned his agreement with Henry, holding it over the kerosene lamp. He said it seemed that Henry just wasn't cut out to be a farmer.

His health failing, Joel was forced to take to his bed. Lorena New and her husband, Lawrence "Humpy" White, had moved to live in the old Wolfe House so Lorena was around to help Olga and Susie Mae take care of their father. Humpy, since the depression, had been laid off from his

work at the Meridian railroad shop. They had two small children, Ina Pearl and Edward Earl White.

When Joel broke out in ulcers all over his body, Dr. Dee Pace had him admitted to the Meridian Sanitarium. He was sixty-seven when he died on February 18, 1931.

All Joel New's children gathered around his deathbed. His next oldest son, Leon New, had driven an old beat-up truck all the way from west Texas to tell his father goodbye. Brother Olan Snellgrove, a Methodist layman minister from Meridian who often preached at Pine Springs, led Joel New's burial service at Pace's Fellowship Baptist Church. They buried Joel there beside the graves of his second wife, Ellie Pratt New, and the little grave of their premature infant, wee Mary Margaret New.

When Joel New died, Henry gave up farming and went to work for the government, handing out food commodities to destitute people who hadn't enough to eat. He and Olga left Pine Springs and rented a house above Center Hill at a village called Shucktown. Later he opened a barbershop down at McComb in south Mississippi.

With Henry New gone, there was nobody on the farm but Joel's three last children, teenagers Joe, Susie Mae, and Irvin. Joe had recently graduated from high school, but Susie Mae was in her senior year and Irvin had two more years to go. Lacking money to operate the school bus, they sold it to Curtis Snowden, their sister Minnie's husband. The Snowdens, who lived a mile away on Fellowship

Deaths

JOEL NEW

Joel New, aged 67, of Pine Springs, died at a local hospital Thursday afternoon after an illness of several weeks.

Surviving him are four daughters, Mesdames G. C. Snowden. W. B. Pace, L. L. White, Miss Susie Mae New; five sons, J. H. New, Joe New, Irvin New all of Pine Springs; E. L. New, San Antonio, Texas, Herman New, Obediah, Miss.

Funeral services were held from Pace's church Friday at 11 a. m. the Rev. Snelgrove officiating. Interment following in the church cemetery.

Active pall bearers—L. L. Ratcliff, J. H. Wells, E. K. Smith, J. W. White, E. J. Trussell, S. D. Kinard.

Honorary — W. E. Chisholm, Ed Hooks, Will Kinard, Jake Smith, John Lovett, W. F. Temple, T. F. Snowden, M. L. Ayers, Prof. H. E. Martin, Dr. R. D. Pace.

James F. Webb in charge.

Church Road, hired Irvin to drive the school route.

In spite of their troubles, the young folks went on with the regular spring plowing. With Humpy's help from the Wolfe house, they planted the sandy fields with peanuts and corn to feed their cows and hogs, and sowed the bottomland with hay for the horse and mules. They didn't fool around with cotton as that seemed useless, but they planted a large vegetable garden and a big pea patch.

"Baby Snooks"—a pet name the boys gave Susie Mae after listening to a program they heard on Irvin's homemade radio—wouldn't graduate from Center Hill until next spring, but all that summer she gathered and canned produce from the garden. Joe urgently prodded her to can more. In addition to canning vegetables, he had her picking blackberries by the bucketful, peeling and drying apples, and canning peaches by the tubful. She wondered why Joe wanted so much food stored, more than they needed. She soon found the reason why. He was about to get married!

After "Snooks" graduated in May 1932, Joe married her schoolmate, Ruby Chisolm. (Ruby was the oldest daughter of Edwin and Sadie Trussell Chisolm who lived a couple miles up the road from the News.) Becoming hired as a taxi-driver, Joe and Ruby moved to Meridian, taking Joe's share of canned goods with them.

The older New family, all married, were concerned about Susie Mae and Irvin being left alone, so young to fend for themselves. Having to think first of their own obligations, they called a meeting to discuss what to do.

At their meeting they agreed to ask their next older brother, Leon New, to come home and take over, providing Snooks and Irvin a home until they came of age and could take care of themselves. In exchange, they would deed him their share of the Pine Springs farm.

Minnie Snowden and Lorena White wrote Leon to offer him the family proposal. Leon, writing back, agreed to come but said he did not have money to move just yet. However, he would send his wife and their two little girls that fall in time to start school, but he couldn't come himself just yet. Next year he would be there for spring planting.

Thus ends the saga of Joel New. The story of Edward Leon and Maebelle Burnham New is told in the next chapter.

The Four Children of Joel and Mamie Wellborn New

I. Joel Henry New

Born: February 2, 1894, Lauderdale County, Mississippi
Died: 1944, Jackson, Mississippi, buried in Dallas, Texas
Married: **Olga Vinona Zienka** in Russia, circa 1918

Growing up on his father's farm in Pine Springs, in 1914 he and his younger brother Leon got jobs before both enlisted in the U.S. Army on February 22, 1915. They were sent to the Philippines but became separated when Henry was sent to Russia with an American Expeditionary Force. At the close of World War I, he was honorably discharged after serving four years. He married a girl from Siberia and brought her home to

Cpl. Joel H. New

join his brother Leon in Texas. Their two children were both born in Dallas.

When his aging father needed him, Henry moved his family to Mississippi to take over the farm. For various reasons this didn't pan out (due to the depression and all that), so Henry moved his family to southern Mississippi where he opened a barbershop in McComb. In 1944 he became ill and was admitted to the VA Hospital in Jackson where he died. His wife Olga had him buried in Dallas where they had lived when she first came to America.

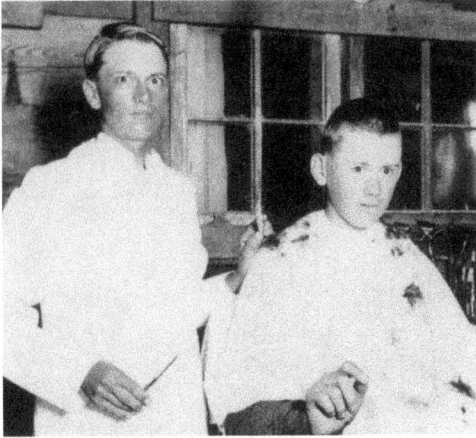

Joel Henry New, barber.
His army buddies called him "Jack"

Children of Henry and Olga New:
1. **MARGARET LORENA NEW** (b. 1920, d. 200_), m.
   (1) **William T. Bond**
   (2) _____
   Children:
   A. **Jack** (b. 1943)
   B. **Henry** (b. 1944)
   C. **Margaret** (b. 1945)
   D. **Bill** (b. 1951)

Joel Henry New, Edward Leon New with a friend –
World War I

Children of Joel and Mamie New:
Minnie Lee, Joel Henry, Marie, Edward Leon

2. **LOUISE NEW** (b. 1922, d. ___), m.
   Randall Carpenter, 1943, Hot Springs,
   Arkansas.
   Children:
   A. **Randall Jr.** (b. 1944)
   B. **Wayne Lanier** (b. 1946), m. **Ann**
      1. Children: **Jefferson Lanier**

Edward Leon New in China

II. *Edward Leon New*

Born: May 6, 1895, Point, Lauderdale County,
Mississippi

Died: April 4, 1955, buried in the Pine Springs
Methodist Church cemetery

Married: **Maebelle Edna Burnham**, Stamford,
Texas, July 29, 1923

Biography of Leon New given in the following chapter.

Edward Leon and Maebelle Burnham New

Children of Leon and Maebelle New:

1. **Edna Mae New** (b. 1924, d. 2004), m.
   Edwin William Shields
2. **Mary Ellen New** (b. 1926, d. ____), m.
   James Monroe White
3. **Constance Amelda New (b.** 1942, d. ___),
   m. **Jay Lee Neil, MD**
4. **Mable Sue New (b.** 1944, d. 1948), died
   young of burns

III. *Minnie Lee New Snowden*

Born: September 7, 1896, Chunky Station,
Lauderdale County, Mississippi

Died: November 27, 1946, buried in the
Fellowship Baptist Church cemetery

Married: December 31, 1913, to **Curtis Gray
Snowden**, son of James G. and Pinkney May
Snowden of Center Hill, Lauderdale County

Curtis bought a farm on Hooks-Fellowship Road in Pine Springs, a half-mile east of Minnie's father. In the late 1920s they covered the old log pre-Civil War house on the place with lumber and painted it white. After the farm was sold, the old house was used by other owners.

Curtis—and Minnie, too—were good managers. Neither was afraid of work, and they prudently husbanded their money. Even in the 1930s during the Great Depression, they seemed to stay a tad ahead of others. No matter how tough the times, Minnie always presented a smiling face, a ready laugh. They had helped her dad when he bought his new school bus and had helped with his hospital bill in his last illness, so Curtis took over the school bus route when Mr. New died.

Minnie was fifty years old when she died of breast cancer. Curtis, in his later years, became a game warden for the Mississippi Wildlife Management Bureau. Still interested in politics and world affairs, he was eighty-nine when he died in 1977.

The Snowdens had four children but only two survived childhood.

Minnie Lee New Snowden

Children of Curtis and Minnie Snowden:
1. **JOEL EDWARD SNOWDEN** (1914–1914), infant, lived one day
2. **MARION RALPH SNOWDEN** (b. January 15, 1916, d. March 11, 1995), m. **Stella Harris**, daughter of E. L. "Pat" and Pearl Bozeman Harris on January 21, 1939. Ralph, valedictorian of his high school class, had an artistic bent, although never developed. He built their first home on four acres of land on a corner of the New's

Curtis Gray and Minnie Lee New Snowden

farm but later sold it back, with the house, to his uncle Leon New. He bought a larger farm further down Pine Springs Road where he built another home, along with several ponds, going into the wholesale minnow business, raising minnows for fish bait.

They had two children: **Sylvia Lynn** (b. October 15, 1940), m. **William Larry Brown**, children, **Daniel Scott** (b. April 1981) and **Jonathan Blair** (b. November 1983); **Ralph Jr. "Butch,"** (b. October 23, 1944), (1) m. **Dorothy Louise Smith**, children, **Theresa Louise "Terry"** (b. April 19, 1961) and **Marion Ralph III "Trey"** (b. August 21, 1962) (2) m. **Brenda Viverett**, child **Carla Snowden**.

Ralph and Raymond Snowden

3. **CURTIS RAYMOND SNOWDEN** (b. May 6, 1918, d. September 1920), he choked on a watermelon seed and died from the surgery that followed.

4. **RUTH EARLINE SNOWDEN** (b. April 28, 1924–____), m. **Earl Bennet Wilson** (d. April 17, 2013) of nearby Obadiah. Earline was born and grew up in the Snowden house on Hooks Fellowship Road. After high school she worked at JC Penny for a year and then stayed home to care for her mother who passed away in 1946. Bennet

managed Singer Sewing Centers, starting in Meridian, then Laurel, Mobile, and Jackson. The last center was in Pensacola where Bennet later retired and passed away in April 2013. Earline still lives alone in the same home near one of her daughters. For her ninetieth birthday, niece Terry Brister hosted a party

Cousins Ina Pearl White and Earline Snowden

for her in the old Snowden home in Pine Springs where she was born and grew up. She still enjoys homemaking, crocheting, and crafty type things.

Bennet and Earline's two children are **Wanda Camille** (b. November 19, 1952), m. Charles McKnight, and **Marsha Elaine** (b. January 13, 1954), m. Barry Hines.

IV. Marie New Pace

Born: September 17, 1898, Chunky Station, Lauderdale County, Mississippi

Died: October 28, 1981, Beaumont, Texas, buried in the Fellowship cemetery, Lauderdale County

Married: Wm. Bennett "Ben" Pace, son of Andrew and Levisa Ann Love Pace, on July 29, 1917. ("Andy" Pace was brother of Dr. "Dee" Pace of Obadiah; Ben was the doctor's nephew.)

Upon her mother's death in 1900, Marie's father took her and her older brothers and sister to live near her Aunt Allie and Allie's husband, Dr. Dee Pace, in Obadiah. As the youngest (age two) of the New children, Marie soon became a Pace favorite, her Aunt Allie's ladylike ways making

Marie New Pace

an impression upon the little child.

When her father re-married and bought a farm in Pine Springs, Marie entered the local grammar school. Upon her finishing eighth grade at Pine Springs, Marie stayed on for a year or two helping with the teaching of English, Latin, and math. Wanting her to go on with her schooling, Joel New made arrangements for Marie to attend the closest high school up in Daleville. She would board with Aunt Allie and Dr. Pace. After a while Dr. Pace didn't want the responsibility of worrying about this attractive teenager, and he sent her home to her father.

Marie was nineteen when she married Ben Pace. At age twenty-nine, he was tall and

Marie New Pace holding James Andrew, Mamie and Elaine

handsome, a likable fellow who loved to talk, not letting truth stand in his way. When spinning an unlikely tale, Marie would quietly reprove, "Now, now, Ben—is that what *really* happened?"

When Ben was young, his father Andy Pace, a timber man, moved the Pace family often so Ben learned little about farming. When he and Marie married, they had no money or land, but share-cropped on various farms. Marie, an excellent seamstress, took in sewing to bolster their meager income. They later moved to Meridian where Ben was hired as a guard/night-watchman. Marie, like her father, spoke frankly, but kindly, as would a lady. She gently corrected her young relatives' grammatical mistakes while not tolerating the unrefined smacking of chew-gum.

Ben Pace was sixty-two when he died in 1951 and was buried at Fellowship Church. Marie went to live with one or the other of her four married

Ben and Marie Pace

Marie New Pace

children. She was at the home of her oldest daughter, Mamie Burkett, when she died in Beaumont, Texas. She was returned home for burial beside her Ben at the Fellowship Baptist Church cemetery in Lauderdale County, Mississippi.

Children of Ben and Marie New Pace:

(Marie used to say that she had six granddaughters with half being named Patricia.)

1. **MAMIE ANNIE PACE** (b. September 1918, d. 199_), m. **Dewey Page Burkett**, a Floridian who arrived in Lauderdale County during the depression years with the CCC, the Civilian Conservation Corps, a federal program formed during the depression to provide jobs for young men hired to build state and federal parks, etc., with part of their pay being sent home to aid their improvident family. Page had no opportunity for formal education, but was a handsome young man, a good talker who had a way with the ladies. Mamie dropped out of school when they married.

After they married Page tried farming but then took up carpentry. They moved to Panama City, Florida, and then on to Vidor, Texas, a town outside Beaumont. Divorcing Page in midlife, Mamie kept their home in Vidor. After her death the two Burkett girls—**Carol Patricia** and **Karen Page Burkett**—chose to remain in Texas.

2. **RORENA ELAINE PACE** (1920–1998), m. (1) **Joseph Ulmer "Sonny" Bozeman Jr.** of Meridian, Mississippi and (2) **D. F. McFarland** in California.

Following high school Elaine worked as a waitress in Joe Bozeman's Café in Meridian where she met and married her boss's son, "Sonny" Bozeman. After having a daughter, little **JoAnn Bozeman**, they moved "out west," where after a time, Elaine and Sonny divorced. Elaine worked her way up in a clothing manufacturing plant in California, becoming a sewing supervisor.

Elaine next married an older man and, after he retired, they went to live near Las Vegas in Boulder City, Nevada. Becoming ill after her second husband died, Elaine went to Vidor, Texas, to live in a rest home administered by her niece, Karen Burkett. Elaine's daughter, Jo Ann Bozeman had married Hughes Courtland, but died before the death of her mother, Elaine, who died at age seventy-six.

Elaine, along with intelligence and ambitions, had also been an artist, her oil paintings drawing favorable comment in the art world. She exhibited her paintings in an art gallery in Las Vegas.

3. **JAMES ANDREW PACE** (1922–1989), m. (1) **Helen Agatha White**, (2) **Ms. Jacquline Everett Woodall**

Enlisting in the U.S. Army in 1942, James served in Germany during World War II, and married Helen in 1946 after the war ended. They had two daughters by 1952 when he rejoined the Army Quartermaster Corps and was sent to an Army Food Service School at Ft. Hood, Texas.

After training he was assigned to food service at Ft. Knox, Kentucky. He served several hitches in the Philippines, Korea, and Vietnam but was returned to Ft. Knox to continue as food service advisor of the 124th Transportation Command. He was promoted to chief warrant officer in 1966, and after serving twenty-three years, he retired from the military in 1969.

Upon being discharged from the Army he returned to Mississippi and bought a small acreage for their mobile home in Obadiah community. Becoming employed by Sears-Roebuck Store, he installed home heating and air-conditioning systems. After their daughters married, James divorced Helen to marry Mrs. Jackie Woodall, a woman with children, and moved with her to Collinsville. At age sixty-eight he died in Meridian's Anderson Hospital. His and Helen's children were **Betty Lou Pace** (b. 1948), m. Rodger Vaughn Whobrey, and **Helen Patricia "Patsy" Pace** (b. 1951), m. Michael Prentis Townsend of Lauderdale County.

4. **RUTH MARIE PACE** (b. September 12, 1928–_____), m. **Dewey Van O'Mire** of Meridian.

After graduating from high school, Ruth married Van who worked for the Sammy Davidson Plumbing Company (today's Southern Pipe Company). They bought a home on Royal Road near Meridian's Highland Park. They had one daughter, **Patricia Kaye O'Mire**. When Van's job took him to Baton Rouge, Louisiana, Ruth became a legal secretary for a young lawyer just out of law school. Over the years as the law practice grew to about 30 lawyers so did Ruth's responsibilities as manager of the practice. When she retired, the first lawyer retired also. Her husband Van's health problems increased with his retirement, which included heart disease and lung cancer. He died in Baton Rouge on April 23, 2006. Ruth moved to Florida to live close to her daughter Kaye who was married to James Ernest Wall. They live in Celebration City, a model city built by Disney.

Six Children of Joel and Ellie Pratt New

I. Vivian Lorena New White

Born: July 14, 1902, Obadiah, Lauderdale County, Mississippi
Died: January 22, 1987, buried in the Pine Springs Methodist Church cemetery
Married: March 1919, to **Lawrence Lavelle "Humpy" White**, son of John Wesley and Lidie Wilson White of Pine Springs

The fifth child of Joel New and eldest of Ellie's six children, Lorena New was born in the Obadiah community and was two years old when her father bought his farm in Pine Springs. Growing up on the farm, she married a neighbor's

Friend Claudia Adams with Lorena
New and Susie Mae New, 1915

son when she was seventeen. Her husband was a genial mild-mannered fellow, apparently content to let Lorena boss him around—not that it did much good. He just grinned and let her think that she was the boss.

Lawrence had acquired his nickname "Humpy" after injuring his back when he and his

brothers helped their Aunt Lee Dabbs build her large fishing pond. His spine grew back crooked and his family, with their usual good-natured irreverent humor, gave him the nickname which he never seemed to mind. He was able to carry on his share of work without physical complaint.

Lawrence and Lorena New White on their wedding day
with Herman, Joe, Susie Mae, and Irvin New

Miss Lorena New and friend
Ollie Calvert, 1918

Lorena New and Lawrence White. Daughters
Ina Pearl and Jackie

When Lorena and Humpy married, he was working at a railroad machine shop in Meridian. In 1930 when their two young children, Ina Pearl (10) and Edward Earl (8), Humpy got railroad passes so they could all ride to Texas to visit Lorena's brother Leon New. Leon had married a Texas girl and they lived on his mother-in-law's goat ranch at Fischer Store, a community on the Guadalupe River a few miles northwest of San Antonio.

They had a wonderful time in Texas, barbequing goat, picnicking, and swimming in the nearby river. It was good that they went when they did; after they returned home, Humpy, due to the increasing hard times, was laid off from his railroad job.

Because of the depression, there were no jobs to be found, so the Whites lived here and there, sharecropping wherever they could find a place to stay. Whenever they moved Lorena's younger brother, Joe New, would come with the mules and wagon to load their belongings. Joe said Lorena moved so often that when he drove into her yard her chickens would run and jump on the wagon's coupling-pole, ready to ride to the next place.

The Whites were living in the old Wolfe house, sharecropping on the New place in 1936, the year their third and last child, Mable Jacqueline "Jackie" White, was born.

In addition to field crops, they usually planted large vegetable gardens, and Humpy sometimes found odd jobs that helped out. His older brother, Ernest White, a motor-grader driver for Lauderdale County's Beat 3, used the machine to clean out ditches along the county's dirt roads and to blade out the deep ruts caused by traffic through the mud. County jobs were much sought after but Ernest, exerting a little 'pull,' was helpful in getting Humpy hired.

When a niece asked Lorena about Humpy's work with the county, Lorena told her that he was a *Pile-it*. Confused, the little girl said she didn't know that the county had airplanes.

"They don't," Aunt Lorena replied. "When a truck drives up with a load of dirt, Humpy points his long stick, saying 'Pile it here' or 'Pile it there!' As I said, he's a Pile-it." Things became better in the 1940s, World War II bringing about an end to the depression. Around 1943 Lorena's oldest sister, Minnie Snowden, became ill with cancer. Her husband, Curtis Snowden, built a new four-room house on his Pine Springs farm near his home for Lorena and Humpy. The Whites lived there for several years, Lorena supervising the housework of both houses while caring for her sick sister. By then Ina Pearl had married and Edward Earl, in the U.S. Army, was fighting overseas in Germany. They had only their youngest daughter, Jackie, remaining at home, a youngster in grade school.

No one ever heard Lorena complain as, with steadfast good humor, she took on added responsibility. Even during dark days when they heard that their son was wounded in Germany, she kept her head up and carried on.

In Germany, Edward Earl had stepped from an army truck onto a land mine, wounding his legs. After a brief stay in an army hospital he was awarded a Purple Heart and allowed a month-long furlough at home, recuperating, before returning to active duty.

After the war ended in 1945 and Minnie Snowden died in 1946, Humpy was hired by a Mr. Ready to manage the dog shelter located at Meridian's Highland Park. The Whites moved into the provided house. Noting how good Humpy was with animals, A. P. Carney offered him a job on his cattle farm east of Meridian. Humpy accepted, and they moved to the Carney farm, not far outside the city.

At last, growing older, they gladly returned to Pine Springs where their son-in-law, L. J. Raley—Pearl's carpenter husband—had built them a

Lawrence and Lorena New White

two-bedroom house of their own on a small land lot behind Lee Ratcliff's General Store, across the road from Pine Springs Methodist Church. It was the only house they ever owned.

Humpy, Lawrence L. White, died in 1974 at age seventy-seven. After he died Lorena lived alone until one night, hopping on one foot while washing the other in the bathroom sink, she fell and broke her hip. Somehow she managed to crawl across the floor to pull on the telephone wire to dislodge the phone from the table. Unable to see in the dark, she dialed a number at random and told whoever answered to call her daughter at the number she gave. The person (whoever it was) called Ina Pearl who came with L. J. to take her to the emergency room.

After that the Raleys moved in with Lorena where they lived with her until she passed on. She died at age eighty-five and was buried next to the grave of her husband Lawrence and their son, Edward Earl, in Pine Springs Cemetery.

Children of Lawrence Lavell and Vivian Lorena New White:

1. **INA PEARL WHITE** (b. February 9, 1920, d. May 2005), m. **L. J. Raley**, a carpenter.

    They had no children but Pearl followed L. J. from place to place, living near the sites where work happened to take him. In the 1960s they bought a land lot in Pine Springs for their mobile home, behind the site where L. J. later built the house for Pearl's parents. When Pearl's widowed mother needed them, the Raleys came to live with her, inheriting her home when she died.

    Later, after L. J. died, Pearl lived alone. Her cousin, Jerry White and wife, Betty, living next door, kept an eye on her, helping when needed. With her health deteriorating, they admitted her to Meridian Rest Home where she died in 2005.

2. **EDWARD EARL WHITE** (b. September 18, 1922, d. August 9, 1969), m. **Doris Florette Brown**, daughter of W. F. and Mary Ellen White Brown of Obadiah.

    Edward Earl was inducted into the wartime U.S. Army before he graduated from high school. Becoming a member of the Wolf Pack Division, he was sent to Germany where he was wounded, receiving the Purple Heart medal.

    At war's end he came home and married his local sweetheart, Florette. Then, taking advantage of the Veterans' G.I. Bill, he entered a school at Belzoni, Mississippi, to learn the craft of watchmaking. Finishing the school, he first worked for Rose Jewelry Store in Meridian, but upon being offered more money, he and Florette moved south to Milton, Florida. They were living in Florida when he died at age forty-seven in 1969. Florette brought him home for burial in the Pine Springs cemetery.

Florette did not remarry but returned to Meridian with their three daughters—**Marilyn**, **Susan**, and **Tina**. (Florettes's mom, Mary Ellen White Brown, was sister of Hetty Jane White who had married Herman New, q.v., and was also a cousin of Lawrence White, Edward Earl's father.)

3. **MABLE JACQUELYN "JACKIE" WHITE** (b. October 5, 1936, d. _____), m.
   (1) **Clyde Thompson**,
   (2) **Richard L. Miles**.

Born in the "Wolfe House" on the New's Pine Springs homestead, Mrs. Jackie Miles writes:

"During my childhood we lived in almost every house in the neighborhood. We attended the Methodist Church (in Pine Springs). Although most of the time we had to walk. No car. This was called the 'good old days.'

"I rode the school bus to attend Center Hill School where I played basket ball and joined the 4-H Club and the Homemakers Club. In the fall of 1952 I met Clyde Thompson and fell in love. We were married January 24, 1953. We had three children, all daughters. Clyde died of a cerebral hemorrhage sixteen days after our 25th wedding anniversary. [Note: Clyde Thompson was cousin of Van O'Mire, the husband of Ruth Marie Pace, q.v.]

"Deciding I wanted to be a nurse, I went back to school and in June, 1964 I was in the first class of students from Anderson Hospital to graduate from Meridian Junior College as a Licensed Practical Nurse. Proud of my Nurses Cap and Pin, I went to work in the office of Dr. Gus Rush.

"I later met and married Richard Miles of Meridian. We live in our home next to the Pine Springs Methodist Church, although we have been active members of Glad Tidings Pentecostal Holiness Church since 1975."

Jackie's daughters were **Regina**, **Judy**, and **Kimberly**.

II. Mary Margaret New

Born: February 5, 1904, Obadiah, Mississippi (premature birth)

Died: May 9, 1904, buried near Grandpa Pratt at Fellowship Church

Her grandma Pratt kept the premature infant alive for a few months when everyone else expected little Mary to not last at all. She was so small her mother's wedding ring could be placed on her wrist as a bracelet.

Herman and Hettie Jane White New

Herman Jackson New

III. *Herman Jackson New*

Born: February 2, 1906, Pine Springs,
Lauderdale County, Mississippi

Died: January 14, 1950, buried Mt. Carmel
Presbyterian Church, Bailey, Mississippi

Married: Hettie Jane White, daughter of Mart
and Sarah White, Obadiah

Herman was born and raised on his father's farm in Pine Springs. The two older New boys left home when Herman was a school boy, eight years old. Their departure left him the next oldest son to help his father in the fields and with other farm chores. After finishing at the local grammar school, he drove his father's mule-wagon to Center Hill High School so he and his younger siblings could continue their education. When his father bought a Ford motor school bus, he became its first driver.

After his mother died in 1926 and his father became ill, Herman took over the operation of the farm. While in his early twenties he married. But his young wife, Hettie Jane, was not happy living on the old New farm. After a year he made arrangements to operate the farm of a childless older widow who lived in Obadiah. He and Het moved to Obadiah where they remained over the next several years.

Herman and Joe New – 1919

When World War II came, Herman hired on as a carpenter to construct new military barracks at Camp Shelby near Hattiesburg, Mississippi, and at the Meridian Air Base at Key Field. (Taking time from his regular job, he built a fine new barn for his older brother, Leon New, who had bought their late father's Pine Springs farm when it was sold for taxes.)

When the war ended, Herman took over a Shell service station on Poplar Springs Drive in the northern edge of Meridian. In conjunction with his gas station, Het opened a hamburger stand, "New's Cafe," which became quite successful. Beginning with only one long bar with stools and three or four small tables, their menu increased as they added full home-cooked meals, causing the cafe to grow until more space had to be added to enlarge the dining area.

In 1950 Herman had gall-bladder surgery. Never fully recovering, he died on January 14,

Herman New riding Old Mack
to church

Joe. K. New

1950, and was buried at Mt. Carmel Presbyterian Church where he had been a deacon.

Het kept her cafe until after she married Everett Snowden of Pine Springs. Growing older, she sold "New's Café" and retired. Keeping the same name, the cafe remains a well-known Meridian eating place.

Children: None.

IV. Joe K. New

Born: April 10, 1908, Pine Springs, Lauderdale County, Mississippi

Died: March 17, 1979, buried in the Forest Lawn cemetery in Meridian

Married: Ruby Katherine Chisolm on March 29, 1932, daughter of Wm. Edwin and Sarah "Sadie" Downey Chisolm, who had moved down to Pine Springs from Neshoba County

In the New's family Bible, Joe's name was written "Jodie New" with no middle name. He always signed himself as "J. K. New," taking his wife's middle initial as his own. Joe New was an avid sport fisherman all his life. It was said that as a lad he kept a Prince Albert tin in the bib-pocket of his overalls, collecting any crickets or worms he came across to save for fish bait. After all, a fella didn't know when a spare moment would come when he could steal away from chopping

Herman and Baby Jodie (Joe) New

179

cotton long enough to check his set-hooks on the old Slough or those on Okatibbee Creek.

In addition to helping his father and older brother with the grueling farm work, Joe and his brother Herman took turns driving their father's mule-team school wagon the five miles to Center Hill High School. Herman graduated not long after their father bought his Ford school bus, leaving Joe the only school bus driver.

After both of their parents died (old Joel died in 1931), Herman, Joe, teenager Susie Mae, and young Irvin, were left alone on the farm. The young people managed to stay in school and planted a crop, but after it was harvested Joe found work driving a taxi in Meridian for a Mr. Phillips. (Phillips owned a gas station on 7th St. in Meridian, a block from the public library. In those days taxis charged passengers ten cents to ride anywhere inside the city limits.) In the spring of 1932 Joe married Miss Ruby Chisolm who lived just up the road from the New farm. They rented a two-room apartment in a private Meridian home.

Joe K. New

Hard times continued but somehow Joe managed to find a better job with the Southern Railroad Company, hiring on as a machinist in their railroad shop. Because of the depression, business remained poor, causing the railroad to make temporary layoffs of its employees. Whenever Joe was laid off, he went back to driving a taxi so they could eat. In time he became a regular employee of the Illinois Central railroad shop in Meridian.

After the Japanese bombed Pearl Harbor in 1942, business picked up. When World War II began, Joe's work became regular. They were able to build a two-bedroom home on State Blvd. on the northeast side of Meridian, where they were living when their two children, a girl and a boy, were born.

Joe and Ruby Chisolm New

Joe New enjoyed his retirement years. He and Ruby remained active members of Highland Baptist Church. Joe spent many happy hours fishing on various local private lakes. Everybody liked Joe, finding him a cheerful man of sound moral character who was genuinely interested in how they were faring.

Joe was in his seventies when he died in Anderson Hospital with a lung affliction. He was buried in Forest Lawn cemetery in Meridian. Ruby New lived to be 101 years old, passing away in April 2012.

Children of Joe and Ruby Chisolm New:

1. **EDWINA GAYLE NEW**, (June 10, 1942–____), m. **Fred Allen "Bill" Gray**, son of Zoia Brown Gray, who grew up in Pine Springs and graduated high school at Center Hill. Gayle New Gray is a registered nurse, now retired from the Lauderdale County Health Department. She and Bill built their home in Pine Springs on land that once belonged to Bill's grandparents, Clarence and Leona Williams Brown.

   The Grays enjoy boating, and Gayle finds contentment landscaping and working with flowers. She is also an oil painter with an understanding of modern art. Their four daughters are **Carla**, **Tara**, **Rosemary**, and **Danna**.

2. **JOEL KEITH "JOEY" NEW** (February 4, 1946–May 1962), while in high school, got a job working in an A&P Grocery Store. Riding his motor-scooter home from work, he was struck by a man driving a car through a stop sign. He was sixteen when he died. His grave is in the Forest Lawn cemetery in Meridian.

Susie Mae New, 1960s

V. Susie Mae New

Born: January 2, 1912, Pine Springs, Mississippi
Died: August 4, 1988, Pine Forest Sanitarium near Chunky, Mississippi, buried in Pine Springs cemetery next to the grave of her brother Leon
Married: No

Born on the New's farm in Pine Springs, Susie Mae was a young teenager (14) when her mother died. She had older married sisters and sisters-in-law that offered a little help, but the brunt of the farm's household management fell upon her young shoulders. She managed to graduate from Center Hill High School in 1930 but remained at home as there was nobody else to carry on the housewifely chores.

Susie Mae New, age 3

After her father died in 1931, her older brother Leon New, living in Texas, sent his wife and children on ahead before coming himself to take over the New farm to provide a home for Susie Mae and young Irvin. When Maebelle New arrived with her young daughters in the fall of 1932, Susie Mae felt that at last she had found a real friend. Maebelle, a few years older than Susie Mae, became the young girl's needed companion and confidant. She sewed Susie Mae new dresses on her sewing machine and embroidered her hand stitched feminine under-garments, making Susie Mae feel like a proper young lady. She never forgot what Maebelle had done for her.

A year or so after Leon and Maebelle came, Susie Mae rented a room in town as she had been hired as a waitress in Sam Shepherd's Hamburger Cafe, kitty-cornered from the new Meridian post office. Back then they sold two hamburgers and a glass of milk for ten cents. Later she was hired by

Meridian's Mayweb Hosiery Mill and earned better money. With her first big paycheck, she bought Leon and Maebelle a battery-operated radio. This was before President Franklin Roosevelt had the Tennessee Valley Dam built for the R.E.A (Rural Electric Association) to provide electricity for rural homes.

Marie New Pace, Susie Mae New, and Lorena New White. Jackie and Ina Pearl, Lorena's daughters

When World War II came, the nation's women, left behind when men were drafted for military service, took the men's places in war material plants. Susie Mae, taking a short course in sheet metal work and welding, was hired by a ship-building dry-dock establishment at Pascagoula on the Mississippi Gulf Coast. There she helped build warships until Japan surrendered in 1945 and the conflict ended.

Becoming dissatisfied with jobs she found in Meridian, Susie Mae went to Riverside, California, the "land of opportunity," where she easily found work as a waitress. After several years in California, she became homesick and, in the late 1960s, returned to Mississippi to live with Maebelle, her sister-in-law and friend. At that time Maebelle was a house mother for girls at a Seventh-day Adventist boarding high school in Chunky. Susie Mae became a work supervisor for the girls in the sanitarium/rest home.

Susie Mae New on the farm, 1918

Susie Mae found that she liked helping hospital patients. Later she was able to go back to school to become a licensed practical nurse. Upon retiring she returned to Pine Springs to live in the home of her widowed

Susie Mae New at Grand Canyon, 1960s

sister, Lorena White. After becoming ill, she died at the Pine Forest Sanitarium at the age of seventy-five. She is buried at Pine Springs cemetery next to her brother Leon.

VI. Irvin Deason New

Born: January 15, 1916, Pine Springs, Lauderdale County, Mississippi
Died: September 14, 1964
Married: October 19, 1942 to **Mildred Louise Harper** of Bonita, outside Meridian in Lauderdale County, Mississippi

Youngest of Joel and Ellie's children, Irvin was born and reared on their Pine Springs farm. His mother died when he was ten, and his father died when he was fifteen. One by one his older siblings had married and moved out until, at last, there were only young Susie Mae and Irvin left on the place. They needed help.

Two weeks before the 1932 school term began, Leon New, the next to oldest son of the family, consented to come from Texas to provide a home for the two teenagers until they could fend for themselves. Not having enough money—the depression, you know—Leon sent his wife and two little daughters ahead and planned for himself to drive back the following year in time for spring planting.

Irvin and Louise Harper New

I remember when I first met my Uncle Irvin. A tired six-year-old, I don't remember much about riding on the big bus, and then arriving at Pine Springs, but that first morning I waked in a strange bed with unfamiliar sounds—a-whump, a-whump—coming through the window. Not seeing Mama or my big sister, I slipped outside and found a young man sitting on the kitchen steps. I timidly watched a moment until curiosity got the best of me.

"What'cha doin'?" I asked, trying to sound cross. "You woke me up!"

The young man turned and said, "Why, I'm so sorry, Mary Ellen! I'm churnin' milk to get butter. Haven't you seen anyone churn before?"

"No," I said. Emboldened by his friendly smile, I sat on the steps beside him to get a better look. To my chagrin an unexpected poot escaped when I plopped down. Embarrassed, I peeked sideways at Irvin, not knowing what he might do. "Well, well," he said mildly, "sounds like you must'a sat on a frog."

Irvin New on the front steps

I immediately fell in love with my Uncle Irvin and was delighted to find that we would be living in his house. Next week when school started, Mama took Edna Mae and me to enroll at Center Hill. I was entered in first grade and was a little worried when I heard that we were expected to ride Uncle Curtis' school bus. But when I found that Irvin was the driver, I was no longer afraid. He had been driving the school bus for a while. Even when his older brother Joe was the driver, Joe would get underage Irvin to drive so that he could sit in the back by his future bride, Ruby. Now Joe had finished school and Irvin was the full-time driver.

Joe, Herman, Irvin New with dog, Ruler

That was Irvin's last year in school as he graduated in the spring of 1933, his last year at home. He and his older brother Leon, having come home from Texas, farmed that summer but that fall his brother Joe got him a job driving a taxi in town for a Mr. Phillips. Later Irvin was able to change jobs, working for the railroad for a while as a boiler maker. Through a friend, Tom Lisle Snowden, Irvin met Mildred Louise Harper from Bonita, a community just east of Meridian, around 1940. They were married October 18, 1942, at Highland Baptist Church. Their baby girl, Mabel Ann, was born July 28, 1944.

With war raging in Europe, in the late 1930s the United States began drafting men to build up its military. Irvin registered with the draft board but was turned down, having developed sinus problems while working on railroad boilers.

As factories had been geared up to meet war needs, in January 1945 Irvin was sent to Oak Ridge Tennessee to work in a defense plant.

On May 7, 1945, Germany surrendered. Everyone celebrated V-E Day (Victory in Europe Day) with wild rejoicing. But there was yet much fighting to be done, warring with Japan on the islands and atolls of the South Pacific.

Everything was kept "hush-hush" at the Oak Ridge plant, workers cautioned to keep silent about any wartime secrets coming to their attention—"Loose Lips Sink Ships" and all that. Irvin didn't know until after August 6, 1945, when the United States dropped a mighty new-type bomb on Hiroshima (Japan) that he had been helpful in developing an atomic bomb!

The second atomic bomb was dropped on Japan two days later on August 8, and on August 14 Japan surrendered. The war was over!

Returning to Meridian, Mississippi, in 1947 after the war, Irvin and Louise took a house in Meridian's "south side," and Irvin went to work for Magnolia Dry Goods Company selling Wrangler and BlueBell clothing as well as bolts of cloth. They were happy when on November 6, 1953, a son, Irvin Dwight, was born.

In 1964 as Irvin was bush hogging a field, he came upon an old fence post in the way. Climbing down to pull it up by hand, he pulled so hard it unexpectedly broke loose and struck him hard in the face. Being determined, Irvin got back on the tractor to drive home with blood running down his face. His sister-in-law Hettie Jane passed him and noticed the bleeding. She stopped him and insisted he go to the hospital. He was admitted for a few days. On the Monday morning he was

expecting to be discharged, he suddenly fell over dead. It was thought that he had a blood clot.

Louise married again in 1989, her second husband being David Marion "Pup" Snowden, a friend of Irvin's from Pine Springs, his boyhood playmate. After Pup died at age eighty-five in April 2002, Louise was placed in a convalescent home where she died on May 23, 2008.

Children of Irvin and Louise Harper New:

1. **MABLE ANN (ANNIE) NEW** (b. July 28, 1944), m. **John A. Kendall**. After Ann graduated from Mississippi State, she met John Kendall who began to call her Annie. They were married on December 29, 1969. They lived in Jacksonville, Philadelphia, Winston-Salem, Oakland, and Los Angeles. After their divorce Annie continued to live in Los Angeles for a time before returning to Winston-Salem where she still resides. She taught first grade until retirement.

2. **IRVIN DWIGHT NEW** (b. November 6, 1953), m. June 19, 1976, **Pamela Jean Hudson**, daughter of Harry L. and Virginia Reynolds of the Dalewood community.

   Graduating from Meridian High in 1971, Dwight received his bachelor's degree in visual design from Auburn University. Working for Communicorp, an advertising and public relations firm in Columbus, Georgia, Dwight has won numerous awards for his artwork designs.

   Their children are **Elizabeth Pamela** (b. 1986), **Christopher Hudson** (b. 1988), and **Emily Catalina** (b. 1990).

This Christopher is the *only male New descendent left* to carry forward the name of "New" in Joel New's line of family.

New Siblings: Irvin, Marie, Susie Mae, Joe and Lorena

Birthday Party for Ellie Pratt New, 1923:
Back row – Marie New Pace, holding Baby James Andrew Pace,
Joe New, Herman New, Minnie New Snowden, Susie Mae New
(in front of ?), Lorena New White.
Middle row – Irvin New, Grandma Ellie New, holding Edward Earl
White, Ralph Snowden.
Front row – Ina Pearl White, Elaine and Mamie Pace

Cousins: Back row – Butch Snowden, Ann New, Margaret Smith (friend),
Sylvia Snowden, Amelda New, Gayle New
Front row - Marilyn White, Jackie White holding Susan White, Ginnie Smith (friend), Joey New

Chapter XII
Edward Leon New
(May 6, 1895–April 4, 1955)

Traveling eight miles or so west of Meridian, Mississippi, heading toward Jackson on 1-20, turn left onto old U.S. Highway 80 at the Lost Gap Exit. Entering what remains of the hamlet of Meehan, turn left again onto the very next paved road. About two to three miles down this road, you will drive over a railroad track on the eastern side of Chunky River. Quickly look to your left before crossing the river bridge. On this narrow strip of land, you may get a glimpse of a lone brick chimney that marks the site of an extinct village that is no longer there. This place in western Lauderdale County which was once called Point, Mississippi.

Point was alive in 1895. True, it was small. A few railroad workers lived there with their families in houses clustered around a water tower beside the railroad track. Perhaps there was even a store. In one of the houses, there lived a happy young couple, the family of Joel and Mamie New.

Joel New was a happy man. He had it all—a reliable railroad job, a loving beautiful wife, and a handsome young raven-haired son, Henry, who had inherited his Mama's big brown eyes. To make life perfect, his beloved Mamie, in good health, was expecting their second child.

The neighborhood often called Mrs. Susan Clark, Joel New's sister, to act as midwife. Susan—Aunt Sis—was sent for that spring day (May 6, 1895) when the baby, Edward Leon New, was born.

As the infant's Grandpa was "Edward" V. New, and his Uncle was "Edward" V. New Jr., Mamie said that there were sure enough Edwards in the family so they should call the baby "Leon." And so they did.

With his boys growing bigger, Joel rented another house near the railroad over at the Chunky Station. It was closer to a school.

Living in Chunky, Mamie New had two more babies, little Minnie and Marie. Miss Mamie, a schoolmarm, had to give up her regular teaching assignments but was sometimes called upon to act as a substitute. On these occasions she took along Leon, a bright four-year-old, although he was a mite young to take learning seriously. She began to teach him to read at home, "just for fun."

Little Leon was five the summer his mama became ill. His father, not knowing what else to do, rented another house and they moved over to Obadiah, a farming community north of Meridian. Hopeful that his Mamie could be nursed back to health by her people, he rented the house directly across the dirt public road from Dr. Pace's home. Dr. Pace was Mamie New's brother-in-law.

It was necessary for Joel to continue working at his railroad job, so he left Mamie and their four children to be lovingly cared for by Mamie's younger sister, Allie Pace, when he reported to work.

Little Leon was only six in April 1901 when his mama died. Young Leon, scared and feeling alone, didn't understand what was happening. He longed for the comfort of his mother's arms.

Young Leon's maternal grandfather, Dr. David Wellborn, had become senile. No longer able to practice medicine, he and his wife, Grandma Esther Wellborn, came to live with their daughter Allie and her husband, Dr. "Dee" Pace. The doctors, Wellborn and Pace, held a mutual respect: after sharing an office and working together, young Dr. Pace said that he had learned a lot from the more experienced doctor.

Little Leon sorely missed his mama. Seeking comfort, he spent considerable time at the knee of his Grandma Esther. Grandma reminded him of his mama, telling him Bible stories and recalling the old days "befo' de wah" when she had been a Southern belle on her father's fine Georgia cotton plantation. She told of the gallant gentlemen who treated ladies with high regard, and she showed Leon how to hold his fork. She reminded him to not speak when his mouth was full. Gentlemen remain standing, she said, until ladies are all seated.

Listening, Leon fixed his blue eyes on Grandma Wellborn's face and drank it all in. Sometimes Grandpa Wellborn would pass through and pat his wife on her shoulder. "You sweet old thing, you!" he would say. He still called her his "Miss Puss."

Leon was a short plump little fellow, and Grandma Wellborn allowed that he was just a "bunch of sweetness." Other family members took it up and gave him his nickname, "Bunch." In later years Aunt Allie said that Bunch was also a peace-keeper; when the children got into a scrap, little Bunch would somehow negotiate a peace treaty.

While the News lived in Obadiah, Leon's father married again. His second wife was Miss Ellie Pratt, another schoolteacher. The first two of Joel and Ellie's six children were born while they lived in Obadiah. The second of the two, arriving early, died when an infant.

Miss Ellie, used to teaching children, treated her four stepchildren as her own, showing no difference in their care. But Leon missed the comforting love that he had enjoyed from his own mother. He respected his new mother and was quick to obey, but he addressed her as "Miss Ellie." He couldn't bear to call her "Mama."

When Leon was nine, his father bought a farm in nearby Pine Springs. When they moved over to their new farm, Mr. New stopped working for the railroad, determined to make his farm provide a comfortable livelihood for his growing family. Joel New, never afraid of labor, set his boys a hard example to follow. The next few years were the hardest that Henry and Leon had ever worked in their young lives.

Joel, knowing it was what his Mamie would have wanted, insisted that his children be educated. He enrolled them in the Pine Springs school, but after classes their farm work at home was laid out. His two oldest sons, Henry and Leon, were Joel's main help as they were the only boys tall enough to hold onto a plow handle.

The farm's eroded fields demanded attention, and the original settler's log house was hardly fit for human habitation. After that first winter spent terracing old washed-out fields and digging ditches for new fields, Henry and Leon helped their papa build a new house to replace the dilapidated log cabin. Come spring they somehow managed to plow and plant their first crop, spending long hours behind mule and plow.

Each morning the boys were awakened before dawn to go feed the mules before sitting down to their own breakfast. Young Henry, always in search of an easier way, got an idea about how they could get some extra sleep.

One evening, enlisting Leon's help, Henry placed the mule feed in buckets, which they then suspended over the feed troughs. Tying the bottoms of the pails to plow lines so they could easily be tipped, they ran the ropes up the length of the garden and through their bedroom window. They went to bed that night excited with the thought that next morning they could get some extra sleep.

Before dawn the next morning Mr. New woke the boys, as usual, so they could go feed the animals. The boys, grinning at each other, pulled on the plow lines. Mission accomplished! They turned over to go back to sleep. It didn't take Papa long to return to the sleeping boys.

"You boys get on up, now. You gotta feed those mules now so we can get plowin' by sun-up 'fore it gets too hot!"

"But Papa, the mules have been fed!" they said, and explained about their automatic mule feeder.

"You boys get on up now and feed those mules right," Joel said gruffly. "I ain't raisin' no lazy young'uns!"

Mr. New had a well dug in the front yard at the new house to make it easier to get water for household use. Henry and Leon, growing tired of bringing the mules up from the barn and waiting for them to drink, thought of digging another well down in the barn lot to save time and trouble.

They got out shovels and had dug four or five feet down when Papa came by and asked them what they were up to. When they told him, he didn't say a word but got on Dixie and rode off down the road. In a bit he returned with a well-pulley and rope, and a well-bucket, all purchased from Lee Ratcliff's country store.

The boys finished the shallow well (fortunately water was near the surface) and Mr. New helped them build a well-shelter and a watering trough. He didn't say much, but they gathered that he was pleased.

Articles appearing in the Meridian newspaper urged farmers to plant crops other than cotton, along with tips on how to better their production by practicing crop rotation. Agriculture was being taught in the county schools, and in 1909 J. R. Ellis, the county superintendent of education, announced a contest for county boys.

To introduce a better strain of hybrid corn, the county offered to furnish improved seed corn to the contestants. Each boy would get the same amount of free seed. At the end of the year, the boy who had produced the most bushels of corn would win a prize.

In the Sunday edition of *The Meridian Star*, on March 6, 1910, Superintendent Ellis announced that 100 boys had entered the corn-growing contest and were getting their ground ready—he had already passed out 12 to 15 bushels of the hybrid seed. When he listed the boys who had entered from RFD Rt. 1, Bailey, (which included Pine Springs), only two boys were named: Henry and Leon New. Sadly, we have found no record of who won the contest.

When the older New boys finished the eighth grade at Pine Springs school, Henry wasn't interested but Leon wanted to continue his schooling. The closest county high school at that time was the boarding school in upper Lauderdale County at Daleville. Being unable to afford the school's room and board fee, Joel New made an arrangement with Cliff Pace. Mr. Pace lived over at Obadiah, which was closer to the school than was Pine Springs. In exchange for Leon's accommodation during school session, Mr. New made hand-rived shingles and, with Leon's help, replaced the old roof on the Pace home. Nevelyn "Jack" Pace, Cliff Pace's son several years younger than Leon, later recalled the time that Leon New lived with them at their home.

Growing up together, the brothers Henry and Leon had a close relationship. Nearing manhood,

Henry became concerned about their future. Leon, at age sixteen, was near to graduating from high school but Henry, who didn't care much for farming, talked Leon into leaving with him to get a paying job.

After school was dismissed for the summer, they both left, against Joel's wishes, to work in a sawmill at Pascagoula down on the Mississippi Gulf Coast. Feeling guilty for leaving Papa with so much work, they both sent a portion of their monthly paydays to Joel for him to hire a plow hand to take their place.

After paying a boarding house and sending Papa money, Leon had fifty cents to spend as he wished. He studied a lot in his free time, trying to learn math. He didn't yet know what he was going to do with his life, but he knew he didn't want to go back to plowing a mule.

The boys wrote their friends back home to tell about the fine time they were having down on the coast. They must have made it sound pretty good as two Pine Springs friends, Ernest White and Luther Bailey, ran away from home to come see them and to get jobs.

The friends stayed in the boarding house with the New boys one night and then went looking for work. The sawmill would hire Ernest but they wouldn't take Luther as he was too young. Running out of money, Ernest had to wire his Uncle Charley Dabbs in Meridian for train tickets for them to return home. In later years Mr. White would laugh when he told how hungry he and Luther became on the long train trip, having no money to buy food.

The New brothers had other guests while on the coast. Miss Cecil, daughter of their Aunt Minnie Wellborn Houston, had married Tom Covington, and the newlyweds, on their honeymoon trip to Mobile, stopped by to say hello. Leon and Cecil, his favorite cousin, continued to write each other and kept in touch for years.

Henry and Leon later found better jobs at a lumber company in Alabama's Geneva County at a town called Sampson, located near the Florida state line. While they were there the sound of the big war that was raging in Europe grew louder.

For years various European countries and parts of Asia had been enmeshed in political conflict. After constant bickering over their national boundaries, in the summer of 1914 a Serb assassinated the heir to the Austrian throne, which triggered an all-out war.

England and France—and later, Italy—became allies against Germany and the Balkan States, and the "Great War" began. (Today we call it "World War I.") While the war raged in Europe, the American president, isolationist Woodrow Wilson, tried to keep the United States out of it.

The greatest challenge to America's neutrality came in February of 1915 when Germany announced that she would use submarines to destroy the Allied merchant ships and warned that neutral countries might suffer as well. The British and French retaliated by declaring a total blockade against all commercial ships to and from Germany. The United States was caught in the crossfire.

The Americans maintained a nervous peace, but the two eldest New boys decided to join the U.S. Army. On February 22, 1915, both enlisted in the Army at Ft. Oglethorpe, Georgia, and were assigned to Company K of the 27th Infantry. Private Joel H. New and Private Edward L. New, still together, were sent to an army camp at Texas City near Galveston for basic training.

On May 9, two months after the brothers enlisted, a German U-boat torpedoed a British ocean liner, the Lusitania, without warning. More than a hundred Americans, among others, were killed. U.S. President Wilson warned that any repetition of that sinking would lead to war. After sinking the Arabic, another British passenger liner, on August 19, the German government gave a definite promise of safety for passenger ships as President Wilson had demanded.

Part of the Army recruits' basic training was to send the men on twenty-mile hikes while wearing heavy G.I. backpacks. While on such a hike the New brothers of Company K were near the coast between Texas City and Galveston when a storm blew in. When night came on they were supposed to pitch their pup tents in the open, but as a fierce gale was blowing, their sergeant said they had best find shelter inside a building.

They went inside an empty brick schoolhouse and sat, listening as the wind became louder and stronger. Suddenly one wall of the school blew in, and it looked as if the entire building was about to go.

"It's every man for himself," yelled the sergeant as they scrambled to get out.

In wind so intense the men could hardly keep their feet, Leon and Henry, along with another buddy, gripped each other's hands as they sought refuge. They hunkered together on a sloping driveway in the lee of a garage. During the night the garage blew away. It sailed out over their heads, leaving the men unharmed.

When the long night ended and dawn arrived, they could see that the city of Galveston was no more. They had survived one of the strongest hurricanes on record.

After doing rescue work around the devastated storm area, the 27th Infantry was loaded onto a ship and sent to the Panama Canal to await transport to the Philippine Islands. In Panama, Leon, hearing that Spanish was spoken in the Philippines, bought himself a book to teach himself the language. He practiced by conversing with the Panamanians.

Upon leaving Panama, the 27th Infantry was shipped across the Pacific on a troop ship, the U.S.S. Logan. As part of an expeditionary force, it was to be stationed at Ft. McKinley at Rizel in the Philippine Islands.

On December 18, 1916, President Wilson, again trying to negotiate peace, secretly talked to the British and to the German governments. The British and their allies were ready for a serious discussion, but the Germans didn't trust Wilson. A month later in January 1917 came the German answer. Deciding to make a last bid for victory with their greatly augmented submarine fleet, the Germans issued a proclamation of unlimited warfare against ALL maritime commerce, the neutral as well as the belligerent.

After this proclamation the president reluctantly asked Congress for a declaration of war to "preserve civilization" and to "make the world safe for democracy."

Under strong pressure from the commander in chief, a Selective Service Act was passed by Congress. With so many raw recruits being drafted into military service, there arose a critical need for more officers.

On April 19, 1918, Corporal Edward L. New, upon passing a test, on which he scored seventh from the top in a class of 200 men, was accepted for the I.O.R.C., the Officers' Training Corps. Upon graduation he was commissioned a second lieutenant and was reassigned to the 15th Infantry, which was stationed at Tientsin, China.

For the first time in their lives, the New brothers, Henry and Leon, became separated.

(Private Henry New was equally as intelligent as Leon, but unlike Leon, was not inclined toward books. Enjoying the camaraderie of his army buddies, he became the 27th Company's barber. After Leon was sent to China with the 15th Infantry, Henry was sent to Russia with the 27th where, during his four years of military service, he met and married his Russian wife, Olga, and brought her home to Mississippi.)

Life was good to 2nd Lt. Edward L. New in China. He had new duties of course, i.e., studying military tactics, ordering non-combatants about as they taught foot soldiers how to don gas masks if attacked with mustard gas, and how to become sharpshooters. Leon became slightly deaf, which he attributed to the constant loud gunfire to which he had been subjected on the rifle range. As a commissioned officer he had records to keep and other secretarial duties, but he found time for sightseeing and other enjoyable social activities.

In China Leon found being "an officer and a gentleman" was different from being a Mississippi plowboy. Back home he was taught to mind his manners and to say "Yes, Ma'am" and "No, Sir," but now he had to learn which spoon to use for soup and which fork to choose for roast duck.

He quickly learned to hobnob with other officers and their wives without embarrassing himself too much. He was grateful to old Grandma Wellborn for teaching him good manners and how to behave as a gentleman.

On the first day of November in 1918, 2nd Lieutenant New was promoted to first lieutenant. This was ten days before a treaty was signed between the American allies and the central European powers. The armistice, signed on the eleventh hour of the eleventh day of the eleventh month, put an end to the fighting. The Great War was over! Back home there was rejoicing in the streets with horns blowing and bells ringing while churches remained open for thankful prayer. Armistice Day, November 11, was declared a national holiday.

Chapter XIII
Leon New in Texas

After spending more than five years in active military service, Lt. New returned to the States to be discharged from the Army at Camp Shelby, Mississippi, on August 19, 1919. In later years one of his small daughters asked why he had not fought with other "doughboys" in France. He replied that the Army sent him to fight in China but fortunately, the war ended before the fighting had advanced that far.

Coming home to family and friends was a joyful occasion. Joel New was glad to have his son back but hid his tears by coughing into his handkerchief. Leon's oldest sisters, Mamie and Marie, had married and already had children, but the younger Lorena had only recently married. Leon's younger brothers, Herman and Joe, had grown to become "big" boys, and his youngest sister, Susie Mae, had recently turned seven. He met his youngest brother, Irvin, for the first time as the three year old had been born while Leon was stationed in China.

To the local girls, his former schoolmates, the handsome twenty-four-year-old officer was a conquering hero. Not interested in the ladies, Leon wanted to continue his education by earning a college degree.

Leon had arrived home in late August, just in time to enroll at college. He was short on money, but he could work, and his uncle, Dee Pace, said he would help with tuition should Leon study to become a doctor. Dr. Pace was looking for

someone to take over his medical practice when he retired.

In September, Leon New enrolled in Mississippi A&M College (today's Mississippi State University) at Starkville. To help with money problems, he enlisted in the Officer Reserve Corps, retaining his rank. In the reserves he was subject to be called to camp duty for two weeks each year, along with one weekend of on-site duty each month. Promoted to the rank of captain he would receive a stipend.

After a year at Starkville, Leon was reading notices on the bulletin board when one of his instructors walked up behind him.

"Look there, New," he said, "Here's a job notice for a bookkeeper at Rule-Jayton Cotton Oil Company in Texas that pays a beginner more money than I make with my teaching degree. I don't know why you're wasting time in school. Why don't you apply for the job?"

Leon wrote to apply and, upon being accepted, he was soon off to his new employment in Texas to become a bookkeeper for a cotton-oil company.

Stamford was a small Texas town with absolutely no place for Leon to live. Another young man, Harry Fuller of Oklahoma, had also arrived there to work and found himself in the same predicament. They went to Mrs. Burnham, the boss's wife, to plead with her to let them board in the Burnham home. They promised they wouldn't drink or smoke, and they would make their own bed so as to not cause her additional trouble.

The Burnham's, Irwin and Harriet, lived in a two-story house on the outskirts of Stamford with their three children, Maebelle, Lyle, and Constance. The oldest, Miss Maebelle, was a lively high school student whom Leon found fetching, but she wasn't yet allowed to have beaus.

Mr. Irwin Cummins Burnham, a corporate lawyer and a former banker, had been named head of the Swift Gin Company in 1918, as well as secretary/bookkeeper for the Rule-Jayton Cotton Oil Company where he had hired Leon New to be bookkeeper.

The Burnham's were among the social leaders of Stamford, a growing railroad town in west Texas. Mr. Burnham, a member of the Masonic Lodge, was not active in church but encouraged his family to participate in the local Methodist Church. He was a son of the retired judge, Albert J. Burnham of Clinton, a town in Custer County in the western part of Oklahoma.

Judge Burnham, a native of Iowa, had been the first justice named to the bench in 1907 when the Oklahoma Territory was established as a state. His oldest son, Fred Nelson Burnham, Irwin's brother, was elected to a seat in the first Oklahoma legislature. Judge Burnham's wife, Irwin Burnham's mother, was Melinda Anne Cummins, a daughter of William and Catherine Cox Cummins who had been one of Iowa's first settlers.

While a law student at Valentine College in Nebraska in 1898, Irwin C. Burnham had enlisted in the U.S. Army to fight in the Spanish-American War. No, he was not a "Rough Rider" who charged up Cuba's San Juan Hill behind Teddy Roosevelt, but he had been a member of the Army Honor Guard at the funeral of William McKinley, our twenty-first U.S. president who was assassinated in 1891. At the funeral they sang the hymn, "Lead, Kindly Light," which so moved Irwin that he requested that it be used at his own funeral.

While young Irwin was away with the Army, his family left Iowa to live on a farm in the Oklahoma Territory where, after his discharge, Irwin joined his parents. Upon passing his bar examination, Irwin became a partner in his father's law firm. (In later years the area of Burnham's farm, incorporated, became part of today's downtown Oklahoma City.)

The young lawyer invested in a land claim in Butler, a community in the Oklahoma Territory near Arapaho, the seat of Custer County. Opening a law office in Arapaho, he ran for and was elected to be the county treasurer of Custer County.

Mrs. I. C. Burnham, Irwin's wife, was the former Miss Harriet Ellen Montgomery, one of the thirteen children of William and Delana Jane Rhinehart Montgomery, proud owners of a substantial Iowa farm.

One of the Montgomery daughters, Miss Harriet, had attended a fashionable ladies' finishing school. She soon became bored with hand painting china and sewing dainty embroidery. Reading about the stylish New York "bloomer girls" who rode bicycles, she wrote and asked her father to buy her a bike. Mortified that one of his daughters would even *think* of such a thing, he gave her, instead, her very own rig—a horse and buggy so she could travel about with ladylike dignity.

Upon becoming "finished," Harriet, a high-spirited young lady who happened to be quite pretty, had returned home and became a widely sought after belle. Afraid of being an old maid, she finally promised one of her suitors, a doctor, that she would marry him. But first, she told him, she wanted to travel south to visit her brother, Walter Montgomery, who had staked a land claim in the Oklahoma Indian Territory and was planning to be married.

When the headstrong Miss Harriet arrived in the territory, it was too late to take part in the Cimarron Land Run (when a fired gun had signaled would-be settlers to begin their race to stake out a claim). However, ever ready to pursue what she wanted, she began looking around for land she could purchase cheaply from some earlier claimant.

While Harriet visited her brother, Walter Montgomery married Miss Mamie Fern Burnham. Knowing Harriet was seeking land, Walter's bride suggested that Harriet consult with her lawyer brother, Irwin Burnham, to help her find suitable land and show her how to file a claim.

Thus, Irwin Cummins Burnham and Harriet Ellen Montgomery met. He helped her buy the land adjacent to his own claim near Butler in the Oklahoma Territory. They were married on April 16, 1903, in Arapaho, the seat of Custer County. Harriet never returned to live in Iowa.

(Harriet's former suitor, Dr. Hiskey of Iowa, disappointed when he heard that Harriet had married and was not coming back, graciously sent them a wedding gift. Her normally quiet new husband howled with laughter when she opened the gift and found it to be a case of the patented "Lydia E. Pinkhams Female Tonic.")

The newlyweds moved onto their combined claims at Butler. Their house was dug into the side of a hill, its roof covered with a thick layer of sod. (The few trees growing in that area made lumber a scarce commodity.) Located in the western Oklahoma cattle country, at times they could hear cows grazing overhead.

The Burnham's first child, Mable Edna, was born in the territory at Butler on February 2, 1904. (The baby was a namesake of Harriet's dear sister, Mable, who had tragically died of tuberculosis when a young wife and mother.)

When little Mable Edna entered school, she found several of her little friends had a "Belle" in their names—Clara Belle, Dora Belle, etc., which prompted the child to change her own name, with her father's permission, from "Mable" to "Maebelle." Harriet never accepted this as her child's name and continued to call her daughter "Mable" all her life.

While living on their claim in Butler, Irwin Burnham went into the banking business by opening a small bank in his law office. Their second child, Lyle Montgomery Burnham, was born in the Indian territory on May 22, 1906.

In 1907, the year that the Oklahoma Territory became a state, Irwin Burnham accepted a position in the Cotton Exchange Bank in Elk City, Oklahoma. The Cotton Exchange was a bigger bank where Irwin was pleased to find it had one of those new contraptions, a mechanical adding machine.

To move his family to Elk City, Irwin rented a house on Broadway, a noisy busy street with many trucks and carts going by. It was not unusual to see loaded freight wagons leaving town being pulled by ten to twenty mules, their high-seated drivers curling long whips in the air, making them crack.

Doing business for the bank, Irwin traveled about in a two-horse buggy to check for land sales. He called upon people who were selling their homesteads, buying them for the bank. He and one T. J. Hawkins became business partners in a miniscule broom company—Hawkins making the brooms with Irwin selling them at the various country stores he passed. He didn't get rich but was soon able to purchase a quieter house on 6th Street of Elk City.

Their new home had space for a small garden and a few chickens. Their third and last child, Constance Beatrice Burnham, was born there on January 6, 1908.

Mr. Burnham was proud of his white Leghorn chickens, each year entering some in the county fair. One year Maebelle and Lyle thought to help

Papa's chickens win a ribbon by giving them a bath. The children added too much bluing to the rinse water and the white chickens turned out to be sky blue!

The Burnham's were active in promoting the American war effort in the 1917–18 Great War. Mr. Burnham spoke at schools and elsewhere, raising the Liberty Bond quota. Mrs. Burnham worked with the Red Cross, making and folding bandages. She had her children chipping up rags and worn-out clothing to make fillers for bandages. She taught Maebelle and Constance to knit, and they both made sweaters and knitted caps for American soldiers in France.

Following the war a group of businessmen approached an Oklahoma financier, J. K. Wooten, to see about forming a new company to build, buy, and sell gins and cottonseed oil. The mills would be scattered about in west Texas near the cotton-growing plains. Mr. Wooten was agreeable, but *only* if they could find a man of integrity to place in charge.

They thought of Mr. I. C. Burnham and went to see if he would consent to being moved to Texas to work for a new company. Upon thinking it over (a sizeable boost in salary being a large inducement), Irwin said "yes" and was hired to become secretary/treasurer of the new company, the "Rule-Jayson Cotton Oil Company" and the "Swift Gin Company" down at Rule, Texas, a small town in Haskell County.

The Burnham's moved to Texas in the summer of 1918. The children were reluctant to leave after listening to their friends who thought that "Texas" was the end of the world, the jumping off place.

One of the first things that Irwin did in Texas was to buy an automobile. His family, of course, thought it a beauty, a 1917 Model T Ford, the first model Ford made that had a hard top. He taught both Maebelle and Lyle how to drive.

Self-starters for cars were not yet invented. One day Irwin was cranking his car when an associate drove by in his buggy. Seeing Irwin, he remarked, "You must plan to go a long way, Burnham, seeing as how you're winding it up so tight!"

In 1920 Irwin's company in Rule moved its main office to Stamford, a larger town that was closer to a railroad. Following Irwin's job, his family also moved to Stamford where Irwin purchased a big house in a quiet neighborhood on Webb Street near the edge of town. For the first time each child had a room of their own. In Stamford the Burnham's were among the town's leading citizens.

Of course, Mrs. Harriet Burnham took all this in stride. Becoming a leader in various ladies' organizations—Eastern Star, Ladies' Aide, etc.—she often invited guests for dinner.

On one fancy occasion Harriet served oysters that she had shipped from the coast by train. This rare treat made quite an impression as oysters were not often seen that far inland. Thereafter, "oyster stew" appeared on other menus, being the "in" thing to serve.

It was about this time, 1921, that our Edward Leon New answered Mr. Burnham's ad and came from Mississippi to Stamford, Texas. He was hired as a bookkeeper for the Rule-Jayton Cotton Oil Company.

After Leon New had stayed at the Burnham's a while and had proved himself a nice man, he was given permission to chauffeur the younger Burnham's on Sunday afternoon jaunts around the countryside in the family auto, the 1917 Ford.

One Sunday the Burnhams entertained an unmarried lady visitor who began to dimple whenever Leon was present. When it was suggested that they go for a ride, the visitor was first in line to be helped into the car's front seat, but Leon gently took her arm. "I'm sorry, but the front seat is for Miss Maebelle," he said, holding the rear door open for the visitor.

Miss Maebelle tried to not show how pleased she was but couldn't control her satisfied expression when Leon assisted her to the favored front seat.

Leon, after saving his money, bought a car of his own, a "man's" car, a two-seater Mitchell Racer. Driving his Racer he began to escort Miss Maebelle, who he was beginning to date, to church and picnics.

When Leon's older brother, Henry New, was discharged from the military and returned home from Siberia with a Russian wife, he wondered where to search for a job. Leon wrote him that he should come to Texas. He had an idea of how they could open up their own business and perhaps make some money.

When Henry and Olga New came to Texas, Leon quit his job with Rule-Jayton. Together the brothers formed a business. They leased a service station on Stamford's Main Street, along with a truck to deliver gasoline for agricultural use to the scattered west Texas farms. Leon pumped gasoline to motorists at the station and did the bookwork while Henry drove their delivery truck.

Business was slow. To further their business contacts Leon joined the "Stamford Independent Order of Odd Fellows Lodge" (No. 52) in March 1923. He also met with the nearby Abilene Chapter (No. 19).

The New gas and oil company was slow in getting started. Henry soon wanted out. He talked Leon into selling their business and moving to Dallas where they were sure to find jobs. Agreeing that they weren't doing too well, Leon said he would go.

The economy was high, but well-paying jobs in Dallas were scarce. Henry found work in a barbershop, thanks to his Army training, but Leon, staying in a rented apartment with Henry and

Olga, continued to read the "help wanted" ads in the *Dallas Morning News.*

Leon answered an ad written by somebody wanting a "pearl diver." It turned out the ad was from a café looking for a dishwasher! In desperation Leon took the job and became a dishwasher on the night shift.

At last Leon found an acceptable job as a shipping clerk at the W. T. Grant "five-and-dime" store in Dallas. Soon he was placed in charge of the stock room, next in line to become the store manager.

There were pretty girls where he worked but, when he found time, he drove his Mitchell Racer out to Stamford to visit Miss Maebelle Burnham. Thinking her special, he called her his "Sunday Girl."

In the spring of 1923, both Maebelle and Lyle Burnham were seniors at Stamford High School. The class was on a field trip when their sponsors received word that Irwin C. Burnham had died following a cerebral hemorrhage. The teachers, not giving Maebelle and Lyle the reason, cut the school trip short to return home a day early. The Burnhams were not told that their papa had died until after they reached home. (Maebelle had wondered why everyone had been treating her extra nice.)

Mr. Burnham died on May 1, two weeks before the school's scheduled graduation exercises, where the Burnhams received their diplomas. Papa was not there, but they knew that he would have been so proud—as he had been with everything they did.

After a brief period of mourning, the Widow Harriet Burnham straightened her shoulders, tightened her corset laces, and began to think of what she could do to earn their income. Her children, although nearly grown, still lived at home.

Harriet took a job with the California Perfume Company (the C.P.C.) to sell toiletries to her wide circle of friends. This proved successful. The ladies were eager to buy Mrs. Burnham's perfumes and face creams. She began to send in such big merchandise orders that her name came to the company's attention. She was offered a new job of being an independent C.P.C agent that traveled to various Texas towns to recruit new salesladies. As a company agent she would make more money—a salary plus a bonus and with her travel expenses being paid. Harriet began to make plans.

Harriet talked her two daughters into loaning (giving?) their brother their shares of the Burnham inheritance. By using all three children's money, Lyle Burnham paid his tuition and entered the Texas University Engineering School at Austin.

Harriet pushed for Maebelle to hurry and marry her boyfriend, Leon New, tho' in this matter neither party needed encouragement. Edward Leon New and Maebelle Edna Burnham were married on July 9, 1923. Following a short honeymoon, they moved into a small bungalow Leon had rented on Henderson Street in the Oak Cliff section of Dallas.

Selling the Burnham home in Stamford, Harriet Burnham made arrangements for her younger daughter Constance, then in junior high, to live with Leon and Maebelle so she would be free to travel with the C.P.C. It is not clear if Mrs. Burnham paid the young couple a little something for their added expense.

With these pressing matters out of her way, Harriet Burnham, the independent business woman, did indeed go "on the road" as a C.P.C. depot agent. She held that position until she retired years later. (In 1936 the name of the California Perfume Company was changed to today's Avon Products, Inc.)

Leon and Maebelle's life together began when they moved into the little frame house that Leon had rented on Henderson Street in Dallas.

Maebelle found herself totally lacking in the art of keeping house. At the market she found it hard to think of which groceries to buy, unable to think of anything to cook. Leon would hint suggestions, telling her what he liked to eat and what tasted good. Slowly she learned.

In their first year of marriage, Leon advanced from being head of the W. T. Grant Shipping Department to become the store bookkeeper. Ever active in church, Maebelle volunteered to help in a Methodist mission, a shelter run by the church to feed and clothe unfortunate people.

On some days when driving around Dallas, Maebelle brought along her sister-in-law, Olga New. The Russian girl spoke a few words in English but needed to learn more. As they drove through the streets, Maebelle pointed out objects—trash cans, names on stores, bicycles—for Olga to repeat in English.

On October 9, 1924, Leon and Maebelle's first baby was born in the Dallas Baylor Hospital. Proud Papa Leon named their baby Edna Mae after her mother Maebelle Edna. He jokingly said he just turned her name around and left off the "racket."

Edna Mae, a tiny baby, delighted her Aunt Constance who treated her as her doll. After Edna Mae began to walk, Aunt "Connie B" (Constance) who liked to sew, dressed her like a miniature "flapper," a girl of the "roaring twenties." For one of her little outfits, Constance made her a white waistcoat with a bright red flannel skirt that ended, as was the fashion, just above her knees. Connie B. enjoyed taking the dainty tot, dressed in her short crimson skirt, to show her Dallas High School friends. Little Edna Mae became their class mascot.

Leon New had served as a first lieutenant when he first joined the Army Reserves in 1919. On February 7, 1925, he was promoted to captain, bringing a rise in his income. That June, after he had fulfilled his annual two-week stint in camp, he moved his Odd Fellow Lodge membership from Stamford to the Oak Cliff I.O.O.F., Chapter No. 27 in Dallas. This chapter, being closer, made it easier to attend their meetings.

When Maebelle found she was pregnant again, they planned for this new baby, as they had their first, to be born in Baylor Hospital. Nearing term, Maebelle went into labor one morning after Leon had gone to work. Judging from her past experience, Maebelle thought she had plenty time. She had Connie help her when she bathed and washed her hair, getting ready.

Suddenly her water broke and labor pains grew stronger. Connie phoned the doctor to see what he thought. It seemed almost at once Dr. Beach arrived. Upon examination he said there was no time to waste and had Connie hand him clean sheets and call the neighbor from next door. Connie also called Leon at work, but the baby arrived before he did.

At 11 a.m. on February 13, 1926, the New's second baby was born, a pudgy little girl. Hiding his disappointment because he still had no son, Leon suggested that they name the baby "Ellen" after the two grandmothers, Harriet Ellen Burnham and Mrs. Ellie New. Disliking the name Harriet, Maebelle chose to name the baby "Mary Ellen."

Around six weeks after her baby came, Maebelle said she didn't feel well. Leon told her to stay in bed that day. Leaving for work, he told Constance to step into their room to check on her sister and the baby before going to school.

When Connie looked in, she found Maebelle's face all red and she was burning with a fever. She immediately phoned Leon and he rushed home.

Leaving Constance to look after Edna Mae, Leon carried Maebelle and the baby to his car and headed for the hospital. In a rush, he was speeding along when a man in a truck ran a stop sign and broadsided their car, flipping it over. Maebelle was not hurt but the baby was bleeding from a head wound. Leon was knocked unconscious.

An ambulance took Leon to Baylor Hospital while some kind lady, witnessing the accident, put Maebelle and infant Mary Ellen into her private car and took them to another hospital. The man who was driving the truck was arrested.

At the hospital Maebelle's illness was diagnosed as scarlet fever, which, they thought, she likely had contracted when she volunteered at the Methodist shelter. In a few days her fever subsided, and she was allowed to go home.

Baby Mary Ellen, her head bloody, was admitted to the children's hospital across the street from Maebelle. She was found to have a shard of glass puncturing her scalp that caused profuse bleeding but, thankfully, narrowly missed her 'soft spot,' the fontanel, a membrane common to all newborns.

Leon wasn't so lucky. In addition to minor cuts and bruises, he had suffered a cracked skull. After a week of bed rest with no apparent permanent damage, he was discharged from the hospital.

Notified of the accident, Harriet Burnham hurried to Dallas to take care of the household, prepared to stay as long as her daughters needed her. Before long all the sick folks were "up and around" and Mrs. Burnham returned to her job with the C.P.C.

Leon continued to meet the requirement of a Reserve Army officer, serving two weeks each year at an Army post. In August 1926 Capt. Edward L. New, having recovered from his head injury, was sent to a camp near Galveston for his annual two week tour of duty. Not wanting to leave Maebelle and their babies alone, he took them with him, renting a tourist cabin near the shore. On his time off they enjoyed driving around sight-seeing and playing in the sand and surf.

Meanwhile, in Mississippi Mrs. Ellie New, Henry and Leon's stepmother, had suffered a stroke and was bedridden. Miss Ellie had always been good to her husband's children, treating them as her own. As they had not been home for a while, the two brothers in Texas thought they should go back to check on their Mississippi family. Besides, they wanted to visit their father; old Joel New was then well into his sixties.

Collecting both of their families, Henry and Leon undertook the long drive from Dallas to Meridian, Mississippi. What a trip that turned out to be! Counting Leon and Maebelle and their two youngsters along with Henry and Olga and their small daughters, Lorena and Louise, there were eight people to drive over 800 miles in the summer heat, cramped into Leon's new canvas-topped Ford touring car.

Although isinglass curtains could be buttoned should it rain, the open four-door car had no glass side windows and insects flew in to pester the riders. This was before cars had rear end trunks, so folding metal luggage racks were attached to the running boards down each side to transport suitcases, cans of extra gasoline, and spare tires.

Streets and roadways were paved through the larger towns, but the highways in between were graveled dirt roads—at least across Texas, that is. Upon entering Louisiana they encountered mostly plain muddy roads. On one narrow road the travelers were sideswiped by a passing vehicle that knocked off a luggage rack, strewing boxes and suitcases along the way. They had to stop to retrieve their scattered clothing from the roadside bushes.

To add to their miseries, Henry's oldest child, Lorena, broke out with chicken pox the day after they left Dallas. Having come too far to go back, they continued the trip. Maebelle, afraid that Edna Mae would catch little Lorena's "pox," began to sponge her daughter with rubbing alcohol. It must have worked because Edna Mae remained healthy although Maebelle later said that Olga wasn't as friendly as she had been. In retrospect she wondered if Olga had been offended when she tried to prevent Edna Mae from catching chicken pox.

Nearing the Mississippi River, the road became even spongier whenever they passed a Louisiana bayou. At one place where they stopped for directions the storekeeper advised them to wait until another motorist came so they could help each other across the next swamp. When another automobile showed up, both cars started out together.

Upon entering the swamp, the road disappeared, leaving only blazed trees to keep them headed in the right direction. First one car and then the other got stuck in the mud but were able to tow each other out. They lost a whole day crossing the eight-mile swamp but at its end they found the mighty Mississippi!

There was no highway bridge to cross the wide river to Vicksburg but a paddle-wheel riverboat made regular runs to ferry automobiles and other traffic across to the other side. Leon drove across the boat ramp and parked on the ferry without incident, and everybody got out of the car to enjoy the boat ride.

Mississippi river ferry

Leon was holding petite Edna Mae by the hand when a stranger, another passenger, remarked, "My, what a lovely little girl!"

Then, turning to Mary Ellen in Leon's arms, he said, "And my, what a *fine* boy!" Leon beamed, never telling the gentleman that he had made a mistake in the baby's gender.

When the ferry docked, they loaded back into the car to drive up Vicksburg's steep concrete levee. The car sputtered and stopped. Its gas tank, located in front over the engine, relied upon gravity to supply the motor with fuel. Due to the levee's steep grade the gravity-fed engine was unable to go forward.

"Turn 'er around and back up!" shouted one of the boatmen, having before encountered this problem.

Leon turned around and backed up the levee without further ado. (Several models later somebody thought to invent a fuel pump for cars.)

After crossing the state of Mississippi, they came, at last, to Meridian and then on out to Pine Springs. Kill the fatted calf! The two oldest sons had returned to the fold!

All Joel New's children—and grandchildren—gathered for a family reunion at his home. Everyone brought food, and the men laid out boards to make a table for all the relatives to eat in the shade of the mighty oaks in the front yard. What a feast!

Henry's Olga was a foreign curiosity and was treated politely, but Maebelle was a "hit" with the younger New family. Having been raised in the country, they were fascinated by her "city" ways, a different style of life. They kept pushing food at her, urging her to sample this or that of their favorite dishes.

Feeling overly full, Maebelle teased them about the News having "gluttonous appetites." For some reason this seemed hilarious. Thereafter the News' "gluttonous appetites" were mentioned

with laughter whenever the family ate together. Could it be that the men were looking for an excuse to go for another piece of their sister Lorena's coconut cake?

In late afternoon the visiting relatives departed to see to their evening farm chores. Maebelle, laughing, was being entertained in the yard swing by young Herman and Joe New, each trying to see who could push her the highest. As it grew dark, the boys had to go milk the cows, and Maebelle went inside to check on her little girls. They were both tucked in and sound asleep. They had had a busy day.

Passing her sick mother-in-law's bedroom, Maebelle saw old Grandma Pratt dozing beside Miss Ellie's sickbed. Seeing that she was not needed, she continued on to help young Susie Mae "ready up" the kitchen.

To Maebelle's chagrin, she found Leon and Mr. New in the kitchen sharing a toddy, Mr. Joel's moonshine jug between them. She couldn't believe it! Before thinking she lashed out at Leon, asking what he was doing, drinking *liquor* while professing to be a Christian! She went outside, slamming the door.

Chuckling, Joel said, "Son, 'peers like you got yourself a tough little wife—puts me in mind of a Banty rooster."

Apparently old Joel admired Maebelle's spirit, finding her amusing. He continued sipping his drink while Leon followed Maebelle to calm her down. Maebelle said that she was sorry. It had been a long tiring trip.

After a week of visiting all his Mississippi relatives—Aunt Allie Pace, Aunt Minnie Houston, and the New family from out at Meehan—Leon and Maebelle motored back to Texas with their two little girls. Henry, with his family, remained with their aging father to operate his Pine Springs farm.

Mrs. Ellie Pratt New died that fall in October after Leon had left. They buried her at Pace's Church (today's Fellowship Baptist Church) beside the grave of her infant daughter. Leon and Miss Ellie had already expressed their goodbyes while he was there; he felt unable to return to Mississippi so soon for her funeral.

The next few years in Dallas were quiet. While living with them, Connie B. graduated from high school. Growing into a natural blonde beauty, she was employed as a model to be photographed while wearing stylish clothing for the Montgomery-Ward catalogue. Later she trained to be a switchboard operator for the Dallas Telephone Exchange.

On school holidays Lyle came over from Texas University, and Mrs. Burnham visited each time her traveling job took her through town. Selling toiletries and needing to keep a youthful appearance, Harriet disliked for Edna Mae and Mary Ellen to call her "Grandma." She insisted they call her "Big Mama."

With these visitors and Leon's "babies" growing bigger, their house in Oak Cliff seemed to shrink. (Leon's children were big kids before he stopped addressing them as "you babies.")

With times being good and with Leon's job being secure, they moved into a larger brick home in Highland Park, a better section of Dallas.

But then—wouldn't you know it—in 1929 the stock market crashed, the bottom falling out of the Wall Street stock exchange. Overnight, millionaires became paupers. This caused panic at local banks as customers rushed to cash in their checking and savings accounts before the money was gone.

Harriet Burnham was one of the lucky ones; she withdrew her savings before the government declared a bank "holiday" and closed all national banks. In a dither she came to Leon to ask him what she should do with her money.

He told her to invest into real estate; as people went broke, they were selling land at a low price. The market wouldn't stay down forever he told her, and when good times returned, she could sell her land and gain a handsome profit.

As always, the idea of making money appealed to Harriet Burnham. She went out and, without an inspection, bought herself a goat ranch!

Big Mama's ranch was situated in the Texas Hill Country a few miles north of San Antonio in a community called "Fischer Store." Its former owner, in better times, had used the ranch as a deer-hunting lodge, his main home and business being in San Antonio.

Sited near the deep canyon walls of the Guadalupe River, the ranch's arid rock soil was good for growing various varieties of cacti and juniper bushes, along with numerous rattlesnakes and burrowing hard-shelled armadillos. A small stock of goats came with the place, which was good, but the old ranch house and barns were badly in need of repair.

Feeling she had made a mistake, Big Mama (Mrs. Burnham) turned to Leon in tears. She couldn't find anyone to operate her ranch and didn't have money enough to pay such a person if she did. She prevailed upon her son-in-law, asking Leon to move out to her ranch to restore it to its former lucrative operation. Maebelle, feeling sorry for her mother, said it sounded like fun. She always enjoyed being in the country.

Thus pressured, Leon, who disliked farming, gave up his city job and moved with Maebelle and the "babies" down to Fischer Store. Connie, now a telephone operator, rented a wee apartment with another working lady and remained in Dallas.

Thinking it would prove handy on the ranch, Leon traded his car for a used truck to move their furniture to their new home. The unpainted ranch house was constructed with rough lumber, its four sizable rooms separated by a wide dog-trot hallway containing a stairway that led to an unsealed attic. Across the length of the house was a wide screened porch constructed of native stone. It made a pleasant place to catch any wayward breeze on a hot Texas day.

There was, of course, no indoor plumbing; water for household use came from a hand-operated pump located in the yard behind the kitchen. A short distance from the house was a brook running through an arroyo where, in one secluded place, the water ran between two flat boulders to form a natural bathtub. The outdoor privy was hidden behind a falling-down log smokehouse.

Off to the right of the house was a rail fence enclosing a barn lot to hold goats and cattle. Behind this was a barn with a haymow, a sheepfold, a corn crib, and a couple stalls for cows or horses. Way down behind all this was a pigpen, far enough away not to bother the house with the smell.

As there was no electric power and no ice route that extended to the ranch, they had no way to refrigerate food. The first time Big Mama visited and had to retrieve the stored milk from the cool brook, she thought something had to be done. She had Leon drive her to San Marcus (the closest little town) where she purchased an "Icy-Ball," an early model refrigerator that operated on kerosene.

The refrigerator was an insulated chest-type model that opened from the top. It had two metal balls the size of basketballs attached to each other, somewhat like barbells. An arm between the balls rested in a slot located just under the lid of the chest, allowing one ball to hang inside and the other outside. For a period of time each day the outside ball was heated by a kerosene heater, which came with the unit, which caused the chemicals inside to freeze. Then the ball, all covered with frost, was reversed to be placed

inside the chest and the heater was then turned off—until the next day when it had to be repeated.

It was a lot of trouble, but the Icy-Ball worked well with no mishaps—until the day Mary Ellen (4) saw the ball covered with tempting frost and decided to steal a lick. To her dismay her tongue stuck—that old ball wouldn't turn her loose! Hearing her loud caterwauls, her mother ran to see what in the world the matter was.

The child's shrill screams also alarmed a farm hand, Edgar, who was just outside. Edgar ran in to help whoever was under attack. Seeing the situation, he wanted to snatch the girl loose but Maebelle restrained him, saying Mary Ellen would lose the hide off her tongue. She began to pour warm water over her child's tongue and slowly the ice melted. Mary Ellen was freed, never again having to be cautioned to keep away from the Icy-Ball.

Leon worked hard on the ranch, re-stacking rock fences where stones had fallen, making them goat-proof. He bought an old L.C. Smith double-barreled shotgun and whenever he left the house he took it along in case he ran into a rattler hiding amid the rocks. He killed the snakes to keep them away from his babies.

Having no horse, Leon took in his neighbor's untrained horses and/or mule colts to train them to pull a plow. For payment he used these animals to plow his own vegetable garden, hay and cornfield before returning them to their owners.

One mule colt was flop-eared, one ear standing askew. Lyle, visiting from college, named the mule "Josephus." He tied its long ears together to make them stand erect. Apparently Josephus didn't want to be dignified and shook his head, breaking Lyle's string.

Giving up, Lyle said, "OK, Joe, have it your way. Go on and be a jackass."

Leon ordered Maebelle baby chicks and turkeys from the Sears-Roebuck catalogue. Having no place to house them, they turned them loose inside the old log smokehouse until they could buy chicken wire for a fence. As the young pullets matured, they had plenty of eggs, which Maebelle swapped with their neighbor for milk. She also traded eggs for a young pig to be fattened up and butchered.

The low ground near the brook was a good place to grow vegetables. Leon plowed and Maebelle planted, priding herself for being a good gardener. One day Maebelle was picking English peas while Edna Mae and Mary Ellen splashed in the brook. Suddenly Maebelle began shouting and calling, and the babies ran over to see what Mama was yelling about. They found her holding the tail of an armadillo she found digging its burro between her cabbages. He was scratching to dig deeper and Maebelle held his tail to keep him back. Neither was winning, but Maebelle held on and kept hollering for Leon.

In a few moments, Leon, in a panic, came running. Using a hoe, he dug the animal out and killed it.

Maebelle, with satisfaction, made a sewing basket out of the animal's dried shell. After lining the shell with shiny pink fabric, she wired the tip of its tail to its nose to fashion the basket handle. Most every home in the community had at least one armadillo basket. Thinking of her blistered hands, Maebelle was sure she had earned hers.

The area around Fischer Store was first settled by German emigrants who had built a Lutheran Church. As people from other church affiliations came, they lacked a church and began to worship in the local schoolhouse. As Leon and Maebelle became absorbed in the community, they met with other Methodists who held Sunday service in the school.

The Methodists wanted to build their own church, but in those bad times they were hard pushed to find money. To raise cash someone suggested they stage a play and charge an admission. Good idea!

So they put on a play in which Leon was picked for the starring role. His character was a convict, and Maebelle sewed him a black and white striped suit to wear as he played the part.

On opening night Maebelle brought the babies to watch Daddy in the play. Halfway through the second act, Leon came on stage in his convict suit and waving a pistol. After some loud talking, he shot off his gun twice and then jumped from the stage and ran down the aisle and escaped out the front entrance. Edna Mae and Mary Ellen were terrified. Maebelle, sitting between her sobbing girls, tried to explain that Daddy was just "play acting" as they sometimes played with their dolls. "Sides, it wasn't *real* bullets but just made a loud noise without hurting anybody."

The babies calmed somewhat, but felt better after the third act when Daddy acted natural while wearing his Sunday suit and talked real nice in his normal voice.

Leon had a German shepherd that kept him company as he worked about the ranch. One day neighboring ranchers came to tell Leon that their sheep were being killed and they had reason to believe that Leon's dog was the culprit. Leon said he didn't think it was Chief, but they insisted, saying it was the "code of the West" that he had to get rid of his dog.

Rather than cause friction between himself and his neighbors, Leon got his shotgun and took Chief to the far side of the ranch. He came back alone. Too late, the ranchers returned to tell Leon that Chief was innocent; they had caught the real sheep killer in the act.

Feeling sorry for Leon, Connie brought him another dog, an Airedale, the next time she visited from Dallas. Leon thanked her but gave the little dog to his babies who named her "Connie."

Connie (the dog) took her job of looking after the babies seriously. A terrier, she became quite adept at killing snakes. Whenever she saw a rattler she would grab and shake it until it died. Sometimes she would get bit but apparently she had acquired immunity to snakebites for when that happened she would appear listless for a few days but would recover. When her muzzle swelled, Leon would remark that Connie must have tangled with another snake.

Playing and gathering wildflowers, at times the children would stray a bit too far and become lost. When Edna Mae said, "Let's go home, Connie!" the dog would turn to lead the little girls homeward. Maebelle said that sometimes she would become worried about her girls but then she would see them coming, walking hand in hand behind their shaggy friend. The dog seemed to know that she was their protector.

In their second year on the ranch, Leon's sister Lorena with her husband, Lawrence White, and their two children, Ina Pearl and Edward Earl, came from Mississippi to visit Leon and Maebelle on the ranch. (Their youngest, Edward Earl, was a year older than Edna Mae.) Lawrence, who worked in the Meridian railroad shop, was issued four round-trip passes for them to ride the train.

The Whites were feted on their first visit to the "Wild West." That weekend all the Burnhams—Big mama, Lyle, and Constance—came to meet Leon's folks, and on Saturday neighbors showed up with food for a get together. They met on the bank of the Guadalupe where all the youngsters went swimming.

That morning Leon had barbequed a young goat, and Maebelle made a tasty Texas barbeque sauce, adding whole peppercorns to make it spicy. At the picnic plain-spoken Lorena commented, "I've never eaten goat before, but I know 'tis goat 'cause I found goat-pills in the sauce!"

After the Whites returned home, Lawrence White, with others, was laid off from his railroad job. Like everywhere else during the Depression, the railroads had to cut back on their expenses.

One of the big front rooms in the ranch house, next to the kitchen, served as a sitting/dining room. It was an activity room where the family gathered. Near the room's wood burning heater was a wide wicker rocking chair where Leon would sit with both babies, one snuggled under each arm, to sing them to sleep.

He made up words for his lullabies, always singing them to the music of the hymn "Come Thou Fount." [Robert Robinson, John Wyeth, Methodist Hymnal] He would sing;

> *Go to sleepy,*
> *Little Babies,*
> *Daddy loves you,*
> *Go to sleep.*
>
> *Now it's time to*
> *Go to sleepy*
> *Close your eyes and*
> *Go to sleep.*

Leon also sat with his little girls on his lap to read them fairy tales or tell them whimsical stories he concocted about raccoons or 'possums or some other small animal. The girls loved Sundays after church when Daddy would read them the colored funnies while Mama put dinner on the table. After dinner the babies took their naps while Daddy finished reading his paper. He liked to keep up with the news.

As Edna Mae grew older, Leon taught her numbers. While on a visit, her Uncle Lyle told her to go in to check on the time. When she said she didn't know how to tell time, Lyle told her that the long hand is named 'Edna Mae' and goes around fast, and the short hand is named 'Mary Ellen' and goes around real slow.

Edna Mae scooted into the house and came back to report, "Edna Mae is on ten and Mary Ellen is on three!"

"Good!" Lyle said, "That means its ten minutes until three o'clock." Then he explained it further.

When Lyle returned to his school, Edna Mae could tell time.

In the fall of 1931 Edna Mae was old enough to start school, but the schoolhouse, four miles distant, was too far away for a small girl to walk. Other children rode horses, but Maebelle couldn't see Edna Mae riding a horse, she seemed so tiny and helpless.

Maebelle asked her mother what to do, and Big Mama said she would sell her ranch, trading it for a house in town. (The ranch wasn't making Mrs. Burnham money, anyway.)

Leon, anxious for his babies to be educated and thinking that in town he could go back to working for pay, said that the idea sure sounded good.

The New family left Fischer Store near the time for the 1931 school year to start; Mrs. Burnham traded her ranch for a spacious antebellum home on North Olive Street in San Antonio. The impressive house had four massive columns across its wide front veranda. In its early days it had been a plantation home before the town had grown up around it. In good condition, it had been converted into four apartments, two upstairs, two down.

Leon New and family moved into a two-bedroom downstairs apartment. Big Mama said they didn't have to pay rent, of course, but Leon could act as landlord to collect her rent from the other tenants when she was away.

Edna Mae was enrolled in first grade at Emerson Elementary School, only a block away from their new home. Maebelle registered Mary Ellen in a free kindergarten class that the city operated at nearby Travis Park. Leon commenced hunting for a job.

Due to the nation's depressed economy, jobs were hard to find. Leon kept looking until he was hired to be a salesman for a real estate company, the National Real Estate Directory. The problem was that while many landowners wanted to sell, none had money to buy.

Running short on money, the company sometimes had to pay Leon with shares of their stock in lieu of a salary. Payment in company stock didn't put food on the table so Leon kept looking elsewhere for work.

After several months Leon was able to go back to work for the W.T. Grant Company in their San Antonio store. His salary wasn't as good as it had been in Dallas, but it was a job. (After Leon left the real estate company it declared bankruptcy, making Leon's stock worthless.)

The house on North Olive was a few blocks from a railroad roundhouse that served several railroads. Often hobos, unfortunate men who "rode the rails" looking for work, came by the big house looking for a handout. Leon, feeling blessed that he had a job, told Maebelle to spare whatever she could from their kitchen to feed the hungry men. Eggs were cheap; she began to scramble up a couple with a slice of bread to serve whenever a hungry man showed up. She wouldn't allow them inside but handed out their plates at the back door and they ate on the back porch. As more men showed up for food she began to wonder if word about her scrambled eggs had been passed around.

After Leon had worked a while at his new job, he surprised his family by showing up in a new car! Well, it wasn't new, but it was a shiny hard-topped dark green Whippet that was manufactured by the Overland Company. He proudly had his folks pile in to go for a ride.

Their ride took them past a drug store where they went in to sit at a little round table to celebrate, each having a bowl of ice cream. Thereafter, whenever they passed the drug store Mary Ellen would nod her head wisely and say, "They have ice cream in there!"

In the summer of 1932, Leon's sisters, Minnie Snowden and Lorena White, wrote to ask if Leon would consider coming back to Mississippi to take over the New's Pine Springs farm. The older New children had married and moved out but after Papa (Joel New) died the two minor children, Susie Mae and Irvin, were left at home alone.

Susie Mae New, in her late teens and unmarried, had just finished high school, but young Irvin New still had a year to go to graduate. The family wanted Leon to come back to provide a home for these two News until they could make it on their own. If Leon would return, they wrote, all the New children would give him their inherited shares of the Pine Springs farm.

Leon didn't really want to go back to farming, but Maebelle said that as he had gone to the ranch to help her family so she thought it only right—and she would be willing—to return to Mississippi to help out his family.

Leon New, sighing, said that he would go.

Chapter XIV
Back on the Farm

Leon New meant it when he promised his relatives that he would come home to take over the family farm. He said it was too late that year for spring planting, but he would return next year in time to put in a crop. He wanted to remain in San Antonio a while longer, collecting a few more paychecks before giving up his job. In August, however, he sent Maebelle and his babies on ahead so the girls could be enrolled in school for the 1932–33 school term. He placed his "women" on a Greyhound bus bound for Mississippi.

The Mississippi family owned no cars, but Ralph, the nearly grown son of Aunt Minnie and Uncle Curtis Snowden, drove the old black school bus to the Meridian bus station to meet the tired travelers. (Uncle Curtis had purchased the old bus from Minnie's late father, Joel New.)

Ralph had parked across the street. As they crossed to get into their school bus, Maebelle suddenly called out in her happy little voice, "Now, just whose little face do I see peeking out that back window? I SEE you!"

Entering the bus they found Earline, Ralph's young sister, who shyly greeted them. Earline was a year older than Edna Mae, but neither little girl remembered the other. After all, it had been over five years since they had first met.

They drove out to the Snowden farm in Pine Springs where Aunt Minnie had their supper waiting. After supper Ralph took them over to the nearby New farm where they were greeted by Susie Mae and Irvin. Edna Mae and Mary Ellen, all tuckered out, hardly remembered being put to bed.

A few days later, Maebelle had Edna Mae enrolled in second grade at the Center Hill school, while she enrolled Mary Ellen, a beginner, in first grade. When school started, every school day morning the little girls and Irvin walked out to the road to wait by their mailbox. Presently the old bus, driven by Ralph, would come by to pick them up to ride with the other students to school, which was five miles away. (The Pine Springs school had closed the year before when it was consolidated with Center Hill.)

Irvin New was a junior in high school while his nephew, Ralph Snowden, a year older, was about to graduate. When Ralph graduated in 1934, the Snowdens hired Irvin to be their bus driver.

While Leon batched alone in San Antonio, Maebelle adjusted to life on the farm. Susie Mae, now age nineteen, had been fifteen when her mother died. She found in Maebelle the friend and confidant she needed. She taught Maebelle how to tend a vegetable garden and how to milk a cow. In exchange, Maebelle taught the awkward country girl how to be more feminine.

Maebelle hand-stitched Susie Mae's first bra along with fancy step-ins made from bleached flower sacks, all trimmed with crocheted lace. Having no money to buy crochet thread, they had used the cotton sewing they saved when they opened feed sacks, winding each string onto a growing ball.

Missing Leon, Christmas that year was a dreary time for Maebelle. They attended the Christmas program at the Methodist Church and then took the little girls home to bed to dream of old "Sandy Claws."

From Meridian's Woolworth Store, Maebelle had managed to buy each of their babies a tiny baby doll—about three inches long—and sewed them wee dresses from scraps of cloth from the "rag-bag." The girls were thrilled when they found the cheap dolls under the Christmas tree. They didn't understand when they found Maebelle crying in the next room.

Susie Mae gave each little girl compacts for face powder with mirrors under their lids. They were decorated with their initials, "E" for Edna Mae, and "M" for Mary Ellen. Edna Mae had to explain to her little sister the meaning of the word "initial."

Spring finally arrived in 1933 and so did Leon. One morning he came driving up in their Overland Whippet while Maebelle was in the garden dusting arsenic on the Irish potato plants to kill the 'tater bugs. All his girls ran to meet him and gave him a big group hug.

Maebelle, her arms about him, began to sob, "Oh, Leon! You've grown so thin!"

Leon had loaded the Whippet with everything he thought they could use on the farm. After filling the backseat, he had bolted a wooden platform with a box across the rear of the trunkless automobile to transport the rest of their stuff.

How exciting it was when Leon had Irvin help unload. Maebelle was relieved when the box containing her silver-plated silverware was opened. She hadn't complained but she hated to eat with the New's outdated black-handled eating utensils, the old three-tined forks making it difficult to eat

peas as they would fall off her fork. She was also relieved to get her sewing machine so she could more easily make dresses for her growing girls.

Leon had brought his old L. C. Smith shotgun along and the .22 rifle that he had purchased before they left the ranch. He also brought Maebelle's big pressure cooker to make it easier and quicker to preserve food. It was the first "steamer" seen in Pine Springs.

Maebelle's spirit was somewhat dampened when she found that most of their china dishes were missing, the set Leon had purchased when a young serviceman stationed in China. Leon said that before he left San Antonio he had the dishes packed and waiting on the back porch when some rascal made off with two boxes.

Leon and Maebelle, as did everyone else, struggled through hard times over the next few years. In Leon's first year back, he had Lorena and "Humpy" (Lawrence) White move into the Wolfe house when Humpy lost his railroad job and they needed a place to stay. Humpy, sharecropping, worked with Leon and Irvin as they planted the fields with corn and cotton. When the cotton was sold, Leon found it was costing more money to raise than it brought in when it was sold. At least they had plenty of corn for cornbread and fodder for the livestock.

The family had no money to spend, but they ate well. They had six or seven Jersey milk cows supplying milk and butter, and food from their garden furnished vegetables. Also, they had three peach trees, as well as apples, pecans, and figs, so they ate fresh fruit in season and canned the excess, enough to last all winter.

The ladies peeled and sliced the apples and then, using the young black walnut tree growing next to the henhouse for a ladder, they gave the little girls an old sheet and sent them shinnying up to spread the apple slices to dry in the sun on the tin roof.

In July wild blackberries growing in the pasture ripened, free for the picking. Taking the girls along, Maebelle and Susie Mae spent mornings picking berries, canning them in the afternoon. Their goal was to put up ninety quarts of berries each season, enough to last a big family all year.

Their problem was that their diet lacked meat. They had no pigs, and their few old chickens were needed for eggs. Leon hungered for some good old beefsteak.

Looking over their cows, Leon thought that Beulah, an old Jersey cow now past her prime, would solve his problem. He spoke to his local sisters, Lorena and Minnie, to enlist their help. Lorena hooted. She said that the old cow's meat would be so tough you couldn't chew it, and besides, hot summertime was not the time to be butcherin'.

In spite of misgivings, they set a date and both sisters brought their families to help their misguided brother.

None of the crew had ever butchered a cow, but they found it was much like cutting up a hog. The biggest difference was that instead of scalding and scraping off the hair as they did with hogs, the tough cowhide was skinned away with sharpened knives. Leon set the hide aside to be dried and tanned for leather. Leather was useful around a farm, being used to make or repair horse reins, bridles, or to resole worn shoes.

The men set aside the fat—the yellow tallow—and sliced the remaining dark meat into chunks of the right size to fit into glass quart jars. As the men worked outside, the women were busy in the kitchen, washing jars and packing them with chunks of lean beef. Adding a dash of salt before screwing on the lids, Maebelle loaded the filled jars into her pressure cooker to be processed for a measured length of time on the hot wood range.

While the grown-ups were busy, Edna Mae and Mary Ellen played with their young cousins,

Ina Pearl White and Erline Snowden. Taking their dolls, they headed for a stand of pines that grew on the edge of the pasture to make a new playhouse in the thick pine straw. Passing behind the farm workshop, they came upon the pile of old Beulah's guts that the men had dumped out in the pasture.

A flock of bald-headed turkey buzzards had collected around the pile of bloody entrails, doing their job of cleaning the pasture by eating as much offal as they could manage. Somehow this didn't seem quite right to the little girls, those stinking old buzzards showing no respect for the dead. Feeling righteous, the girls looked around for sticks to chase the birds away.

The birds flew up into the trees, all save one that, somehow, Erline had managed to hit, making it flop around on the ground. Filled with curiosity, the girls stepped closer and began poking sticks into the smelly pile of intestines.

Edna Mae suddenly exclaimed, "Look! Old Beulah was goin' to have a calf!"

Erline asked what she was talking about.

Edna Mae pointed to a moist calf head protruding from a membranous sac. "See, she was pregnant!"

Erline, who had been told that cows got calves by finding them in the woods, didn't believe what Edna Mae said. Edna Mae had to explain the "miracle of birth" that her mama had told her. Erline didn't believe her but Mary Ellen backed her sister's story.

The sisters told that once their Aunt Constance's Persian cat was attacked by dogs and their mother, Erline's Aunt Maebelle, had cut its dead body open to see if its kittens could be rescued. The undeveloped kittens could not be saved, but Maebelle then told her girls about where real babies came from and they, accepting it as an ordinary "fact of life," thought nothing more about it.

Ina Pearl, oldest of the group, had already guessed where babies came from and wasn't paying much attention. Watching as the bird's flopping ceased; she soundly announced that the buzzard was dead. She understood death; the memory of Grandpa Joel New was still fresh on her mind.

"We must give Mr. Bird a funeral," Ina Pearl said.

The little girls, using their hands, scratched a hole for a grave in the sand of a worn towpath where they placed the corpse. The large body still stuck out so they scooped more handfuls of sand from down the path. Tips of feathers still showed so the mourners gathered bouquets of Black-eyed Susan's and other wildflowers to hide them.

Ina Pearl, the self-appointed preacher, led the mourners in a hymn they often heard at church. Following the song service, the preacher remained standing to deliver the sermon. The cries of the sobbing mourners grew louder, the preaching more eloquent. The exhorting sermon spoke of hellfire and damnation for those who turned not from sin. One of the bereaved, overcome by emotion, howled as she rolled about on the grass.

The funeral ended abruptly when the congregation heard parents calling. It was time for the visitors to go home.

Each family that had helped was given a roast to take home for immediate use, along with several jars of canned beef to enjoy later. To Lorena's surprise the steam cooking had rendered the delicious chunks of beef quite tender.

Leon invited Grandma Pratt (the elderly mother of his late stepmother, Ellie New) to come for a visit and to show Maebelle and Susie Mae how to make homemade soap. Grandma Pratt, in her eighties, was living with her other daughter, Mrs. Bettie Pace, but often visited with Ellie's

children. She had lived in frontier days when they hardly knew what "store-bought'n" soap was.

Grandma Pratt had them combine tallow from the butchered cow with lye made from oak wood ashes and cook the mess outdoors in the big iron wash pot. When it had cooled, it solidified and they sliced it into useable bars of soap. This soap was not successful for body use, but it did well when used for washing dirty work clothes.

Leon went trading and came back with a pair of pigs. The sow would bring piglets and, come winter, the boar could be butchered for meat and lard. Next winter, God willin', they would have sausage and bacon to eat with their hot biscuits and homemade 'lasses, and sow-belly to cook with their peas.

In January 1934 there came a notice that the yearly land tax had not been paid for the past two years. This year if the tax was not paid, the farm would be sold to the highest bidder.

Leon did not have the money to pay the taxes.

Leon's family had said that if he came back to make a home for Susie Mae and Irvin, they would sign over their share of the farm to him. On January 27, 1934, Leon asked his brothers and sisters to sign a notarized warranty deed to him for their undivided interest on the estate of Joel New, deceased, their shares of the 168-acre New farm in Pine Springs. [Located in S.4, T–7. R–15E.] To keep it legal Leon gave each heir one dollar. His siblings all signed the deed—all except two.

Henry New did not sign. He had been offered the farm by his now deceased father, but when old Joel New disposed of their written agreement, Henry lost interest. Henry had recently moved down to south Mississippi to work in a barbershop. He wouldn't sign the deed because he thought Leon was making a terrible mistake.

Young Irvin New was the other New heir who would not sign. He said the farm was the only thing he had that belonged to his father. He would probably lose it, but he couldn't give it away.

The New farm, sold for back taxes, was purchased by the Federal Land Bank of New Orleans. On January 17, 1935, Leon bought the farm back from the bank by signing a promissory note to pay off the lien in ten annual payments. The mortgage was $1,862 (plus interest) but from somewhere Leon came up with $172.41 cash (probably the last of his savings), which left a balance of $1,689. In addition to his annual loan payment he was expected to pay the yearly land tax. Where in the world could he come up with that kind of money?

To make matters worse, Leon—Capt. Edward L. New—received notice from the Army Reserves that his services were no longer needed. Due to drastic budgetary cuts, the U.S. military had to curtail its services; the R.O.T.C., finding it could pay two lieutenants for what it cost to pay one captain, had given Capt. New an honorable discharge.

Leon knew that the farm income alone would not be enough to pay the yearly mortgage payment. He had to find a job.

Hoping to work for the U.S. Postal Service, he easily passed the written civil service exam to become a railway mail clerk. His name was added to the *long* list of men already waiting to be called. Meantime, the U.S. Census Bureau had a part-time job opening for a local man who owned a car. Leon jumped at the chance.

The census (Leon called it his "gin job") required Leon to make monthly visits to each cotton gin in Lauderdale County to record how many bales of cotton they had baled that month. It took only a few days to make his rounds, leaving most of his time free to farm. It didn't pay much, but 'twas better than no job at all.

Maebelle had an idea that she could sell the extra produce they raised from their vegetable garden. She could also sell eggs as her white Leghorn pullets were beginning to lay more than the family needed. (They had bought baby chicks the year before from Long's Hatchery in Meridian, choosing the Leghorn breed because of their reputation for being good layers.)

Leon and Maebelle went to town in the Whippet each Saturday where Maebelle went house-to-house selling farm produce while Leon waited in the car. Knocking on a door and using her happy little voice, she would say, "Would you be interested in buying some fresh tomatoes?" (Or butter beans, bell peppers, etc., whatever.) "These are extra nice, just picked this morning."

Most Saturdays Maebelle sold everything she had, which added a bit to the family income. She developed regular customers who looked forward each week to buying fresh vegetables from Miss Maebelle, that nice cheerful lady who delivered them to their door.

The corner grocery stores showed small interest in buying vegetables, but became good customers for her fresh eggs and butter. Using milk from their cows, Maebelle made at least two churnings a week to make butter, feeding the extra buttermilk to their pigs and chickens.

Maebelle used a mold to shape her butter into half-pound bars, wrapping each stick in a square of waxed paper, ready to be sold.

One Saturday a store clerk said that a customer had returned Maebelle's butter, saying that it was not fresh. Maebelle was mortified. She had not sold any butter that she had not churned the day before. She knew it wasn't HER butter that had gone bad but she couldn't prove it.

To prevent this from happening again, Leon took out his pocketknife and carved the letter 'N' on her butter mold. Thereafter all Maebelle's butter was marked so it could not be mistaken for butter coming from another source. Housewives began asking for the big "N" butter as it was always fresh.

In the 1930s there were around four automobiles in all of Pine Springs—most folks had to walk when they needed to go somewhere. Leon and Maebelle never failed to stop to offer a ride whenever they passed a neighbor on foot. As word got around that the News went to Meridian every Saturday, neighbors began hitching rides to town with them. Some days when the Whippet was already filled, Leon would stop for another pedestrian, telling them to just hang onto the running board to get a lift.

After driving Maebelle around on her peddling route, Leon had a habit of parking near the corner of the Help-Yourself Grocery, kitty-cornered from the new Meridian post office. The folks that had hitched a ride knew that around 4 p.m. the News would leave for home.

Sometimes the riders would find another way home, but there were usually some waiting on that corner to ride back to Pine Springs in the Whippet. The News charged no fee for their "bus" service. Times were hard and they were glad to help their neighbors any way they could.

Edna Mae and Mary Ellen were usually left with Susie Mae when their parents went to Meridian. As they became older, they began to go along on the Saturday trips. After parking, the girls were allowed to walk the few blocks to the Temple or Strand Theaters to watch the Saturday movies. The matinee admission was six cents apiece for the girls to see a cowboy movie, the latest installment of a serial movie, a couple cartoons, and the latest news. They could spend half a day for less than a dime at the "picture show."

Cousin Edward Earl White, living nearby in the old Wolfe House, often came to play "cowboys and Indians" with the girls. They bent sticks to make six-shooters and galloped after each other, yelling "Boogety! Boogety!" to show they were riding a horse. Edward Earl was always Tom Mix or Ken Maynard, the cowboy in the white hat, or he wouldn't play.

The great drought of the early 1930s was one of the worst on record when the southern Great Plains became the "dust bowl." By 1935 the lack of rainfall in the West caused widespread damage to crops and the extinction of livestock, bringing about further hardships. Farmers and ranchers, unable to make a living, were leaving in droves to find somewhere else to live.

With water holes drying up and grazing land becoming arid, herds of beef cattle were dying. The United States started a program to help the cattlemen by offering to buy their cattle for $15-$20 per head. The plan was to save the livestock by shipping them back east to more verdant pastures.

Leon New, who was always aware of the news, signed up to take around fifty head of the starving western cattle to fatten up on his Pine Springs farm. The government would ship the cows by railroad to Meridian, but it would be Leon's responsibility to move them the twelve to fourteen miles out to his farm.

When the cows arrived in Meridian, it was round-up time! Having no money to hire a cattle truck, Leon proposed to drive the cows on *foot* from the Meridian stockyard out to Pine Springs via the public road.

They started off with Maebelle slowly driving the Whippet down the road behind the cattle. Leon and Susie Mae rode on the car's rear platform, ready to jump off to head the cows in the right direction. (This was the same platform that Leon had built when he came back from Texas—it had proven so handy for hauling sacks of seeds and fertilizer that he had never taken it off.)

Their old mule, Lucy, had gotten so old that Leon thought that this would be a good chance for her cheap replacement, hence, along with the other livestock there was a western saddle horse.

An old saddle from home had been brought along, and Leon placed it on his new horse. He had Edward Earl ride the horse out to the farm, herding the cattle all the way.

Edward Earl was in seventh heaven! He was riding a horse and herding cattle just like a REAL cowboy!

It had been a long tiring day, but at last they reached the farm and turned the cows out into the green pasture. The only mishap had been when Leon, riding on the platform, suddenly called out "STOP!" When Maebelle slammed on the brakes, Leon fell off onto the road. His sprained wrist was painful for a time, but he soon got over it.

Edna Mae claimed the horse to be hers and named her "Tiny." She would ride Tiny in the evenings to bring up the milk cows. She was quite pleased with the way the horse knew how to herd cattle. The horse, trained to drive cattle, knew what to do without being guided.

Susie Mae New's first job was working as a waitress in Sam Shepherd's hamburger joint, a hole-in-the-wall in Meridian near the corner where the News usually parked. As a treat, Leon would sometimes buy his babies their supper at Shepherd's Cafe. Susie Mae would wait on them, and they could each buy two hamburgers and a glass of milk for fifteen cents.

Having no way to get to work from the country, Susie Mae and another young lady rented a small apartment in Tuxedo, an older section of Meridian south of the railroad tracks. Shepherd's Cafe was closed on Sundays and Mondays, so Susie Mae usually rode home on Saturday evenings with Leon and Maebelle to spend her time off.

After making hamburgers a while, Susie Mae landed a better paying job at Maywebb Hosiery Mill that manufactured socks and stockings. With her newfound "wealth," she bought a battery-operated table radio for the News to enjoy on the farm.

In the afternoons the girls stopped playing long enough to listen to the children's programs—"Little Orphan Annie" or "Jack Armstrong, the All American Boy." Leon and Maebelle laughed together over the antics of "Amos 'n Andy" and the escapades of "Lum and Abner" in their "Jot 'em Down" store. On Saturday nights Susie Mae and Irvin would have friends over to listen to the "Grand Ole Opry" being broadcast from Nashville. They would serve homegrown popcorn and parched peanuts at these informal parties. Sometimes they made pulled molasses taffy, but not often. The candy was fun to make, but it was a mess to clean up.

They all learned to shush when it was time for evening news. Leon, much into local and national politics, kept abreast of what was going on. Slightly hard of hearing, he would sit facing the radio with his hand behind his ear, listening to every word. If the girls got too loud he would say, "You babies be quiet, now!"

Every other week Maebelle would stop by the Meridian Public Library to check out four books for her girls, two for Edna Mae and two for Mary Ellen. Both loved to read; each would read the books checked out for her and then read the books checked out for her sister. They read the entire *Bobbsey Twins* and *Motor Maids* series, as well as other books—*Black Beauty*, *Pollyanna*, the glad girl, and *Anne of Green Gables*. They averaged reading eight books each summer month, but when a new school year began Maebelle cut back on their reading so they could spend more time on lessons.

Leon and Maebelle had moved their church letters from San Antonio to Pine Springs Methodist Church in 1933, the year that Leon had come home. They faithfully attended church services—Sunday school, preachin', and prayer meetings—whenever the church doors opened. Edna Mae and Mary Ellen, if they didn't have two broken legs, were also expected to attend. The New family rode the mile to the church in the Whippet, stopping, as usual, to give those on foot a lift. They were often a little late, but most times the services were not started until the News arrived. (Lorena said that Leon New would be late for his own funeral.)

Upon request, Leon began teaching the adult Sunday school class. He was there every Sunday and was a good talker who explained the lessons well. Maebelle said he should have been a lawyer.

Maebelle was also given a job teaching the intermediate children. She enjoyed working with young people. She said adults had already had their chance; she chose to work with youngsters who still needed help.

A small church, Pine Springs Methodist was on a circuit with other churches. Its circuit-riding pastor was there only twice each month. On Sunday nights when no preaching was scheduled, older folks stayed home, but the teenagers, with nothing better to do, showed up at church to sing hymns.

Maebelle became a councilor for the host of young people who met at church. She helped them join the Epworth League, a Methodist Episcopal youth society. Each chapter elected its officers from their group and young committee members took turns selecting a new program to be presented at the next week's meeting.

(In 1939 the branches of the Methodist Church combined to form the United Methodist Church after which, in 1941, the name Epworth League was changed to today's "Methodist Youth Fellowship.")

Not many grown-ups took the time to meet with the Epworth League. Mr. Stacy Snowden and young Mr. Adolph Johnson with his wife, Jerusha

Mae, came each Sunday night to help Maebelle with her youngsters.

(Stacy was cousin of Curtis Snowden. His farm was near the church where he sponsored a teenaged baseball game that played in his pasture on Saturday afternoons. The Johnsons, whose farm was adjacent to the News, were Adventists but worshipped with the Methodists when they were home from college. These adults played an important role in developing the characters of the local youths.)

Mrs. Evie Gramham, who lived on today's Allen Swamp Road, was the church pianist, but when she wasn't there, Maebelle played piano for the hymn singing. Maebelle just adequately played the hymns but was by no means a concert pianist.

It must have been around 1935–36 that Mrs. Mavis Harabour, who lived up near Kemper County, was hired by the Federal Works Projects Administration (the W.P.A.) to teach music at Center Hill school. The W.P.A. gave jobs to people who, due to hard times, could not find jobs elsewhere. Mrs. Harabour, in addition to her government check, charged each student a dollar a month for the weekly piano lessons.

Maebelle was overjoyed when the music teacher became available for her girls. When Leon fretted about having to come up with two dollars each month to pay for their lessons, Maebelle declared that her girls would learn to play the piano even if she was forced to take in washing!

Seeing that it meant so much to his wife, Leon relented and his babies began to study piano. He even made an arrangement to purchase an old upright piano for them to practice.

By the time Edna Mae and Mary Ellen reached their teens, they and Nettie Ingram (another teenager) took turns at playing piano for Sunday night church services. They were shy, but Miss Maebelle insisted. Edna Mae and Nettie played by note, but Mary Ellen learned to play by ear. She never learned to read music, just enough to fool her teacher.

In the late 1930s Leon New was finally called up to become a railway mail clerk, the postal job he had so long wanted. He had passed the written test, but now he had to pass a physical. He went to Dr. Wilson, a country doctor who lived up the road.

Dr. Wilson found Leon's blood pressure alarmingly high. At that time there were no effective drugs to combat hypertension, so the good doctor told Leon to go on home and get his affairs in order—he wouldn't last much longer. He was apt to have a stroke at any time.

Well, this scared the "bejeezus" out of Leon. In an effort to lose weight, he placed himself on a strict diet. Leon was told that garlic would lower blood pressure. He began to eat fresh cloves of garlic until his perspiration smelled like an Italian kitchen. Fortunately, garlic was plentiful—it had become a nuisance in the News' backyard after it spread wild from Miss Ellie's old herb garden.

By not passing his physical, Leon missed out on being hired as a railway mail clerk, but he still had his part-time "gin job."

After the neighboring Johnson boys saved enough to return to college, Adolph, the last one to leave, sold the Johnson's old Farmall tractor to Leon. The old model tractor had iron cleats on its wheels instead of rubber tires, but its motor still ran well. It had no plows but Leon was only interested in its belt pulley. He wanted to use the power takeoff to operate other machinery.

Leon bought a Hammer-mill to be powered by the tractor motor. The mill paid for itself when Leon chipped up fodder for his cows and mules. As word about his Hammer-mill got around, other farmers brought their fodder to be chipped for animal feed. Leon charged them a toll.

Curtis Snowden's old rotting barn was about to fall down. He told Leon that he would help him pay for a new one-man sawmill if Leon would saw Curtis' logs to build a new barn. Leon jumped at the chance and at once ordered the sawmill. It would be operated by a belt from Leon's tractor.

When the little sawmill came, they set it up behind the Snowden's home where Curtis and Ralph were felling their trees and dragging them up to the site. With his new sawmill, powered by the old tractor, Leon cut the boards and Curtis and Ralph built the Snowdens a fine new barn.

The original log mule barn on the New farm had finally rotted away and the newer cow barn (which old Joel New had built) was inadequate for both mules and cows. Leon proposed to use the existing cow barn as a shelter for his mules and build another barn for his growing herd of milk cows. After he sawed the lumber for Curt Snowden's barn, Leon brought his sawmill home and set it up behind his house.

The land on the north side of the New's farm was owned by a Mr. Whitaker of Meridian whose spoke mill, back then, was located at the present site of today's Okatibbee Lake Pine Springs swimming area. The mill, which manufactured wagon-wheel spokes, was operated by steam power. All through the work week local residents could hear, in the background, the steady beat of the steam engine—"SUR-come-stances, SUR-come-stances." At four o'clock the mill whistle would blow, sounding like a train, and the mill would shut down for the night. On days when the young New girls visited their friends, Maebelle would caution, "Y'all come home when the whistle blows, you hear?"

Leon sold the oaks and sweet gum trees that grew on the back of his farm to spoke woodcutters who hauled wood to the spoke-mill. While there Leon had them cut down the trees that would make good saw-logs and hired the spoke-wood hauler, Ab Stephenson, to haul the saw-logs up through the pasture to pile them next to his saw-mill. (Ab, with his wife and four kids, lived nearby in a "company" house next the spoke-mill.)

Leon New managed to get his logs sawed and his lumber stacked and had poured the cement foundation for his new barn when, at last, the U.S. Corps of Engineers offered him a better paying full-time civil service job. He had to leave home; his new barn unfinished.

Edward L. and Maebelle Burnham New

Chapter XV
The End of Our Line

In the worldwide depression years of the 1930s, one Herr Adolph Hitler, a member of the German Nazi Party with a psychopathic personality, had become the fascist dictator of Germany. He believed the Aryans were the master race that was entitled to dominate, and he set about to annihilate all Jews. He wanted the area of Germany expanded to include all Europeans of German descent, and he had no scruples about the methods he used.

In 1935 Hitler began compulsory military service and re-militarized the Rhineland. In 1938 Germany annexed Austria and by 1939 the Germans occupied Czechoslovakia and took over Poland. Germany, with Italy its ally, continued with more acts of aggression.

In May 1939, with the turmoil in Europe, President Franklin D. Roosevelt opened a campaign to repeal the U.S. Neutrality Acts of 1935–37 so that American supplies would be available if war came, but for the time being, Congress would not agree. If England and France gained another ally, it would have to be Russia.

That fall, on September 3, 1939, British Prime Minister Chamberlain and French Chancellor Daladier gave formal notice to Germany that a state of war between them existed. The long armistice of 1918–1939 was over!

When war was declared in Europe, our national leaders determined to remain neutral but began to strengthen the American military force. The thought of Europe being dominated by Germany frightened Congress; a modest expansion of the Army became the first order of business. In 1940 Congress passed the Selective Service Act, which produced an inflow of draftees committed to a year of military training. By mid-summer of 1941 more than 1,150,000 American men were in uniform.

Camp Shelby, near Hattiesburg, Mississippi, had been a small camp when Leon New had been discharged from the military back in 1918. Now, with the large number of men entering the Army, the small camp had to be enlarged. The civil service job offered Leon was with the procurement office of the U.S. Corps of Engineers, where building materials and war supplies were ordered to enlarge Camp Shelby.

Passing the written application was no problem for Leon, his real test came when he had to pass his physical. Knowing that he was hypertensive, Leon starved himself, not eating for three days before he reported to the doctor. His blood pressure was still a mite high, but he scraped by and was hired.

After a brief indoctrination at Grenada, Mississippi, Leon was sent to Camp Shelby. Leaving the Whippet home for Maebelle's use, Leon stayed in the camp during the week, riding the Greyhound bus home on weekends. After drawing a few paychecks, he hired one of his brothers, Herman New, to build his new barn with the lumber he had already cut.

Rev. Jeff Hunt and his wife, Belle, a childless black couple who lived on the edge of Okatibbee Swamp, moved into a tenant shack Leon had built down in his pasture. Jeff, with Leon away, helped Miss Maebelle tend the livestock, cut firewood, and kept her garden plowed while planting twenty-four acres of cotton for himself. Belle helped Miss Maebelle milk cows (along with the young teenagers Edna Mae and Mary Ellen). She also helped Miss Maebelle do the laundry while helping her husband chop cotton and hoe the cornfields.

"Humpy" and Lorena White had moved from the Wolfe house, but his brother, Claude White, had moved in with his wife, Lela, and their two half-grown children. A tenant farmer, Claude planted six and a half acres of cotton to be grown on "shares." With all the new soldiers, the price farmers got from cotton made planting worthwhile.

Many of Leon's Pine Springs family and friends, after pinching pennies so long during the depression, happily found good paying jobs with the government. Neighbors Jake Smith, Ollie Calvert, and Leon's brother Herman New—among others—were hired as carpenters to enlarge Camp Shelby and build new Army barracks at Meridian's Key Field. The airport runways were lengthened to accommodate heavy military aircraft as more barracks were constructed for men of the Army Air Force and the expanded Mississippi Air National Guard.

When the Selective Service began inducting young men into the Army in 1940, the cousins Irvin New and Ralph Snowden were the right age to be drafted. Irvin had left the farm right after he graduated from school and was driving a cab in Meridian. When called up for draft, he was classified '4-F,' not physically fit for military service.

Embarrassed, he wouldn't speak about it but, it was guessed it was because of his flat feet. As a youngster he had stepped into hot coals around the wash pot, and his feet were badly burned.

Ralph Snowden was not accepted when called. He had lost sight in one eye when it had become infected following a schoolboy accident. Also, a year before, in January of 1930, he had married Miss Stella Harris who lived a half-mile south of the Pine Springs Church. He was working at the Flintcote Company, a building material factory in Meridian.

Two of Leon New's nephews, Edward Earl White (Lorena's son) and James Andrew Pace (Marie's son), were too young for that first draft, but both were in the Army before the war ended. Edward Earl was wounded in Germany.

When the Camp Shelby upgrade was complete, the civil service transferred Leon to Greenville, Mississippi, where the airport there was being enlarged for a military landing field. This air station in the Mississippi delta in the northern part of the state was too far away for Leon to ride home on weekends by bus. His old Whippet, held together by "chewing gum and baling wire," was unsafe to travel that far from home, so he rented an apartment in Greenville.

A. T. "Ab" Stephenson (spoke-wood hauler) went car shopping in Meridian and found a used '37 Dodge Deluxe coach model he liked at the Motley Motor Company. After trading in his old '31 model Chrysler, he still owed $300. After sobering up a bit, Ab realized that he really didn't want to be obligated to make car payments.

Leon happened to come home that weekend and Ab showed him the Dodge. Well kept, it looked like new. Somewhat streamlined, it had a slanted windshield instead of being straight up and down like the Whippet, and it had an automatic gear shift! It was just what Maebelle and Leon needed.

The following weekend Leon traded in his old Whippet, having car-dealer Mr. Motley transfer the ownership of the Dodge from Ab to his name. The agreement was that Leon pay the company $21.38 each month for the coming year. He also paid Ab Stephenson $63.44 for his interest in the car.

When school turned out in the spring of 1941, Maebelle and the girls drove the Dodge to Greenville for a week-long visit with Leon. She let her girls take turns at driving along the highways, but took the wheel herself when they passed through a town. They also learned to read maps.

The girls felt quite grown up driving a car! Edna Mae had just finished her junior year in high school and Mary Ellen had just completed the tenth grade.

Leon, promoted to be the head purchasing agent at the Greenville Air Base, was kept busy at work, but it was a lonely time for him being away from his family. He enjoyed having his folks there on their visit. It was nice having Maebelle there in his apartment to cook him a decent meal, and it was wonderful having all his "women" around the table to eat with. While they were there, they went sightseeing along the river. Leon drove them over the bridge into Arkansas so the girls could brag to their friends that they had visited another state. They rented a rowboat and went fishing. They had lots of fun but they didn't catch any fish.

Too soon, it seemed, the visit was over as Maebelle had to get back to see how Belle and Jeff were doing on the farm. That summer Maebelle and the girls made more weekend trips to Greenville but, after school opened that fall Maebelle went alone. She asked neighbor Martha Johnson to stay with Edna Mae and Mary Ellen while she was gone. (Martha was a retired nurse who lived alone next door on the old Johnson place.)

Maebelle was in Greenville on December 7, 1941, when it was broadcast that Japan had launched a surprise attack on the United States by bombing Pearl Harbor, its American Naval Base, and the surrounding air fields in Hawaii. The next day, December 8, President Franklin D. Roosevelt answered with a stirring speech. He called the attack "a dastardly deed" and announced that the United States was declaring an all-out war against Japan and Germany. Forthwith, England, already at war with Germany and Italy, also declared war against Japan.

Thus the United States entered World War II!

With war came gasoline rationing, which limited Maebelle's trips to Greenville. The government had hastily formed a Ration Board that issued each family a coupon book to prevent citizens from hoarding food and other supplies needed to wage war. Shoes, sugar, spare tires, etc., became rationed—no ration coupon, no sale. Even with a coupon a fellow had to turn in his old tire to purchase a new one as used tires were retreaded or their rubber salvaged to be re-used.

As the Army paratroopers needed nylon for their parachutes, ladies' nylon stockings were practically unattainable. Ladies began to color their legs with suntan lotion to make them appear to be wearing hosiery. (Some even used an eyebrow pencil to paint a seam down the back.)

Families were encouraged to plant "victory gardens" to save their grocery coupons. School children collected scrap metal, depositing it in conveniently located places, to be melted down to make war equipment. Wives saved their used kitchen grease to be donated to make explosives. Green dyes and paint, used for soldier uniforms and to camouflage army equipment, became scarce. Lucky Strike cigarettes, normally wrapped in dark green paper, changed its packaging to white, advertising, "Lucky Strike Green Has Gone to War!"

America's patriotic spirit remained high. As more men enlisted or were drafted into the armed services, the women began to take over the men's jobs. Surprisingly, they learned to build military aircraft, Jeeps, warships, guns, and tanks. A popular song heard on the radio was, "Rosie, the Riveter."

Susie Mae New quit her job in the knitting mill to take a course in welding at a Meridian vocational school. She then left for the coast to work on warships at a Pascagoula shipyard. Irvin New took a wartime job in a factory at Oak Ridge, Tennessee, where they manufactured bombs. He didn't know it at the time, it being all secret and hush-hush, but at the end of the war he was surprised to find he had worked on the atomic bomb!

After Maebelle's visit to Greenville when the war began, she was amazed to find that, after sixteen years, she was *pregnant*! Her teenaged daughters had long begged for a brother, and Leon was delighted because he still longed for a son. Joking between themselves, the girls vowed that if the baby was another girl they would pinch off her head!

Talking it over, Leon and Maebelle thought it best to leave Jeff and Belle Hunt to manage the farm while they moved to Greenville. Leon rented a little unfurnished house there on Inez Street, and they made plans to move. After the school term ended in 1942, the government paid the expense of moving the New's household goods to Greenville. Leon hired Ab Stephenson to move them in his old beat-up truck. (Well, it was wartime and one did the best he could.)

Come September, Edna Mae and Mary Ellen both enrolled in Greenville high school, Edna Mae a senior, her sister a junior. Changing schools without difficulty, Edna Mae took typing and shorthand and joined the student diversified occupation (D.O.) class. The school found her

a part-time job in the office of a local furniture store to learn how to do clerical work.

Becoming a physical education teacher appealed more to Mary Ellen. It sounded like fun! To do this, the school counselor suggested she take a course in chemistry. Both girls took a Spanish class; a year of a foreign language was required to graduate. These subjects were not offered to students at Center Hill.

On September 20, 1942, Maebelle's baby was born in Greenville's Kings Daughters Hospital. Sure enough, it was another GIRL! Leon found Maebelle crying; she was afraid the family wouldn't love the baby, but she needn't have worried. They all fell in love with the infant, passing her from hand to hand. Instead of being "spoiled," the baby was probably glad when they placed her in her crib to sleep.

Maebelle said the big girls could name the baby. They both chose to name her in honor of their idol, their Aunt Constance. They couldn't think of a second name until Mary Ellen remembered her former teacher whose name was "Amelda." They agreed it was a pretty name, if unusual, so the baby was christened "Constance Amelda New." They called her Amelda.

Maebelle was late in sending birth announcements to the folks back home. Lorena, thinking that the baby was overdue, wrote to ask for news. Hearing that they wanted a boy, she wrote that they were watching the Okatibbee Creek for the headless body of a girl baby to come floating by. Maebelle hastened to mail the birth notices.

After enlarging Greenville's Air Base, Leon was transferred a few miles further east to enlarge the landing field at Greenwood, another small Mississippi delta town. The government packed them up and moved them to a house on the edge of the new town.

Edna Mae remained in Greenville because in just two months she would graduate and receive her high school diploma. Leon found her room and board in the home of an elderly lady and her grown daughter. They were good folks, members of the same Methodist Church the News attended. For the first time in their lives, Edna Mae and Mary Ellen became separated.

The family drove back to Greenville the Friday she received her diploma. After graduating, Edna Mae remained in Greenville, taking the full-time job offered by the store where she had worked as a student. She wanted to save her money to enter college the next year.

And the war raged on! Casualty lists were high. The names of Gen. Douglas MacArthur, the Bataan Peninsula, Solomon Islands, Corregidor, Wake Island, Guadalcanal—and others—became familiar to families whose sons were sent to the South Pacific to serve in the U.S. Army and Marines. They got down their old geography books to look for the unfamiliar places they heard about in the news.

In May 1942, Gen. Dwight D. Eisenhower was appointed commanding general of the American forces allotted to fight in the European war arena. On July 4 American aircraft began flying with England's Royal Air Force to bomb the Netherlands, the first of the U.S. operations in Europe.

(In passing: Howard White, son of Ernest and Minnie White of Pine Springs had joined the Mississippi National Guard, along with others, at Key Field in 1939. A turret gunner on a B–20, making dangerous flights over Germany, his plane was hit by flack, and the pilot gave the order to jump. Checking to see that his crew had bailed out, he found Howard still on board; his parachute was damaged and he couldn't jump. Not willing to leave him behind, the pilot returned to the cockpit. "Coming in on a wing and a prayer," he flew the limping airship back across the channel and landed safely in England. We'll hear more about this White family later.)

The ground troops of the British Allies in Western Europe and North Africa were in danger of losing the war. Before the Americans entered the war, Germany had invaded Norway and seized Denmark. Germans had invaded the Netherlands and Belgium, and on May 14, 1940, the Dutch Army surrendered.

On June 6, 1940, British soldiers, chased by Germans, evacuated Europe at Dunkirk, crossing the English Channel in wild confusion. When Paris fell, Germany and France signed an armistice.

In February 1941 trapped Italian troops surrendered to the British, which prompted Hitler to send Gen. Rommel to take over the North African campaign at Tripoli. In November the British began a second invasion of North Africa, and Rommel withdrew to Egypt.

In desperate warfare the British 8th Army, commanded by Brig. Gen. Bernard Montgomery, chased the Germans out of Egypt with Rommel losing half his forces. Later, Gen. Montgomery was knighted by King George VI for this brilliant accomplishment.

Nearly a year after the United States declared war on Japan and Germany, in November 1942 Gen. Dwight D. Eisenhower, commander of the U.S. Army in the European Theatre, launched an invasion of Tunisia to aid the British. After months of planning, he sent Gen. George Patton with tanks to fight in a desert war against Rommel's Germans and Italians. Under orders of Gen. Eisenhower, Gen. Patton joined Gen. Montgomery.

In May 1943 the American and British forces declared a victory in Africa and began their next campaign against Italy, beginning in Sicily and, two months later, they gained a foothold on Italian soil at Salerno.

In August 1943 the Corps of Engineers paid Tri-State Transmit Company to move Leon New's family from Greenwood to a base at Birmingham, Alabama. Leon had rented a two-bedroom upstairs apartment on 12th St. North near downtown Birmingham.

Edna Mae did not move with them to Birmingham. Instead she went to live in Meridian with Aunt Allie Pace, widow of Dr. "Dee" Pace, and in September she enrolled in Meridian Junior College. To help pay her tuition, she found employment in Lyle Corey's law office.

When school began that fall, Mary Ellen enrolled in the big Birmingham high school that boasted 4,000 students. Instead of a school bus, she had to ride a city bus, transferring to another transit bus on the corner of the Birmingham post office. She didn't like the new school, telling Maebelle it was like a disturbed ant hill, little ants running everywhere with no time to talk.

While transferring to another bus at the post office corner, Mary Ellen spotted posters urging girls to enlist in the Women's Auxiliary Corps, the W.A.A.C. Having no brothers in the armed services, she would be Daddy's "son" to help with the war!

In patriotic fervor she went in to join but was told she had to be twenty-one. She was only seventeen.

Her cousins Edward Earl White and James Andrew Pace were both serving in the Army. As the New family leaned more toward girls than boys, these two were the only men of old Joel New's family that were of the right age and/or physical fitness to serve in America's armed services. (Also, her Uncle Lyle M. Burnham, her mama's brother, having earned his engineering degree at Texas University, was a captain in the U.S. Army, serving as an Army engineer.)

On another poster Mary Ellen read, "ENLIST TODAY IN A PROUD PROFESSION! JOIN THE CADET NURSE CORPS!" Pictured was a pretty girl wearing a sharp cadet nurse dress uniform. She would become an Army nurse! But first she had to graduate from high school, and she was only a senior. The war would be over before she could join!

Maebelle, seeing her daughter so unhappy, spoke to Leon. He arranged for Mary Ellen to return to Pine Springs to stay with Aunt Lorena White so she could graduate from Center Hill with her former classmates. She had known them since first grade.

Lawrence and Lorena White were living in a four-room house that Curtis Snowden had built on his farm in Pine Springs so Lorena would be there to take care of her sick sister, Minnie Snowden. (Aunt Minnie had developed breast cancer and was bedridden.) The older Snowden and White children had all grown up and gone, but Jacque, Lorena's youngest daughter, was a beginning student at Center Hill.

Living with Aunt Lorena, Mary Ellen rode the school bus to Center Hill each day with her little cousin, little "Jackie" White. Missing Edna Mae, she was glad to be back among her old friends.

Around the time Mary Ellen left Birmingham, Maebelle found that she was pregnant—again! Also, just after Mary Ellen left, Leon, still plagued with high blood pressure, suffered a stroke. Fortunately he suffered no paralysis, but he was forced to take a long sick leave.

Returning to Pine Springs, Leon, Maebelle, and little Amelda moved back into the old house. He had paid off the mortgage on the farm a couple of years before so at least he didn't have that to worry about.

Edna Mae remained in Meridian with Aunt Allie to be nearer the college and her work, but Mary Ellen came home from Aunt Lorena's to live with her parents. The last half of Mary Ellen's senior year while she lived at home, Ralph

Snowden hired her to drive his school bus. (Ralph had taken over the school route from his father.)

Ralph and Stella Snowden, who had a little daughter Sylvia, were expecting their second baby. Wanting to have a home of their own, Ralph asked his uncle, Leon New, to sell him enough land for them to build a house. In 1944 Leon gave him four unused acres of his farm that were located along the public road in the southeast corner of the old New homestead. Ralph commenced immediately to build a home. They were able to move into their new home later that year with their new baby, Ralph Jr.—proud papa Ralph Sr. called him "Butch."

A flooding rain came the day Mary Ellen was to receive her high school diploma, in 1944. The birth of Maebelle's new baby was imminent, so Leon didn't think it prudent for them to go to her graduation exercise. Resolutely, Mary Ellen donned her tasseled cap and robe and drove the old family Dodge over the slick muddy country roads to the schoolhouse. To keep her company, Aunt Marie Pace and her youngest daughter, Ruth Marie, rode along to cheer when she was handed her diploma. (Ruth Marie, her cousin, was two years younger than Mary Ellen.)

It was a good thing that Aunt Marie and Ruth were with her. While driving slowly up a steep rain-slicked hill, Mary Ellen felt the car gradually sliding toward the deep roadside ditch. Aunt Marie told her to stay in the car and drive slowly while she and Ruth stepped out to push the rear end of the car back toward the middle. Little by little the car, going sideways, made the hill, and they continued on their way. Mary Ellen felt guilty because Aunt Marie and Ruth's Sunday shoes were ruined by mud.

Mary Ellen had applied to join the Cadet Nurse Corps, and her teachers wrote good recommendations. At about the time she graduated, she was accepted by the Charity Hospital in New Orleans and the Physicians & Surgeons Hospital (the P. & S. Hosp.) in San Antonio. At Maebelle's request she chose the P. & S. so she could look in on Big Mama from time to time. Big Mama was getting on in years.

Baby Mable Sue New was born in the Meridian Sanitarium on May 10, 1944, near the time that Mary Ellen was to leave for her nurses training class in San Antonio. Mary Ellen felt guilty at leaving her mother with all the household chores to do while taking care of the new baby. She was consoled by thinking that Belle Hunt, living in their tenant house, would be there to help, and Edna Mae would be there on weekends.

Mary Ellen's nursing class in San Antonio was to begin on July 1, 1944. She rode the train to Dallas where she spent the night with Aunt Constance before catching the Greyhound bus to San Antonio. While in Dallas, Aunt "Connie B." took her to Neiman-Marcus to see a style show. Not having a nice dress to wear, the country girl was embarrassed to see all the ladies wearing such expensive clothes—it made her feel like the rag-picker's daughter.

Aunt Constance, seeing her distress, told her that whenever she was in a fancy place that made her feel uncomfortable, she should just put on a big friendly smile and folks wouldn't mind what she was wearing. Mary Ellen took this lesson to heart and began to smile.

Leon New, having recovered from his mild stroke, returned to his civil service job. They sent him to a base in north Mississippi where he took Maebelle and their two youngest children, Amelda and baby Mable Sue.

On April 12, 1945, President Roosevelt died at Warm Springs, Georgia. Harry Truman, the vice president, became the president of the United States. The heavy bombing of Germany continued.

Gen. Patton with his American ground troops continued to pursue the Nazi Army across

Germany, taking over town after town. On April 28 the Italian Dictator Mussolini was captured and killed by Italian partisans. On April 30 as the Americans were entering Berlin, Germany's capital, Adolph Hitler committed suicide. A few days later on May 7, the German high command surrendered all European forces unconditionally. That left only Japan to fight, as Japan refused to surrender.

Japan changed its mind after seeing the damage an atomic bomb could do. The United States dropped two of these new bombs on Japan, and on August 12, 1945, Japan surrendered. On September 2, 1945, about two weeks later, Japanese representatives signed an instrument of surrender aboard the USS battleship "Missouri" in Tokyo Bay. The war had ended!

After helping build Army bases and airfields, Leon New's job after the war was to tear them up. The civil service sent him to the base at Gulfport, Mississippi, to dismantle or move the unneeded war supplies. Some things were discarded or moved to another facility for storage, but some things were sold to private individuals who opened "Army surplus stores" to sell small items to the public. Some of the larger items, such as Jeeps, could be purchased at a bargain.

Leon moved his family to Gulfport to an apartment that had been converted from an old barracks. While they were there, Ralph Snowden wanted to know if his Uncle Leon was interested in buying back the four acres he had given him. On it Ralph had built a snug two-bedroom house that had a nice bathroom with hot and cold running water. It wasn't a big house, but it was well built. He himself had made a stone fireplace in the living room using native stones and had even built a barn big enough for two milk cows.

Ralph wanted to sell because he had a chance to buy a bigger Pine Springs farm just down the road. It would give him more room. Rodgers

Creek ran across the back of his new place, and he had an idea that he could raise and sell minnows to local fishermen.

Leon and Maebelle New. Daughters Edna Mae, Mary Ellen, Amelda, Mabel Sue, 1944

Leon didn't have the money to buy Ralph's house without going into debt, and he didn't know when he would have another stroke. However, Big Mama came to visit and heard that Ralph wanted to sell. Always looking for a good bargain, she bought Ralph's house for Maebelle. She was tired of her daughter having to live in the drafty old house that Joel New had built so many years ago. Why, it didn't even have a bathroom!

Going on vacation, Leon and Maebelle with their two youngest daughters and Mrs. Burnham drove back to Pine Springs to move into their new house. They were quite pleased with their new home.

After graduating from Meridian Junior College, Edna Mae had visited SMU (Southern Methodist University) in Dallas to enroll to become a social worker. She didn't have enough money for tuition, so she went to the dean's office. Seeing that she was sincere and intelligent and appeared to be worthy, he gave her a small scholarship, which lowered her tuition. He also gave her a job in the girls' dormitory cafeteria to pay for her room and board.

In San Antonio, Mary Ellen was having exciting new experiences in training to be a nurse. She had to study a lot, and working in the hospital was tiring, but she made lifetime friends with some of her fellow students. All in all, she found it most interesting and enjoyable.

Just before Christmas in 1946 Mary Ellen phoned her parents at Gulfport to tell them that she was married! She had married James M. White, her childhood sweetheart from Pine Springs. Leon and Maebelle were surprised—shocked—at the news. They would have liked it better if she had waited until she finished school. However, she could still graduate; she had only six more months before she could take her state board exam to become a registered nurse, and they knew that James was a nice boy.

James was the second son of Ernest and Minnie White of Pine Springs whom Leon had known most of his life. When the recent war began, James had enlisted in the Army transport service and was on an ammunition ship that saw combat in the South Pacific. On the USS G.W. Pasley he was promoted to become a bo'sun (boatswain). After the war he was given an honorable discharge.

After the war James had returned home and got a job in Meridian. On his Christmas holiday, he went out to San Antonio to visit Mary Ellen, and they just couldn't wait to be married. A machinist, James easily found a job, and they rented an apartment in San Antonio. After she married, Mary Ellen passed her state board exam and became a registered nurse.

Leon was fifty-two in 1947 when he had to give up his job at Gulfport because of his hypertension. Trying to keep his pressure down, he tried to take life easy and went back to eating garlic. He retired with a small pension, hardly enough to live on, so Maebelle got a job in a sweltering Meridian "sweat shop" garment factory—the first paying job she had in her life. She was then forty-three.

In the fall of 1948, Amelda started school. Entering the first grade at Center Hill, she waited for the school bus at their mailbox each morning while Maebelle drove the car to work. Leon looked after four-year-old Mable Sue during the day, and they became "buddies." She was a cute little tyke.

In the summer of 1948, James and Mary Ellen White returned to Pine Springs. When Mary Ellen found she was pregnant with twins, she wanted to live closer to her mother. James got work with a local building contractor, and they rented an apartment in Meridian.

Edna Mae, still at SMU in Dallas, came home for the 1948 Christmas holidays. Leon had gone to a trustee meeting at Center Hill school one evening. When Maebelle came home from work, Edna Mae was in the kitchen getting supper ready and had let the fire in the bedroom heater burn low.

Amelda and Mable Sue were wearing only their panties as they played with their dolls. Amelda was on the bed whereas Sue was on the floor, closer to the stove. As the late sun went down, the house was becoming noticeably chilly. Maebelle, thinking to restart the fire, put some green wood onto the hot coals in the heater.

Seeing that the wood was slow in catching up, she poured some kerosene onto the logs. (Leon always had the kerosene can close by the wood box to start the heater on cold mornings.)

As the fire started up, Maebelle, still holding the kerosene can, stood by the heater talking to Edna Mae in the next room. As the fire caught on, suddenly the fumes from the almost empty can exploded! Flames around the heater went all over Maebelle's legs. Worst of all, they engulfed Mable Sue who was standing nearby, near-naked.

Maebelle screamed and commenced beating out the flames on little Mable Sue, and Edna Mae came running in to help Maebelle douse the flames on Maebelle's legs. The fire, which had not spread, was quickly put out.

Leon had not yet returned from the trustee meeting at Center Hill with the car. Having no phone, Edna Mae ran as fast as she could up to their neighbor, Talmadge Smith, who drove Maebelle and Mable Sue to the emergency room at Meridian's Anderson Hospital. When they got there, someone phoned Mary Ellen to tell her what had happened. Edna Mae waited with Amelda for Leon to return home and then followed them to the hospital.

James and Mary Ellen's apartment was just three or four blocks from the hospital. They didn't have a car but Mary Ellen hastened as fast as she could to the hospital. Leon and Edna Mae arrived shortly after Mary Ellen. He saw that his wife and young daughter had been admitted to the hospital. They had admitted mother and daughter to the same room.

Mary Ellen came prepared to stay the night to act as their private duty nurse. She talked Leon and Edna Mae into going on home, saying they should get some rest and come back in the morning. They reluctantly agreed.

Maebelle, with deep blisters on both lower legs, was in agony, but little Sue, in shock, was semi-comatose. She had breathed in the flames, and her lungs were filling. She died at five o'clock in the morning of December 24, 1948, the day before Christmas.

They buried Mable Sue in the Pine Springs Methodist Church cemetery. Maebelle, still in the hospital, was unable to go, so Mary Ellen stayed with her while Edna Mae took Leon and Amelda to the funeral.

Maebelle's legs below her knees were badly burned and required skin grafts. Taking pinches of healthy skin from her upper legs, they grafted her deepest burns. In a few days she was allowed to go home.

Feeling that her daughter needed her, Big Mama, in her eighties, sold her house in San Antonio and moved to live in Mississippi. It was questionable whether she was a help or a hindrance.

It took several weeks, but Maebelle's legs eventually healed, her scars hardly noticeable. With bills mounting up, as soon as she was able, Maebelle returned to work at her job in the garment factory. She hated to go off each morning and leave Leon, Amelda, and Big Mama alone. They all needed her.

His heart failing, Leon couldn't get much done without stopping to catch his breath. He sold all his livestock except two cows that were his job to milk each day. His mind was still active, and he remained interested in politics and what was going on in the world.

Around 1950–51 the government farm bureau began a program that made it possible for farmers to build ponds to water their livestock. Leon signed up for a grant and soon large earth-moving equipment showed up to build Leon a pond. Sited in a vale about 150 yards from the back of his house, they created a pond that roughly covered three and a half acres.

Leon was no fisherman, but he stocked the new pond with White Bream and Grass Perch minnows from the state's fish hatchery outside Meridian.

Pleased with his pond, Leon ordered a cheap wooden rowboat from Sears. The boat came, but it had to be assembled and painted. Not physically able to do the job himself, his neighbor Joe Hodges was glad to help him put the boat pieces together.

Not one to fish, Leon did enjoy, at times, drifting around in his new boat. Little Amelda enjoyed swimming and had no fear of water, and someone gave her six or seven baby ducks that swam with her. Both her parents insisted that she wear a life jacket when she went to the pond, but she was spotted several times in the water not wearing her jacket. She would hold onto her floating jacket while on it the little ducks took a ride. She had learned to swim by imitating a frog.

Upon completing their education, two of the neighboring Johnson children returned to Mississippi to run a rest home near Chunky in western Lauderdale County. Dr. Rueben Johnson was a medical doctor and Dr. Adolph Johnson held his masters in agriculture. Devout Christians of the Adventist faith, they planned to open an outpatient clinic with their rest home, along with a boarding school for high school Adventist students. For tuition the students were expected to work in the rest home as nurses' aides or work in the school cafeteria. The boys were expected to work in the school's adjoining fields.

The Johnsons, who had grown up next door to the New farm, felt great kinship with Leon. After little Mable Sue died, they came to Pine Springs several times to offer prayers and condolences to her sad parents.

In the summer of 1953 the Johnsons invited Leon and Maebelle to attend an outdoor Adventist camp meeting being held in a big tent just outside Meridian. They both came. Before the summer was over both Leon and Maebelle, who were Methodist, joined the Seventh-Day Adventist Church.

In the early 1950s Maebelle New had a "tough row to hoe." Coming home exhausted from her factory job, she had to take care of the needs of her sick husband and her aging mother, and to "be there" for her ten-year-old daughter. She asked the Lord what to do and he sent her help.

The Johnsons needed a housemother for the girls' dormitory at Pine Forest Academy, the Adventist boarding school near Meehan Junction. Adolph Johnson—the students called him "Prof"—asked Maebelle to take the job. As housemother, she and young Amelda would share a private bedroom and sitting room in the girls' dorm, while Leon and Mrs. Burnham would be admitted as patients in the adjoining rest home.

This all sounded good to Maebelle, especially as they offered Maebelle a small stipend in addition to the family's room and board. Her duties would be to operate the girls' dorm and much later to act as receptionist in Dr. Reuben Johnson's outpatient clinic.

The News rented out their home in Pine Springs and moved to Pine Forest Academy in 1953. Leon, with his congestive heart failure, was nearly bedridden, while Mrs. Burnham (Big Mama), in her 80s, remained up and around, enjoying visiting with the other ambulatory patients.

They were still living at Pine Forest in the spring of 1955 when Leon had another stroke. This time it was a big one. Maebelle tried to phone Edna Mae in Burma where she and Edwin were doing missionary work for the Methodist Church. For some reason the call wouldn't go through, so she wrote them a letter, which they received a few days later.

James and Mary Ellen with their two small children were living in Savannah, Georgia, when Maebelle wrote that Leon had suffered another stroke. Planning to move back home anyway, they sped up their plans and came as quickly as they could.

As soon as they arrived, they went to the hospital to see Mary Ellen's daddy. His speech was gone, and he couldn't say a word, but he squeezed her hand and watched her as if he understood what she was saying. She told him that they were moving home and planned to build a house out there on the old farm so they could stay closer to both of their families. The old house on the farm was rotting and falling down, so they planned to salvage its timbers to use on a new house. Leon's eyes shone, and he seemed to know they were moving back.

James took Mary Ellen and their two kids out to spend the night with James' folks, the Ernest Whites, who still lived in Pine Springs. After breakfast the next morning they started out to go back to Pine Forest to visit Maebelle and see how Leon was doing.

They were halfway there when a car honked to stop them. It was Irvin who was coming to tell them that Leon had died that morning.

Maebelle wanted to bury Leon in the Pine Springs cemetery near the grave of little Mable Sue. As his funeral procession moved slowly from the mortuary out to the country, the panel truck full of wreaths and flowers in the front of the hearse had a flat tire. The tire was quickly changed while the family waited. Later, Lorena quipped, "I always said that Leon would be late for his own funeral."

When Edward Leon New died on April 4, 1955, he was a month shy of being sixty years old. He was sorely missed. He had been for so long a part of our lives. As the poet Edwin Markham wrote, "He went down as when a lordly cedar, green with boughs, goes down with a great shout upon the hills, and leaves a lonesome place against the sky."

Mary Ellen, Edna Mae, Mable Sue, Amelda New – Leon and Maebelle's four girls

My Daddy, Edward Leon New, always wanted a son, but instead he had four daughters. He loved his four girls very much and was proud of everything they did. My mother, Maebelle New, also loved us and called us her "four roses." (I once remarked to my sister, "Do you suppose she thinks we are her four bloomin' idiots?")

Edwin and Edna Mae New Shields
Children Eddie and Kathi

I. Edna Mae New Shields

Born: October 9, 1924, Dallas, Texas
Married: **Edwin William Shields**, Pine Springs
Methodist Church, Meridian, Mississippi
Died: December 9, 2004, Rush Hospital,
Meridian, Mississippi

With only 16 months difference in our ages, Edna Mae and I grew up as "twins." Mama dressed us alike, and when one got a new toy her "twin" got another just like it. We had a happy childhood, growing up on the farm in Pine Springs.

This ended in 1944 when our father, Leon New, who worked for civil service, was transferred to Greenville, Mississippi. We all moved to Greenville, but a short time later the civil service sent Daddy to Birmingham. As Edna Mae was just a few months from graduating from high school, our parents made an arrangement for Edna Mae to remain in Greenville long enough to receive her diploma. I, who had a whole year to go, moved with our parents to Birmingham. It was the first time in our lives we were separated.

The husband of Edna Mae, Edwin Shields, wrote the following:

I met Edna Mae for the first time in September 1944. Each of us had finished high school in May, she in Greenville and I in Meridian. We were attending Meridian Junior College and the class was Freshman English, taught by Dorothy Beswick. I was impressed by her abilities and she was impressed by my smart aleck attitude. By the time our sophomore year began, we wound up together in a zoology class. Since it had a lab, I asked her to be my lab partner. She proved to be very capable. On one occasion when my finger went through the hide of a poorly preserved starfish and I turned somewhat green, she took over and did the dissection while I returned to normal. When the year ended the two us and our classmates—sixteen in all—were graduated from Meridian Junior College in June of 1947.

I had worked part-time and Saturdays in the drafting room at Flintkote Company and moved up to full-time after graduation while Edna Mae was finding secretarial work in town. At the end of the summer I left for Mississippi State in Starkville while she continued working in Meridian. I came home at the end of spring term in 1947 and got a job at Meridian's Merchant & Farmers' Bank.

Sometime during that summer Edna Mae made a trip to San Antonio to see her sister, Mary Ellen, graduate to become a Registered Nurse. Leaving San Antonio she went on up to Dallas to visit the Dean of one of the schools at Southern Methodist University [SMU]. She must have made a good impression; she came away from the meeting with a variety of jobs which allowed her to live in the dorm, earn her tuition, and attend classes!

Upon returning to Meridian, Edna Mae continued working while she collected her clothing and then headed for Dallas and SMU in the fall of 1947. The school terms of '47–'48 and '48–'49 were spent at SMU. [She happened to be home for the Christmas holiday in 1948 when her youngest sister, Mable Sue, died from burns on December 24, 1948.] She once told me that she never drank a Coke during that time—she didn't have the fifty cents to spare. But there were good times, too. There were the football games with Doak Walker running. There were concerts; her favorite stars, Jeanette McDonald and Nelson Eddy, each gave one, and there were Methodist Student meetings. She liked to talk about them. In the fall of 1949 she received her college degree, a bachelor of arts degree in social group work.

And then—off to Nashville, Tennessee, to the Scarritt College for Christian Workers. By then she had the attention of the women's division of the Board of Missions and Church extensions of the Methodist Church and they began paying her way. She was working toward a master's degree in social studies and she enjoyed her classes, the professors and their surroundings. In the summer of 1950 she spent class time at the Crossville campus of Scarritt where she was able to do practical work in pottery metal work as well as fieldwork in social work.

The 1950 fall semester was to be her final at Scaritt, following which she would receive her master's degree and would probably be assigned to work in South Georgia. HOWEVER … What occurred between this paragraph and the previous one was unplanned by Edna Mae, unplanned by Ed, and to each and to both appear to be divine intervention. Two days previous, Ed had been sitting on the porch on 14th Street (his parents' home) when a horn sounded from up the street and he looked to see Edna Mae driving past, smiling and waving at him from a baby-blue Buick convertible. [The car was borrowed from Edna Mae's sister Mary Ellen and her brother-in-law, James White.] He waved and smiled back and he thought that this was the girl he had pursued for some time, with no apparent success. He gave it more thought and later that day he called and extended an invitation to a benefit baseball game on the fifth of September. The invitation was accepted, and the following evening after they watched the Quacks and Shysters battle each other in the game, Ed headed up the hills to the south where lights of the city could be seen. I guess it was the right time … we looked at each other and thought "How? What?" And the next day when we met, we began to plan the rest of our lives together!

Edna Mae went back to Scarritt and I returned to State. She came home once we told our folks our plans, and I made a trip to Nashville to meet her friends. It was so good just to be alive! I wrote to the personnel secretary with whom I had been making plans to go as a single short-term missionary. I told him there would be two of us, and he gladly changed our schedule.

We celebrated Christmas that year in two places; in Meridian with my mother and dad Shields and at Pine Springs with her mother and dad New and young Amelda New, her little sister. All this time we were making plans for our wedding in June.

Ed Shields graduated from Mississippi State in May 1951, and two weeks later, on June 10, 1951, Edna Mae New and Edwin W. Shields were married in the local Pine Springs Methodist Church. The bride's dress was hand sown by the bride and a large lacy hand-crocheted tablecloth, also made by the bride, was placed under the wedding cake.

Edwin Shields went on to tell that soon after their wedding the young couple received word from the Methodist Missionary Board (in New York) that while more teaching experience would be desirable, they were needed in the field—but first they needed to take specific training courses for missionary service that would take a year-long stay at the Kennedy School of Missions at the Hartford Seminary Foundation in Connecticut. That fall they packed their bags and went by bus to Connecticut, taking side trips in Washington and New York for sightseeing.

Indeed, their year in Hartford was quite an experience for the young couple. They took courses in linguistics, health, anthropology, and readings in Burmese history, and seminars on customs foreign to life as they knew it. That fall they enjoyed playing in the snow and were allowed a quick visit by bus at Christmas.

Come spring they were commissioned to be missionaries to Burma by a Church Bishop and were sent home to Meridian to pack their household goods to have them shipped to New York to await passage to Burma.

Sunday, July 13, 1952, was Ed Shields' birthday. The Whites (James and Mary Ellen) held a big birthday dinner for him by celebrating with a family reunion that was held under a grove of big oak trees growing beside their apartment at Key Field.

Two weeks later on July 27, Ed's elderly father, Mr. Shields, woke Edwin and Edna Mae to tell them that Ed's mother was sick. He woke them before 6 a.m., and she died before 7 o'clock.

Within a week word came from the Missionary Board that their visas to enter Burma had been denied. The board was appealing, of course, and hoped for success.

Edwin wrote:

This presented us with a pair of problems, but one of which we quickly envisioned as an opportunity as well. In the first instance, we had never planned to go off and leave a single parent alone—two, yes; they would care for one another. This may have been unrealistic, but we had no experience in such. The obvious thing would be to postpone our leaving for such an amount of time that they/we could organize things suitably. Then, almost immediately, there was another factor, which came to both of us at once.

We both knew we wanted children. We knew, even before we were married, that any children we had would have to be adopted. In the time we had up to now there had been no time for adoptions, at least a year would be needed. Now, if we wanted a year we could take a year. A letter went off to the board telling them to put us on leave without a salary and I'd get a job until we received our visas. This was done.

I began a search for employment, and Edna Mae at once began a search for adoption agencies. The responses to her queries were mostly, "Well, we can put you on the list, but it may take several years."

Most were just negative. One of the places we inquired was the Methodist Home Hospital in New Orleans. They gave us names of other places to try, which turned out to be non-productive. Edna

Mae finally called them back and said, "Look, you are Methodist, and we will soon be commissioned to serve as Methodist missionaries. Once we leave this country, we are not going to have a chance to adopt a child until we come home on leave four years from now. Can't you help?"

Faced with a clearly determined person, they agreed to help but said they didn't have a child available right then.

In August I went by the employment office and was told to go see the superintendent of education at the courthouse. They needed a science teacher at one of the Lauderdale County schools.

The school was Martin High School, ten miles out from Meridian. The schedule was seven periods a day, and I taught math and science in all of them. Edna Mae recalls that she was widowed, as my time was spent in making lesson plans, marking papers, and not much else. She spent her time cleaning house. (With the likelihood of a social worker expected to inspect our home, the house got a cleaning it had not had for a long time.) I came in from school one afternoon to find my wife glowing. A social worker had come by that day and found her busy making cookies! She had seemed impressed.

On one March day in 1953, we had a call from New Orleans. It was the worker there with whom we had talked, telling us that we could come down and pick up our son!

We borrowed James and Mary Ellen's Buick convertible and drove down to New Orleans. The next day little Eddie (Edwin Wm. Shields Jr.) less than a year old, rode on the seat between us, his new mother feeding him ice cream as we sped back to Meridian, a family complete.

The visas for the Shields to enter Burma finally came through in the fall of 1953. On the last day of October, they caught the train from Meridian for New York. There they sailed via MV Britannic to Liverpool, England, where, after two weeks, they sailed via the Salween for Rangoon, Burma. Edna Mae wrote her folks about how pleased the Salween's captain was that little Eddie had taken his first steps aboard his ship.

The missionaries' ship arrived at Rangoon in Burma two days before Christmas in 1953, and they were given temporary quarters in the Scotts Kirk Manse where they stayed with the Hollisters. After the Yuletide holidays, they began taking lessons to learn the Burmese language, and Edwin began to teach at the Methodist English School in Rangoon. They stayed with the Hollisters until April 1954, when the Mission Board found them a home, which was located on 321 Godwin Street in Rangoon.

After their first year in Rangoon, in March of 1955 the Shields spent their first one-month vacation in the cool hills of the Southern Shan state town of Kalaw.

Edwin Shields wrote:

In the first week of April we set out to return to Rangoon, 400 miles to the south. We had arrived by plane but we had the opportunity to return by road as the lady missionary appointed to Kingswood School had come to the end of her term and wished to return her car to Rangoon. She had decided that we could all go together if I would drive, and I happily seized the chance.

We set out early on an April morning; Etha Nagler, her Burmese cook, Edna Mae,

Eddie, and myself, the car fully loaded and all of us feeling as this was the start of a great adventure, singing "blue skies smilin' at me, nothing but blue skies do I see." Down the hill to Mekila we joined the main highway to Rangoon.

We were making pretty good time but somewhere near Pyinmana where there had been a former mission station, we came to a bridge which was being worked on. In trying to detour around it, we got stuck. Although this sounds like a serious problem, it wasn't. There were farmers about, and although they had no mules, they did have water buffalo and were happy to pull us free (for a small fee) and send us on our way.

We hadn't lost much time, and there was lots of daylight left, so we continued on to see just how much more we could cover before it got dark. We were having a good adventure! A few miles on, almost to Toungoo, I spotted a truck/bus stopped and what appeared to be a soldier beside it. As we approached he waved the truck on and gestured for us to stop. We did so and he came up to the car as I was searching my pockets for papers, assuming it was some sort of checkpoint. Suddenly, he was thrusting his rifle against my chest, exclaiming, "Thoung dour'! Thoung dour'!" which I didn't understand as my slight knowledge of Burmese had vanished with the sight of the gun. The cook interjected, "He's saying three thousand!"

I said, I didn't have three thousand and proved it by emptying my pockets and producing a ten kyat banknote. This had the effect of really irritating him. He prodded me with the gun, and I could smell him and there was a strong smell of alcohol.

The thought briefly ran through my mind that this was the height of ridiculous: "God, I've travelled halfway round the earth to get shot by a drunk, angry bandit!"

I pulled off my wedding ring, gave up my watch, and Etha produced a 100 Kyat note. The bandit's assistant insisted that Edna Mae also had a ring, but she had gotten it off. (She was sitting on it.) They stepped back and waved us on and we went down the road in a hurry. I expect they disappeared into the woods since they had to know that the truck he had stopped would have given the alarm at the next police post. The next little town was Thawatee where we made a report to the police.

Next we came to Tougoo, located the government Bungalow, and spent the night. I can't remember the next day; it was without incident. It would've had to take a good bit to be more impressive than what we had just experienced.

About the time they returned from vacation, they received bad news from Mississippi; Edna Mae's father, Edward Leon New, had suffered another stroke and had died on April 4, 1955.

After the Shields had been in Burma for nearly five years, they wanted to take off a year from their work to return to the United States, their reasons being twofold. Edwin's old father, Edwin Pace Shields, was ill and was not expected to live much longer, and his son wanted to see him again before he died. Edwin also wanted to take a year off from work to go back to school to earn his master's degree.

Edna Mae (along with Edwin) wanted to find another baby to adopt to raise along with young Eddie. From experience she felt she needed a year to make this happen.

The Shields flew by Pan Am for Hong Kong where they shopped for two weeks before boarding the USS President Cleveland, to sail via Japan, Hawaii, and then on to San Francisco. From there they took the train down to Los Angeles and then on to Phoenix to visit Mg Tin and other Burmese students, then on to the Grand Canyon to visit Edna Mae's old college friends.

Returning to Phoenix, they took the Greyhound to Dallas where they spent a couple of nights with Edna Mae's Aunt Constance. The last of their long journey home was to Meridian, Mississippi, where they were met by Edna Mae's mother, Maebelle New. (After Leon died, Miss Maebelle and young Amelda had stayed on at Pine Forest Academy where she was housemother in the girls' dorm.)

Edwin Shields wrote:

Dad was in the nursing home at the Pine Forest Sanitarium [in May 1958]. He'd been moved there about a year before. I think the doctors there were just trying to hold onto him until I got home. He had tubes in and out. I visited him daily but never got a response. He just looked at me with his "eagle eye'" but showed little emotion. My son Eddie got the only sign … he came back one day and announced that "Granddaddy laughed at me."

One day toward the end of the month I was called down early at 2 a.m. and sat with him for a while. A few days later I got a similar call, but this time he was gone by the time I got there. I think rational life had ended some time before. When we left home back in 1953 his last words had been, "Son, I didn't think you'd do this to me." I have lived with those words.

The following month the Shields went to New York for Edwin to begin the summer session at the teachers college of Columbia University. As quickly as they could, they both met with an adoption agency who had seemed interested when Edna Mae had written earlier from Burma.

June and July of 1958 was summer school for Edwin while Edna Mae had visitors from CAS social workers to see what kind of home they had. (Been there—done that.) Evidently they were satisfied but told Edna Mae they didn't have a child yet. Edna Mae told them, "You will."

On October 17, 1958, they adopted baby Kathryn Edna, who had been born that year on August 12. Christmas that year they celebrated as a COMLETE family. Joy!

Soon after Christmas the Shields were told that when they returned to Burma they would be going to Kalaw where Edwin, with his new master's degree, would be principal of the Kingswood School. Both the place and the job were exciting, ideal for the young family.

Taking a nonstop flight to San Francisco, the Shields took up temporary residence with Mary Ellen, James, and family at nearby San Jose. It became a grand reunion when Maebelle and Amelda drove out to California from Mississippi. They brought along Edna Mae's grandmother, Big Mama (Mrs. Harriet Burnham) and had stopped along the way to pick up Aunt Constance at Dallas. While they were there, Uncle Lyle Burnham drove down from his home in Oregon for a weekend visit.

When the Shields finally got their permit for Burma in July, 1959, they flew out on a plane that stopped in Guam, Wake, and finally, Manila. They had a quick visit in Manila with one of Edna Mae's former schoolmates on the July 4 holiday—it was HOT!—and then on to Hong Kong and Rangoon.

They spent nearly a week in Rangoon sorting through things they had earlier left in storage, picking out what they would need at their new home in Kalaw. Their worst finding was in a large steamer trunk in which they had stored papers, photos, and some articles of clothing that looked OK, but as soon as it was opened they found much of the contents had been reduced to dust by termites. They made their selections of immediate needs and set out for Kalaw.

The next six years, spent in Kalaw from 1959 through 1965, were a happy time; the Shields family all together and content. They were 400 miles from Rangoon with its committee meetings, government supervision, etc., all together on their own.

This began to change in 1962. The military seized power from the elected government officials, bringing about a number of changes. By 1964 it became clear that the new communist government was not going to allow expatriate workers to continue to stay in Burma. The Shields left Burma on March 30, 1965, knowing they would have to continue their work in other places.

Since the Shields had no out-of-station leave for six years, the board allowed them to take their time in getting home. They visited India (the Taj), Egypt, Athens, and arrived in London shortly before Easter in time to meet Mother New when she flew in from the States. They arranged to buy a British Dormobile (a camper) and set out on a 7,000 mile jaunt through France, Monaco, Italy, Switzerland, Austria, Liechtenstein, Germany, the Netherlands, and back to the UK, and finally to Southampton where they sailed on the MV Rotterdam for New York.

In the summer of 1966 the Shields were told that their next assignment was to be in Sarawak, a British colony of Malaysia that was on the island of Borneo. They drove their camper to California to visit Mary Ellen and her White family again before setting out for Sarawak. They boarded a twelve-passenger Norwegian freighter, the Sunnyville, to sail to Manila. From Manila they flew to Sibu in Sarawak.

(On the trip aboard the Sunnyville they had teased young Kathy by telling her that she might miss her birthday on August 12 since that might be the day they crossed the dateline. When she awoke on the twelfth, every signal flag on the ship had been hoisted and the sky was filled with colorful flutter. In the evening there was a party with birthday gifts for Kathy as the guest of honor.)

Following their arrival in Sarawak, the Shields took a riverboat down to Sarikei where they were to teach. Edna Mae had agreed to teach two classes of English in the mornings; in the afternoons she homeschooled young Kathy. They took a look at the house where they were to live and lunched at a teashop on the way back. They had wanted Eddie to have a look at their new home since the teenager had to return to Singapore to start eighth grade in a boarding school, the Singapore American School.

The Methodist Secondary School in Sarikei was two miles from where the Shields lived. They bought two bicycles to travel to and from school. At the end of the year Edwin figured they had biked over 1,000 miles. "No wonder I'm so tired!" Edna Mae replied.

At the end of the first year in Sarawak (1967), Edwin was made school principal. He taught fourth and eighth standard English classes, some scripture, earth science, and health science. Edna Mae stopped teaching, being involved in Planned Parenthood activities in Sarikei plus helping the choir at church and other town activities. Kathy was ten in 1968 when they sent her to Singapore to live in the Methodist hostel with Eddie, Mrs. Snead being the hostel mother. That was the year Edwin bought a secondhand 90cc Honda motorcycle, which was a help since he often had to make several trips a day to school.

After Eddie graduated from the Singapore American School in June of 1971, all the Shields left Asia on a leave to the United States. It was the last one-year leave from Malaysia they were to take; about this time the Malaysian parliament passed a law that expatriates would only be allowed to work in the country for a maximum of ten years.

Eddie was to begin his college studies at Springfield College in Massachusetts while the others lived in Ithaca, New York, so Edwin could study Indonesian and other Southeast Asian history and cultures at Cornell University.

While Edwin was in school, Edna Mae and both children visited the Burnhams, Edna Mae's Uncle Lyle and Aunt Becky who lived in Portland, Washington. While there Edna Mae bought a car.

After a pleasant year at Cornell and a Christmas visit from Mother New, the Shields drove down for a visit in Mississippi. Leaving Eddie with the car, ready to return to Springfield, Edwin, Edna Mae, and Kathy returned to Sarawak.

Upon reaching Sarawak, Kathy was returned to her school in Singapore and Edwin returned to his teaching. Unfortunately, the school was passing students for a variety of reasons (political?) and, at the end of the year Edwin was transferred to Sibu where he was posted to teach science at Pilley Memorial Methodist High School. Edna Mae found a variety of areas in which she could be of help to the school and community as well. She was very involved in Wesley Church, and an English/Chinese expatriate young group, particularly women's activities such as the Women's World Day of Prayer.

Edwin wrote:

It was during this period [1973–75] just after Easter when Kathy was home for spring break that Kathy came running in from her room as I was dressing to tell me. "A man has mother locked in my bathroom!" I headed to Kathy's room, pausing a moment as I passed the telephone to call the police, and found the bathroom door locked. I put my shoulder to it but it was well-made. I called out to Edna Mae, and she answered in Burmese, telling me that the man had a gun. Immediately there was muttering and she switched back to English so the intruder could understand. She relayed his demands: $2,500 in cash and an air ticket to New York, and I was not to call the police. I told him I'd see what I could do, not mentioning that I'd already called the police.

I called Mr. Burr at the Mission Office and told him what was happening. I talked to the police who were already prowling around and asked them to be inconspicuous. They agreed to remain concealed. I talked with the bandit through Edna Mae and asked if there was anything else he wanted. He wanted a Coke. So I fixed him one with the cap off with some sleeping pills put in and the cap replaced. We passed it up thru the bathroom window.

We finally agreed that I would have the car backed out and started and I would toot the horn and he would bring Edna Mae out to get in the car and I would take them to the airport. The tickets arrived and the money was passed to him through the window.

Meantime, Kathy had dressed and I had led her out of the house and back to the back fence and had helped her over, telling her to follow the road out and come the way around the block to Methiah's house. By then there were hidden police all over the place. Following instructions, I went down and started the car and drove it to the front steps and tooted the horn. In a moment the bandit appeared at the front steps dressed all in black with a hood over his head with Edna Mae walking in front with her hands tied behind her back. They moved down the steps and as they stepped toward the car, suddenly there were police everywhere. A shot was fired, and the bandit was on the ground and it was all over. Edna Mae was off to one side, and the bandit was being hammered and kicked by the police. It turned out that the gun was a toy, though it looked real enough. The shot fired by the police had gone into the bandit's thigh from the rear. The chief officer asked if I could take them down to the hospital and, after I unwound the electric cord from Edna Mae's wrists, we went off with the chief telling me "Drive slowly, Edwin. Drive slowly!"

By 1975 Eddie had finished three years at Springfield College and became fed up with things that seemed to have no relevance to soccer (which he loved). He quit Springfield College and joined the Army. He had also found a prospective mate while at Springfield. He and Diane Deyoe of Framingham, Massachusetts, planned to be married in September.

So, when Kathy's junior year in high school ended at Singapore, the Shields flew off to Framingham to meet the bride's parents, Frank and Rita Deyoe, and attend their son's wedding.

In the following year Edwin and Edna Mae were still doing their thing at Pilley School while Kathy finished high school in Singapore. They flew over to Singapore to see Kathy graduate and then put her on a plane to fly alone to Mississippi. She and her mother had looked at several schools in Mississippi and had finally selected Wood Jr. College near Starkville. Aunt Mary Ellen, who

lived near Meridian, helped get her settled in, and she spent the next two years there before entering Mississippi State University.

While Edwin was acting as principal at the Pilley School in 1978, the government of Malaysia informed him that his time limit for living and working in Malaysia was going to expire in November. They began to pack their belongings and get ready to leave.

On their final day in Malaysia, Edwin was at school signing report cards when the phone rang. It was Kathy calling to introduce Edna Mae to her fiancé, John Howard Patton, and also saying that when they came through Singapore, if they wanted, they could pick up some white Chinese brocade for her wedding dress.

The Shields bid farewell to Malaysia in mid-November and flew to Singapore for a week of shopping, and then to Burma and Kathmandu to visit friends. Then they flew to Frankfurt, Germany, where Eddie's wife Diane met them and took them to Nuremburg where Eddie was stationed. In Nuremburg they had a chance to meet their first grandchild, Eddie's baby daughter, little Laura Mae Shields.

After visiting in Germany for two weeks with Eddie's family, they flew to New York where they were met by Edna Mae's younger sister, Amelda Neil. Amelda and her husband Jay Neil introduced them to a friend who sold the Shields a Volvo station wagon for $800.

They drove by Framingham to see Eddie's in-laws, the Deyoes, and then on to Nashville to visit a contributing missionary congregation, and then on to Mississippi. In Mississippi they stopped at Durant to meet Kathy's future in-laws, the Pattons, and then stopped at Starkville to meet Kathy's intended, John Howard Patton. The wedding was set for June in the Chapel of Memories located on the Starkville campus.

Finishing their furlough in 1979, the GBGM (General Board of Global Ministries) sent the Shields to Kathmandu in the country of Nepal to open a hostel for the children of Christian ministers. They operated the hostel over the next few years.

The Shields were nearing retirement age in 1985 when, while in America the GBGM offered them a posting in the Southeast Jurisdiction of the Methodist Church for a two-year period of time. So they came home from overseas work.

Edwin Shields wrote:

From 1985 to the end of 1987 we were to live and work out of Atlanta, covering the southeast from Mississippi to the Atlantic, from the Gulf of Mexico to Washington, D.C. We got into all those states, some more than others, mostly by car. We did "saturation" coverage, speaking to groups in various places and sometimes covered several churches on Sundays, Edna Mae going one way, I going another. It was both exhausting and exhilarating. I still hear from some of the people.

After we moved back to Mississippi in 1987, we still received opportunities to visit churches but were ready to start building our retirement home. Over the years we had drawn and re-drawn our house plans, and Mrs. New had given us a share of the old New farm located outside Meridian in the Pine Springs community. We cleared a space for our floor plan, marking it roughly with sapling trunks and then, with the direction of a good, retired carpenter, arranged the outlines and drove the post for the corners.

The site was on a slope, just where the old New home (built by Edna Mae's grandfather Joel New) had stood, where

Edna Mae had lived when she, Mary Ellen, and their parents first came to Mississippi 'way back in 1932. A neighbor had brought a motor grader and dug a hole so we could have a basement (a bit unusual in that community) and when he was done our part of the work began. The building went on, and in May 1989, with funds exhausted, we were able to part company with our carpenter, 'Deb' Ivey, and we moved in on our anniversary on June 10. In July we drove to an annual missionary conference, and at the end, we officially retired.

In 2003 we drove to Starkville to see Kathy's son, John Alden Patton, playing the field as a wide receiver on the football team. Edna Mae didn't feel like going, so Kathy's new husband, Charles, and I went together. John Alden got the ball and ran the entire length of the field and scored a touchdown!! Joy!!

Edna Mae was already in bed when I got home. The next morning, Kathy had to be off to attend a training class in West Point. I, ready to get back to Meridian, was loading the car. Edna Mae was just ahead of me as we went out the door to the garage … WHEN IT HAPPENED!

I spoke to Edna Mae, "Watch out for the cat!" (Kathy had a couple of cats that were not supposed to go outside, but they were rather crafty.) Maybe it was the tone of my voice … whatever …, my wife EXPLODED!

I don't recall her words, but in any case, it wasn't Edna Mae. It was somebody I didn't even know. She stalked out of the garage, down the drive, and then made a turn toward a neighbor's house, and all the time I was trying to persuade her to come back to the house, but she was protesting that she was being kidnapped!

By now Charles was with me. With one on either side we got her up to the house, but she was still struggling. She was trying to reach out for things to throw. I asked Charles to pass me the phone. While I talked on the phone, she pulled my right arm up to her mouth and chomped down on it. I dialed 911 and asked someone to come help take a woman to the hospital. A pair of men came very soon and strapped her onto a gurney, and I asked Charles to lead me to the hospital, and we followed in my car. When we got to the hospital, I told them what had happened, but they didn't seem too surprised. They said they had sedated her, and if I wanted they would give her more sedation, and I could put her in the car and take her to Meridian. Having just witnessed an explosion, I asked if we could have the ambulance take her to Rush Hospital in Meridian, and I would meet them there. They agreed.

When I arrived at Rush Hospital, they had admitted her to a room. She was awake and was not quite sure why she was there. I talked with a doctor, and I don't recall what he said, but he suggested that they admit her to the nearby Alliance Hospital in what he termed the "geri-psych ward." I guessed he meant the nerve disorders of the aged. So I took her over there and she went placidly enough. I don't know if she was sedated or not.

They made more tests there and adjusted her medicines, suggesting that she be admitted to a nursing home. I made inquiries and visited several. Someone suggested I visit the King's Daughters Home, so I went out to see. I was much impressed with their care and their charges sounded possible, so I chose that place.

Eddie came down from Massachusetts, and together we went and got her. She made no protest and for the next fourteen months she seemed happy at King's Daughters. I was never quite sure that she knew the relation between us, or even if she clearly knew who I was. Much of the time she was satisfied—I won't say happy—but smiling at times and never really quarrelsome as some of the other patients were.

The chief thing that made her smile was her little dog Patches. We came every day except Sunday. Patches acquired a taste for ice cream as the attendants would sometimes bring around little plastic cups, and he would always be given one.

Once when Amelda and Jay came down for a visit from New Hampshire, she and Mary Ellen were "jollying" their big sister and she smiled. Jay took their picture and an enlargement hangs in my bedroom.

On October 9, 2004, I made fresh peach ice cream and took it out for her eightieth birthday. On December 9, two months later, my phone rang at 3 a.m. The nurse on duty was calling to let me know that Edna Mae had vomited during the night and had sucked some of the vomit into her lungs. They had taken her to Rush Hospital.

I went to the hospital and spent the day. Edna Mae was conscious but not very active. I talked to various doctors, and they were noncommittal. Dr. Abney finally said something that caused me to ask, "She *might make it or not, but don't count on it?" He nodded.*

As the sky started to darken, the nurses were asking if any visitors wanted to spend the night. I finally realized that if I were going to spend the night a shower and some more comfortable clothing would be desirable, so I left and headed for a quick trip home.

I hadn't been there long before my phone rang. It was Edna Mae's niece, Jan Ash—Edna Mae was gone.

We had a good life. AMEN.

Children of Edwin W. and Edna Mae New Shields:

1. **Edwin W. "Eddie" Shields Jr.**
   Married: **Diane Deyoe**, daughter of Frank and Rita Deyoe of Massachusetts
   Children: **Laura Mae Shields Pidgeon**, **Karen Marie Shields Baldwin**, and **Julie Shields**

2. **Kathryn Edna "Kathy" Shields**
   Married: (1) **John Howard Patten** and (2) **Charles Hester**
   Children: **John Alden Patten**

II. *Mary Ellen New White*

Born: February 13, 1926, Dallas, Texas
Married: **James Monroe White**, December 23, 1946, San Antonio, Texas
(Her autobiography is the next chapter)
Children: (As listed in following chapter)

1. & 2. **Peggy Jean and Patsy Ann White** (twins)
3. **James M. "Jim" White Jr.**
4. **Janice Ellen White**
   (See final chapter)

Jay and Amelda New Neil
Children: Jay, Jr., Joel Edward, June

III. *Constance Amelda New Neil*

Born: September 20, 1942, Greenville, Mississippi
Married: **Jay Lee Neil M.D.**, June 1961, Pine Forest Academy, Lauderdale County, Mississippi

Amelda New Neil's life story follows, which she wrote in 2008:

In 1942 as World War II was going on, my father was working for the Civil Service Corps of Engineers helping build air bases around Mississippi and Alabama. Mother took their two older daughters and moved to Greenville, Mississippi, to be with him, so that September I was born in Greenville instead of Meridian. Edna Mae was a senior in high school, Mary Ellen a junior, and I was a much loved, held, and played with baby. Three mothers! This has given me a security and a feeling of being loved that I have always valued.

About my first birthday, my father had his first stroke, which was the beginning of a long, slow downhill battle, both mentally and physically, until his death when I was twelve. This was the greatest loss of my life, as I knew him more as a kind grandfather. I missed not having a father.

When I was in first grade, age six, there was a fire in my parent's bedroom that resulted in severe burns for my mother and the death of my little sister, Mabel Sue, age four, from smoke inhalation. This also had a big impact on me.

When I was about seven or eight, Roy Wolf, who was from our Pine Springs community and had gone on to become a fine Methodist preacher, came back "home" to have a revival meeting in our little Methodist church. Our New family was always there whenever the church doors opened, so of course we went to the meetings every night and to both meetings on Sunday. The only thing I remember Roy Wolf saying that week was in response to the folks chuckling at some humorous point he had made: "Now watch out, or I'll take your picture and put it in my pickle patch!" But my heart was responding to another voice I was hearing—I had heard it before in my mother's and later in Pearl Harris' Sunday school lessons, and now I responded to it when Roy Wolf made a call. I went forward to give my life, my love, to Jesus. This was the greatest decision of my life.

My childhood on the farm in Pine Springs was happy. I spent a lot of time by myself playing in our pond and in the woods and fields around our home with dolls, books, farm animals, my horse Tiny (whom I had claimed after Edna Mae left home), my paper dolls, and a great imagination. The highlight of those years was when Mary Ellen and James or Edna Mae and Edwin would come out from town to visit or when I could visit them.

My mother, who had to get a paying job after Daddy became ill, felt that my young life was a little too unsupervised, so my fifth grade year in school was spent with Edna Mae and Edwin in town attending Meridian's Witherspoon School instead of our country school, Center Hill. Mother would take me home on weekends. That way Edna Mae would see that I settled down and did my studies.

Well, she sure tried—but I missed my mother and home. I don't know if Edna Mae ever forgave me for the afternoon I took off for home (ten miles out in the country) without telling her. After school she and Ed looked all over for me and were on their way out to face my mother with the horrible fact that they didn't know where I was when Mother and I met them halfway to town. I had had an easy time getting home. A neighbor, seeing me walking along the road alone, had given me a ride home, and now Mother was taking me back to Edna Mae. I was happy—but it sure felt good to have Mother there to explain to Edna Mae what had happened. Punishment? How do you punish a child that has only gone to her mother?

As my father's health worsened, Grandmother (Mother's mother, Mrs.

Harriet Burnham) came to live with us when I was still a carefree seven or eight year old. I was not learning much responsibility because Mother was working long hours at a garment factory in town. Our family needed help!

Adolph Johnson and his wife Jerusha invited Mother to become the dean of girls at the Seventh-day Adventist boarding school, Pine Forest Academy, which was about twenty-five miles away at Chunky, Mississippi, in the western part of the county. This seemed, and proved, to be a godsend. Daddy and Grandmother moved into the nursing home that was connected with the school while Mother and I moved into the girls' dorm, a stone's throw away. All the students were expected to work; the school put me to work at once carrying meal trays to the patients. We were all together with all our individual needs being met and we were able to contribute.

My next eight years were spent at Pine Forest Academy where I learned not only schooling, but also how to work. I gained a much-needed direction for my life, and I loved every minute of it.

Pine Forest Academy was small, having about forty to fifty high school students. We were more like a big family. When I was a sophomore, a young man, Jay Neil, entered the school for his senior year. He wasn't ordinary. A natural leader, he preached his first sermon that year. Being so responsible and smart, he made the other boys look immature. I was only a sophomore, so young, but I enjoyed being around him.

When three years later, taking a year out of college, he returned to Pine Forest to be the boys' dean, he made known his

desire to get to know me. I was amazed. By then I was eighteen and through school. When he asked, of course I said "Yes!" We were married June 18, 1961.

Jay's schooling and starting our family occupied the next several years. Our son Jay Neil Jr. was born in 1962. Jay Neil Sr. graduated as a physical therapist from Loma Linda University in California in 1964, the year that our second son, Joel Edward Neil, was born. Jay was chief therapist at Hialeah Hospital in Florida for three years while he finished his pre-med college requirements. Also, while in sunny Florida little June Evelyn Neil joined our family in 1966.

From Florida we returned to California so Jay could go to medical school. He graduated in the top ten of his class in 1971 and the next four years were occupied by his orthopedic surgical training at Loma Linda University. This sounds like Jay's story instead of mine, but this formed the framework around which my life revolved.

After Jay became a doctor, we lived in beautiful northwest New Jersey for four years, along with short stretches of time spent in northern California, Chicago, and Mississippi. In 1982 we made our home in New Hampshire.

Jay Jr. finished medical school, married Terri Dickenson, and completed an anesthesia residency. They gave us our firstborn grandchild, beautiful Jenna Renee Neil, who is now in high school. Her brother, charming Mason Elliot Neil, is now in seventh grade. Bangor, Maine, is their home.

Our Joel Edward Neil received his master of divinity degree and married

Sonya Gully. Their graceful daughter Caroline Grace Neil came first and is now in high school. Their son, keen and clever Clayton Edward Neil, is now acing the seventh grade near their home in Collegedale, Tennessee.

Our daughter June is a nurse midwife. She married Dr. Wayne Dysinger and had two sons—Stephen Neil, our first grandson, and William Joel Neil, our youngest grandchild. William is a high achieving Down syndrome darling.

Young Stephen was an unusually outgoing boy, passionately engaged in life, who faced cancer and death at age thirteen with great peace. "What's the big deal? I close my eyes, next time I open them I'll see Jesus." June and William now live in Atlanta, Georgia.

It sounds as though my life is defined by my family and, in a way, it is. That is how I wanted it. My life has been filled with many enjoyable pursuits—family, church activities, sewing, flower gardening, and freedom to follow my nose at times. The verse, "Let me live in a house by the side of the road and be a friend to man," has always appealed to me. I have written no books, performed no great deeds, nor earned any degrees—but my life has been great! I have cared for my family and tried to give a helping hand to those who passed. "She hath done what she could." [Mark 10:8]

Children of Constance Amelda New and Jay Neil:

1. **Jay Neil Jr.** (1962–), m. **Terri Renee Dickenson**
   A. **Jenna Renee Neil**
   B. **Mason Elliot Neil**
2. **Joel Edward Neil** (1964–), m. **Sonya Lorraine Gully**
   A. **Caroline Grace Neil**
   B. **Clayton Edward Neil**
3. **June Evelyn Neil** (1966–), m. **Wayne Dysinger, M.D.**
   A. **Stephen Neil** (d. July 2006)
   B. **William Joel Neil**

IV. Mable Sue New

Born: May 10, 1944, Meridian, Mississippi
Died: On December 24, 1948, from burns and smoke inhalation when their Pine Springs home caught on fire. Buried in the Pine Springs Methodist cemetery.

Chapter XVI
And Me – Mary Ellen
(born February 13, 1926)

I, second daughter of Leon and Maebelle New, was born in Dallas, but I don't remember much about living in Texas as we moved to Mississippi when I was six years old. Entering first grade, I remember riding the school bus each morning with a bunch of other kids, and meeting my teacher, Miss Clayton. Once when she was helping me learn to write I told her that she smelled just like my Big Mama. I hope she didn't take it as an insult. Big Mama always smelled like Avon's "Cotillion Toilet Water."

There was a cute little boy named James in my class that I liked. He must have liked me, too, 'cause most every day at recess he would go across the road to Avery's Store and bring me back a five-cent Baby Ruth candy bar. His daddy, Mr. Ernest White, worked for the county, so he had spending money for his lunch. My daddy just farmed, so Mama had to make biscuit and egg sandwiches for my sister Edna Mae and me to eat at lunch recess. (Nowadays they have a school cafeteria.)

When I was in second grade my class put on a play for the whole school in the big auditorium, a play about a wedding of the flowers. I was given the part of a tulip so Mama took the pattern they gave her and made me a tulip dress out of crepe paper. My little boyfriend, James White, a sunflower, wore, like the other boys, a pleated bright yellow ruffle around his neck. I was so glad James and I were partners when the tulips and sunflowers marched on stage. I still remember the songs we sang.

Me:

> *Tulip Red, Tulip Red,*
> *Waken, waken, lift your head!*
> *Spring is here! Spring is here!*
> *So the merry Robin said.*

James:

> *Marching, Marching, Marching*
> *straight and tall.*
> *Marching, Marching, Sunflowers all.*
> *Looking above to the sun so high*
> *We turn to salute it in the western sky!*

After completing twelve years in school, I was ready to graduate with the class of 1944. At that time World War II was in progress, and I dreamed of being an Army nurse to take care of our gallant brave boys who had been wounded. I was accepted and joined the government's cadet nurse program at a school of nursing in San Antonio. The war ended before I completed my nurse training, but I continued and became a registered nurse.

James White was not accepted for the U.S. Army because he had a perforated eardrum. He joined, instead, the Army Transport Service and his ship, an ammunition ship the USS Pasley, was deployed to the battle zone in the South Pacific. In

James M. White, Sailor

Mary Ellen New, Cadet Nurse

the coming months he was promoted from being an able body seaman to a boatswain. Discharged after the war he returned to Mississippi where he got a job with a building supply plant in Meridian. We had been writing each other all during the war, and now he wanted to come to see me in San Antonio.

As luck would have it I was working on the 3–11 shift in the newborn nursery when his wire came. He wired to tell me to meet him at the Greyhound bus station at 8 o'clock. I called the nurses home and arranged for two of my classmates to meet him because I had to work.

Mary Lou Cleverly and Lovie Sparks offered to go pick James up and bring him to the dorm to wait for me to get off duty. Around nine, Mary Lou came over to the hospital to report.

"I declare, New, that's the *handsomest* man I ever saw! The minute I laid eyes on him my drawers rolled up like window shades!"

James had a week off from his job for the Christmas holidays. We decided to not wait for me to graduate but go on and get married right away. Frank Hovell, who dated another of my classmates, took James down to the courthouse for him to get a wedding license. On my next day off, on December 23, 1946, we were married in the small prayer chapel of San Antonio's Travis Park Methodist Church with two of my classmates witnessing. My best friend, Margie Johns, was hurt because she hadn't been told I was getting married. She had been out of town at that time. She and I were roommates.

James, a trained machinist, had no trouble locating a local job. He was hired by the Blue-White Diamond Instrument Company, a small company that made diamond-coated dental drills. We had no car, but the city bus stopped right in front of his plant's office.

We quickly rented an apartment near the hospital so I could continue my nurse's training. I had to study for my state board nurse exam, but I passed without any problem. Cleverly and I were the only two of our class who passed the entire exam the first try without having to go back and take part of it again.

That summer Edna Mae came to visit us and to see me graduate. After graduating from Meridian Junior College she was on her way to Dallas to see about enrolling at SMU. We enjoyed her visit and eagerly listened at what was going on back home. I think James and I were both homesick.

In June (1947) James and Edna Mae saw me graduate and receive my nurse's cap and pin while wearing my first long-sleeved white uniform. I was a full-fledged registered nurse!

Edna Mae went on to Dallas, and James kept on working at his job. I began to take private duty cases where I had only one patient to care for. It seemed so easy taking care of only one patient after having to worry over a whole ward. And the pay! As was the custom, private duty nurses were paid a dollar an hour, *eight dollars per day*! I never felt so rich in my life!

Upon discovering that I was pregnant, I wanted to go home. We moved back to Mississippi and rented an apartment in Meridian close to Anderson Hospital. James got a job working for a building contractor who was building a new factory for the Wire-Bound Box Company.

On September 23, 1948, I delivered twin girls. James and I were so proud! We named them Peggy Jean and Patsy Ann. Our joy was short lived, however, because both infants survived less than a day. We had our babies buried in the cemetery out at Pine Springs.

Meantime, the Box Company that James had helped to build was completed and ready to begin operation. James, on the spot, applied for a job in its maintenance department. He, the number one employee of the local Meridian Company, was sent to Rockaway, New Jersey, for factory training. He returned after three months to become the head of the new Box Company's maintenance department crew in Meridian.

We found another apartment that had been converted from an old Army barracks at Key Field. It was next door to James' work. I got a regular job with the Mississippi State Department of Health in a public health project that had its office at Key Field. (It had been opened to combat a statewide epidemic of syphilis that could be cured by the new drug called "penicillin.") A former Army barracks had been renovated for the clinic along with a men's and women's dormitory. Each Monday loaded busses of infected people from across the state came to spend a week and go home cured.

With both of us working, we decided to buy a car. We both fell in love with a (used) light blue Buick Road Master convertible. Driving it around I felt like Mrs. Aster-butt, or at least like a movie star. Never mind that it was three years old when we bought it, it looked like new.

On March 7, 1950, our son, James M. White Jr., was born. We decided to call him "Jimmie." In the following year, in 1951, our daughter was born in November. We named her Janice Ellen, and we called her "Jan." They were both our pride and joy, and both were "spoiled" by their four grandparents.

Dissatisfied with his job at General Box Company, James wrote to the parent company in New Jersey to see if they could place him in another of their companies. Immediately they wrote back and offered him a job at another of their plants, which was located at Decatur in northern Alabama. It sounded good so James took the offer. They even paid for our furniture to be moved.

I, of course, being a nurse, had no problem in being hired by the Decatur General Hospital. (Registered nurses were in short supply.) I took the 11–7 night shift so James could watch our kids at night and I could take care of them during the day.

That snowy winter turned out to be especially cold. Little Jimmie became so croupy that we had to admit him for a short stay in the hospital.

Fed up with cold weather, we determined to move further south.

Calling a storage company to pick up our furniture and put it in storage, we quickly packed our bags and got ready to move. The storage people came so fast that I was hardly finished with defrosting our refrigerator. (They promised to store it with its door open until it had completely dried.)

We went to Florida in the wrong time of the year. It was full of tourists, and James couldn't find a job. We were fast using our meager cash for rooms in tourist courts. About halfway down Florida we turned around and headed home.

We were driving along near Panama City, Florida, on the coastal highway when I saw a hospital sign pointing out across a field to a big brick building. I quickly backed up and headed toward the hospital. James asked me where I thought I was going. I told him I was going to work.

I parked and went in and asked to speak to the director of nurses. She looked at my registered nurse card and asked me if I could start that day. I told her that I had my family along and would have to find them a place to stay. She directed me to a tourist camp just up the highway. She wanted me start work that same afternoon at 3 p.m. on the medical ward.

We found the tourist camp without trouble, it being right on the beach. James checked us in. I dug out my white uniform and shoes from my suitcase and, leaving James in charge of the children, I reported to work at my new job.

What a fine time we had in Panama City! We stayed there about a month with mornings spent swimming, playing in the sand, or flying kites. I worked on the swing shift, 3–11, while James put the kids to bed each night. Our cabin had a small kitchen where we cooked our meals. James had to make supper each night for himself and the 'chilluns,' and he didn't know how to cook. I understand that he became quite adept at making fried biscuits and 'lasses.

Unable to find a job, James' male ego couldn't stand it that his wife was making his living. He wrote to New Jersey again, and they found him another job at a box factory over in Savannah, Georgia.

We rented an apartment in downtown Savannah. Leaving Jimmie and Jan in a day care nursery, James worked at his new job, and I worked at the Southern Railroad Hospital.

Savannah was an interesting city, the oldest town in Georgia. After seeing all the sights, it was a boring place to live. While there somebody stole our car, but insurance helped us get a new one. The new car was a used two-door, hard-top Oldsmobile "Ninety-Eight" model that was three years old.

Fed up with living place to place, James and I together thought that we would like to go home to stay. We talked it over and decided that if my father would give us three acres of the family farm we would attempt to build our own house in Pine Springs. About that time, however, Mama wrote that Daddy had another stroke and was in "bad shape." We burned our bridges in Savannah and hurried home as fast as we could.

My Daddy, Edward Leon New, was very sick. He couldn't speak, but his eyes shone when I told him that James and I were moving home and planned to build a house. I felt he knew who I was and what I was saying but was unable to respond. I was glad we made it home in time to say goodbye; he had another stroke that very night and died before morning on the fourth day of April in 1955. He was laid to rest in our family plot in the Pine Springs cemetery near the graves of his little daughter Mable Sue New and our twin babies, Peggy Jean and Patsy Ann White.

When James and I and our two children moved back to Mississippi, we stayed with James' parents, Ernest and Minnie White, who lived less than a mile from where we planned to build. Mr. Ernest and Miss Minnie were a mite crowded, but they didn't seem to mind. They put us up in their spare bedroom that had two double beds. Helping out with the groceries, we planned to live with them while James built our home.

While the building project was going on, I was hired by the Riley Hospital in Meridian because we needed all the money we could get. They had me running the night shift on the third floor surgical ward.

First of all, we borrowed a book from the Meridian library that showed how to frame a house. It gave information on how to build a house that had a flat roof instead of a house with a pitched roof with gables. As James had never built as much as a doghouse it seemed a simple way to put up a building. We didn't have enough money to hire a real carpenter. They say that fools rush in where angels fear to tread.

I had no qualms or fears that James couldn't do the job. He was always good with his hands and usually did what he set out to do. Mr. Ernest, however, was a mite uneasy. He showed up with James when the foundation and floor joists were being laid, but after a while he saw that James

could do without him. Shaking his head, Mr. White went back to his regular job, driving a road machine for Lauderdale County.

The foundation of the old house that Grandpa Joel New had built fifty years before had about rotted away, but most of the studs and other framework was still in good shape and usable. He had no way to haul the lumber but piece by piece James tore away the boards and toted them on his shoulder the quarter mile down the road to his building project.

James was a man of average height and was muscular, but I still don't know how he did it. In addition to his carpenter work, he took little Jimmie and Jan along with him each morning where they amused themselves while he nailed boards. They all walked back to the Whites to eat lunch where he left the little ones to take an afternoon nap with their Granny White while James returned to his building activities.

James salvaged the glass panes from the worn window sashes to make a large picture window in the living room. He hired Robert Williams, a neighbor from up the road, to bring his table saw to cut two-by-fours to frame the glass from the old windows. When it was finished it looked quite impressive.

While James was building our house, I continued working. To get more money, I applied for work at the East Mississippi State Hospital, a mental institution in Meridian. (They paid more.) They hired me to be head nurse on Building C, a women's ward that took care of bed patients. I had been there a couple months when the hospital's director of nurses resigned. They offered me her job, so I took it and became the new director of nurses over the entire large state hospital.

Our house was almost finished when James and Jimmie together dug a well. When the hole got too deep to simply toss out the dirt with his shovel, James got a well pulley and rope and hoisted the soil out by bucketful to young Jimmie who emptied it outside and dropped it back. It was good that they struck water when the hole was only about eight or nine feet down.

After five months the inside of the house was almost done but the outside was still covered with black tarpaper waiting to be covered with asbestos shingles. We figured that the house was finished enough for us to move in so we sent for our furniture stored in Decatur, Alabama.

We were so proud of our new home. It was small—it had three small bedrooms and a bath, a living room with a dining area in the roomy kitchen. The house was separated from a one-car garage by a breezeway that made a nice place to sit. We had enough furniture, but we needed a range for the kitchen. We went to Sears and bought a new Kenmore cook stove on credit. We hated to go into debt, but it was a nice propane gas range that had an automatic lighter—you didn't have to strike a match to turn it on.

Proud, we wanted to show off our new house, so we invited my cousin Ruth Marie and her husband, Van O'Mire, out to spend a Sunday afternoon with us. They came and we made popcorn and lemonade for refreshment. Coming back into the kitchen, I saw a tiny flame coming from the pilot light on my new stove. I managed to turn it off and thought no more about it.

When our guests left, I was not ready yet to go to bed. There was a Disney movie showing at the drive-in, so I asked James if he would like to go. He said for me to go with the children but he was tired and wanted go to bed.

We were watching the movie when Van came to get us. Someone had called looking for me because our house was on fire, and we should go home, which we did. When we arrived, our house was just a bed of red hot embers.

We were never sure what started the fire, but it had awakened James, but it was too late to do

anything about it. I have always thought that it was caused by the pilot light on our new stove.

The people at church for the Sunday night singing heard what was happening and had all come running. They were too late; old dry lumber burns fast. They couldn't get to the well to get water because the well was right beside the house. It was a total loss. The only thing we had left were the clothes we were wearing, not even having a toothbrush to brush our teeth. (Years later the Pine Springs Volunteer Fire Department was organized.)

Our friends and neighbors were unbelievably kind. Gifts poured in from everywhere—clothes, bed linens, pots, dishes, and even some pieces of furniture. I'll always remember how they all pitched in to help us.

We rented a small house near the hospital where I was working. James wanted to work, but he couldn't find a job in Meridian. He called the company in New Jersey, and they at once sent him to a job opening over in Bainbridge, Georgia. A new box factory was opening, and they needed a good maintenance man.

James immediately left for Georgia, but I wasn't ready to give up my director of nursing position at the state hospital.

Jimmie, Jan, and I were staying in our little rented house when September (1956) came, and it was time for six-year-old Jimmie to begin school. It was nice that we lived just a few short blocks from Highland Park Elementary. I found a young black girl to stay with Jan while her brother and I were away at work and school.

That Christmas I gave up my job and moved to Bainbridge. James had rented a two-bedroom house just down the street from the Methodist Church, but the grade school was too far away for Jimmie to walk. I would have to drive him to school in the car.

James' employer in Bainbridge owned part interest in the local hospital. Hearing that I was a nurse, he wanted me to work for him as his director of nurses as there were no other registered nurses in the small town. I regret to say that I took the job.

I was used to larger hospitals, but the small Bainbridge Hospital proved to be too much. In addition to my nursing duties, I was expected to help in the lab and X-ray—and other things I had not been trained to do. I was afraid I might make a mistake and kill somebody and get sued. I stuck it out for about two months before I resigned.

Truth to tell, neither James nor I cared much for Bainbridge. We had no friends. The town was full of "quality" folks that treated us like we were "Georgia crackers." Even the church down the street did not make us feel welcome. I never could tell why they thought themselves so "special."

After living there for nearly two years, I told James that I was ready to move on. He agreed. We had never been out west, and I said I'd like to see California.

James went back to the phone and called New Jersey. They told him they really needed a maintenance man in San Jose, California. James asked when they wanted him to start. "Last week!" they said.

James, Jimmie, Jan, and I loaded up the car with "stuff" and headed back to Mississippi. It happened that my sister Edna Mae was already there visiting Mama. She and her husband, Ed Shields, (Methodist missionaries from Burma in Southeast Asia) were home on furlough. James went on to California and left us behind with the car so we could visit with our relatives.

After a nice long visit, I told everyone good-bye and prepared to drive the kids and me to California. One sister-in-law marveled that I planned to drive all that distance alone with two young children. She said that she hesitated to drive to downtown Meridian with her brood.

Nevertheless, Jimmie, Jan, and I set out on our adventure. The first day we made it to Corpus Christi, Texas, where we stopped to visit my old nursing school companion, Jan and Frank Hovell. She and her husband took us to the beach where the kids and I had a marvelous time. We stayed with them nearly a week.

Next was a short drive to San Antonio where we spent an afternoon and night with another friend. Then we headed across west Texas. One doesn't realize how BIG Texas is until they drive across it. It goes on forever!

We went a little out of our way to see that enormous hole in the earth, the Grand Canyon. While we were marveling at the sight, eight-year-old Jimmie found a small group of young Indians who lived in the area. He said he was tired of driving so he would just stay there and live with his new friends. He said they told him how they trapped little animals and made them pets. California couldn't be better than that so he would just stay. I had to talk fast to tell him how sad his daddy would be if we left him behind.

Driving on a dirt road back to the highway, I hit a sharp rock and a tire went flat. Never mind, we had a spare. I got it out but the bolts that held the tire on were very tight. I had a tire wrench, but I couldn't get it to turn. What to do?

Looking over the flat plain I could see some sort of a house. There wasn't much tourist traffic that early in the morning, but I hesitated to leave the car, and I doubted if six-year-old Jan could walk that far, especially as the day grew hotter. The only thing to do was to point out that only house and send young Jim there for help. Scary thought!

With misgivings I watched my boy start off. He had walked but a few yards down the road when I saw a dust cloud coming toward us as someone left the house. As the truck came closer, I was relieved to see that it was a park ranger who said he had been watching us with his binocular. He changed the tire, and we went on our way. At the next town I stopped to buy a new tire.

Without further ado we made it to San Jose where we met James. We eventually bought a house in nearby Santa Clara and remained in California for thirteen years, James working for the Owens-Corning Fiberglass Company, and I working on the surgical ward at Doctor's General Hospital in San Jose.

We enjoyed life in California. On one side we had the Pacific Ocean to play in and on the other side we had the mountains where we went fishing and camping. James especially enjoyed the fishing where he learned to fly-fish to catch trout. He took courses at San Jose State College (English, math), and I took a course in oil painting. Jimmie and Jan were growing, fast becoming teenagers and enrolling at Santa Clara High School.

In the late 1960s our real worries began. More and more reports of high schoolers were found, of all things, to be sniffing glue! It became such a fad that we became concerned that our own children would be tempted. Also, at that time, James was concerned about his parents back in Mississippi who were getting old. He felt that they needed him.

Finally, in 1969 we gave up. We resigned our jobs, sold our house, and returned home to Mississippi.

Getting ready to return home, we were able to find an old 1-ton Dodge truck with a new Ford engine that a fellow sold us for $400. James, using plywood, covered the truck bed and loaded it with furniture. Behind the truck he towed the largest U-Haul trailer that he could rent.

James, with Jan serving as his copilot, drove the truck while I followed in my car, a 1966 Ford Mustang. Behind my car I towed James' car, a small 1965 English Ford station wagon with a luggage rack on top. On the front seat of the station wagon was a birdcage with a pair of parakeets and a Siamese cat in a box. A big Weimaraner dog named Diana was tied to the rear door so she couldn't reach the birds. Together we made quite a caravan. We had moved and left furniture before, but this move we took along everything we owned.

(Not quite everything. We left one of our best treasures, our son Jim White, age eighteen. He was ready to enter Santa Clara Jr. College with his buddies and then go on to the University of California at Santa Cruz. To pay his own way, he and a friend went into business together to build houses.)

I drove in front of our parade because James' truck was so loaded that it could hardly make it up steep hills. Like the rabbit and the tortoise, I would zip right on up and wait for him at the top. If he wanted to confer with me about anything, he would have Jan signal me by waving a towel out her window and I would pull over.

We ran into trouble at Albuquerque, New Mexico. I had zipped up a hill and waited for the truck at the top—and waited and waited. At the next crossover I turned around and went back looking. I found them parked on the shoulder waiting for me. The old truck's transmission, not used to such a heavy load, had played out. I told them to sit tight—I would go for help.

I left the highway and found a garage that could fix the transmission. Their big truck towed them in and, unhooking the trailer, pushed the old Dodge up onto the grease rack. Next question was, could the grease rack raise such a heavy load? Somehow they managed to lift it up, one end at a time, and installed a new transmission. They wouldn't take our check until they called our bank in California to make sure it would clear.

On our way again, we entered the plains of west Texas. Stopping at a roadside park to eat lunch, we tied Diana to a post so she could make her "pit stop."

Thinking to let our cat (Mei Ling) out of her box to let her stretch her legs, we took the birds out of the car so as not to tempt the cat. We sat their cage on the picnic table when along came the Oklahoma wind "sweeping down the plain." It blew the birdcage over and both birds, out of their cage, got caught in the flow. Last we saw them they went out of sight headed for Mexico at a fast clip.

The trip had been an adventure, but our caravan finally reached our final goal, Pine Springs, Mississippi, where we planned to stay.

Okatibbee Dam is located on Okatibbee Creek in Lauderdale County, Mississippi, about seven miles northwest of Meridian. Authorized by the Flood Control Act of 1962, its construction was initiated in June 1965 and was substantially completed in 1968 at a cost of around eight and one half million dollars. This dam created a lake whose water covers an area of 352 acres.

Before construction could begin, government agents, using the Right of Eminent Domain, began to buy the land of landowners who happened to own the land that was needed for the lake. They were not paid as much as the land was worth, but what else could they do?

Maebelle New was, after her husband Leon died, the sole owner of the New's Pine Springs farm. She was forced to sell most of her farm to the government. Out of her 160-acre farm she was allowed to keep about thirty-three acres. She felt lucky that the land she was able to keep was sited on the Pine Springs Road that contained her home.

After my younger sister Amelda married her classmate, Jay L. Neil, and moved away, Mama remained at Pine Forest Academy where she continued as house mother at the girls' dorm. While working in the medical office of Dr. Reuben Johnson, James and I moved into her vacant house at Pine Springs. We planned to stay there while our home was being built.

As we were ready to build and Edna Mae and Edwin were about to retire from the mission field to come home, Mama divided what was left of her land into three parcels so each of her three daughters would have a home-site. She deeded each of us a little over eleven acres of land. James and I were deeded the middle plot between Amelda and Edna Mae. Amelda's lot contained Mama's house, but she and Jay, going off to school, were not ready to settle down.

After we returned to Pine Springs, James found work as head of the Sanitation Department of Meridian's Smith Bakery after sending him to State College for a course on entomology and the related courses required for a pesticide license. I went to work as a nurse at Meridian's Anderson Hospital. I was able to find time to take a course on drawing blueprints and drew the plans for the new home we planned to build.

Looking for building contractors, we found one that fit our slim budget. Using my blueprint, Mr. Ball started building our house on the eleven acres that Mama had given us. We selected the site where the old log Wolfe house had stood, next to the three-acre pond that my father had built.

Mr. Ball did a lousy job in building our new house. He would come in near noon each day with what appeared to be a hangover. In places the doors were visibly lopsided and had to be re-done. I caught him sealing outside walls with none of the specified insulation. We finally fired him, and James and his younger brother, Dusty White, finished the job. Dusty was a roofer by trade, but he did a pretty good job at making kitchen cabinets. My cousin James A. Pace (married to James' sister Helen) worked for Sears. He installed our central air conditioning.

We celebrated Christmas in our new home in 1972. It was a happy time.

In the fall of 1975 James was cutting grass in our big yard with our garden tractor. He ran over a nest of bumble bees and was stung several times. He thought nothing more of it, but a few days later his back was so painful that he could hardly move. He was admitted to Anderson Hospital where he was diagnosed with rheumatoid arthritis.

James' condition progressed from bad to worse. He gradually became so crippled that by 1977 he could no longer work. That year on June 4 he took an early retirement from Smith Bakery and began to draw his social security. He was fifty-six.

Finding it hard to walk, for years James sat on the sofa in our living room and watched life go on around him. He especially enjoyed talking to his young grandson, Jimmy Ash. They became best buddies. (Jimmy was our daughter's young son; she and her husband, Vernon L. Ash, later had two more little boys—Brian and John Ash.)

At times James would be enjoying a conversation with guests when he would say, "I've enjoyed all this that I can stand," and would take another pain pill and retire to his bedroom.

Developing pneumonia, we admitted James to Anderson Hospital where he died on May 27, 1993. His suffering over, I believe he was glad to go.

But how I miss him! Sweethearts all our lives, we were married for forty-six years. James and I were never rich nor famous. But we had what many long for—we were loved.

Thus ends the saga of my particular branch of the New family. Having no son named New, there are none to carry us forward. Other branches of our New family tree have sons to carry the name, but, sadly, all we had were daughters. I write this record to keep our family from being forgotten through the misty pages of time.

James M. and Mary Ellen New White

Children of James M. and Mary Ellen New White:

1. & 2. **Peggy Jean and Patsy Ann White**
   Born: September 23, 1948, Meridian, Mississippi
   Died: September 24, 1948, buried Pine Springs Methodist Church cemetery
   Married: No; died as infants

3. **James Monroe "Jim" White, Jr.**
   Born: March 7, 1950, Meridian, Mississippi
   Died:
   Married: **Beverley Gist** (divorced)
   Jim continued to live in California after high school when the rest of his family returned home to Mississippi. He built homes with a friend while off and on attending college. He returned to Mississippi after his father became ill, and

James M. "Jim" White, Jr.

Janice started selling Avon, taking after her Great-grandmother Harriet Ellen (Montgomery) Burnham. She then worked for Nina Heidelberg where she quickly picked up all the skills of a florist. Years later she made the flower arrangements for all of her sons' and her brother Jim's weddings to include boutonnieres and corsages. Vernon always said she should have been an interior decorator due not only to her skill in knowing colors, which was amazing, but also for the fine way she always kept their house decorated.

Janice started attending Meridian Junior College and was ready to start the nursing program the upcoming spring. However, when her son Jimmy was born, she changed her priorities. Janice later went to work at Peavey Electronics about the time they started their electric guitar

there he married Beverly. Jim worked for a number of years running a maintenance crew for the Meridian Water Department. After his divorce, he moved to Destin, Florida, where he became head of Destin Water Users Maintenance Department. Jim took early retirement due to health problems.

Children: None

4. **Janice Ellen White Ash**
   Born: November 21, 1951, Meridian, Mississippi
   Died:
   Married: September 8, 1978, to Vernon Lee Ash from Pennsylvania, a sailor stationed at Meridian Naval Air Station

   Upon returning with her folks to Mississippi from California in 1969 (and getting over the culture shock),

Vernon, Janice White Ash, Jimmy, Brian, and John

line. Some of the guitars somewhere out there have her signature inside the neck. Upon the upcoming arrival of her next two sons, Brian and then John, Janice quit work and devoted herself to raising her three boys. Vernon and Janice built their home in 1992 on a two-acre parcel of land given by her folks, which was a small piece of the property Joel New had purchased from Tommy Wolfe.

Children:

A. **James Vernon "Jimmy" Ash,**
   (1) m. **Michelle Larice Parker**;
   (2) m. **Kristyn Summer Overby**

   Jimmy was born as James Barthel, named after his grandfather James and his father Barthel Doan Waggoner. When Vernon adopted Jimmy, he had his name changed to James Vernon Ash. Jimmy joined the Mississippi Air National Guard after high school and served four years in security police. He later rejoined the Air Guard following the events of September 11, 2001, where he served a year in vehicle maintenance. While married to Michelle, Jimmy attended EMCC and earned a degree in mortuary science. He worked for the Robert Barham, Stephens, and Webb Funeral Homes, both in Meridian and Philadelphia, Mississippi. After a few years he took a break from the funeral service business, only working on a part-time basis. Meanwhile he went to work full time in the minnow business, first with Rodgers Fish Farm, then with Covington Fish Farm. During this period working on the minnow farms, Jimmy married Summer, and Elijah was born. They moved to Daleville, Mississippi, and

Jimmy went back to work full time with Webb Family Funeral Home.

Children of James and Michelle:
1. **Ainsley Parker Ash**
2. **Gavin James Ash**

Children of James and Summer:
1. **Elijah Seth Ash**

B. **Brian Lee Ash**, m. **Deborah "Debbie" Kay Etheridge**

   Brian joined the Mississippi Air National Guard after high school and served his hitch in aircrew life support. Brian was mostly self-employed, first as an insurance agent, then becoming a private contractor constructing portable buildings, carports, and installing metal roofing. Brian later went on to work a sales route for DuFour Battery. Brian's wife Debbie is a registered nurse and works for Rush Hospital. They live in Enterprise, Mississippi, where they enjoy their family, which includes many grandchildren.

Stepchildren:
1. **Les**
2. **Candice**
3. **Geordan**
4. **Laurel**
5. **Conner**
6. **Kara**

C. **John Vincent Ash**, m. **Kathleen DeShee O'Donoghue**

   John and Kathleen both attended Mississippi State University where they met. They got married in college and, after graduating with engineering degrees, took jobs in the oil and gas industry in Houston, Texas. Their children, Jacob and Matthew, were born in Clear Lake, Texas. They live in Tomball, Texas.

Children:
1. **Jacob Vernon Ash**
2. **Matthew Roland Ash**

John, Brian, James (Jimmy), Jan and Vern Ash

Index

The numbers in this index indicate the chapter where each individual can be found. It may be that they are written about in detail, or simply mentioned in a list of children or grandchildren. Women are listed under their married names rather than their maiden names.

We invite you to view the complete
selection of titles we publish at:

www.ASPECTBooks.com

Scan with your mobile
device to go directly
to our website.

Please write or email us your praises, reactions,
or thoughts about this or any other book we publish at:

AB **ASPECT Books**
www.ASPECTBooks.com

info@ASPECTBooks.com

ASPECT Books titles may be purchased in bulk for
educational, business, fund-raising, or sales promotional use.
For information, please e-mail:

BulkSales@ASPECTBooks.com

Finally, if you are interested in seeing
your own book in print, please contact us at

publishing@ASPECTBooks.com

We would be happy to review your manuscript for free.

www.ingramcontent.com/pod-product-compliance
Lightning Source LLC
Chambersburg PA
CBHW050358110426
42812CB00006BA/1734